MW01259244

TURNER PUBLISHING COMPANY
FRONT LINE OF MILITARY HISTORY
412 Broadway, P.O. Box 3101
Paducah, KY 42002-3101
Phone 502-443-0121

Copyright © 1995. 1st Cavalry Division
Vietnam 1965-1969
All rights reserved.
This book or any part thereof may not be reproduced
without the written consent of the Publisher.

1st Cavalry Division Association Officers:
BG Art Junot, USA (Ret), Executive Director
Lorinda Stout, Editor/Office Manager
Edward L. Daily, Board of Governors
President, 7th U.S. Cavalry Assn.

Reprinted by:
Turner Publishing Company
Dave Turner, President
Robert J. Martin, Chief Editor

Library of Congress Catalog Card No.: 95-60330
ISBN: 1-56311-180-2
Printed in the U.S.A.

1st AIR CAVALRY DIVISION

— • —

Memoirs of

THE FIRST TEAM

Vietnam

August 1965—December 1969

— • —

Foreword

This volume can be many things to many people—a book of memories, a souvenir, a pictorial essay on air-mobility, or simply a story of gallant men at war. It can be many things, but one thing it is not, nor does it pretend to be—a complete history of the 1st Air Cavalry Division in Vietnam.

The task and burden of history must lie with the objectivity of future generations, far removed from contemporary pressures and restraints. It is true, of course, that much research for this book has been done from available official records, the ultimate source of written history. But even more has been drawn from the vivid recollections of the Cavalrymen who fought, tasted the brassy bile of fear, shared the fierce exhultation of victory or were drenched in the dark despair of death.

This is the story of the small, close world of fighting men in action, men who even at this writing still are fighting. This volume contains the memoirs of a fighting team—THE FIRST TEAM. It is a memory of combat; no doubt it is imperfect as all memory, but none-theless real for those who were there, for those who can fill in the inevitable gaps.

It does not presume to be more than that.

1

To the 1st Cavalry Division Skytrooper

Phuoc Vinh

12 February 1970

Men of the Cav:

This is your story—the story of the FIRST TEAM from its reactivation at Fort Benning through the years of fighting in Vietnam. Those who worked and trained in the days of the test division at Fort Benning before coming to Vietnam will find a memory included here, too. This book is more than a history; more than an illustrated after-action report. It is the story of men, told in words and in pictures, men who have fought valorously and who have carried the banners of the FIRST TEAM proudly on to new and greater honors. It is, in effect, a book of memories.

Since the vivid recollections of a man who served in an infantry battalion differ from one who served in an artillery battalion, and because the outlook at brigade level is substantially more detailed than the view at the top, this book has been organized to give several perspectives. There is a section devoted to each battalion and separate company in the division, a section for each brigade and one for the division as a whole.

I will not attempt to summarize the history contained in this book, but I would be remiss not to pay reverent respect to those fallen Skytroopers who have given their lives in the service of their country. It is to their memory that this book is dedicated. All profits from the sale of this book will go to the Education Foundation of the 1st Cavalry Division Association to provide educational scholarships for the children of our comrades who made the supreme sacrifice in Vietnam and once again paid the price of freedom.

To every Skytrooper who has faithfully served this division, it is my sincere hope that in years to come this book will stimulate reminiscences and will always serve to remind all that in Vietnam, as it was in World War II and Korea, the FIRST TEAM remained—ALWAYS FIRST!

E. B. Roberts

E. B. ROBERTS
MAJOR GENERAL, USA
Commanding

Contents

GENERAL
CREIGHTON W. ABRAMS
COMUSMACV

GENERAL
WILLIAM B. ROSSON
DEPUTY COMUSMACV

4

LIEUTENANT GENERAL
THOMAS MILDREN
COMMANDING GENERAL USARV

LIEUTENANT GENERAL

JULIAN EWELL

COMMANDING GENERAL

II FIELD FORCE

1ST AIR CAVALRY DIVISION COMMANDERS

MAJOR GENERAL
HARRY W.O. KINNARD

MAJOR GENERAL
JOHN NORTON

MAJOR GENERAL
JOHN J. TOLSON

MAJOR GENERAL
GEORGE I. FORSYTHE

BRIGADIER GENERAL
GEORGE W. CASEY
ASSISTANT DIVISION COMMANDER-A

BRIGADIER GENERAL
ROBERT M. SHOEMAKER
ASSISTANT DIVISION COMMANDER-B

ASSISTANT DIVISION COMMANDERS

MAJOR GENERAL
RICHARD T. KNOWLES

MAJOR GENERAL
JOHN M. WRIGHT, JR.

MAJOR GENERAL
WILLIAM A. BECKER

BRIGADIER GENERAL
GEORGE B. BLANCHARD

LATE BRIGADIER GENERAL
ALFRED J.F. MOODY

BRIGADIER GENERAL
EDWARD H. DESAUSSURE, JR.

BRIGADIER GENERAL
RICHARD L. IRBY

BRIGADIER GENERAL
OSCAR E. DAVIS

BRIGADIER GENERAL
WILLIAM E. SHEDD, III

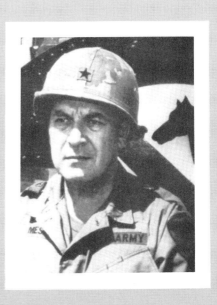

BRIGADIER GENERAL
FRANK MESZAR

9

DIVISION CHIEFS OF STAFF

Colonel George S. Beatty
Colonel Herbert E. Wolf
Colonel George W. Casey
Colonel George W. Putnam, Jr.
Colonel Conrad L. Stansberry
Colonel Robert N. MacKinnon
Colonel Robert M. Shoemaker
Colonel Joseph P. Kingston

DIVISION COMMAND SERGEANTS MAJOR

Command Sergeant Major Chester R. Westervelt
Command Sergeant Major Kenneth W. Cooper
Command Sergeant Major W. O. Marshall
Command Sergeant Major Jack Moore
Command Sergeant Major Vern O. Peters
Command Sergeant Major Lawrence E. Kennedy

THE FIRST CAVALRY DIVISION

1921 • • 1965

The First Cavalry Division
1921—1965

The 1st Cavalry Division was activated as a Regular Army division on September 12, 1921, under the new National Defense Act. Three days later the 7th and 8th Cavalry Regiments were assigned to the division. The 5th Cavalry Regiment was assigned on December 18, 1922. Until 1932 the 1st Cavalry Regiment was assigned to the division, making the Cavalry a "square" division. In 1932 the 12th Cavalry Regiment replaced the 1st, and remained with the division until the March 1949, reorganization, when it was disbanded as the division assumed the "triangular" (three-regiment) configuration of a regular infantry division.

In addition to three of the four regiments of cavalry the original organization included the 82nd Field Artillery Battalion (Horse), the 8th Engineer Battalion (Mounted), the 13th Signal Troop, the 27th Ordnance Company, Division Headquarters and the 1st Cavalry Division Quartermaster Train, which later became the 15th Replacement Company.

Major General Robert L. Howze was assigned as the first division commander.

In 1923 the division assembled in the Camp Marfa area in Texas for its first maneuver and for the next four years was engaged in training and patrolling the Fort Bliss, Camp Clark and Camp Marfa area, again engaging in combined maneuvers in 1927.

The division engaged in maneuvers in 1936 at Camp Marfa, Texas, and in 1938 and 1939 at Balmorhea, Texas. Following the Third Army maneuvers in Louisiana in 1940, the division (less the 1st Brigade) constructed cantonments for 20,000 anti-aircraft troops at Fort Bliss and took part in the development of the El Paso Air Base.

In 1941 the entire division was assembled at Fort Bliss for extensive field training. The strength of the division was increased by the activation of the 61st Field Artillery Battalion as the first

medium support artillery of the division and the authorized personnel strength was increased from 3,575 to 10,110 men.

WORLD WAR II

In 1942, troopers of the 1st Cavalry Division were still horse soldiers.

The changeover from horses to jeeps came in February 1943 when the division received orders assigning it overseas. Under the command of Major General Innis P. Swift, it arrived in Australia on July 26 and went through six months of jungle and amphibious training at Camp Strathpine, near Brisbane. Early in 1944, the division moved to Oro Bay, New Guinea, where final preparations were made for an assault into the Admiralty Islands north of New Guinea and west of the Solomons.

On the morning of February 29 a shattering naval bombardment preceded the 2nd Battalion, 5th Cavalry, as it led the rest of the regiment into Hayane Harbor on Los Negros Island. Waves of landing craft filed through a dangerously narrow channel under fire. But the location of the landings had been a surprise to the Japanese; their defenses were oriented toward the larger Seeadler Harbor on the other side of the island.

Before they could shift their concentrations eastward to meet the onrushing Cavalrymen, the Momote Airstrip and much surrounding territory was in American hands.

The Japanese infiltrated the perimeter at night and launched a series of bloody, although futile, counterattacks. But as one prong of the American advance swept northward up the Mokerang Peninsula, the other squeezed the Japanese back against their useless defenses around Seeadler Harbor, nearly annihilating one battalion. By this time 1,400 enemy dead had been counted.

Attention then shifted to Manus Island, a much larger land mass just west of Los Negros. At its northeast corner, near the village of Lorengau, was the only airstrip in the Admiralties still held by the Japanese. At dawn on March 15 the 2nd Brigade combat team stormed ashore well west of Lorengau, supported by two battalions of artillery emplaced on tiny Hauwei Island.

Again the 1st Cavalry Division had outflanked the main Japanese line of resistance, which in this case ran along the beach directly in front of Lorengau. There were moments of fierce jungle fighting when the enemy opened fire from camouflaged pillboxes. However, by nightfall on the 17th, the 8th Cavalry had taken the airstrip. The brigade crossed the Lorengau River under fire and entered the village on the following day.

In its first fight the 1st Cavalry Division had done outstandingly well. When the Admiralties Campaign ended officially on May 18, 1944, the troopers had killed 3,317 of the enemy, while suffering

casualties of less than one-tenth that size.

When the tide of war swept westward across the Pacific, the division, as part of X Corps, Sixth Army, was instrumental in liberating the Philippines. On October 20 the division's LCV's landed on the east coast of Leyte near Tacloban. On the 21st the troopers entered the city and began sheltering and feeding thousands of refugees.

After breaking out of Tacloban the division, now commanded by Major General Verne D. Mudge, moved northwest up the rich Leyte Valley in two prongs, aiming at the fishing town of Carigara on the island's nothern coast. Carigara fell; the valley had been cleared. However, Japanese reinforcements had landed in the Ormoc Valley on the other side of the mountain range, and were now menacing the X Corps flank from the southwest. Accordingly, the 1st Brigade advanced into the mountains.

The battle through the mountains was the outstanding achievement of the campaign. Record rains flooded the island. Supply lines were stretched to the breaking point. The Japanese were dug in on the reverse slopes of the knife-edged ridges, almost immune to artillery fire. Patrols slipped behind enemy lines, were isolated for days, fought without support, and withdrew battling for each clump of jungle foliage. But in spite of all hazards the troopers of the 5th and

12th Cavalry broke through in nearly a month of sustained heavy fighting, climaxed by the capture of Hill 2348 on December 2-3.

Meanwhile, the 7th Cavalry had been knocking out Japanese strongpoints on the fringes of the Leyte Valley and the 8th Cavalry, which had landed on the neighboring island of Samar on October 24, had been waging a brilliant campaign of its own.

At first the 8th Cavalry advanced slowly north toward Hinabangan, near a junction with the east-west road connecting Wright and Taft. Hinabangan was occupied on December 7. The troopers pushed on and captured Wright on the 13th. Then they took the left-hand fork and raced westward to Catbalogan, where they were halted temporarily by defenses on the Magbag River. Pressure against this line convinced the Japanese that they could not hold Catbalogan, and on the 19th the Cavalrymen entered the objective unopposed. Taft soon fell; by the 21st the Samar portion of the campaign was over.

When the Leyte-Samar Campaign ended the 1st Cavalry Division had eli-minated 5,937 Japanese while losing 241 of its own men.

Without pause, the now battle-tested division entered the fight for Luzon and the capital city of the Philippines, Manila. It played a key role in the Sixth Army's drive to fulfill the promise General MacArthur had made three years before —to return and liberate the islands.

The FIRST TEAM landed in the Lingayan Gulf on January 27, 1945, and moved 30 miles inland to Guimba. On January 31 MacArthur gave the following order to MG Mudge: "Go to Manila. Go around the Nips, but go to Manila. Free the internees at Santo Tomas. Take Malacanan Palace and the Legislative Building."

This meant that a flying column would have to knife through 100 miles of enemy-held territory, churn through mud, ford rivers where the bridges had been blown, fight or by-pass an enemy whose dispositions were largely unknown and crash into the defenses of a major city. Under the command of Brigadier General William C. Chase, the troopers did it in 66 hours. There was fighting at Angat, the "hot corner" at Novaliches,

and other places, but on February 3 the column entered Manila. The 3,700 people who had been imprisoned in the Santo Tomas camp for three years were freed.

"First in Manila" became one of the highlights of Cav history.

By March 3rd the resistance in the capital had ceased. During the latter stages of the battle the 2nd Brigade combat team challenged the formidable defenses of Antipolo, with an aim of preventing Japanese reinforcements from reaching Manila.

MG Mudge had been wounded at Antipolo, so when the division turned south on March 21 toward the Batangas peninsula it was commanded by Brigadier General Hugh F. T. Hoffman. The XIV Corps plan of attack called for an envelopment, with the 1st Cavalry Division and the 11th Airborne Division converging on the main north-south road at Lipa.

The towns of Santo Tomas, Tanauan, and Lipa were captured in sharp fighting by March 29. Then the Cavalrymen moved east and linked up with the 43rd Infantry Division, severing all north-

south communications. The Japanese holed up in strongpoints, fighting when attacked but otherwise remaining fairly immobile. The Bicol peninsula was cleared in April and a stronghold at Mt. Malepunyo was slowly reduced. Around the Katapalan Sawmill in eastern Luzon the last major battle of the war was won in early May. When the campaign officially ended on June 30, the 1st Cavalry Division had accounted for 14,114 enemy dead and 1,199 prisoners.

The shooting war was over for the Cavalrymen. However, their outstanding services made them eligible for a final honor: That of being the first unit to enter the surrendered Japanese capital.

On the morning of September 8 the division marched into Tokyo. GEN MacArthur was escorted by the 2nd Battalion, 7th Cavalry. Amid ceremonies celebrating the newly-won peace, the FIRST TEAM, which was to remain in Japan as part of the 8th Army until 1950, staged a triumphant parade, as "First in Tokyo" was entered in the proud roll of 1st Cav achievements.

KOREA

On July 18, 1950, when the 1st Cavalry Division landed at Pohang-dong, South Korea, within the rapidly shrinking Pusan perimeter, it was one-third under-

strength. Supplies were scarce. But there was no time for additional preparation. The division was being deployed as part of the Eighth Army in a desperate attempt to salvage a war that had been three-quarters lost. When the troopers waded ashore from their LSTs, Communist lines were only 25 miles away and moving closer day by day.

Under the command of Major General Hobart Gay, the division occupied the key sector of the perimeter, straddling the main road from Pusan to Seoul, the capital of South Korea. The troopers first contacted the enemy on July 22 when a probing North Korean patrol clashed with the 1st Battalion, 8th Cavalry.

The following morning an artillery and mortar barrage heralded the first major ground attack against the Cavalry positions. With unrelenting ferocity, the North Koreans hammered at the U.N. forces for the following month, forcing them to yield ground grudgingly but steadily. Lacking manpower, the division was forced to leave gaps in its front. The Communists infiltrated through the gaps, sometimes hiding themselves in the crowds of refugees, flanking the Allied units and maintaining offensive momentum.

However, once the Cavalrymen took up positions behind the Naktong River fronting the city of Taegu, the cumula-

tive effects of heavy casualties and over-taxed supply lines began to tell on the North Koreans.

They succeeded in punching across the Naktong, but only at suicidal cost. An attack on August 4 against the 7th Cavalry Regiment cost the enemy 1,500 counted dead out of a force estimated at 1,700. Reinforcements bolstered the strength of the Eighth Army. Republic of Korea (ROK) units were integrated with 1st Cavalry units, and by August 28 the division was back to full strength.

September 1950, a month in which the 1st Cav had shown virtuosity in both defense and attack, ended with a quick United Nations victory apparently in sight.

On October 9, the troopers received orders to continue the advance across the border. The town of Kumchon on the road leading to the North Korean capital of Pyongyang was captured in the face of the stiffest resistance the enemy was able to mount on the entire front. The 7th Cavalry and the 27th British Commonwealth Brigade trapped some 5,000 Reds further north in the vicinity of Sariwon, assuring a triumphal entry into Pyongyang.

On October 19 Pyongyang fell and the third historic "first" for the FIRST TEAM was consummated. Pyongyang followed Manila and Tokyo in the roll of enemy capitals occupied by the 1st

Cav.

As the cold Korean winter began to set in the Cavalrymen remained in the Pyongyang area while the front swept forward. During this lull they refitted and mopped up the remaining pockets of resistance. On October 28, however, an I Corps order ordered them forward again. By November 1 the 5th and 8th Cavalry were in position around the town of Unsan, on the Kuryong River.

That night a probing attack was launched with sudden force against elements of the 8th Cavalry. Hardly had this been beaten back when the main Red Chinese offensive, carefully prepared and backed by inexhaustible manpower reserves, began in a barrage of rockets and mortar shells.

Blowing bugles, hoardes of Red soldiers appeared out of the night, climbing over piles of their own dead. The 3rd Battalion, 8th Cavalry, was surrounded and only a few Cavalrymen were able to escape from the pocket. Other units retreated to avoid the same fate. The division took up a temporary defense line to the south along the Chongchon River.

On November 22, after the expected Chinese follow-up attack failed to materialize, the 1st Cav went into Eighth Army reserve. On the 26th its units were moved to the Taedong River, and renewed contact began on the 28th. The II ROK Corps, hit hard, was forced to withdraw, and the Cav moved to plug the gap. The 2nd Battalion, 5th Cavalry, defeated an estimated reinforced regiment after crossing the river.

During the month of December, four planned withdrawals were carried out. While supplies and reinforcements were massed in the rear, a fluid, yielding United Nations line screened major movements, inflicted casualties, and prevented an actual breakthrough. Space was traded for time. The 1st Cav crossed the 38th Parallel on December 11 and 12, and began to construct a defense in depth along the Han River in the vicinity of Seoul.

One New Year's Eve the forward units at the 38th Parallel were hit by the Chinese juggernaut. Crossing the frozen Imjin and ignoring fearsome losses, the Communist troops clawed fanatically through minefields and barbed wire. The United Nations forces fell back to their second line of defense on the Han, abandoning Seoul. The city was evacuated on January 3, and more than a million refugees began the freezing

trek south. The enemy drive began to lose momentum when it crossed the Han. After the fall of Seoul a lull fell over the front in January 1951.

Eighth Army, wondering what the enemy's intentions were, began probing northward in late January. The 3rd Battalion, 8th Cavalry, rebounding from its losses at Unsan, was included in Task Force Johnson, which conducted a reconnaissance on January 22 and encountered few Communist soldiers. The entire division was ordered to probe northward through the snow toward the Han, reaching a series of phase lines; for two weeks gains were slow but steady.

On February 14 the 7th Cavalry seized Hill 578 in spite of heavy resistance. Phase line objectives had been reached. The division prepared to go back in reserve, but at that moment the long-delayed Red blow fell on X Corps, surrounding the 23rd Infantry Regiment and an attached French battalion at Chipyong-ni. The 5th Cavalry organized Task Force Crombez, painting its tanks like tigers to give the rescue dash maximum psychological effect.

The 1st Cav then took up positions north of Chipyong-ni, moving through a snowstorm on February 18 and occupying Line Yellow. It was assigned limited-objective attacks in support of an offensive by two Corps: X circling west and IX east in a double envelopment. However, torrential rains and floods in late February blunted the thrust. At this point Major General Charles D. Palmer

took command of the FIRST TEAM.

On March 14 the 3rd Battalion, 8th Cavalry, crossed the Hangchon River under fire. Enemy resistance had begun to melt away, and north of the Hangchon the tracks and boots of the Cavalrymen crossed one target line after another. Seoul fell in the middle of March. The Communists pulled their lines back across the whole front, abandoning the plains and trying to reorganize in the mountains.

The offensive began on April 22. The 1st Cav troopers, who had been taking a well-deserved rest in the I Corps reserve, halted the threat by committing the 5th Cavalry Regimental combat team in support of the 6th ROK Division.

During the first half of the month the Reds slackened their pressure; licking their wounds, they prepared for a "Fifth Phase" offensive which was initiated on May 18 and 19. It smashed head-on into prepared defenses, multiple gun emplacements, and a seemingly inexhaustible barrier of lead. Brute numbers could not prevail against that kind of firepower. The assaulting masses were thrown into confusion and routed; troopers pursued them down the steep mountainsides.

On the 19th the division, without pausing, swung into the attack and advanced to Line Topeka, six miles ahead. On the 25th a three-day drive was begun to Line Kansas, seizing commanding ground from which the Allies could overlook the lowlands of central

Korea. By the 28th, the 1st Cav first harassed the railway network of the "Iron Triangle" formed by the cities of Chorwon, Kumwha and Pyongyang, and then advanced nine miles to Line Wyoming. The successful defense of Seoul had demonstrated the value of a prepared defense line.

On July 18, one year after the 1st Cavalry Division entered the war at Pohang-dong, it assumed a reserve status.

On the nights of September 21-22, the 2nd and 3rd Battalions of the 7th Cavalry were attacked by waves of Communist soldiers who were driven back only after hand-to-hand fighting. But this was just a warmup for the kind of effort that would be required by the 1st Cav during Operation Commando, part of a general Eighth Army offensive designed to drive the Chinese from their well-prepared winter line of defense. The division was given the task of rooting almost an entire Chinese Army from elaborate trench lines, caves and reinforced bunkers carved into steep hills.

The Chinese defensive line was redesignated Line Jamestown. On October 3 the division moved out from Line Wyoming. Immediately it came under fire, and for the first two days hardly any progress was registered. When a hill was taken counterattacks often recaptured it. Nonetheless, by the third day the enemy line in front of the 7th Cavalry showed signs of cracking. On October 5 the 8th Cavalry took Hill 418, one of the flanking hill masses upon which the line was anchored. The Chinese flank began to be rolled up from north to south.

The southern portion of the line proved a tougher nut to crack. B-26 bombers dropped their heaviest ordnance upon the bunkers and tunnels. This did not prevent the enemy from counterattacking against the 7th Cavalry on October 10 and 11, but it did lead to the capture of Hill 272, the central pivot of the line, by the 8th Cavalry on October 13.

Gradually the night raids diminished in strength. Indeed, the Cavalrymen who had stormed "Old Baldy," a sheer hill mass in Line Jamestown, had seen the 1st Cavalry Division's last major combat in Korea. Artillery harassed the Reds as they tried to build a new line, but most of the sector was quiet as reconnaissance parties from the 3rd Infantry Division visited the area to prepare for a changeover. On December 16 the division was relieved.

The battle-hardened troopers took over the defense of Hokkaido, Japan, after adding another chapter to an illustrious combat record that saw its beginning with the sabre-swinging horse soldiers of the Indian Wars. Six members of the division had received the nation's highest award for heroism, the Medal of Honor.

By late January 1952 all units of the 1st Cavalry had arrived at Hokkaido, and after settling into its new quarters the division began a program of winter training. The climate and terrain of Hokkaido were ideally suited to instruction in Artic survival techniques.

In war the business of an army is combat, and in time of peace its business and duty is preparedness. So it was that the 1st Cavalry Division spent the years between winter 1952 and summer 1957 in almost constant training with a series of regimental and division size maneuvers. Despite the work of new training and review, the years were a well deserved rest from the hard grind of the Korean War.

Commanding the division, from June 1953 through April 1959, were MG Armistead D. Mead, BG Orlando Troxel, MG Edward J. McGaw, MG Edwin H. J. Carns, MG Ralph W. Zwicker, MG George E. Bush and MG Charles E. Beauchamp.

On August 20, 1957, the division was reduced to zero strength and transferred minus equipment to Korea where, on September 23, the 24th Infantry Division was redesignated the 1st Cavalry Division. Assuming a defensive posture along the Demilitarized Zone—known as "Freedom's Frontier"—the 1st Cavalry remained poised to counter any aggressive moves by Communist forces. Between 1957 and the beginning of the Vietnam War, the 1st Cavalry Division was the only division in the Army which faced an armed and ready enemy.

The years at Hokkaido and the subsequent return to duty in familiar Korea were not years of war and trial for the division, but they were years of learning and cautious defense.

The year 1965 would mark the beginning of another long chapter of war for the division, a yet unfinished chapter in Vietnam that would reflect Douglas MacArthur's tribute to the 1st Cavalry following the Pacific Campaign of World War II:

"No greater record has emerged from the war than that of the 1st Cavalry Division—swift and sure in attack, tenacious and durable in defense, and loyal and cheerful under hardship. It has written its own noble history."

The Cav, as the northernmost unit in Korea after the end of hositilties, of Freedom.
maintained diligent watch over the Korean DMZ, known as the Frontier

AIRMOBILE ANTECEDENTS

"...freed forever from the tyranny of terrain."

The 1st Air Cavalry Division possesses a uniqueness among Regular Army Divisions—apart from some rather obvious differences—with a duality of antecedents. Woven into the rich fabric of traditional Cavalry history is the bright and bold thread of the airmobile concept.

Thus it is that while the 1st Cavalry Division's historical background can be traced in a conventional manner, the background of the airmobile portion of the division title relates directly to another division, the organizational parent of the 1st Air Cav—the 11th Air Assault Division. Intellectual parentage of the Air Cav, is, however, considerably more difficult to pin down.

The origins of dreams of airmobile operations are obscured in the past. The pre-history of air assault certainly must take cognizance of pre-World War I thinkers who suggested that military aviation was properly a function of the cavalry arm. Instead it grew up through the Signal Corps, became a separate combat arm and eventually an independent service. Note too must be taken of the innovative ideas of air pioneers like Colonel Billy Mitchell, who actually began detailed planning in late 1918 for an infantry division combat parachute assault behind German positions.

More recent pre-history involved the visions and thinking of officers who came out of World War II convinced that something had to be done to overcome the weight of firepower and the dependence of mechanized armies on ponderous, ground-bound trains. In the latter days of the Korean conflict the helicopter became ubiquitous. There were tentative and primitive tests of sky cavalry and aerial artillery concepts in the years immediately following the Korean War.

By the 1960's the drive and enthusiasm of countless officers, some of them rated pilots but more who were not, began to exert an influence on Army thinking. Much of the thinking was crystalized in the writings of Generals James M. Gavin and Hamilton H. Howze. In a few hectic and hard-working months the "Howze board" established the rationale and requirements for an air assault division.

In late 1962 Secretary of Defense Robert S. McNamara ordered the Army to conduct a series of field tests to seek out the advantages and limitations of the airmobility concept. On January 8, 1963, Brigadier General Harry W. O. Kinnard, the assistant division commander of the 101st

Airborne Division, walked out of the office of the chief of staff of the U.S. Army, General Earl K. Wheeler. His head was buzzing with ideas. He had just been told to create an air assault division and test it to "see how far the Army can go—and ought to go—with the airmobile concept."

The stage was set for the beginning of recorded airmobile history. And the one main thread holding the pattern together for the first 38 months was the dynamic and inspired leadership of one man. This part of the airmobile story is also the story of this man, Harry William Osborne Kinnard. Never before had one man been able to fashion an operational reality from a vision and a dream and then command it in combat. Not even in the heyday of the birth and development of the airborne divisions of World War II did one individual accomplish a similar feat. The men who dreamed the dreams of airborne assault tactics did not get to test them in combat as division commanders.

The vehicle chosen for the airmobility test was the 11th Airborne Division. It was recalled to active duty February 15, 1963, and redesignated as the 11th Air Assault Division (Test). MG Kinnard was the first Skysoldier on the division's rolls. His chief of staff, Colonel E. B.

Roberts, who now commands the 1st Air Cav, was the second.

The division's beginnings were humble and the first units were small. Men and equipment were levied from all over the active Army to start a single battalion at first. That battalion was the 3rd Battalion of the 187th Infantry, and it was commanded by Lieutenant Colonel John J. Hennessey, the man who had commanded the battle group that had worked with the Howze Board at Fort Bragg.

Aircraft and pilots came from Fort Bragg and Fort Lewis. The aviation battalion of the 4th Division provided enough aircraft and pilots to form A and B Companies of the 227th Assault Helicopter Battalion, the fledgling division's first lift battalion.

Preceded by individual and small unit training and by two division-controlled problems named EAGLE STRIKE and EAGLE CLAW, the division took to the field for its first test, AIR ASSAULT I. This took place in the vicinity of Fort Stewart, Ga., during late September and early October of 1963 and involved almost 4,000 Sky Soldiers and about 175 aircraft.

While AIR ASSAULT I was in progress, the division continued its buildup to a brigade-size force. Two infantry battalions, the 1st of the 188th and the 1st of the 511th, were added along with a corresponding increase in combat support and combat service support units. On October 1, 1963, the 187th Infantry, Company A of the 127th Engineers and Battery B of the 6th Battalion, 81st Artillery, were officially designated as airborne units, thereby giving the air assault division a limited airborne capability.

Very early in the game MG Kinnard realized that these initial moves were but a step in the right direction. Recognizing the need for fresh, new ideas, he established the Division Idea Center in January 1964, thereby creating an intellectual climate in the division that was receptive to bold thoughts and startling techniques. Of these innovations, unusual as they may have seemed then, many are now accepted, combat-tried methods and techniques in the Air Cav Division.

The Grover E. Bell Award, given annually for research and experimentation in the field of helicopter development, was awarded to the 11th Air Assault Division on January 21, 1964. At the Honors Banquet of the American Institute of Aeronautics and Astronautics, the 11th Air Assault Division was cited for its pioneering work in application of the rapid mobility and firepower provided by the helicopter to extend the Army's ground combat capabilities.

The tests went on. There was HAWK ASSAULT I, followed by HAWK ASSAULT II, and then HAWK STAR I. All were observed closely by hundreds of distinguished military and civilian visitors. The frequency of the visits and the intense scrutiny to which the the division was subjected led MG Kinnard to quip: "Never have so few been observed so often by so many."

On July 2, 1964, three infantry battalions, two artillery battalions and a brigade headquarters from the 2nd Infantry Division were formally attached to the 11th Air Assault Division—the wedding of two fine units which was, one year later, to produce a strapping offspring known as the airmobile division.

Through this testing period, the division, brigade and battalion staffs pitched into write tactics and techniques handbooks and SOPs. It was an exhilarating feeling in those days to know that a new textbook was being written and each individual had a part in the writing.

Ideas were tested, accepted, revised or rejected. With each innovation often came changes in organizational structure. One of the crucial aspects of the airmobile concept was that it had to be more than merely providing infantry troops with helicopters for simple lifts to and from a combat area. Ground personnel began thinking in terms of air vehicles; commanders and staff substituted space and distance measurements with time intervals. Aviators became familiar with problems faced daily by ground troops. New concepts in supply and evacuation were developed; techniques in communications and control of widely dispersed units were perfected.

One of the innovations was in the marking of aircraft. It was felt by division thinkers that if aircraft could be readily identifiable by ground troops it would not only speed up combined operations, but develop a closeness and rapport otherwise unobtainable. So markings for each air unit were devised, and these markings, by and large, still exist today in the 1st Air Cav. The familiar box, triangle and circle originated during this period. Markings were carried on to even a more finite degree. Platoons within lift companies were given color codes and each aircraft in the platoon was assigned numbers. These colors and numbers were proclaimed by a color plate affixed to both sides of the aircraft.

An air assault infantryman, watching a bird come in with a blue colored circle and with a white color plate

Testing of the airmobile concept was conducted in 1965 at Fort Benning, Georgia, prior to the division's deployment to Vietnam. Here troops board helicopters in the final phases of the test program.

bearing the numeral one, would know immediately that this was the lead aircraft (probably the platoon leader) of the second platoon of Charlie Company, 229th Assault Helicopter Battalion.

Lift units developed personalities and ground troops identified with aviation elements. A key factor in developing air assault espirit was the Air Assault Badge. Worn by all members of the division who met certain prerequisites, the badge symbolized the excitement of the bold experiment.

For the 2nd Division soldiers joining the air assault ranks for the first time, the badge was a source of amusement—at first—then as the Indianhead troops became involved in the training intraca-

A sergeant involved in test exercise SKY SOLDIER I in 1965 loads a 2.75 inch rocket into the weapons system mounted on an earlier model Huey, the UH-1B.

Army Sergeant Philip Maddox, 1st Squadron, 9th Cavalry, learns rappelling techniques as he makes his third jump from a 35-foot tower at Fort Benning, Georgia.

cies of combat assault, rappelling and rigging, the Air Assault Badge became a coveted possession.

The summer of 1964 was spent preparing for the division tests in the Carolina maneuver area. This was to be the payoff; the demonstration to hundreds of highly critical eyes that airmobility was here to stay.

The tests, AIR ASSAULT II, were administered by Test, Evaluation and Control Group from Combat Developments Command, and the entire show was monitored by U.S. Strike Command.

AIR ASSAULT II tests pitted the 11th Air Assault Division against the 82nd Airborne Division, which had been reinforced with two mechanized battalions from the 2nd Infantry Division.

The 11th, even with the augmentation from the 2nd Division, still had only six maneuver battalions that operated for the most part under the 1st and 2nd Brigades, although the 3rd Brigade, working with a planning headquarters staff but no troops, was allocated two maneuver battalions for an operation late in the exercise.

By November 15, the tests were over and the division had returned to Fort Benning to await results of the tests. Umpires, test directors and commanders put in long hours threshing the results about and came up with some solid conclusions about the airmobile division. The tests showed conclusively that the division's elements could seek out an enemy over a very wide area, find him, and then rapidly bring together the necessary firepower and troops to

destroy him. In a low intensity war, the division would be ideally suited for controlling large sectors; in a high intensity war, it could serve superbly as a screening force or as a mobile reserve.

It was one of the paradoxes of this development of airmobility that the main thrust of the tests was within the parameters of a medium or high intensity combat environment and not in a counterinsurgency situation. The division's early TOE reflected this thinking. For example, at one time the division artillery boasted a Little John rocket battalion in addition to three 105 mm artillery battalions and an aerial rocket artillery battalion.

The organization of the lift units was influenced by the need to maintain tac-

(Continued on P. 259)

The USNS Croaton waits in port at Mobile, Alabama, for the 1st Air Cavalry troops and equipment bound for Vietnam. The ship was one of several used in the deployment of the Army's first airmobile division.

The birth of the 1st Air Cavalry Division (above) was also the end of the 11th Air Assault Division (Test). The "changing of the colors" ceremony took place at Fort Benning's Doughboy Stadium on July 3, 1965. As the colors of the 11th Air Assault Division (Test) were cased, inactivating the division, the colors of the 1st Cavalry were brought onto the field. The "airmobile concept" had become reality. Major General Harry W. O. Kinnard, first commanding general of the 1st Air Cavalry Division, troops the line of review (below) during the ceremony at Fort Benning upon his departure for Vietnam.

THE FIRST AIR CAVALRY DIVISION IN VIETNAM

Somewhere in the annals of military organizations there may have been outfits activated, organized and moved 12,000 miles to combat all within the space of 90 days, but none comes immediately to mind.

That the 1st Cavalry Division (Airmobile) successfully did just that, not only is a remarkable achievement, but a tribute to men of the division who devoted an unbelievable amount of time and effort to accomplish their missions.

The story began on June 16th, 1965, when the secretary of defense announced to the nation that the Department of Army had been granted authority to organize an airmobile division at Fort Benning. At the same news conference, he made the sobering declaration that the division would be "combat-ready" in eight weeks.

He also named Major General Harry W. O. Kinnard to command the division. It was an obvious choice. MG Kinnard had, of course, commanded the 11th Air Assault Division, the bulk of whose assets would go into the 1st Air Cavalry Division structure.

Subsequent orders to the division gave it less time than eight weeks. Concurrent with reorganization from resources of the 11th and the 2nd Infantry Division it was told on July 1 to achieve REDCON-1— Readiness Condition of highest combat priority—by July 28. The problems involved seemed insurmountable. As of reorganization date, the division was short substantial numbers of officers, warrant officers and enlisted men. Other complication factors included a major increase in the number of airborne spaces (the entire 1st Brigade was to be airborne qualified) and the high number of division members who were nondeployable under announced criteria. Because of the sensitivity of the mission, guidance concerning criteria for deployment was sketchy.

Another herculean task was the requirement to locate nearly 7,500 families of division members. Advance planning was, of course, done in secret, but in the final stages, the job was accomplished by the Infantry Center's Army Community Service Agency, working in conjunction with the division's own family assistance groups.

During the early days of July, despite the obviousness of preparations, there had been no official word from Washington. There were rumors, of course, but most in the division simply did not believe it really ready for deployment to combat. In fact, there was the story told of a captain who had been waiting for nearly a year for on-post housing to open up. Early in July, when an apartment came open, he assured his family that the division would not possibly be deployed before fall and moved from comfortable off-post housing. Needless to say, he moved again—in four weeks.

The official word came on the date the division was to achieve REDCON-1, July 28. President Lyndon B. Johnson, in a nation-wide address, told the world, "I am today ordering the airmobile division to Vietnam."

There was little idle time aboard the ships loaded with Skytroopers on their way to Vietnam, as training schedules were made to help maintain combat effectiveness. Members of the division (below) got their first glimpse of Vietnam as the fleet, loaded with an entire division, sailed into Qui Nhon Harbor.

Stepping foot on foreign soil (below) created a mixture of emotions. For some there was exhilaration, for others uncertainty, or maybe fear. But those landing knew one thing. The trek across the ocean was behind them. As the Cav patches walked onto solid ground, there was relief. And there was an evident confidence. The "Cav" had come to fight.

MG Kinnard told newsmen who swarmed to the division's Harmony Church headquarters following the announcement: "I have no misgivings whatever about the ability of this division to perform superbly in Vietnam in any way that may be required. I believe we will make the Army and the country proud of us."

Now that the cat was out of the bag, work began in earnest. While POR/POM processing was handled at a central location using the county-fair system of stations to handle 850 persons daily in the big field house at Harmony Church, the vast training requirement for the entire division was accomplished by means of centralized direction and decentralized execution.

The major training task was to qualify the entire division on the M16E1 rifle which replaced the M14 as the main individual arm. In addition to the general infantry training, the division, because of its peculiar composition, had to conduct or arrange for certain specilized training. The Airborne School at Fort Benning conducted a special 10-day intensified airborne qualification course which graduated 659 new paratroopers. The Aviation School at Fort Rucker, Alabama, conducted two special classes —a UH-1 transition class for 89 aviators and a UH-1 aerial weapons firing course for 120.

Operational planning was conducted apart from normal division functions, and ultimately five operational plans were developed. The division was fortunate in this area in that, since January, its G-2 and G-3 sections had been war-gaming with studies based on the very area of Vietnam into which it was scheduled to be deployed. This six-month lead time permitted an orderly buildup of intelligence files, preparation of Order of Battle studies and compilation of weather, enemy and terrain information.

Decisions were made daily that were to have long-reaching effects on both the division and the Army. Most were in the fields of tactics and doctrine, but some were not. The men of the division, accustomed to the requirements of garrison life, sported blazing yellow Cav patches and white name tapes. Under shorts, T-shirts and handkerchiefs were position-revealing white. Many of the fatigue uniforms were faded to a near grey. No jungle fatigues were available for issue; the division would deploy with what it had on its back. So a decision

was made to dye all fatigues and white underclothing. The color chosen was a dark green. Much of the burden was assumed by the quartermaster laundry at Benning, but many Skytroopers found it convenient to buy the dye and do it themselves . . . at home or in laundromats.

Every packet of green and black dye in Georgia was snapped up. The sewage effluent at Columbus, Ga., and Phenix City, Ala., was said to have turned green and stayed that way for weeks. But the division's uniforms toned down. White name tapes were further dulled by magic marker pens. The yellow patches turned into a green and black patch. and from this color combination was born a further idea: the manufacture of OD and black patches and rank and branch insignia. MG Kinnard ordered some special patches made by a Japanese firm and after the 1st Cav arrived in Vietnam, the trend swept the division like wildfire. Of course, it eventually spread to other units in Vietnam, and, ultimately, the entire Army.

Late in July the division began to curtail training to pack its equipment and supplies. General cargo and aircraft departed from eastern and gulf coast ports in late July and early August, and equipment that was to accompany troops left Benning about one week prior to the movement of the troops.

At the end of these harried weeks commanders tried to give every man a few days leave before actual departure; a few days to spend with their families before the long, hard year ahead. For the troopers and families both, leave provided a tremendous morale boost before

the men were to leave their country, their loved ones, their families, for at least a year—and for some of them, forever.

Movement of personnel was accomplished in three increments. An advance liaison planning detachment of 32 key officers and men, led by Brigadier General John S. Wright, the assistant division commander, departed on August 2 by commercial air. An advance party of 1,030 officers and men and 152 tons of cargo was deployed by the Military Airlift Command from Robbins Air Force Base during a six-day period beginning August 14th. The advance party landed at Cam Ranh Bay and then flew to An Khe where work was begun on the division base.

It was at this time that the base got its name "Golf Course." BG Wright assembled his men shortly after their arrival and told them they were going to create a base and that it was going to be done without the use of bulldozers or power equipment. This was, he said, because earth moving equipment stripped the land of its protective grasses and bushes and, with 435 helicopters soon to arrive, the base would quickly become a vast dust bowl or a gigantic mud pie, depending on the season. BG Wright then picked up a machete, tied a cloth about his forehead and, to the horror and chagrin of the assemblage, led the way into the scrub jungle to carve out a helipad that would be as he put it, "as clean as a golf course."

For several months afterwards, veterans of that advance party, colonels and privates alike, could be distinguished by the callouses on their palms.

An aerial view of the 1st Air Cav's newly established basecamp at An Khe in I Corps shows typical Army orderliness, even when located in a combat zone. This picture is of the rear section area of the 1st Battalion, 8th Cavalry.

A CH-47 Chinook of the 228th Assault Support Helicopter Battalion off-loads Skytroopers of the 3rd Brigade into an already secured landing zone during Operation MASHER in early 1966.

The bulk of the division moved by Military Sea Transport Service troop ships. The first ship, with the 2nd Brigade, two infantry battalions and one artillery battalion, left on August 15th.

A total of six troop carriers, four aircraft carriers and seven cargo vessels were employed in the over-water movement. The 1st Brigade loaded out on the USNS Geiger, the 2nd Brigade on the Buckner, the 3rd Brigade on the Rose. The remainder of the division loaded on the Darby, Patch and Upshur. More than 470 of the division's aircraft were crowded on the carriers USNS Kula Gulf, Croaton and Card. The USS Boxer had more than 220 aircraft, including the four CH-54 Flying Cranes from the attached 478th Aviation Company.

Four weeks at sea provided little idle time. Additional training and preparation for jungle warfare filled the hours. Physical fitness was emphasized through daily PT sessions on the hatch covers, and open decks. Skull practice in counter-guerrilla tactics, patrolling, jungle navigation and other pertinent subjects kept skills sharp. Weapons testing and familiarization was carried out from the after decks of the troop carriers. On the Buckner, for example, the chief

engineer rigged out a floating target that demonstrated amazing stability despite the turbulence of the ship's wake.

The division celebrated its 44th anniversary September 13th, on the high seas. But the following day, USNS Buckner with the 2nd Brigade, dropped anchor in Qui Nhon harbor. Two days earlier the Boyer had arrived and Cav birds already were flying to shore.

Combat elements of the division closed on the An Khe base on September 14th and the Viet Cong wasted little time in probing the base defenses. While the valley and the route into the base was secured by the 1st Brigade of the 101st Airborne Division, the resposibility for defense remained with the division.

Although the division supported the 101st's brigade with air and ground combat elements on September 19th in Operation Gibralter, just east of An Khe, the official date for the 1st Air Cavalry Division assuming complete responsibility for defense of the An Khe area and the division's tactical area of responsibility was September 28.

This was 104 days from the date Secretary McNamara announced the formation of the 1st Air Cavalry Division and just 90 days after the general orders

activated the unit on July 1st, 1965.

Meanwhile, the 17th Aviation Company, detached from the 10th Aviation Brigade at Fort Benning, was winging its way around the world. The 18 twin engine CV-2 Caribou aircraft worked out of Camp Holloway at Pleiku and provided the Cav the continuous, responsive fixed-wing lift support it needed in those vital early days.

Just west of An Khe on Highway 19, in 1954, the most mobile unit in the French forces, Mobile Group 100, was ambushed and destroyed by a Viet Minh Regiment. One of the first missions of the Cav was to open and secure Highway 19 from Deo Mang pass on the east to Mang Yang pass on the west. In clearing brush from the sides of the road, Skytroopers discovered a memorial obelisk commemorating the brave French and Vietnamese soldiers who had bled and died on that spot 11 years earlier. It was a sober reminder of the worth of the enemy and the fact that others had tried before and failed.

On October 10th, the 3rd Brigade kicked off the first self-contained combat operation in the war for the FIRST TEAM. Dubbed Operation SHINY BAYONET, the five-day thrust into the Suoi Ca Valley east of An Khe gave Skytroopers their first taste of a combat assault under fire. Quipped some veterans of Air Assault Division tests: "We call it AIR ASSAULT III . . . with bullets."

It was a good shakedown for the three battalions involved. Other battalions began to flex their muscles in early October, moving into the Vinh Thanh valley and spreading the Cav oil slick in the valley around the An Khe base.

The number of "firsts" racked up by the Cav in those early days was staggering. The first full division in Vietnam, the first airmobile division, the first unit to deploy CH-47 Chinook helicopters into combat, the first unit to use CH-54 Flying Crane choppers, and so on, ad infinitum.

Being first had become a habit. But there was no "first" of more significance than being the first division in the Vietnam conflict to earn a Presidential Unit Citation (PUC).

The story of the PUC is more than a story of valor, although that is an indispensable element for the award. There have been many combat actions in Vietnam since then in which many units—in and out of the Cav—have exhibited a high degree of courage.

But the Pleiku Campaign—the name given to the 35 days of airmobile operations that swept across the plateau country west and south of Pleiku—was precursory.

The Pleiku Campaign was the first real combat test of the FIRST TEAM as a full division and for the fledgling airmobile concept. But the campaign was more than just the triumph of a concept. It marked the first major confrontation between a U.S. Army division and a North Vietnamese division. Again, however this "first" by itself was not overly significant.

It is only when considering the results of the battle in the context of the strategic and political implications of the enemy actions that the Pleiku Campaign looms as a monumental feat of arms.

It all started on October 19th, just a couple days after SHINY BAYONET had terminated, and while other Cav battalions were just beginning to test their wings.

The Special Forces Camp at Plei Me, some 35 miles south of the key provincial capital of Pleiku, was beseiged by a strong enemy force. The force later was identified as the NVA 33rd Regiment.

This was the lure.

Intelligence quickly picked up the presence of a second NVA regiment, the 32nd, deployed along the road from Pleiku to Plei Me Camp. Any relief column sent to assist the besieged camp surely would have to run a bloody gauntlet.

This was the ambush.

The enemy's plan was to smash the relief column, and then move both regiments against Plei Me. The enemy operation order set a time estimate for the reduction of the camp—just one hour.

Since a large ambush was fully anticipated by allied commanders, it was decided to commit reaction forces of sufficient strength to foil the ambush and punish the enemy.

This was the Cav's opening scene in the drama that was to ensue. A battalion task force, including airmobile artillery, was flown from the Cav's base at An Khe to Pleiku and given a reinforcement mission. As the ARVN armored column moved down the road to Plei Me, Cav artillery leapfrogged in a series of air-moves to keep the column under cover of the 105 milimeter howitzers.

The battle at Plei Me was not a haphazard engagement generated by local enemy forces. It was the outgrowth of a master plan by the enemy—a campaign to secure and dominate a major portion of the Republic of Vietnam. The plan envisaged the committment of three NVA divisions in the northern and central portion of the Republic.

One such division was to conduct the Tay Nguyen (Western Plateau) Campaign and to attempt to seize Kontum, Pleiku, Binh Dinh and Phu Bon Provinces. The lure and the ambush at Plei Me was the opening gun in the struggle for the vital highlands.

On the 23rd of October, when the ARVN relief column smashed through the ambush and relieved Plei Mei, the two NVA regiments broke contact and began moving toward sanctuaries along the Cambodian border.

At this point a significant and historic decision was made. General William C. Westmoreland, the COMUSMACV, along with Lieutenant General Stanley Larsen, the commander of I Field Force, visited the 1st Brigade command post at LZ Homecoming. Present at the meeting were key members of the division staff, and, of course, MG Kinnard.

Realizing that only bold and decisive action would keep the enemy from retaining the iniative, GEN Westmoreland gave the Cav its head. He ordered the division to pursue, seek out and destroy the enemy.

The Cav's mission was then changed from one of reinforcement and reaction to that of unlimited offense; its area of operation was changed from a tiny, constricted zone to a vast arena, con-

Cavalrymen from Company A, 1st Battalion, 5th Cavalry, move toward a thatched Vietnamese home to search for contraband items that might be stored there. The men were on a search and destroy mission near the division's basecamp at An Khe in I Corps, late 1965.

taining 2,500 square miles of trackless jungle.

The 32nd Regiment, located between Plei Me and Pleiku, managed to slip to the west relatively unhampered by the division, which concentrated its efforts on the final relief of Plei Me. The 33rd Regiment, which had tarried too long around the camp before beginning its retreat, paid dearly for that error.

The pursuit of the 33rd by the battalions of the 1st Brigade and the 1st Squadron, 9th Cavalry, introduced to the enemy a new concept in warfare. His retreat from Plei Me to the Chu Pong Massif on the Cambodian border became a nightmare.

North Vietnamese regulars were routed from their hiding places, hounded and pursued, fragmented and destroyed in terrain they had believed would be their protector. Nothing in their background or training had prepared them to cope with the full effects of an unleashed airmobile pursuit.

On the 9th of November, a lull came to the battlefield and MG Kinnard decided to bring in the 3rd Brigade, fresh and spoiling for a fight. At the same time, the NVA division was introducing new troops to the battle. Fresh from the infiltration trail, the 66th NVA Regiment moved into staging areas in the valley of the Ia Drang and along the edge of the Chu Pong Massif.

On the morning of the 14th of November, the 1st Battalion, 7th Cavalry, air assaulted into a landing zone codenamed "X-Ray." There it met the 66th Regiment head-on.

For the next three days, LZ X-Ray became the scene of some of the most violent combat ever experienced by Cavalrymen in any war. The 66th and remnants of the 33rd Regiment tried again and again to overrun the tiny perimeter.

The combination of conspicious gallantry and massive firepower of the FIRST TEAM inflicted hideous casualties on the enemy. But more was yet to come.

On the 17th of November, the decision was made to maneuver away from the Chu Pong hill mass to permit a close-in B-52 air strike—the first time in history that strategic bombers were used in support of the ground scheme of maneuver.

The 1st of the 7th was airlifted to Pleiku. The 2nd Battalion, 5th Cavalry, moved overland to an LZ named Columbus, where two artillery batteries were located. And the third battalion that had fought on LZ X-Ray, the 2nd Battalion, 7th Cavalry, began moving toward a map location known as Albany. A battalion of the 66th Regiment also was on the move to nearly the same location.

The two battalions collided.

Mere words never can convey the agony that was Albany that afternoon, where two well-armed, determined and aggressive forces fell upon each other in a dense jungle; where friend and foe were intermingled; where it was rifleman against rifleman.

Then came another lull, and again, a change in brigades. This time the 2nd Brigade was brought in. But the NVA had had enough, and the 2nd Brigade chased the remnants of the 33rd and 66th Regiments back into their Cambodian sanctuaries. At this point the ARVN Airborne Brigade had been brought into the battle, and it remained for it to drive from the Ia Drang the survivors of the 32nd, the last regiment of the NVA division that had opened the Tay Nguyen Campaign so confidently 35 days earlier.

In those 35 days, the 1st Air Cav killed 3,561 North Vietnamese soldiers and detained 157 others, literally annihilating two of the three regiments of the NVA division. The Cav captured 900 individual weapons and 126 crew served weapons and enough munitions to completely arm an NVA battalion.

Above all else, history will record that there were two things achieved in the Pleiku Campaign. North Vietnamese regulars sustained their first major defeat ever, forever disrupting a well-conceived plan of conquest, and the 1st Air Cav

Division engineered the triumph of a concept.

When Secretary of Defense Robert McNamara reviewed the results of the campaign, he called it an "unparalleled achievement." He declared: "Unique in its valor and courage, the Air Cavalry Division has established a record which will stand for a long time for other divisions to match."

MG Kinnard noted that remark when he wrote: "The only higher accolade possible is the award of the Presidential Unit Citation."

In the Rose Garden of the White House in October 1966, a full year after the opening gun of that fateful campaign, a grateful government concurred.

But, of course, the Cav did not rest on its laurels, either present or projected. There were other areas that needed the immediate services of a tested airmobile division. Attention was directed to the east of An Khe, first to provide security for the establishment of the Republic of Korea Capitol Division's basecamp at Binh Khe, and then into an area that was becoming quite familiar to Skytroopers—the Soui Ca Valley. Operation CLEAN HOUSE was conducted from the 17th to the 30th of December and was marked by short but fierce engagements in which the enemy attempted to break contact immediately after it was made.

1966

Operation MATADOR was the next show for the division, and involved opening Highway 19 to Pleiku as well as conducting spoiling attacks along the Cambodian border in both Pleiku and Kontum Provinces.

It was on January 25th, 1966, that the division launched its longest and largest operation to that date. Operation MASHER/WHITE WING, also known as the Bong Son Campaign, lasted for 41 consecutive days as the division moved into the northeast and eastern portions of Binh Dinh Province. Reliable intelligence built up over several months said that this portion of Binh Dinh contained another NVA division, the Sao Vang (Yellow Star) or 3rd Division. As the operation developed it became apparent that there were three regiments subordinate to the 3rd Division—the 18th, the 22nd and the 2nd VC. These units were to be the Cav's main adversaries for most of 1966. They were primarily concentrated in the central-coastal plain north of Bong Son and in the mountains north, west and southeast of Bong Son.

MASHER/WHITE WING was conducted in five phases in which each one of the division's brigades participated in one or more. For the first time, the FIRST TEAM worked in conjunction with other Free World Forces. Additional support came from the III Marine Amphibious Force, the 22nd ARVN Division reinforced by an airborne brigade, and the ROK Capitol Division.

The first phase began as a 3rd Brigade operation and lasted only three days. It was geared at deceiving the enemy as to the true intent of the Cav in Bong Son as well as increasing the security on Highway 1 between Qui Nhon and Bong Son. The bulk of the activity was south of Bong Son itself.

Phase II kicked off with a bang when the 3rd Brigade conducted air assaults into the lowlands north of Bong Son. The ARVN Airborne Brigade was to the east along the coast while 3rd Brigade battalions attacked north to the west of Highway 1. Two enemy battalions of the 22nd NVA Regiment were located, fixed, hit and finally flushed. The division quickly combat assaulted blocking forces to the west and north of the contact.

guration of tributary valleys.

In this phase the division perfected a new technique for finding, fixing and destroying the enemy. The 3rd Brigade combat assaulted elements of three battalions onto the outer limits of each of the tributary valleys, placing ambush positions at key terrain features along exfiltration routes out of the valley. Simultaneously the remainder of the brigade assaulted into the center of the valley along its floor and began sweeping outward toward the ambushes. These "beater" forces flushed the enemy into the kill zones of the ambush positions. For more than three days ambushes were sprung and the enemy casualties mounted.

The capture of a battalion commander of the 22nd NVA Regiment led to a major battle in a strong NVA defensive position south of Bong Son, dubbed the "Iron Triangle." The 2nd Brigade was

A giant CH-54 "Flying Crane" hovers over LZ Laramie, located near An Khe in I Corps. Helicopters were used exclusively to supply the mountaintop base.

Carrying a pair of souvenir sandals picked up during Operation WALLOWA, a 3rd Brigade soldier and his platoon move to a new location.

Heavy fighting took place for two days, and when Phase II terminated on February 3 the NVA had paid dearly for their exposure to the Cav—556 killed and 215 captured.

Phase III had the 2nd Brigade moving into the An Lao Valley, long a VC stronghold. The plan also called for elements of the III MAF, the 9th Marines in particular, to assault down the valley from the north. The Marines, working without the support of Naval gunfire, found themselves under the shield of Cav artillery and gunships plus, for the first time in history, the support of airlifted 155 milimeter howitzers.

Bad weather forced a two-day delay on D-Day and the enemy seized the opportunity to escape. As a result, the attack into An Lao was disappointing and met with only slight resistance. During the operation, the division's psychological operations people were busy broadcasting and dropping leaflets to inform the people of the valley that the Cav could not remain and that if they chose to leave the valley the opportunity was present. Approximately 4,500 of a total population of 8,000 elected to leave and most were flown to freedom by Cav Chinooks.

The fourth phase of the operation was initiated to exploit intelligence reports of an enemy buildup in the Kim Son Valley, dubbed the "Eagle's Claw" or "Crow's Foot" because of the confi-

tasked to reduce the stronghold and after three days of continuous, hard fighting, the broken remains of the 22nd Regiment hurriedly departed, leaving 313 dead behind.

Meanwhile, the 1st Brigade had replaced the 3rd Brigade in the Kim Son Valley and continued to maintain pressure on the enemy there. A major contact in one tributary valley deprived the 18th NVA Regiment of its 12.7 millimeter anti-aircraft guns and its recoilless rifles and most of the personnel in its heavy weapons company.

The fifth phase of the campaign, from March 1st to the 6th, was aimed at destroying the enemy forces in the Cay Giep mountains to the east and south of Bong Son. This phase ended with 50 enemy killed and another 30 captured.

When MASHER/WHITE WING terminated March 6 the bulk of the Cav's forces were back in the area south of

Bong Son where the first phase had started 41 days earlier. The division had operated in 360 degrees around Bong Son in which enemy contact was maintained during each of the 41 days. The campaign also dissipated any residual doubts about the airmobile division's capability to conduct sustained operations under adverse weather conditions and at substantial distances from a basecamp. The campaign proved beyond a doubt that the victory scored in the Pleiku Campaign was no fluke.

The statistics of the operations are impressive: 1,342 enemy killed by the Cav, with an additional 808 killed by Free World Forces. Five of the nine enemy battalions engaged were rendered ineffective and three field hospitals had been captured.

From March through April the FIRST TEAM ran several battalion and brigade-size operations. While heavy contact

with resultant enemy losses was minim the division gained valuable intelligen of infiltration routes and rest stations well as uncovering a few sizable cache

While two of these operations were progress—LEWIS and CLARK a DAVY CROCKETT, the airmob division experienced its first change command. MG Kinnard, who pi neered the air assault concept with t 11th Air Assault Division at Fort Be ning, and who brilliantly led the Air Cavalry Division in its first mont in Vietnam, relinquished command Major General John Norton.

On the 6th of May, MG Nort trooped the line of colors and a new e for the division began. MG Nort was no stranger to the Cav, nor to t airmobile concept. He served with t FIRST TEAM in Korea in 1959-60 a battle group commander and, in 19 as the Army Aviation Officer for Conti

A pack-laden Skytrooper takes a break while patrolling the An Lao Valley near An Khe during Operation PERSHING in 1967.

ental Army Command, he served on the Howze Board, which gave birth to the airmobile concept. Like his predecessor, MG Norton was an old airbornetrooper, campaigning with the paratroops during World War II. He came to the Cav after a successful tour as commander of MACV Support Command, the forerunner of U.S. Army Vietnam.

Operation CRAZY HORSE kicked off on May 16th, scarcely giving the new Cav chief time to get unpacked. When the operation, which was centered in the mountains between the Vinh Thanh and Soui Ca valleys, ended on June 5th, a total of 507 enemy from the Yellow Star division were dead. There was tragedy too. Sam Castan, a senior editor of Look Magazine, was killed while on assignment with the 1st Brigade. (Of the hundreds of correspondents who have covered the FIRST TEAM since its arrival in Vietnam, Mr. Castan is the only one to have lost his life while on assignment with the division.)

During a 90-day period, beginning in mid-June, the "old" FIRST TEAM rotated back to the United States and new replacements, eager to become part of this famous team, arrived, were oriented and integrated into the fold. From a personnel and logistic stand-

point, the rotation was a task of the first magnitude. Although attrition had pared the division's rotational hump somewhat, there still were 12,000 Skytroopers due to DEROS during this period.

The smooth flow of replacements in and veterans out was handled with a shuttle of Air Force C-141 Starlifters between Travis Air Force Base, California, and Pleiku. The Cav established a liaison office at Travis and handled all outprocessing at Pleiku, thus bypassing normal replacement depot channels.

Operations DECKHOUSE and NATHAN HALE in the area around Tuy Hoa in Phu Yen Province, followed by HENRY CLAY in Phu Bon and Darlac Provinces gave the division ample opportunity to weld the newcomers into a finely tuned airmobile machine. By August the Cav was ready to return to its old haunts in the Ia Drang-Chu Pong area for the fourth time in less than a year.

Operation PAUL REVERE II followed the now-familiar pattern of extensive search and maneuver interspersed with brief periods of intense contact. Since the division had been in the area three times previously planners had

a pretty good idea of what to expect of both enemy and the terrain. It was the weather, however, that was unexpected and unusually severe. MG Norton described it as some of the worst weather he had ever seen for airmobile operations. Only a few hours a day were available for lift and resupply and even during these periods flying was hazardous.

But despite the hazards the Cav fought on, and when the operation drew to a close the enemy had lost 861 men to Allied Forces. As PAUL REVERE terminated, a task force with the 2nd Bn, 7th Cav, was formed and placed under the operational control of IFFORCEV on Operation BYRD. The task force was sent to the southernmost part of II Corps Tactical Zone to support the Vietnamese Revolutionary Development Program in Phan Thiet. This task force remained on this mission through the close of 1966.

On the 13th of September, the division's organization day, THAYER I kicked off with five infantry battalions combat assaulting into a circular configuration around the Crow's Foot area. It was the beginning of a 17-month campaign to pacify Binh Dinh Province.

The battalions did not make major troop contact, but did dig up significant caches and, more importantly, by staying and dominating the valley, prevented the enemy from using the bases he needed to stay combat effective.

Other 1st Air Cav units meanwhile had moved east from the valleys and maneuvered into position to trap the enemy in a coastal pocket. There evolved Operation IRVING, which, in a sense, was a battlefield within a much larger battlefield. Because of the tight cordon maintained, the enemy had two choices: to stand and fight or try to exfiltrate. In either case he lost.

In 22 days the FIRST TEAM, working with Free World Forces, compiled some overwhelming statistics. In both operations, the enemy had lost 2,063 killed, 1,930 captured and returned 141 to GVN control. In particular, IRVING was unique in that the Cav captured, interrogated and processed more enemy than in any previous operation. Also, for the first time since the division began operations in Vietnam, the number of enemy captured exceeded the number killed.

THAYER II was but a logical extension of the preceeding operations in the Bong Son area as part of the all-out effort to pacify eastern Binh Dinh Province. Division forces in these operations ranged from a brigade with two maneuver battalions to three brigades with eight battalions. The division now boasted nine battalions, with the 5th Battalion, 7th Cavalry, having joined the FIRST TEAM from Fort Carson, Colorado.

The Christmas truce ended violently when in the early morning of December 27, LZ Bird in the Kim Son Valley erupted with mortar and small arms fire. The 22nd NVA Regiment had taken advantage of the truce to move into position around the LZ. The attack was pressed hard but in the end the 22nd lost more than 200 killed.

The year 1966 closed during the second two-day truce period around the U.S. New Year. On December 31st, THAYER II was in its 68th day, the longest operation undertaken by the division in Vietnam. It was to last considerably longer.

1967

The new year of 1967 began for the 1st Cavalry with a new approach to its enemy. In 16 months of being chased

and chopped by a relentless air assault cavalry, the enemy became reluctant to meet the FIRST TEAM head-on. The enemy was loathe to show himself in massed forces. He slipped into elusiveness. He began to spread out and spread thin. The division countered by easing off on its chase. Instead, the Cavalrymen were prepositioned near known enemy haunts; platoon ambushes were widespread and frequent and long range patrols overwatched principal enemy locations while "stirring forces" were used to generate enemy movement, to mix his simmering pot of activity. The enemy was prodded and herded into "coming to us."

Operation THAYER II lingered through January and saw the 1st Cavalry straddling a large II Corps area. The 1st

A convoy (left) fords the shallow An Long River as the trucks make their way toward Camp Evans in I Corps.

"Garry Owen" troopers of Company D, 2nd Battalion, 7th Cavalry, dash toward the helicopter that will carry them to yet another location. Once there they will search near Khe Sanh, as part of Operation PEGASUS. The action occurred in April 1968.

A Chinook waist gunner aboard the last Cav ship to leave the A Shau Valley looks back on the scarred and torn valley floor where so many fierce battles raged, where ghastly numbers of the enemy died and where many Cavalry troops made the highest sacrifice possible for their comrades-in-arms.

Brigade was stirring enemy action in the central and southern Kim Son Valley. The 2nd Brigade beat the bush to flush enemy troops in northern Kim Son, the Crescent Area and in the Nui Mieu and Cay Giep mountains.

The heaviest January contact came on the 27th northeast of Bong Son when elements of the 2nd Battalion, 12th Cavalry, air assaulted on top of an NVA battalion. By dark they had been reinforced with four rifle companies, two platoons from the 1st Squadron, 9th Cavalry, and elements of the ARVN and Vietnamese Marines. The fight flared and flashed through the night. At dawn the Allied soldiers rose to sweep the area and finish off pockets of resistance. Seventy-two enemy lay dead and 11 were taken prisoner.

THAYER II was the division's longest operation to that date in Vietnam—111 days. In the end, when the operation was finished and tallied, the division's soldiers had killed 1,757 enemy soldiers in that time.

From February to the end of April the division was able to concentrate its forces for the first time in the pacification of a single province. The division began dominating the lush, densely populated Binh Dinh Province with Operation PERSHING after THAYER II terminated February 11. Main force enemy units were encountered primarily on the Bong Son Plain and in the An Lao Valley. Under Cav pressure North Vietnamese and Viet Cong units were eventually forced to withdraw into Quang Ngai Province north of the II Corps boundary. With PERSHING began the Phase IV of the Binh Dinh Pacification Campaign.

When the enemy had been driven back into his base areas north of the province border in April, the 2nd Brigade's two battalions were deployed for the first time outside II Corps to conduct Mission LEJEUNE. In 16 days of fighting along the coast, they killed 176 enemy soldiers.

When PERSHING was launched on February 12, the rich rice areas were to see the first signs of waning Communist control. It had been an area closed in the fist of Communist domination, but when PERSHING ended in January 1968, that grip had been pried open and wrested loose.

The first division-size operation conducted by the FIRST TEAM, PERSHING pitted the Army's unique airmobile division against the 3rd North Viet-

35

namese Army Division, a match which cost the Communists more than 6,000 killed.

Suffering from earlier defeats, the enemy refused to actively engage the Skytroopers, but he was hounded relentlessly as the division dogged his footsteps. Only once would the enemy stand and fight, at Tam Quan in December, and then he would lose 650 men from the 22nd NVA Regiment.

Operation PERSHING was largely unglamorous. The division began the monotonous task of cordon and search operations that would break the VC political stronghold in the villages. The division's capabilities were greatly enhanced by the attachment of three companies from the 816th National Police Field Force (NPFF). Elements of

the division conducted pre-dawn cordons and the NPFF would sweep through and search villages and hamlets for VC. The process of physically rooting out the Viet Cong had begun. Some 2,400 of the enemy were detained during the year.

While the day to day footwork of the infantry lacked glamour, the spectacular flying of the 1st Sqdn, 9th Cav, and the brigade scout helicopters made its job easier. As the NVA rice gathering elements attempted to steal crops, reconnaissance helicopters engaged them and a pattern of aerial death was established. After being spotted, the enemy could expect aerial rocket artillery, tube artillery, infantry, and the slashing miniguns of gunships to descend on them.

The 1st Sqdn, 9th Cav, with its ability

to react immediately to any situation, accounted for 38 percent of the division's kills during Operation PERSHING, cutting down some 1,700 of the enemy, and maintaining a kill ratio of 38 to 1. Additionally, it detained 602 enemy soldiers and captured 203 weapons.

Important rice production areas were closed to the enemy. In the An Lao Valley thousands of refugees were relocated from the area, depriving the NVA and VC those crops. The Kim Son and Suoi Ca were also made denial areas, forcing the enemy into the plains to find food. Denial areas were pounded by artillery at night, making rice gathering after dark a dangerous proposition.

Though only 18 major engagements were made during PERSHING, the division took a heavy toll of the enemy as gunships caught food producing units moving down from the mountains. As hunger gripped the NVA, entire companies and battalions attempted to leave their hiding places for the lowlands and were interdicted by swift movements of the Skytroopers.

As the pacification program pace increased, the division physically blocked VC attempts to regain influence in the villages. The PERSHING area of operations extended over 1,600 square miles and the FIRST TEAM's ability to hold such a large area displayed the capabilities of a well deployed airmobile division. Major General John J. Tolson took the reins of command from MG Norton in April. A career soldier for 31 years, the new "First Skytrooper" participated in every jump the 503rd Parachute Infantry Battalion made in World War II, including the recapture of Corregidor in 1945. He also was an Army Aviator of long standing.

May 31 saw 96 of the enemy from the 9th Battalion, 22nd Regiment, killed as they came west down from the mountains to the Bong Son Plain near An Qui. In June both the 2nd VC Regiment and the 18th NVA Regiment took heavy losses near the Dam Tra-O Lake and the Suoi Ca.

By early summer the 1st Cavalry Division faced a highly demoralized enemy. Hoi Chanhs and detainees spoke of the terror that ARA and armed helicopters wrought and of the rapid decay of morale among the VC and NVA cadre.

The 1st Battalion (Mech), 50th Infantry, joined the division in September, providing a heavy punch against heavily fortified emplacements as their APCs

A tired but stiff-lipped soldier moves forward, unaware of the destructive symmetry passing him by, as he completes a routine patrol with a headquarters element of Company A, 2nd Battalion, 7th Cavalry, near Op Dai Phu hamlet, located north of Hue.

rumbled against the NVA in the 506 Valley, Dam Tra-O Lake, Suoi Ca and Bong Son Plains in a quick introduction to combat for the fresh-from-the-states mechanized battalion.

The 6th to the 20th of December saw the 1st Brigade return from Operation MACARTHUR at Dak To to engage the 2nd NVA Regiment in the much publicized battle near Tam Quan.

Two scout helicopters from the 1st of the 9th spotted a hut sporting an antenna and, when they wheeled to investigate, were engaged by machine-gun fire. Two infantry platoons from the squadron were inserted and quickly became heavily engaged.

The division's quick reaction force, Bravo Company, 2nd Battalion, 8th Cavalry, air assaulted into the area and was later joined by the 1st of the 50th APCs, which proved to be the equalizer for assaulting the bunkers and entrenchments of the NVA.

The 40th ARVN Regiment blocked to the north and south of the enemy headquarters at Dai Dong Village and elements of the 1st Battalion, 8th Cavalry, began assaulting the fortifications of the village.

Returning from Dak To, the 1st Battalion, 12th Cavalry, kept the pressure on the 22nd Regiment, and the Skytroopers overran the fleeing command post.

As the enemy slipped back to the Cay Geip Mountains the 2nd Bn, 8th Cav, got a new fix on the NVA across the Bong Son River and quickly engaged the remnants of the 22nd Regimental Headquarters. Allied forces had killed 661 enemy.

The Army Chief of Staff, General Harold K. Johnson, visisted the Tam Quan battle site and highly praised the 1st Brigade and the 40th ARVN Regiment for their ability to take the battle to the enemy, disrupting the NVA's plans for the Tet Offensive in the Bong Son Plains and for the exceptional performance of the FIRST TEAM in Operation PERSHING.

Vietnamese civilians, most of whom had been raised under the Viet Cong, witnessed a great transition as Operation PERSHING crushed the VC. Under the direction of the Saigon government, elections were held for the first time on September 3, with 95.7 percent of the registered voters in the PERSHING AO participating, against 81 percent nationwide. Schools, hospitals and refugee centers were constructed. Perhaps of more importance, Highway

Working in the Que Son Valley during Operation PERSHING, Specialist Four Joe F. Reyna of Company D, 2nd Battalion, 12th Cavalry, waits and listens for enemy movement while on patrol.

1 was opened for commerce through Binh Dinh for the first time in many years.

When the 2nd Battalion, 7th Cavalry, arrived in Binh Thaun Province, the southernmost province in II Corps, at the end of August 1966, the entire area was in danger of falling into the hands of two Viet Cong battalions. The government had receded to the immediate area of Phan Thiet, the province capital and the center of profitable fishing and fish sauce manufacturing industries. Cavalrymen were committed to mission BYRD.

Of unique political significance was the fact that Ho Chi Minh had once taught school in Phan Thiet.

Sixteen months later the "Garry Owen" troopers had run up a body count of 929 enemy, while losing only 39 of their own men.

More importantly, they had cleared the populous "triangle" area north and west of Phan Thiet for Government of Vietnam administrators to begin development work on a dozen "New Life" hamlets.

The roads around Phan Thiet opened gradually as the battalion's operations fanned out from the capital. Perhaps the biggest success of BYRD's last two months (which ended in mid-January 1968) was the reopening of Highway 1.

Lieutenant Colonel Joseph T. Griffin, the battalion commander, recalled the effect of the road's opening. "The word spread like wildfire. Shops along the highway suddenly came to life again with goods sent up from the south, and lobster, fish and fish sauce were on the way to Saigon by truck."

A task force from the 2nd Bn, 8th Cav, participated in BOLLING September 17 through October 14 west of Tuy Hoa. Contact was scattered with the Skytroopers accounting for 21 enemy killed during the period.

The division's 3rd Brigade entered Quang Tin and Quang Nam provinces during the first week in October for a three and a half month stay that ultimately cost the 2nd North Vietnamese Army more than 2,400 men killed. Three times during the operation 20 or more Viet Cong became Hoi Chanhs due to the relentlessness of Cavalry air and ground pressure.

The 3rd Brigade began the 125 mile move north from its Binh Dinh Province headquarters on October 2 into an area 20 miles southwest of Da Nang, beginning Operation WHEELER/WALLOWA.

The NVA never knew what hit them. Cavalry companies popped up all over the area, decimating the North Viet-

Skytroopers check part of an enemy weapons cache, one of many captured by the division during Operation JEB STUART III. This cache contained Communist mortar and rocket rounds.

namese that tried to escape. Cav helicopters and gunships from the 1st Sqdn, 9th Cav, created havoc among their ranks.

"On my first day flying here," recalled Major Lewis B. Beasley, then B Troop's commander, "I saw a column of NVA walking in the open with weapons and packs. I knew we were going to do some business in this area."

When the operation was three months old, B Troop had killed 834 NVA, roughly half a regiment, while losing three men. Airmobile infantry tactics brought similar results.

1968

The 1st Air Cav has never had an easy year in Vietnam, or a year when it wasn't at the forefront of Allied actions. Even so, it would be hard to find a year that exceeded 1968 for operations that made news, made history and, most importantly, made life tough for the North Vietnamese and Viet Cong. From the walls of Hue to the jungles of III Corps, Skytroopers relentlessly pursued the enemy.

The division began 1968 by terminating Operation PERSHING, the longest of the 1st Cav's Vietnam actions. For nearly a year the division scoured the Bong Son Plain, An Lao Valley and the hills of coastal II Corps, seeking out enemy units and their sanctuaries. When the operation ended on January 21, the enemy had lost 5,401 soldiers and 2,400 enemy had been detained. Some 1,300 individual and 137 crew served weapons had been captured or destroyed. With PERSHING concluded, it was time for the division to move.

The new area of operations for the Cav was in eastern I Corps, Vietnam's northern most tactical zone. Camp Evans, north of Hue, was the division's new basecamp. As the 2nd Brigade continued actions against the enemy in the old PERSHING AO, the rest of the division began Operation JEB STUART.

JEB STUART started as a normal operation. The enemy made it something special when they launched their Tet Offensive in late January. Some 7,000 enemy, primarily well-equipped, crack NVA regulars, had blasted their way into the imperial city of Hue, occupying all but a few strongpoints held by U.S. Marine and ARVN forces. To the north a sapper platoon penetrated Quang Tri, the capital of Vietnam's northernmost province. They initiated acts of sabotage and terrorism early in the morning of January 31. Two hours later five battalions of NVA and VC assaulted the city.

The division's 1st Brigade had been located to the south and west of Quang Tri when the attacks began. From 4 a.m. to noon on January 31 ARVN troops successfully resisted the enemy attacks, but the resources of the Vietnamese soldiers were being strained to the limit. At noon the 1st Brigade was called in. By four in the afternoon the Cavalrymen were helicoptered to landing zones near enemy infiltration and support positions.

Three companies assaulted into LZs around the village of Thon An Thai, east of Quang Tri. All elements received heavy enemy fire initially, but the Sky-

troopers couldn't be stopped.

The heavy weapons support of the NVA battalion to the east of Quang Tri was nullified. In a closing vise between ARVN and 1st Cav forces, the enemy unit began splitting into small elements to escape.

The ground troops and the hard hitting aerial rocket artillery created pandemonium in the ranks of those enemy who had moved up alongside Highway 1 for the attack.

As the day darkened, the shattered Communists strove to break contact on all fronts and withdrew. They dissolved into small groups. Fighting erupted through the night as they were spotted.

By noon on February 1, Quang Tri City was cleared of the enemy. The 1st Brigade immediately initiated a pursuit that continued through the first 10 days of February. During the week that started with the enemy attack the 1st Brigade killed 381 enemy, while losing

Aerial rocket artillery (ARA) rounds set fire (above) to the grass surrounding the landing zone just prior to the first lift's touch down. Upon reaching the ground, the soldiers immediately fan out to protect other incoming birds. Before moving too far, however, the soldiers pop smoke (below) and wait for their company commander (below left) to give orders to move. Hours later a tired Skytrooper (lower left) crosses a stream, knowing there will be many more combat assaults and more days just like this one.

only four of its own men.

The 3rd Brigade was given the assignment of driving the enemy from Hue and its environs. That effort began on February 2 when helicopters, flying at treetop level because of fog, air assaulted the 2nd Battalion, 12th Cavalry, just outside PK-17, an ARVN outpost 10 kilometers northwest of Hue. Advancing on February 5, the battalion spotted enemy soldiers on the other side of a broad rice paddy in the hamlet of Thon La Chu.

During the next hours the battalion moved across the paddy and was soon in a savage firefight with nearly 1,000 NVA soldiers in the hamlet. The battalion's officers called for artillery support but it was not available for several hours. Two aerial rocket artillery helicopters braved the dense fog to spew 2.75-inch rockets at NVA positions. This permitted battalion elements to

occupy trenches abandoned by NVA guards, but a reinforced NVA battalion in bunkers put out a devastating fire from small arms, heavy machineguns and mortars. For two days fire and counterfire ripped the air between the two positions, as lack of food, water and sleep added to the Skytroopers' discomfort.

At 8 p.m. February 4 the battalion undertook a daring night march to outflank the enemy. At six the next morning the battalion's soldiers climbed a hill overlooking the valley surrounding the hamlet. The battalion now was behind the enemy and in a position to overlook and interdict his movements.

By February 11 the enemy was blocked on the north and on the south. A night patrol behind enemy lines convinced the battalion's officers that the enemy on the south was too strong to attack. After an assault on the north met with only limited success, the 3rd Brigade waited until February 21 to try again, and then the Cavalrymen moved swiftly through the hamlet. On February 22 the brigade finished sweeping Thon La Chu. The battle had disrupted an important enemy headquarters and severed a major NVA and VC supply and reinforcement route.

With the sweep of the hamlet finished the final push to Hue began. The 2nd of the 12th moved at night, getting within three kilometers of Hue when the NVA opened up with automatic weapons, rockets, recoilless rifles and mortars. During the next two days the battalion was in almost constant contact as it moved toward the city. The 5th Battalion, 7th Cavalry, was pinned down by heavy enemy fire a kilometer from Hue. After artillery pounded the position, the battalion moved past it the next day, meeting its Bravo Company, which had been airlifted inside the city. The northwest wall of Hue was secure.

The 1st Battalion, 7th Cavalry, broke through heavy resistance to meet its fellow "Garry Owen" battalion at the southwest wall. With this part of the wall secured, enemy resistance in the city collapsed, although the pursuit of the fleeing enemy continued for several days. By the end of the operation the 3rd Brigade had killed 404 enemy, 359 of them NVA. Bravo Troop, 1st Squadron, 9th Cavalry, accounted for another 156 enemy.

Three days after the 3rd Brigade finished its operations in Hue, the 2nd Brigade completed Operation PERSH-

ING II. The brigade then joined the rest of the division in I Corps where throughout March the Skytroopers pursued the shattered forces that were the remnants of the enemy's dreams for a Tet victory.

Before the month was over the division received a new challenge: Drive the enemy from the hills around the Marine base at Khe Sanh and reestablish an overland supply route to the embattled outpost. For months the enemy had cut off Highway 9, forcing all supplies to come by air to the Marines, who also suffered constant poundings from NVA artillery in Laos.

The 1st Sqdn, 9th Cav, was the first division unit to enter the valley.

Unaffected by the message given them by the enemy, these Cavalrymen display their find with pride. The signs were contained in a weapons and food cache discovered during an operation in III Corps, 1969.

The squadron's helicopters flew into the valley March 26, and the NVA greeted them with heavy anti-aircraft fire. The NVA fire was self-defeating, for in addition to general reconnaissance the squadron had been assigned the task of seeking out anti-aircraft positions and directing artillery and air strikes to destroy them before the division assaulted in force.

Operation PEGASUS, as the action was named, officially started April 1 when dozens of helicopters carried the 3rd Brigade into a series of landing zones within five miles of Khe Sanh. Not a shot was fired at any of them, so efficient had been the work of the 1st Sqdn, 9th Cav. At two day intervals, the

2nd and 1st Brigades and a three battalion ARVN force were air assaulted south and west of the Marine base. A total of 15,000 men were deployed in the valley.

The 2nd Battalion, 7th Cavalry, fighting its way to Khe Sanh to take over the defense of the base, battled for four days against an enemy force entrenched in positions it had been fortifying for months. The enemy finally left 94 bodies and more than 70 weapons on the battlefield. The battalion marched into its objective to the cheers of Marines, and put up a sign: "Khe Sanh under new management."

Although the Khe Sanh post had been reached, the operation wasn't over. In one action 1st of the 9th gunships killed 50 NVA. The two 1st Brigade battalions that landed on LZ Snapper April 5 had several sharp fights as they pushed north toward Khe Sanh and then west toward the Laotian border and the CIDG Camp at Lang Vei. The camp, captured by the NVA in March, was retaken by the 1st Battalion, 12th Cavalry, after a day of fighting. The 1st Brigade also discovered numerous supply caches, including one stockpile of 50,000 rounds of AK-47 ammo and 1,600 mixed mortar rounds.

The division's artillery batteries slammed tens of thousands of rounds into enemy positions during PEGASUS. An almost unbelievable 500 tons of ammunition a day was hauled by the 228th

Assault Support Helicopter Battalion to feed the guns. The enemy's heavy artillery in Laos shelled LZ Stud, the division forward command post, and once the 2nd Brigade's LZ Tom. Both times enemy observer teams were spotted in the hills. After division artillery was turned on them, the shellings stopped.

Operation PEGASUS ended April 15. The division and its opcon units had relieved Khe Sanh, killed 1,259 enemy and captured 540 individual and 216 crew-served weapons.

Yet another major operation was waiting for the division. The A Shau Valley is a slit in the mountains 45 kilometers west of Hue. Close to the Laotian border, remote and usually hidden from the air by thick clouds, the valley was a major way-station on the Ho Chi Minh trail, a North Vietnamese Army base and was the jumping-off point for the enemy's Tet Offensive against Hue. Since a CIDG camp pulled out of the area in 1966, no Free World Forces had penetrated the valley.

Operation DELAWARE, as the division's invasion of the valley was named, changed all this. The men of the 1st and 3rd Brigades began to enter the valley on April 19. Mobile 37 mm guns camouflaged in the jungle and capable of hitting targets at an altitude of 25,000 feet poured out their fire, and .50 caliber machineguns added a wall of red tracers. Despite the resistance, the division's battalions successfully secured landing zones.

The three Garry Owen battalions hit the valley first. An overturned truck loaded with 200 rifles was found on April 20. This was the first indication that Operation DELAWARE would be a gigantic treasure hunt, punctuated by small, sharp clashes with scattered enemy units.

On April 24 the 1st Brigade seized the A Luoi airstrip, clearing the long unused field so vital resupply could come by air. The strip was renamed LZ Stallion. On the 25th the men on Stallion heard the rumble of a truck motor. From the north bounced a green vehicle, covered with waving Skytroopers. They had found five Russian-made trucks and driven one back.

As the days went by the finds mounted: Huge arms caches, more trucks, food, uniforms, rockets, gasoline. Exploring one cache on April 29 a company came under fire from an enemy tank. It knocked out the position with two light antitank weapon (LAW) rounds.

A wounded Skytrooper rides the "lifeline" to an awaiting 15th Medical Battalion helicopter. He is framed by bamboo shoots that abound in III Corps jungles.

During May the two brigades crisscrossed the valley floor and searched out its corners, uncovering more supplies at every turn. On May 17 the operation ended as the brigades moved back to Camp Evans. What the enemy had regarded as an inviolable sanctuary had been raided by the FIRST TEAM, who had destroyed the enemy's bunkers and fortifications and stripped the valley of his supplies. The division had captured or destroyed 2,371 individual weapons, 13 anti-aircraft weapons, 42,000 large caliber rounds, 169,000 small arms rounds, 40 tons of food, two bulldozers, 73 wheeled vehicles, three tracked vehicles and a tank. In addition 737 enemy soldiers were killed.

Resettled in the Hue and Quang Tri area, the division undertook Operation JEB STUART III, with the twofold mission of denying the enemy access to the rice growing coastal plain and up-

rooting him from his strongholds.

The largest battle of JEB STUART III was fought by the 2nd Brigade June 27-30 in the coast eight miles north of Quang Tri. Elements were moving across a beach near the village of Binh Anh when they were hit by enemy fire from the village. In 10 minutes, gunship from the 1st Sqdn, 9th Cav, ranged over Binh Anh, cutting down any NVA who tried to flee as ARA, tube artillery, naval gunfire and eight tactical air strikes hit the village.

Battalion elements moved in for the kill, cordoning off the village. The trapped NVA tried to filter through American lines under cover of darkness. In the morning Skytroopers closed the trap. Bulldozers caved in enemy bunkers and 17 more air strikes completed the destruction. Some 233 NVA had been killed and 44 captured.

Command of the division was passed

from MG John J. Tolson to Brigadier General Richard L. Irby on July 14. BG Irby served as an officer in Burma in 1945, and was a 1st Cav battalion commander in the Korean conflict. The general also held various positions in armored units. Prior to assuming command BG Irby was assistant division commander.

Major General George I. Forsythe replaced BG Irby as division commander on August 19. MG Forsythe came to the division from MACV, where he was assistant to the deputy commander for CORDS. The general started his military career in World War II, first as an infantry officer in the Pacific and later in Europe, where he helped plan the Allied invasion. As a colonel, he commanded the 502nd Airborne Infantry in 1956 and 1957. His first tour in Vietnam came in 1958 when he was the first senior advisor to the ARVN Field Command. He earned his first star in 1963 and became a major general in 1966. Like his predecessors, he was an aviator, but unlike them, he had earned his wings just prior to taking command of the division.

On October 25, the 1st Air Cavalry Division area of operations was quiet. At Camp Evans, in the brigade bases, in isolated forward positions, Skytroopers looked out over an expanse of "Cav Country" they had tamed in nine months of bitter fighting. They had seized NVA caches in the razor-sharp, jungled mountains bordering the A Shau Valley. They had crippled the VC infrastructure and denied the enemy rice and recruits on the sandy, half-flooded plain between Hue and Quang Tri. They had provided safety and shelter for refugees. Charlie was on the run.

During the summer there had been rumors of a move. But no rumors were current when the order came to move the whole division—more than 19,000 men, hundreds of vehicles and helicopters, tons of supplies—south to a new area of operations northwest of Saigon.

The Cav moved. The equivalent of a medium-sized U.S. town tore itself up by the roots, took wings, and landed at the other end of South Vietnam. Within days, the division was conducting combat operations in III Corps; within two weeks, everything was back to normal. Supplies were circulating. Paperwork flowed. And the enemy, once again, was on the run.

During the move, the division had to fight on two fronts 350 miles apart,

overcoming staggering problems of control. Three operations were in progress simultaneously.

The 3rd Brigade spearheaded the advance south. The 1st Brigade remained in the northern provinces until November 3, wrapping up Operation JEB STUART III, which had lasted 171 days and cost the Communists 2,016 men. The 2nd Brigade continued to participate in Operation COMANCHE FALLS in the jungle 25 miles from the DMZ. With elements of the 1st ARVN Division and the 5th Infantry Division, the Blackhorse troopers formed a cordon 16 kilometers in circumference around the My Chanh District to weed out the Viet Cong infrastructure. COMANCHE FALLS, which ended on November 7, resulted in more than 100 enemy killed.

In the midst of this, the brigades had to adapt to a new kind of task organization. The 3rd Brigade occupied the northeastern section of the new AO, with a base at Quan Loi. The 1st Brigade followed, funneling through Quan Loi and establishing bases to the southwest, in the Tay Ninh area. The 2nd Brigade came last, taking up a central position between the other two brigades. The new division base was established at Phuoc Vinh. Altogether, the FIRST TEAM assumed areas of responsibility in the provinces of Phuoc Long, Binh Long, Tay Ninh, and Binh Duong.

The move was clearly a logistical triumph. By the evening of October 31, 2,600 men and 61 helicopters had arrived in Quan Loi. By November 10,378 air sorties had been flown from Camp Evans with more than 9,200 men aboard. Some 3,600 tons of vehicles and equipment had moved by air. The Navy's LSTs had carried 2,800 passengers, 11,000 tons of equipment, 1,750 wheeled

vehicles, and 27 helicopters. The rest of the Cav was coming fast.

As the 1st Infantry Division moved out of its bases, the Skytroopers moved in, setting up communications networks, making contact with ARVN units and Special Forces-advised CIDG groups, and learning as much as possible about the local enemy.

Charlie was already feeling the pinch, despite his sanctuary in nearby Cambodia. By November 9, the 1st Air Cav, joining other Allied units in the Toan Thang offensive, had killed 109 enemy soldiers. On November 14, Cavalry firepower helped the 3rd Battalion, 36th ARVN Rangers, repel an NVA assault on LZ Dot with almost 300 enemy killed. After a month in III Corps, the division by itself had accounted for more than 1,100 VC and NVA dead. Large bunker complexes stocked with munitions had been uncovered around Loc Ninh and along the Saigon River. ARA and tube artillery disrupted traffic on the enemy's major supply routes.

Sporadic action continued in December. Forty-five enemy were killed by Allied units on December 4; 50,000 rounds of ammo were captured December 8; 46 enemy died on December 9; 42 lost their lives on December 18; 18,000 pounds of rice were seized December 21; and in a flurry of action after Christmas 155 VC and NVA were killed.

Hue, Quang Tri, Khe Sanh, A Shau, III Corps. The Cav was used to fighting and important victories, but 1968 was, even by Cav standards, a year of unique achievement in the face of unusual challenge.

(Continued on P. 247)

INFANTRY

FIRST BRIGADE

COMMANDERS

COL Elvy B. Roberts .... July 1965—October 1965
LTC Harlow G. Clark Jr. .... October 1965—November 1965
COL George S. Beatty ....November 1965—December 1965
COL Elvy B. Roberts .... December 1965—February 1966
COL John J. Hennessey .... February 1966—July 1966
COL Archie R. Hyle .... July 1966—November 1966
COL James C. Smith .... November 1966—April 1967
COL Donald V. Rattan .... April 1967—March 1968
COL John F. Stannard .... March 1968—October 1968
COL Robert J. Baer .... October 1968—March 1969
COL Joseph P. Kingston .... March 1969—September 1969
COL Joseph E. Collins .... September 1969—

The unit was constituted in the Regular Army as the 1st Brigade August 29, 1917, and organized in February 1918 at Fort Sam Houston, Texas, as an element of the 15th Cavalry Division.

Campaign participation credit was earned in World War II, including the New Guinea, Bismarck (with arrowhead), Leyte (with arrowhead) and Luzon Campaigns.

The 1st Brigade prior to the Vietnam conflict had been decorated with the Presidential Unit Citation, streamer embroidered LUZON; and the Philippine Presidential Unit Citation for October 17, 1944 through July 4, 1945.

On September 20, 1965, the 1st Cavalry Division's 1st Brigade debarked from the troop ship USNS Geiger and marched ashore at the city of Qui Nhon, Republic of Vietnam. In its ranks were three airborne infantry battalions, the 1st and 2nd Battalions of the 8th Cavalry and the 1st Battalion, 12th Cavalry, with a direct support artillery battalion, the 2nd Battalion, 19th Artillery. The brigade did not tarry but loaded quickly into helicopters and moved inland to the division's basecamp at An Khe.

The men of the brigade entered the Vietnam war with the flavor and traditions of airborne troopers—the brigade's slogan "All the Way" stems from its early airborne status—and they would need all the spirit and determination implied in that slogan in the coming months. It had been the last of the three brigades of the Cav to be organized, owing to the difficulty in filling it with qualified airborne personnel, and the last replacements had arrived just before the unit had departed Fort Benning for combat. Many of the companies, platoons and squads had never been in the field together, but their commander, Colonel E. B. Roberts, had faith in the airborne spirit and knew that it would sustain them through the first difficult months in Vietnam.

It was not long after the brigade's arrival before that spirit was tested. An enemy attack on the Special Forces Camp at Plei Me set the stage for the brigade's first trial by fire which was later to be known as the Pleiku Campaign of October 23—November 9, 1965. In a series of massive search and destroy operations kicked off with Operation ALL THE WAY, 1st Brigade units air assaulted to support an ARVN relief column winding toward the besieged camp. When the enemy's encirclement had been broken and his units began withdrawing, the brigade forward command post at LZ Homecoming was visited by General William C. Westmoreland and the order of the day was changed. Lieutenant Colonel Harlow G. Clark, then the acting commander of the brigade in COL Robert's temporary absence, was to conduct a brilliant pursuit campaign with this new concept called airmobility. As the retreating 3rd NVA Regiment raced overland for Cambodia and sanctuary, LTC Clark's men made daily air assaults to catch and cut into the fleeing enemy, smashing chunks out of his strength as he tried to get out from under the blanket of the

Cav.

It was hard, exhausting work. During this time the brigade's tactical area of operations covered more than 1,200 square miles of tangled jungle, and that was a lot of territory for Charlie to get lost in. But the pursuit kept track of him; artillery batteries were leap-frogged forward by Chinook helicopters to provide support as the infantry was constantly air assaulting into positions blocking the enemy's path.

If the drive was relentless and exhausting for the 1st Brigade, it was far worse for the harried and much less mobile enemy. By November 9, when the All the Way Brigade gave up its AO to the fresh 3rd Brigade, the 33rd Regiment had lost 826 men killed and another 119 captured by LTC Clark's troops.

The next challenge the 1st Brigade was to face was Operation MASHER/WHITE WING, a tactical program which spanned the period from January 29 to March 6, 1966. This operation was destined to evolve into the largest joint-service and Allied operation up to that time in the Vietnam conflict. MASHER/WHITE WING centered on the Bong Son Plain in the eastern portion of Binh Dinh Province along the tidal coast of the South China Sea; it was a campaign that drew virtually every combat and support element of the division into play. For the 1st Brigade the most significant period of the operation began on February 27 with a series of sharp battles fought south of Bong Son along Highway 1.

The enemy forces involved had been threatening the cities of Bong Son, Quang Nai and the vital port city of Qui Nhon, and they were dealt a crippling blow in the less than 40 days of MASHER/WHITE WING.

On March 25 the brigade returned to the Ia Drang Valley for the highly productive Operation LINCOLN. The enemy lost 480 killed and, for the first time, Cav units penetrated the Chu Pong Massif.

In mid-May of that year the brigade had overwatch responsibility for the newly-built CIDG camp in Vinh Thanh Valley, a jungle bowl ringed by mountains just east of An Khe. Thus, when one of the CIDG forces came in contact with an enemy of unknown strength in the mountains it was decided to commit one of the rifle companies from the An Khe base defense force into the area to develop the situation. It was Bravo Company, 2d Bn, 8th Cav, that was selected

and the company combat assaulted into an LZ on a mountain ridge overlooking the CIDG Camp. The Skytroopers of Bravo Company wound their way up the ridge to the top of one of the mountains and smashed into an enemy battalion.

This hilltop fight triggered Operation CRAZY HORSE, a campaign that was never designed but which took shape quickly in the heat of a few expedient hours. Exploiting the situation, during the next three days the brigade deployed five maneuver battalions to do battle with what turned out to be the 2nd VC Regiment and the 12th NVA Regiment. The enemy's plan of smashing the CIDG camp in fiery commemoration

of Ho Chi Minh's birthday on May 19 desintegrated as the 1st Brigade joined by ARVN and ROK forces, quickly surrounded him and sealed off his escape routes. It was not to be the last time that the Cav, with its ability to react with lightning speed to a promising situation, would smash an enemy plan before it could even get off the ground. Airmobility was coming of age.

When CRAZY HORSE terminated on June 5, 1966, the enemy—who had entered the area and opened the fight with such grandiose plans—had been badly mauled. Skytroopers under the command of the All the Way Brigade had killed some 350 enemy troops, but the capture of a Viet Cong political indoctrination center was a dividend of more lasting importance. The documents taken enabled the national police to put a substantial dent in the VC infrastructure in Binh Dinh Province.

Of passing interest is the operation that had been sidetracked by the impromptu CRAZY HORSE. The brigade planned to conduct a multi-battalion operation which was to have included a battalion-sized combat jump in the area west and south of Tuy Hoa. CRAZY HORSE caused the scrapping of those

These 1st Brigade Skytroopers have just moved into position outside the perimeter of LZ Stallion in the A Shau Valley. They were part of the Cav's Operation DELAWARE, which marked the first deployment of U.S. troops to that valley in many months.

A 1st Brigade machinegunner relaxes his trigger finger just long enough to fix the enemy's location and then immediately resumes firing. The firefight took place in the Que Son Valley jungle.

plans, and though the brigade ultimately campaigned in the Tuy Hoa area later in June, the operation was not quite what the brigade planners had envisaged in early May.

The months that followed found the brigade participating in Operations NATHAN HALE and HENRY CLAY. NATHAN HALE brought the 1st Brigade into the Tuy Hoa area in a reaction role, and it was during this period that the "Jumping Mustangs" of the 1st Bn, 8th Cav, won the Presidential Unit Citation.

In the second operation, HENRY CLAY, the brigade experimented with a technique designed to search for the enemy over a wide area with a minimum of forces. This technique was called "saturation patrolling" and it found its first implementation when the 2nd Bn, 8th Cav, was broken down into 54 six-man reconnaissance teams and spread over an area covering 100 square miles.

Following HENRY CLAY the brigade returned to An Khe and the base defense mission in early August and planning commenced for Operation THAYER.

Intelligence reports indicated that elements of the 3rd NVA Division, which was a mixture of VC and NVA units, had moved back into the Kim Son Valley. To counter this threat THAYER was launched on September 13, 1966, with three battalions being air assaulted into positions along the high ground south and west of the Crow's Foot network of valleys along the Kim Son River. The brigade then aggressively sought the enemy out until the operation came to a close on October 1. By this time 191 enemy soldiers had been killed by the lightning strokes and determined fighting of the All the Way Brigade. The enemy was forced from his bases and kept constantly on the move despite his best efforts to stay under cover and minimize losses.

When the enemy realized that he could not remain in the area and continue to sustain the losses he was taking, he looked for a way out. Elements of the Cav were north, west and south of him, so there was only one direction he could go—east, toward the South China Sea and there, unknown to the enemy, the 1st Brigade waited. When this move began exactly

A CH-54 "Flying Crane" helicopter prepares to lift a defective 155 mm howitzer out of the Vinh Thanh Valley near An Khe in May 1966. The howitzer was supporting 1st Brigade operations in the area and was manned by members of Battery C, 1st Battalion of the 30th Artillery. Operation CRAZY HORSE was in full swing at the time.

as predicted, the brigade met the enemy units, closed in on them, and piled on. It was October 2, 1966, the beginning of the short and furious Operation IRVING. As the enemy force fell into the brigade's blocking force, the first six days of fighting accounted for 397 enemy dead. An incredible figure of 321 enemy soldiers were captured during this week, and by the time the operation was completed on October 24 the numbers of enemy killed and detained had doubled.

One of the problems encountered during IRVING concerned the thousands of civilians endangered by the wave of battle violence. A massive PSYOPs and civic action campaign was launched to forestall this danger and in the end less than 10 civilians had been accidently killed in the 22 days of the operation.

The next major operation in which the brigade participated was PERSHING which began on February 13, 1967 in the Bong Son Plain. The first days were punctuated by actions at Tuy Au on the 18th, Tan An on February 27th, and Hy Van on March 19th. In these and related actions the enemy lost 161 killed and seven were detained by the All the Way Brigade.

Later in the same operation a battalion of the 69th Armor was attached to the infantry and greatly enhanced the effectiveness of the brigade's maneuver units, particularly against fortified positions. Many valuable lessons were also learned about the employment of airmobile infantry with armor, and these were to find application time and time again during the later years of the war.

At An Qui the brigade committed three infantry companies from the 2nd Bn, 8th Cav, and the 1st Bn, 12th Cav, with supporting gunships from A Troop, 1st Squadron, 9th Cavalry, along with tanks against a battalion of the 3rd NVA Division. The fight that followed left 96 dead enemy soldiers on the battlefield.

In Tuy Au the opposing force was the 8th Battalion of the 22nd NVA Regiment. This time it was the Skytroopers from the 1st Bn, 8th Cav, who met them, and the enemy was driven out of the village and nearby hills with a loss of 86 KIA.

In 1967, for the third time in as many years, large North Vietnamese Army forces infiltrated across the Cambodian and Laotian borders during the month of November to threaten Allied outposts in the highland jungles of Pleiku and

Private First Class Joseph Lake, of the 11th Path Finder Company assigned to the 1st Brigade, directs the landing of a UH-1D Huey helicopter in August 1968. The landing zone belonged to the 1st Battalion, 12th Cavalry, and was instrumental in the successful operation known as JEB STUART III.

Kontum Provinces. On each occasion the 1st Air Cavalry's 1st Brigade was called upon to respond to the threat. The enemy target for 1967 was the large U.S. basecamp at Dak To. A force estimated to be four well equipped regiments had maneuvered into positions around the camp and were being engaged by elements of the 4th Infantry Division and 173rd Airborne Brigade when the first Skytroopers arrived. The 1st Bn, 12th Cav, had been called for rapid deployment to Dak To.

Within 24 hours the battalion had responded and was relieving the beleaguered 4th Division units on Hill 724 west of the Dak To camp, together with a platoon from Company A, 8th Engineer Battalion.

The 1st Brigade headquarters and the 2nd Bn, 8th Cav, soon joined the task force in support of Operation MACARTHUR and together with attached units assumed the responsibility for its own AO.

The fighting was reminiscent of the tactics employed in Korea. Cavalrymen advanced directly behind their supporting fires to push the enemy from the strategic high ground. The men fought through some of the most rugged terrain in Vietnam, crawling through dense bam-

boo and underbrush to within 10 meters of the enemy position before they could bring effective fire on the Communist soldiers concealed in camouflaged bunkers and lashed to the tall trees.

The brigade's role in MACARTHUR was concluded after only 11 days and the massive attack planned by the Communists never materialized.

The year 1967 ended with the brigade still in the Bong Son Plain, An Lac Valley and the coastal highlands, coordinating closely with ARVN forces and teaming with armor whenever the situation was favorable.

PERSHING terminated on January 18, 1968, and at the end of the month the brigade moved to Quang Tri Province in southern I Corps, establishing firebases to support offensive operations in Base Area 101 and the Ba Long Valley. This was Operation JEB STUART, and from its headquarters at LZ Betty the brigade watched the drama of Tet 1968 unfurl.

As the NVA threat to Quang Tri grew during the first week of February, the brigade redeployed to that city to prevent its seizure during the country-wide enemy offensive that developed during those fateful days.

(Continued on P. 258)

SECOND BRIGADE

COMMANDERS

COL William R. Lynch .... July 1965–March 1966
COL Marvin J. Berenzweig .... March 1966–October 1966
COL George W. Casey .... October 1966–April 1967
COL Fred E. Karhohs .... April 1967–October 1967
COL Joseph C. McDonough .... October 1967–May 1968
COL Robert H. MacKinnon .... May 1968–November 1968
COL Conrad L. Stansberry .... November 1968–April 1969
COL Byron D. Greene, Jr. .... April 1969–October 1969
COL Edward C. Meyer .... October 1969–

The unit was constituted on August 29, 1917, as the 2nd Cavalry Brigade at Fort Bliss, Texas. It was organized at the same post on December 27, 1917, as an element of the 15th Cavalry Division. The 15th Cavalry Division disbanded May 12, 1918, and the 2nd Cavalry Brigade was demobolized July 9, 1919, at Fort Bliss.

August 20, 1921, the unit was reconstituted in the Regular Army and organized at Fort Bliss as an element of the 1st Cavalry Division.

The unit was redesignated and converted July 15, 1963, as 2nd Brigade, 1st Cavalry Division, and was activated on September 1, 1963, in Korea. In July 1965, the brigade became part of the 1st Cavalry Division (Airmobile).

The brigade participated in the New Guinea, Bismarck Archipalago (with arrowhead), Leyte (with arrowhead) and Luzon campaigns in World War II, and received the Philippine Presidential Unit Citation, (October, 17, 1944, to July 4, 1945). In Vietnam the brigade participated in the Defense; Counteroffensive; Counteroffensive, Phase II; Counteroffensive, Phase III; and the Tet Counteroffensive campaigns, and was decorated with the Presidential Unit Citation (Army), streamer embroidered

Mortarmen with the 2nd Brigade, during Operation WHITE WING in the Bong Son area, cover their ears and duck out of the way as a mortar fire mission pounds a suspected enemy location.

PLEIKU PROVINCE.

It was in Vietnam that the 2nd Brigade came to be known as the "Blackhorse Brigade." Colonel Marvin J. Berenzweig, brigade commander from March to October of 1966, had a black horse on a yellow background painted on the floor

near the entrance of the brigade tactical operations center. A 50-cent fine imposed on anyone who stepped on the horse helped the new brigade symbol make a strong impression, and the nickname stuck.

The 2nd Brigade, 1st Cavalry Division (Airmobile), arrived in Qui Nhon, Republic of Vietnam in September of 1965 aboard the troop ship USNS Buckner.

The 2nd (Blackhorse) Brigade began its combat activities by providing base and road security in the area of Camp Radcliff, the 1st Air Cav Division's basecamp.

In October and November of 1965 the division fought its first major

A lift ship approaches LZ Brass, a 2nd Brigade firebase opened during Operation MASHER/WHITE WING, February 1966.

Vietnam campaign in the vicinity of Pleiku and the Ia Drang Valley, a campaign that would win the entire division the first Presidential Unit Citation awarded in Vietnam.

Through the early part of the operation the 2nd Brigade was assigned the task of keeping Highway 19 open. Its success in this mission prevented the North Vietnamese Army from severing this single link between Pleiku and the sea.

On November 20, 1965, the 2nd Brigade relieved the 3rd Brigade in the Chu Pong Massif area. Working with an ARVN Airborne brigade, the 2nd Brigade swept through the area around Duc Co, making contact primarily with isolated remnants of NVA units reeling from earlier battles. In less than a week, it became clear that the NVA had abandoned plans for a major offensive. The enemy gathered what was left of his forces to return to Cambodia.

From Duc Co and the area near Pleiku, 2nd Brigade moved east and began to operate against the NVA on the Bong Son Plain. LZ Two Bits and LZ Brass served as headquarters for the brigade units as they participated in the Skytroopers first division-size operation of the war, the Bong Son Campaign. The operation began in late January 1966; the 2nd Brigade's role began in early February.

The brigade moved into the area of

of operation to establish blocking positions east of the An Lao Valley and attack areas, while ARVN and U.S. Marine elements blocked other escape routes. Inclement weather, however, permitted the bulk of the enemy forces to evacuate the area. On February 19, 2nd Brigade units 12 miles south of Bong Son had a fierce firefight with what was estimated to be a regimental headquarters and supporting troops. With the help of artillery and B-52 strikes the brigade broke the back of the Communist units. Enemy resistance ceased, and the final enemy body count was 313. After 41 days of contact with the enemy the Bong Son Campaign ended March 6, 1966.

On October 31, 1966, the Blackhorse Brigade moved into the PAUL REVERE IV area of operations. Elements of the brigade carried on extensive search and destroy operations in the Chu Pong-Ia Drang area and along the Cambodian border. Contact was generally sporadic and light through the operation's end on December 27, 1966.

In April of 1967 the Blackhorse Brigade replaced U.S. Marine units in the northern section of the Bong Son Plains, specifically in the Duc Pho area. Along with extensive search and destroy missions, the 2nd Brigade, with Marine units still in the area, participated in a variety of civic affairs projects. Refugees were aided, security was provided for the harvest of some 66 tons of rice (which, ironically, had been planted by the VC), classrooms and houses were built, and medical care for civilians provided. One publication said of the area around Phu My and Hoai An District, that after the brigade's operations, "the area is widely recognized as having probably the most successful pacification program in Vietnam."

In late 1967 the Blackhorse Brigade moved into the Que Son Valley, once a virtually unrestricted playground for the 2nd NVA Division. The brigade's operations severely cut back the NVA freedom of movement, and entire hamlets of former Viet Cong sympathizers and supporters rallied to the government of South Vietnam.

In early 1968 the 2nd Brigade halted

A member of the 11th Aviation Group's Path Finders (left) pops smoke and guides a UH-1H Huey into a clearing near Song Be in III Corps. Troops wait in the background for their ride out of the area.

Troop ships hover just off the ground as 2nd Brigade soldiers jump to the ground, where they immediately fan out to secure the site for further lift arrivals.

the A Shau Valley, where huge caches of enemy equipment were found. Men of the 2nd Brigade assaulted along the ridges of the valley taking a large toll among the surprised NVA.

By now the headquarters of the brigade felt established in the newly built LZ Jane; the men were told this was home, but those wise in the concept of airmobility knew better. As Operation JEB STUART III began, the brigade headquarters shifted to LZ Nancy in May 1968. Meanwhile, the maneuver battalions of the brigade were fighting at Wunder Beach. In one three-day battle 233 NVA were killed and another 44 detained.

Moving further north, just south of Quang Tri City, the Blackhorse Brigade kicked off Operation COMANCHE FALLS, designed to root out the NVA troops from the steep rugged hills and dense jungle. As the brigade mopped up the COMANCHE FALLS Operation, it was faced with a new problem, simultaneously managing an area of operations some 350 miles to the south near the Cambodian border in III Corps.

In late October, the brigade headquarters moved temporarily to Phouc

(Continued on P. 254)

the 2nd Viet Cong Regiment's contribution to the enemy's Tet Offensive before it could get started. In three separate engagements over a five-day period the Cavalrymen battered the three battalions of the 2nd VC, part of the 3rd NVA Division.

The contacts were made on three sides of Phu My, the district capital that was already the hub of bustling South Vietnamese revolutionary development program, thanks to security provided by the 2nd Brigade.

Apparently the Communists' intention was to attack Phu My, but the Skytroopers hit the enemy before they could take the offensive. The regiment was able to assemble only one ground probe on district headquarters, which was easily repulsed.

The fighting cost the NVA 190 soldiers killed and 58 weapons captured. U.S. units lost four men killed.

In April 1968 the 1st Cavalry Division was called upon to spearhead the drive to lift the siege of the Marine base at Khe Sanh. Elements of the Blackhorse Brigade were there. They also participated later that month and in May when the 1st Air Cav drove the NVA from their longtime sanctuary in

Vaulting from lift ships becomes "old hat" after the first few times, but going into an insecure LZ still stimulates the heart and mind. When dense growth prohibits the choppers from touching down, it's simply a matter of getting yourself onto the ground as quickly and safely as possible.

THIRD BRIGADE

COMMANDERS

COL Thomas W. Brown .... July 1965–December 1965
COL Harold G. Moore, Jr. .... December 1965–July 1966
COL Charles D. Daniel .... July 1966–December 1966
COL Jonathen R. Burton .... December 1966–June 1967
COL James O. McKenna .... June 1967–November 1967
COL Hubert S. Campbell .... November 1967–May 1968
COL Charles H. Curtis .... May 1968–November 1968
COL Karl R. Morton .... November 1968–July 1969
COL John P. Barker .... July 1969–December 1969
COL Robert C. Kingston .... December 1969–

The 3rd Brigade was constituted on August 29, 1917, as a cavalry brigade in the Regular Army, and was organized in December 1917 at Camp Harry J. Jones, Douglas, Arizona, as an element of the 15th Cavalry Division. The 15th Cavalry Division disbanded on May 12, 1918; and the 3rd Brigade was demobilized on July 15, 1919, at Camp Jones. The unit was reconstituted in the Regular Army on August 20, 1921, as the 3rd Cavalry Brigade, 1st Cavalry Division.

On October 15, 1940, the unit was activated at Fort Riley, Kansas. The brigade was converted and redesignated 9th Armored Division Trains on July 15, 1942.

The brigade was relieved from assignment to the 9th Armored Division on July 15, 1963, and converted and redesignated 3rd Brigade, 1st Cavalry Division. September 1, 1963, the brigade was activated in Korea. It was assigned to the new 1st Cavalry Division (Airmobile) in July of 1965.

The 3rd Brigade has participation credit for the Rhineland, Ardennes-Alsace and Central Europe campaigns of World War II. The unit has been decorated with the Meritorious Unit Commendation, streamer embroidered EUROPE 1944, and the Meritorious Unit Commendation, streamer embroidered EUROPE 1945.

A fire started by Cav artillery rounds hitting an enemy ammunition cache continues burning as Skytroopers move into the Chu Pong Massiff area in Pleiku Province. The mountains and foothills of the province were to see some of the fiercest fighting in the war.

The men of the 3rd Brigade, 1st Air Cavalry Division, debarked from the USNS Maurice Rose at Qui Nhon, Republic of Vietnam, on the morning of September 17, 1965. They were flown by CH-47 Chinook helicopters to their new home, the division basecamp at An Khe in the central highlands.

The brigade's original battalions were the 1st and 2nd Battalions, 7th Cavalry, thus providing the impetus for the slogan "Garry Owen."

Less than a month after landing, the brigade moved to the Suoi Ca Valley for its first major action in Vietnam: Operation SHINY BAYONET on Oc-

tober 14. The operation ended in four days as brigade headquarters returned to An Khe, having destroyed major enemy staging areas.

On November 9, 1965, the brigade command post moved to the northern edge of the Catecka Tea Plantation southwest of Pleiku. The brigade had been committed to the battle for the Ia Drang Valley, for which the 1st Cavalry Division (Airmobile) would receive the Presidential Unit Citation.

The action of the 3rd Brigade units in the Chu Pong Massif area and the Ia Drang Valley showed how massive fire support and the combat skill of

American infantrymen could achieve victory over the combined Viet Cong-NVA enemy. The combat power brought to bear on the newly infiltrated 66th Regiment and the remnants of the 33rd Regiment resulted in near annihilation of both organizations.

The 3rd Brigade (the Garry Owen Brigade) saw heavier action than any other 1st Cav Division unit in the middle and later stages of the campaign. The battle for LZ X-Ray began on November 14. For three days elements of three 3rd Brigade battalions beat back attacks by units from two NVA regiments. By the end of the engagement the enemy had lost 834 by body count. A day later Garry Owen battalions killed some 400 NVA at LZ Albany.

Operation CLEAN HOUSE closed 1965 for the 3rd Brigade. The brigade controlled the operations in a valley north east of Binh Khe in Binh Dinh Province. Several hundred enemy were killed and much valuable intelligence information was gathered.

The Bong Son Campaign was the first major action for the 3rd Brigade in 1966. The area of operation included the entire eastern half of Binh Dinh Province, an area in excess of 1,600 square kilometers. Much of the fighting was concentrated in the An Lao Valley, which the Viet Cong had claimed would be theirs for all time.

The fighting began on January 29, 1966, when elements of the 3rd Brigade air assaulted into the middle of a Viet Cong battalion less than four miles north of Bong Son. Three days of hard fighting ended when the brigade over-ran the VC positions. The enemy attempted to flee to the north. Two days later, 10 miles north of the first fight, a combined 3rd Brigade—ARVN Airborne brigade force caught up with the retreating VC and decimated the enemy regiment. The three days of battle cost the enemy more than 500 dead.

The campaign continued through March, with the fighting shifting from one portion of the area to another as the enemy unsuccessfully tried to avoid the search and clear operations of the Skytroopers. By the end of the campaign more than 140,000 Vietnamese had been returned to government control. The Central Coastal Plain had been, at least temporarily, cleared of Viet Cong. More than 50 percent of the population (4,500 Vietnamese), availed themselves of the chance

A "Garry Owen" pointman (above) checks his compass while humping through triple canopy jungle near the Cav's 3rd Brigade basecamp at Quan Loi in III Corps.

3rd Brigade soldiers (below) heft their rucksacks to their backs, as they prepare to continue a reconnaissance mission near FSB Vivian in III Corps.

to escape from VC control in the An Lao Valley.

The 3rd Brigade continued to be a highly effective force throughout 1966, participating in numerous other operations designed to drive the enemy from Vietnam's II Corps region. Between the battle of Ia Drang and June of 1966 the 3rd Brigade was responsible for some 3,200 of the 4,500 enemy killed by the 1st Cavalry Division.

Colonel Harold G. Moore, the brigade commander during that period, twice delayed his departure for the United States in order to be with the Brigade until completion of Operation NATHAN HALE, in which an NVA battalion was rendered ineffective.

COL Moore and the 3rd Brigade developed the "hunter-killer" technique of having small units find and engage the enemy, and then piling on more forces to destroy him. The Chicago Daily News described the effectiveness of the brigade under COL Moore as "unmatched" in destroying the enemy.

The 3rd Brigade began 1967 providing road and base security for the division at An Khe. On February 11 the Garry Owen Brigade was committed to Operation PERSHING, aimed at clearing once again NVA regulars and VC main force units from the An Lao Basin and the Bong Son Plain.

PERSHING was the division's longest operation of the war, running from Feb-

A "Garry Owen" trooper (above) makes a mad dash across a bridge north of Hue, while his buddies supply cover fire.

ruary of 1967 to January of 1968. The brigade also participated in other operations in 1967, including Operation WHEELER-WALLOWA when the "Garry Owen" battalions were under operational control to the Americal Division.

In January of 1968 the NVA attacked LZ Ross and LZ Leslie, both occupied by 3rd Brigade units. The enemy failed to overrun the bases and lost 289 men in the attempts.

In February the enemy began its Tet Offensive and 3rd Brigade forces moved to the I Corps area, charged with the task of driving the enemy from their dug in positions around the old imperial capital of Hue. In fighting hampered by poor visibility and bad weather throughout the entire period, the Garry Owen troopers pushed the enemy from their fortified blocking positions along the approaches to Hue and paved the way for liberation forces. After fierce fighting the Cavalrymen sealed their cordon around the city on February 25. Resistance inside

Specialist Four Anthony Williams of the 5th Battalion, 7th Cavalry, hurls a grenade at the enemy. The Cav's 3rd Brigade was then moving toward the imperial city of Hue.

the city collapsed the following day.

Hue was the first of several major actions in 1968. In April the 1st Air Cavalry Division was assigned to lift the seige of the Marines at Khe Sanh. The 3rd Brigade's 2nd Bn, 7th Cav, spearheaded the drive.

As the Garry Owen troopers moved up Highway QL9 they encountered stiff resistance; however, the enemy crumpled after two companies of the 2nd Bn, 7th Cav, were air assaulted behind the Communist force and engaged it from the rear. Brigade elements led the way into the Marine base, then fought for two weeks eliminating the enemy from the surrounding hills, using LZ Stud as a base of operations.

Evidently, the Marines were happy to see the Skytroopers. Said Master Sergeant Jack E. Shroyer, 2nd Bn, 7th Cav, "The Marines seemed pretty happy to see us. They were standing on top of their bunkers, waving at us, taking our pictures and throwing us C-rations."

The brigade's next mission was the mist-shrouded A Shau Valley, long a major supply route and staging area for

An NVA flag captured by 3rd Brigade Skytroopers is displayed northwest of Hue during Operation JEB STUART, at that time the Army's northern-most area of operations.

the enemy. Despite the problems of poor visibility, rain and heavy fog the men of Garry Owen soon sent the enemy reeling accross the border into Laos, and captured tons of equipment, small arms and foodstuffs. Among enemy supplies taken were Russian-built two and a half ton trucks, 37 mm anti-aircraft guns and machinery for mass producing booby traps.

From May through October of 1968 the brigade engaged in a variety of operations aimed at denying the enemy sanctuaries, staging areas, supply areas and rest and training centers that he had once considered secure. These months were characterized by light contact and the capture or destruction of many tons of enemy supplies.

In fall of 1968 the division moved south into III Corps to block the enemy's infiltration routes to Saigon. Once again the 3rd Brigade spearheaded the operation, arriving at the rubber plantation base of Quan Loi on Halloween night. By November 1 three companies had made the Cav's first III Corps air assault into a marshy field five kilometers from the Cambodian border, and constructed the first Cav-built landing zone in III Corps, LZ Billy.

Contact began immediately. On November 2 brigade units fought an entrenched enemy less than a kilometer

Bound for III Corps as part of the division's massive logistical and tactical move to its new area of operations, these 3rd Brigade soldiers board a C-7A Caribou. And their sign goes with them.

(Continued on P. 255)

FIFTH CAVALRY

With the increase of frontier forces a new Army unit, the 5th Cavalry Regiment, was authorized on March 3, 1855. Marching to Texas, it hastened into battle with the Kickapoo, Lipan and Apache Indians, fighting some 40 skirmishes during the next few years.

The outbreak of the Civil War in 1861 found the regiment torn by sectional loyalty. One of the regiment's first commanding officers, Lieutenant Colonel Robert E. Lee, resigned to lead the armies of the South. Then at the end of the war troopers of the 5th Cavalry Regiment sat on their horses at Appomattox to watch their former commander surrender the Armies of the Confederacy.

Action in the west continued. During the next 10 years the regiment defeated the Apaches in 94 engagements, these in the days of Chief Sitting Bull, Crazy Horse and Joseph. Chief Crazy Horse's Cheyenne were trapped in 1876, marking the last great battle with organized Indian warriors.

The regiment sailed to Puerto Rico in 1898 for the Spanish—American War, earning the Maltese Cross for outstanding performances in skirmishes with the Spanish at Les Marias and Hormigueros.

In 1917 the regiment, which had been stationed in the Philippines, participated in actions against the Navajo in northern Arizona and southern Utah and took part in the Punitive Expedition into Mexico. The 5th Cavalry Regiment saw action against Pancho Villa near Juarez, Mexico, in 1919.

The regiment became part of the 1st Cavalry Division, headquartered at Fort Bliss, Texas, on December 18, 1922.

Among the unit's decorations are the Presidential Unit Citation (PUC), streamer embroidered LOS NEGROS; the Philippine Presidential Unit Citation for October 17, 1944, to July 4, 1945; the Republic of Korea Presidential Unit Citation, streamer embroidered WAEGWAN —TAEGU; the ROK PUC, streamer embroidered KOREA; and the Chryssoun Aristion Andrias (Bravery Gold Medal of Greece), streamer embroidered KOREA.

In Vietnam both battalions own the Presidential Unit Citation for the Pleiku Campaign. In addition Companies A and C of the 1st Battalion were awarded the first Oak Leaf Cluster for the PUC for action on October 2 and 3, 1967. Company A of the 1st Battalion earned a third Oak Leaf Cluster on March 20, 1967.

The 2nd Battalion earned the Valorous Unit Award for an action on March 11, 1967.

The shield is gold with a sable moline cross. The crest has a background wreath of the colors gold and black with a bundle of five black arrows tied with a rattlesnake skin having five rattles.

The shield is yellow for the cavalry. The moline cross symbolizes the charge of the regiment on Longstreet's troops at Gaines Mill in 1862, a charge that saved the Union artillery. The moline cross itself represents the iron pieces of a millstone. The black chief of the shield with the maltese cross is for the Puerto Rican Expedition of 1898. The partition line is embattled to suggest the castle on the Spanish arms. The crest is for the Indian campaigns and the number of arrows corresponds to the numerical designation of the regiment.

Often muddy under the surface, Vietnam streams offer little cooling comfort in crossing them, as a man must work twice as hard to reach the other side. Skytroopers of Company A, 1st Battalion, 5th Cavalry, begin "wading in" near An Khe in October 1965.

The "Black Knights" of the 1st Battalion 5th Cavalry, debarked the USNS William O. Darby at Qui Nhon harbor, Republic of Vietnam, on September 13, 1965. They were airlifted from the shore to the division base at An Khe. Their first mission was to defend the basecamp greenline and conduct patrols and ambushes outside the perimeter. In September Bravo Company made the Black Knights' debut under fire in repulsing the Viet Cong's first probe of the division perimeter. Through October the battalion gained experience as it conducted counter-insurgency operations in the Vinh Thanh "Happy Valley," the jungled slash between mountains east of An Khe.

Then came the Pleiku Campaign.

The afternoon of November 17 found Alpha Company, attached to the 2nd Battalion, 7th Cavalry, struggling with a regimental size element of NVA regulars. Captain Walter B. Tully's Bravo Company moved up to provide reinforcement and linked up with Alpha. At 6: 25 p.m. Bravo Company reported that Company A had 12 wounded personnel. The directive was given for the two companies to join in a tight perimeter for the night and prepare to sweep towards nearby friendly elements at the first break of light.

Machineguns and grenades flashed through the night. Enemy fire and lack of light made aerial evacuation of casualties extremely difficult. At nightfall 22 wounded personnel still remained within the element's perimeter.

At first light on the 18th the remainder of the wounded and dead were evacuated by helicopter. Patrols sent out to search finally reached the third platoon of Alpha Company. At 2 p.m. the two companies were ordered back to LZ Columbus to rejoin the battalion. Marching overland under the sun, they arrived at 5 p.m. The battalion then established a perimeter around the LZ. Behind them lay blood-soaked ground and 350 enemy dead. The men were looking forward to a breather, a hard won break.

The breather did not last long. At 5: 35 p.m. observation posts manned by men of Company B spotted and took under fire the lead elements of NVA forces moving in to attack their positions. A few men from the second platoon sector scrambled forward to assist the observation post as soon as the firing broke out. Within 10 minutes, heavy mortar and machinegun fire was raking the land-

FIRST BATTALION FIFTH CAVALRY

COMMANDERS

LTC Frederick Ackerson ....July 1965—March 1966
LTC William B. Ray ....March 1966—August 1966
LTC Robert H. Siegrist ....August 1966—January 1967
LTC James H. Mapp ....January 1967—June 1967
LTC Daniel S. Rickard ....June 1967—December 1967
LTC Robert L. Runkle ....December 1967—April 1968
LTC Clarence Jordan ....April 1968—June 1968
LTC Gregory Troutman ....June 1968—December 1968
LTC Robert J. Peterson ....December 1968—July 1969
LTC Robert R. Rasmussen ....July 1969—January 1970
LTC James L. Anderson ....January 1970—

ing zone across its width.

"It's strange, but I recall that I was not scared except during the mortar barrage that preceded the first assault," CPT Tully reminisced. "I could see the rounds creeping toward my hole."

The battle area was searched the next morning and 27 NVA bodies were counted around the perimeter. More than 20 enemy weapons were captured.

The battalion spent January 1966 performing security operations along Route 19 and at Camp Radcliff and then deployed to Bong Son to participate in Operation MASHER/WHITE WING.

In March the Black Knights resumed the mission of securing Route 19 and remained in this capacity throughout the spring, in addition to participating in Operations MOSBY II and DAVY CROCKETT.

After standing down at An Khe for less than 48 hours, the 1st Bn, 5th Cav, air landed at LZ Hereford, northeast of the Vinh Thanh Valley where elements of the 1st Brigade had been in heavy contact with a large VC force.

Company B, 1st Battalion, 5th Cavalry, Skytroopers creep cautiously down an enemy trail during a sweeping operation near Tay Ninh City in III Corps Tactical Zone. Contact was made just around the bend in the trail.

Troops of the 1st Battalion, 5th Cavalry, wait in front of the ship that will extract them from the freshly-cut pick up zone (PZ), while another man jumps from the ship to take his stint in the field. The doorgunner looks to the rear to insure the safety of the ship.

After landing at LZ Hereford, the rifle companies began search and destroy operations to the east. They repeatedly encountered harassing sniper fire. The snipers were attempting to delay the friendly forces in order to gain time for a large VC force to move out of the area. This type of harassing and delaying tactic persisted throughout the operation. Several grenade and small arms attacks also were launched by the VC against the battalion command post. They continued to search and clear to the northeast through heavily vegetated, mountainous terrain. The battalion airlifted back to An Khe on May 31.

On July 12, the battalion became the first in the division to convert the combat support company, Company D, into a rifle company. This was accomplished by using personnel and equipment within the battalion. The additional rifle company greatly enhanced the combat effectiveness of the battalion, and the other battalions in the division soon followed suit.

In August 1966 the battalion was involved in Operation PAUL REVERE II. Elements made contact on the 14th and 15th with an enemy unit estimated to have been of battalion or regimental strength.

In September the battalion conducted "show of force" operations in the Bong Son area to ensure that the VC did not disrupt the national elections.

In the fall of 1966 the 1st Bn, 5th Cav, gained distinction uncovering numerous caches. Alpha Company located major enemy stores of food, ordnance and medical supplies on a daily basis.

In the village of Tan An, Binh Dinh Province, on March 20, 1967, Company A was given the mission to air assault into a landing zone in the Soui Ca Valley and then to move north to set up a blocking position. Landing operations were completed, and the company was moving toward Tan An with the first and second platoons leading, the command group and mortar platoon following, and the third platoon echeloned to the left rear. After moving approximately 400 meters over relatively open, sandy terrain, the the entire company came under heavy enemy fire from a well-concealed, well-positioned force, estimated to be two companies of North Vietnamese. The first platoon was the most heavily engaged element, having entered an open graveyard area only meters from a treeline of palms and the village of Tan An where the enemy was positioned. Several of the men became wounded early in the fight, including the platoon leader and platoon sergeant. The weapons squad leader took charge with help from the platoon medic, Specialist Four Charles C. Hagemeister.

Hagemeister's platoon suddenly came under heavy attack from three sides by an enemy force occupying well-concealed fortified positions, supported by machineguns and mortars. Seeing two of his comrades seriously wounded in the initial action, SP4 Hagemeister unhesitatingly rushed through the deadly hail of enemy fire to aid them. Learning that the platoon leader and several other soldiers had also been wounded, Hagemeister continued to brave the withering fire and crawled forward to render life-saving treatment and to offer words of encouragement.

Attempting to evacuate the seriously wounded soldiers, he was taken under fire at close range by an enemy sniper. Realizing that the lives of his fellow soldiers depended on his actions, Hagemester seized a rifle from a fallen comrade, killed the sniper and three other enemy soldiers who were attempting to encircle his position, and silenced an enemy machinegun that was pinning his element down. Unable to remove the

Only minutes after shooting this picture of his wounded Company C, 1st of the 5th, buddy being loaded on a helicopter for evacuation, Specialist Four Chuck Harris, a battalion stringer for the division's information office, was himself hit by shrapnel. He, too, was Medevaced for treatment.

wounded to a less-exposed location and aware of the enemy's efforts to isolate his unit, he dashed through the fusillade of fire to secure help from a nearby platoon. Returning with more men, he placed them in positions to cover his advance as he moved to evacuate the wounded forward of his location. These efforts successfully completed, he then moved to the other flank and evacuated additional wounded men despite the fact that his every move drew fire from the enemy.

As the platoon fought to stop a flanking movement by the enemy, the company commander called in supporting artillery fire. Although the command post was pinned down in an open area, the company commander maintained his position and began maneuvering his platoons.

Meanwhile, the enemy force, realizing that reinforcements were moving in, had intensified their efforts on the first platoon's left flank in a last-ditch attempt to encircle the element. The third platoon successfully linked up with the first platoon, and with the added fire support and strength, the first platoon extracted its wounded and shifted its positions to the east to establish a defensive posture with the remainder of the company. Although mortared during the night and harassed by sporadic sniper fire, the company did not regain contact and maintained its tight defensive perimeter until the following morning. A thorough search of the area revealed 50 well-built bunkers with overhead cover, of which 15 had cement castings.

Equipment, supplies, and the size of the area gave evidence that a large enemy force had been opposing Company A. The manner in which Company A reacted and the unit's ability to gain fire superiority and outmaneuver a numerically superior enemy force clearly indicated that Company A had soundly defeated the enemy and turned what might have been disastrous defeat into decisive victory.

For this action the company was awarded the Presidential Unit Citation and SP4 Hagemeister was awarded the Medal of Honor.

Bravo Company was operating in Binh Dinh Province when a helicopter crashed near its position on June 21, 1967. One platoon rushing to the aid of the downed crewmen was taken under fire by a large enemy force just as it arrived at the crash scene. The fire team led by Specialist Four Carmel B. Harvey, Jr., was directly in the path of the enemy onslaught. Two of Harvey's companions were wounded in the initial burst of fire.

The platoon medic, Specialist Five Edgar L. McWethy, was making his way across the fireswept area to help the platoon leader and his RTO. After being patched up the platoon leader was able to continue his command. "Doc" McWethy then headed across the open area in response to a call from SP4 Harvey's squad. On the way he was wounded in the head and knocked to the ground. He regained his feet and continued on but was hit again, this time in the leg. He dragged himself to the side of his comrades and treated their injuries. Another wounded Skytrooper lay in the

Three grunts from the 1st Battalion, 5th Cavalry, move to the other side of the stream to provide security while their comrades take time out to for a refreshing bath.

(Continued on P. 265)

SECOND BATTALION FIFTH CAVALRY

COMMANDERS

The strain of battle, both mental and physcal, is mirrored on the face of this tired Company C, 2nd Battalion, 5th Cavalry, trooper.

The main body of the 2nd Battalion, 5th Cavalry, disembarked the USNS General Simon B. Buckner at Qui Nhon, Republic of Vietnam, on September 13, 1965. It proceeded by air to join the advance party which was constructing the division base at An Khe.

In October the battalion conducted Operation COBRA to clear and secure the Song Con "Happy Valley" region. November found the battalion taking part in the Plei Me Campaign in the Ia Drang Valley. The highlight of the battalion's operations there was the November 15 blitz, both by air and march, into LZ X-Ray to relieve the embattled 1st Battalion, 7th Cavalry. The "Black Knights" were rotated back to An Khe to close out 1965 securing Camp Radcliff.

The battalion took part in several operations in the beginning of 1966, but did not make significant contact until Bravo Company engaged an NVA battalion on the morning of February 17.

In that action Sergeant Gary B. Gorton, a weapons platoon squad leader, moved his mortar sections forward under heavy fire. Scrambling everywhere to see that the tubes were correctly adjusted and aimed, Gorton was a one-man dynamo as he tried to supervise the 10 men under his command. Disdaining the enemy's concentrated fire toward his positions, he directed a heavy concentration of mortar fire that fell upon the well dug-in enemy force, causing a deadly toll. The mortar ammunition ran out, so Gorton deployed his men as riflemen and maneuvered close enough to use hand grenades against the enemy, knocking out a .51 caliber machinegun.

The sergeant was killed by a sniper before he could return to the company perimeter. Bravo was reinforced by A and C Companies, which air assaulted

Waiting for helicopters to extract them from mountainous terrain near Khe Sanh during Operation PEGASUS, these 2nd Battalion, 5th Cavalry, soldiers take some comfort in lumpy rest on rocky ground.

Sweat-soaked clothes and steamy jungle do not keep Specialists Four John Codron and Robert E. Wilken of Company B, 2nd Battalion, 5th Cavalry, from taking this enemy B-40 rocket out of the weapons cache they found during Operation JEB STUART III.

Private First Class Stephen Hanh, an RTO with Company B, 2nd Battalion, 5th Cavalry, informs his company commander by radio of his platoon's situation during operations northeast of Tay Ninh in III Corps.

to link up with the embattled Skytroopers. By 4 p.m. the contact had been reduced to isolated sniper fire as the overpowered NVA unit scampered northward.

Through the summer of 1966 the elements of the 2nd Bn, 5th Cav, were engaged in securing Camp Radcliff, the new airfield at Kontum and the Pleiku installation. The Black Knights made raids and conducted cordon and search operations along Highway 19. Sporadic encounters with small enemy elements continued through the close of the year.

Until the early part of February 1967, the battalion continued securing Camp Radcliff while at the same time conducting local patrols to insure that any enemy within striking distance of the base would be discovered and routed.

February 11 marked the beginning of Operation PERSHING, an operation designed to search and clear populated areas from the Nui Mieu Mountains to the South China Sea, to control the use of Highways 1 and 505, and to interdict and harass the operations of the 2nd and 3rd NVA Divisions.

On the morning of March 11, Company C moved into a blocking position near the village of Phu Ninh while elements of the 40th ARVN Regiment conducted a sweep of the interior. The sweep had progressed smoothly, and at 10 a.m., Captain Don Markham, the company commander, instructed the third platoon, led by First Lieutenant Dana Gerald, to conduct a local patrol to the south to insure security to the rear. After moving about 1,300 meters from the rest of the company, Staff Sergeant John Kriedler, the platoon sergeant, spotted a man running from them down a trail. He took aim and killed him. The man turned out to be a local hamlet guerrilla armed with several hand grenades.

SGT Kriedler and Specialist Four Jose Garza continued to root around some small huts near the trail when one enemy with an automatic weapon opened up and killed the Americans on the spot. LT Gerald, located about 200 meters away, reacted quickly and brought the remainder of the platoon to the sound of the latest shots.

When he arrived, all seemed clear, but another well-concealed soldier fired and killed Gerald and four other men. The platoon took cover and contacted CPT Markham. He estimated the platoon was pinned down by one squad of VC. He could not have known that the

lieutenant had stumbled into the front door of the 18th NVA Regiment.

The regimental headquarters had occupied the high ground (Hill 82) directly south of Phu Ninh, where the initial contact had been made. About half way down the hilltop was a 600-foot long trench that was the main defense for the hilltop . . . filled with enemy soldiers. There were numerous boulders that served as intermediate cover positions for the enemy troops occupying the hill below the trench.

Markham moved the remainder of the company to the vicinity of the hamlet, but repeated attempts to relieve his platoon failed because of the enemy's superior fortifications and firepower. Aerial rocket artillery (ARA) was called in to determine the enemy's strength and location in relation to the beleaguered platoon and to neutralize their more vulnerable positions. The view from above gave CPT Markham a more conclusive picture of the enemy situation. Gunship cover allowed a seven man rescue force to crawl up to assist the pinned Skytroopers.

Descending to a small clearing below where they will begin operations, 2nd of the 5th Cav Skytroopers (upper left) watch the thick jungle below, knowing the enemy may be waiting in ambush.

Another of the battalion's troopers jumps from the lift ship that has dropped him into a small section of Vietnam jungle real estate. The doorgunner leans forward to check tail rotor clearance.

Grinding his belly into the ground to get low, this soldier watches to his front. His platoon is moving into a suspected enemy bunker location.

While the rescue effort was in progress, Company D, commanded by Captain Richard N. McInerney, was airlifted to assist Charlie Company by establishing a blocking position to the east of their location. The plan was to effect the rescue of the platoon and then force the enemy off the hill by employing air strikes and artillery fire.

The rescue force succeeded in drawing close enough to the men in the platoon to place effective fire on the enemy positions, while each man individually crawled to safety beneath the thick underbrush.

Both of the companies pulled back slightly and fanned out to complete their blocking positions. Then Air Force fighters came on station to drop their ordnance on the hill. The action literally cast a stone in a hornet's nest—the enemy soldiers swarmed off the mountain into the hands of the two companies.

Sporadic clashes with the furious and frightened enemy erupted throughout the night.

By the following morning, the enemy units had left the battlefield, carrying their dead and wounded with them. Later, 36 bodies were found and 145 NVA were captured. A subsequent analysis of documents taken from an NVA political officer identified the unit as the 7th and what remained of the 9th Battalions of the 18th NVA Regiment. The detainees revealed that the unit was nearly wiped out.

After a period of pulling security operations, Operation LEJEUNE commenced on April 7. The battalion spearheaded a brigade task force that, at the end of only 12 days, killed 177 enemy soldiers and established two fully-operational hardtop airstrips, two major roads, plus one of the 10 busiest seaports in all of Vietnam. This operation was the first conducted with the Marines in I Corps.

Cache finds and minor incidents continued through the summer. On June 21 Alpha and Bravo Companies wiped out an enemy company which had been acting as an advance party for the 18th NVA Regiment. They had been moving into the Nui Mien Mountains.

In August Company A began working in the rockpile area in what became known as "Pratt's Corner." The area was named for Captain Clayton A. Pratt, who commanded Alpha Company in a two-week offensive, which destroyed the effectiveness of the 8th Battalion, 18th NVA Regiment. The campaign netted

Sniper fire sends this Skytrooper rushing to aid a wounded friend. The action occurred shortly after the platoon of Company A, 2nd Battalion of the 5th Cavalry, had combat assaulted into the location near An Loc in III Corps.

a total of 35 killed, 45 detained and 16 wounded, with 70 weapons captured.

For the remainder of 1967 the Black Knights interspersed security operations with a variety of patrols, making frequent light contacts. Intelligence gained during this period helped provide early warning of the enemy's greatest drive of the war, the 1968 Tet Offensive.

As 1968 began, the 2nd Bn, 5th Cav, continued combat operations in the vicinity of the Bong Son coastal plain. The area was large and presented the battalion with quickly changing tacti-

cal situations, but through continuous operations and full utilization of the airmobility concept, the enemy threat in the AO was greatly reduced. The enemy had dwindled in force from fortified regiments to small, ill-equipped, poorly motivated bands wandering about in search of survival. A few enemy soldiers were killed and several rallied to the Skytroopers.

It was a different story when in mid-February the battalion moved north to Camp Evans, just 21 kilometers from

(Continued on P. 286)

SEVENTH CAVALRY

Within a gold horseshoe showing seven nail holes, the heels are upward and the opening between the heels is closed with a blue ribbon bearing the words "Garry Owen" in yellow letters. The crest of the regiment is azure in color. In the center a buckskin-clad hand grasps an old style United States Army sabre.

The horseshoe is symbolic of the cavalry. Its color, gold, is the color of the old United States cavalry uniform facings. It is still retained as the color of the cavalry arm.

The words "Garry Owen" are the title of an old Irish song, known and sung as the regimental song since the days of General Custer and the Indian Wars.

The arm, taken from the crest of the Regimental Coat of Arms, symbolizes the spirit of the cavalry charge. At the time of the organization of the 7th Cavalry Regiment this position of the arm and sabre was known as "Raised Sabre" and was taken at the command, "Charge". The sabre itself is of old cavalry type used in the Indian Campaigns.

The 7th Cavalry Regiment was formed in 1866 at Fort Riley, Kansas—its ranks filled with a hard-bitten crew of trappers, war veterans and frontiersmen, many of them Irish immigrants. The influence of the Irish on the regiment is noted in its famous drinking song "Garry Owen" which the unit adopted as its own.

Until 1872 the regiment rode against the Sioux, Apaches and scattered remnants of the Cheyennes who had so decisively been defeated at the Battle of Washita in 1868. In 1874 the unit moved to the Black Hills of South Dakota to afford protection for railroad construction parties. Hoards of gold seekers and farmers followed the newly-laid tracks and the influx brought on new troubles with the Sioux. In 1876 the 7th Cavalry and its dashing leader, Brevet Major General George Armstrong Custer, joined in a concerted drive to break the power of the tribes once and for all.

In 1877 the regiment returned to action against the wiliest of all Indian generals, Chief Joseph of the Nez Perces. During a bloody four-day battle the might of the great chief was broken.

By 1906 the regiment had served two tours of duty in the Philippines and in 1916 joined the Mexican Punitive Expedition. It returned to Fort Bliss, Texas, and remained there until it was assigned to the 1st Cavalry Division on September 13, 1921.

The unit had been decorated with the Presidential Unit Citation, streamer embroidered YONCHON, KOREA (1st Battalion cited); the Philippine Presidential Unit Citation, streamer embroidered October 17, 1944, to July 4, 1945; the Republic of Korea Presidential Unit Citation, streamer embroidered WAEGWAN—TAEGU; the ROK PUC, streamer embroidered KOREA; and the Chryssoun Aristion Andrias (Bravery Gold Medal of Greece), streamer embroidered KOREA.

In Vietnam the 1st Battalion has been awarded the Vietnamese Cross of Gallantry with Palm for heroism in the Ia Drang Valley November 14, 1965. Both the 1st and 2nd Battalions share with the division the Presidential Unit Citation for gallantry in the Pleiku Campaign, October 23 to November 25, 1965.

Watching Air Force bombers in the hands of today's Rickenbackers, Scotts and Mitchells is an exciting experience, one which draws the attention of even the veterans of several months in the field. Troopers of the 1st Battalion, 7th Cavalry, while they had the chance at LZ X-Ray in the Ia Drang Valley, take such an opportunity.

FIRST BATTALION SEVENTH CAVALRY

COMMANDERS

LTC Harold G. Moore ....July 1965—December 1965

LTC Raymond L. Kampe ....·.....December 1965—March 1966

LTC Herman L. Wirth...........................March 1966—July 1966

LTC Edward M. Markham III ....July 1966—December 1966

LTC George W. Orton ....December 1966—July 1967

LTC Edward M. Pierce ....July 1967—February 1968

LTC Joseph E. Wasiak ....February 1968—July 1968

LTC William D. MacMillan.....................July 1968—January 1969

LTC Guinn E. Unger ....January 1969—June 1969

LTC Robert E. Justice.......................June 1969—September 1969

LTC Robert L. Drudik ....September 1969—

In August, 1965, the 1st Battalion, 7th Cavalry, sailed for South Vietnam, arriving at Qui Nhon on September 18.

The battalion warmed up to its first decisive engagement when the Cavalrymen entered the Plei Me area in Operation SILVER BAYONET on November 9. On the morning of November 14, 1965, the 1st Bn, 7th Cav, met its rendezvous with destiny.

The battalion commander, Lieutenant Colonel Harold G. Moore, received the mission to air assault into a location near the Chu Pong Massif to conduct search and destroy operations. Bravo Company was on the ground at LZ X-Ray one mile north of the Massif by mid-morning.

But by the time the slicks returned with their fifth load of troops, LZ X-Ray was ablaze with enemy fire. Bullets ripped into Major Bruce P. Crandall's chopper, killing three infantrymen and wounding three. However, by the time the LZ got too hot for further flights, the bulk of the battalion was on the ground. The tactical situation was that some of the NVA field assault elements had been using the Chu Pong Massif as a base and were staging for an offensive when COL Moore's battalion landed in their midst.

Alpha Company, commanded by Captain Ramon A. Nadal II, landed on the LZ and its first platoon, led by Second Lieutenant Walter J. Marm, fanned out. COL Moore ordered Captain John D. Herren's Bravo Company to move up to the fingers of a slope to avoid any ambush in the draws. At the H-Plus-1 hour Bravo Company ran into stiff enemy resistance and one of its platoons found itself cut off and tangling with an entire NVA company. In a hellish confrontation that lasted 20 hours, the 40 man platoon was reduced to a few wounded survivors. The enemy lost 72 dead. Bravo Company was forced to pull back.

Meanwhile, LT Marm was on his own and ordered his men to withdraw. At the base of the hill, Marm received orders to go up the slope to relieve the surrounded Bravo platoon. Sniper fire rang out, but LT Marm's platoon moved forward under an umbrella of artillery and aerial rocket artillery fire.

The rigors of the three-day-long battle at LZ X-Ray show on the face of this 1st Battalion, 7th Cavalry, trooper as he and other Garry Owen soldiers inspect Communist weapons captured during the fierce fighting.

Marm moved slowly up the hill, firing short bursts from his M-16. He dashed across to the right flank where his men were receiving extremely heavy fire. Suddenly three North Vietnamese soldiers emerged from the brush. Marm whirled and emptied his weapon at them.

The attacks came in waves, and LT Marm moved from one position to another held by his platoon. It was late afternoon when Platoon Sergeant George B. McCulley, Jr. and the machinegun teams appeared on the scene. With a platoon from Bravo Company that also had worked itself up an adjoining slope, the Skytroopers battled the well-entrenched enemy. Marm ordered walking casualties back down the hill.

"We're surrounded, lieutenant," reported Sergeant Charles P. Tolliver, a squad leader, when he returned back up the slope with several wounded men. Enemy troops had slipped behind the platoon.

Marm concentrated on the platoon's immediate problem, a seven foot bunker which had pinned down his men. One trooper crawled over to Marm with a light-weight anti-tank weapon. Marm triggered the LAW which obliterated the left side of the bunker, but the machinegun continued to blast away at the platoon.

"Hold your fire!" Marm shouted. Jumping to his feet, the pintsized officer dashed toward the bunker, yanking the pin from a grenade. Dodging the enemy fire, he pitched the grenade through the gun port and hit the ground. The grenade exploded and Marm rushed around the left side of the bunker, jabbed his M-16 into the entrance and triggered off a long burst. Then he scrambled back to the side of the bunker and gestured for his men to move up.

"On the double!" he yelled, just as an enemy bullet slammed into the left side of his jaw and drilled through his mouth. A medic ran up and administered first aid.

Alpha Company plunged ahead, thanks to LT Marm's act of bravery for which he was later awarded the Medal of Honor—the 1st Air Cavalry Division's first in Vietnam.

In the two days that followed, the battalion again engaged the NVA, during which time it drove back four human wave attacks.

During the fierce three day battle to gain ground from the enemy, the 1st

A Company C, 1st Battalion, 7th Cavalry, trooper lofts a grenade into an enemy position, while others hug the sandy bank near LZ Baldy. The unit was operating in an area little explored by American forces.

Bn, 7th Cav, and supporting units were credited with killing 834 NVA, with approximately 1,215 more North Vietnamese regular forces either killed or wounded by supporting arms.

For their courageous fighting and decisive victory over the enemy forces, the 1st Bn, 7th Cav, was awarded the Vietnamese Cross of Gallantry with Palm on August 22, 1966, by General Cao Van Vien, the chief of the Joint General Staff, Republic of South Vietnam Armed Forces.

In January 1966, the battalion worked as barrier defense at Camp Radcliff in An Khe. The period from the end of January through February was spent on operations MASHER and WHITE-WING in the northeastern sector of Binh Dinh Province.

The battalion operated around the Chu Pong Mountains in April, participating in Operation LINCOLN/MOSBY, and returned to find a more peaceful LZ X-Ray. During June the battalion se-

cured Highway 19 from its junction east of the An Khe Pass to Mang Yang Pass in the west.

In July the battalion participated in Operation HENRY CLAY around Dong Tre and Chung Son.

Then came PAUL REVERE, and once again the "Garry Owens" were back in the Ia Drang.

Soon after noon on August 8, 1966, A Company made contact with a large enemy force in the Ia Drang Valley. The third platoon was on point and made the initial contact with several NVA. They aggressively pursued and were immediately hit by several heavy and light machineguns, cutting them off from the rest of the company. Reinforcements were requested, and B and C Companies were air assaulted east of the contact area. In the meantime, the third platoon made its way back to link up with the main body company, aided by several individual acts of heroism. Sergeant Major Richard Schaaf was killed while exposing himself to enemy fire to cover the withdrawal of those pinned down and wounded. Platoon Sergeant Francisco Roig led the platoon to safety while personally beating off several attacks on his beleaguered men.

Once in the company perimeter, artillery was effectively placed on the enemy. Several human wave attacks by the Communists were beaten off, largely through the efforts of two valiant machinegunners, Private First Class David Frederick and Private First Class George Hamilton, who fired with deadly effectiveness until their guns were put out of action. Captain Robert A Wands, the company commander, was wounded and First Lieutenant Jeffery White, the executive officer, took command. Although wounded himself, he rallied the unit to beat off the attacks. The wounded were taken care of by Private First Class Elvin L. Polk, who moved from man to man to give aid during the attacks, even going outside the perimeter to gather additional medical supplies.

Shortly after 3 a.m., with more rein-forcements enroute, the enemy force broke contact and fled. The three companies then set up a perimeter for the night. Darkness prevented a search of the battlefield but the enemy casualty figures were estimated to be at least 65 killed.

In September the battalion once again became responsible for barrier defense at Camp Radcliff at An Khe.

Operation THAYER II lasted from October through the end of 1966. During this operation the 1st Bn, 7th Cav, operated in the Phu My District, working off many landing zones in the area.

January and February of 1967 were spent in Operation DAZZLEM securing Highway 19. From the end of February to the beginning of October the battalion took part in Operation PERSHING, working across the Bong Son Plains and in the An Lao Valley.

Throughout October 1st Bn, 7th Cav, chased the NVA up the South China seacoast, twice killing more than 100 men in a single day.

On October 27, 1967, the battalion began offensive operations against an an enemy command post and hospital complex west of LZ Baldy, near the South China seacoast and Highway 14. Charlie Company air assaulted into the complex followed by A and B Companies. An aerial scout observed enemy positions to the north of the LZ. Company C advanced toward the location and made heavy contact shortly after leaving its landing zone. Bravo Company maneuvered northwest to support Company C and also made heavy contact.

With both companies heavily engaged, Alpha Company moved in to flank the enemy and the North Vietnamese force soon found themselves surrounded. Companies C and B rolled over the enemy positions from the west, and then joined in mopping up operations which continued until dark.

As Company A had advanced on the west flank, searching well-used trails, the lead platoon made contact with several of the enemy in camouflaged bunkers. They were quickly eliminated. Company A continued to advance on

Covered by the stone walls common around Hue, these 1st Battalion, 7th Cavalry, Skytroopers throw lead at the enemy nearby. The imperial city of Hue was then held by the Communists.

Eyes ever-peeled for signs of the enemy, this Garry Owen machinegunner prepares to move into heavy jungle in III Corps.

line with Bravo and Charlie and then set up a perimeter for the night. Just at dusk the unit received heavy automatic weapons and mortar fire from an enemy company dug into the front and one flank of their position. The enemy positions were immediately engaged by artillery and aerial rocket artillery and then the Skytroopers assaulted and overran the enemy positions.

Subsequent intelligence reports indicated that the 1st Bn, 7th Cav, had, in one day of battle on the 27th, rendered one North Vietnamese battalion totally ineffective—killing or wounding all personnel.

The beginning of 1968 found the Garry Owens participating in Operation WHEELER/WALLOWA in the Que Son Valley, located in Southern I Corps, on the border of southeastern Quang Nam and northeastern Quang Tin Provinces.

From the end of February to the end of March the battalion was active in Operation JEB STUART. This operation was carried out around the city of Hue and later in the coastal area known as the "Street without Joy".

On April 19, 1968, the 1st Bn, 7th Cav, spearheaded the U.S. drive into the A Shau Valley, landing at LZ Vicki.

On April 21st, the battalion made light contact and killed three NVA. Working east to establish a new LZ, the battalion found two enemy bulldozers, one with USSR stamped on it. It became apparent that engineer units of battalion size had been working in the area, building and repairing the

The damaged, deserted structure in the rear is a backdrop, a stage, for this Company C, 1st of the 7th Cavalry, Skytrooper. He is sweeping with his platoon into the imperial city of Hue, February, 1968.

vital road network. The Skytroopers took the bulldozers with them to their new LZ.

A few days later Alpha Company found three flatbed trucks with 37 mm anti-aircraft weapons mounted on them. Three days later Charlie Company found four more trucks in the same area.

From May 1968 through October of that year the Skytroopers from the 1st Bn, 7th Cav, participated in Operation JEB STUART III. This operation was conducted around the Camp Evans area and along the "Street without Joy."

Participating in Operation TOAN THANG I, which began November 3, 1968, the 1st Bn, 7th Cav, continued to compile an outstanding record of achievements. After deploying to the III Corps Tactical Zone and before the battalion had settled into its new rear area at Tay Ninh, the Garry Owen troopers were deployed to LZ St. Barbara and initiated combat operations in War Zone C. Intelligence soon indicated that NVA forces were massing in the northwest corner of Tay Ninh Province near the Cambodian border. In response to this threat, the Garry Owen battalion was airlifted to LZ Ann.

While most of their time was spent searching for the enemy in the jungle, part of each company's time was spent in defense of the battalion firebases.

Several times, while the 1st Bn, 7th Cav, was operating near Quan Loi, the enemy—frustrated in their attempts to travel through the Garry Owen area of operations—tried to break the Sky-

An aerial view of LZ Joy shows the isolation of a 1st Cav firebase. On June 12, 1969, Companies D and E, 1st Battalion, 7th Cavalry, beat back a devastating attack by an estimated NVA battalion. The enemy, reluctantly, seldom returned after that. The firebase was shortly afterward closed down. It had outlived its usefulness.

A 1st of the 7th Cav RTO (left) relays a message to battalion headquarters for his commander. He reports, "Negative activity here."

A mortar crew (above) lofts rounds out of their firebase to support 3rd Brigade troops operating north of Quan Loi.

SECOND BATTALION SEVENTH CAVALRY

COMMANDERS

Arriving at Qui Nhon, South Vietnam, on September 16, 1965, the men of the 2nd Battalion 7th Cavalry, the "Garry Owen" battalion, boarded aircraft for a flight to a small village located in the jungles of the central highlands named An Khe, the 1st Air Cavalry Division's first home in Vietnam.

Late in the afternoon of November 14, 1965, Company B, commanded by Captain Myron Diduryk, was air assaulted into LZ X-Ray in the Ia Drang Valley to support the 1st Battalion, 7th Cavalry, which had tangled with the 66th NVA Regiment.

Bravo Company went under the operational control of the 1st of the 7th and extracted from LZ X-Ray with that battalion on the 17th, thus being spared the agony that was incurred at LZ Albany.

The remainder of the 2nd Bn, 7th Cav, which had moved overland to LZ X-Ray from LZ Columbus on the 16th, moved again through the jungle toward a location along the Ia Drang Valley that was to be known as LZ Albany. The battalion compensated for the loss of its Bravo Company by picking up Alpha Company, 1st Battalion, 5th Cavalry. The column was almost to its destination when it ran across an NVA patrol. The lead elements of the battalion killed two, captured two, but at least two got away. That was the flank security for an NVA battalion that was on the move toward LZ Columbus.

The two battalions collided. For more than four hours it was rifleman against rifleman in hand to hand fighting of unparalleled intensity.

When the battalion finally pulled itself into a perimeter, the worst was over. Bravo Company was air assaulted into LZ Albany to assume a reinforcing role. There were still Skytroopers outside the perimeter during a night which was filled with sounds of scattered fighting.

Although the battalion took heavier casualties than in any previous engagement of the war, General Westmoreland proclaimed the action "an unprecedented victory." When the smoke from the battle cleared, the enemy had left over 350 of their crack troops dead on the battlefield. The battle of Ia Drang Valley was over.

On January 25, 1966, the battalion was called upon to participate in Operation MASHER. On January 28 Company C conducted an air assault into LZ 4, a sandy, open graveyard surrounded on three sides by tall palm trees. Immediately upon landing, Charlie Company came under intense automatic weapons and mortar fire from well fortified enemy positions in the treeline. Company C was scattered over the entire landing zone and suffered moderate casualties during the initial hours of the battle. At 3 a.m. on January 29, Charlie Company conducted a night withdrawal south across the landing zone, carrying its wounded, as artillery fired into the treeline. Later that morning

Rice paddies (right) afford little cover from sniper fire, causing men of the 2nd Battalion, 7th Cavalry, to scurry where they can find some. The action took place near Phan Thiet in Binh Thuan Province in II Corps.

Skytroopers scoot under barbed wire to advance toward an enemy bunker complex located in the trees beyond. Bong Son was the place, 1966 the date and MASHER the operation.

and into the afternoon, artillery fire and air strikes were delivered on the enemy positions. When the action was over the enemy dead numbered 81 with an estimated 112 more killed.

The Garry Owens began Operation WHITE WING in the An Lao Valley, on February 7. At 9 a.m. on the morning of February 15 Company B made contact with a well dug-in enemy force.

By using air strikes and artillery, the company was able to overrun the enemy positions and by nightfall had accounted for 57 dead Viet Cong. Bravo Company succeeded in capturing the Viet Cong battalion commander and thereby obtained valuable intelligence information.

On August 1 the battalion was com-

Arriving at the landing zone with a full load of supplies, this helicopter is guided down for off-load. The 2nd Battalion, 7th Cavalry, trooper (below) serves as receptionist.

Marines watch men of Company C, 2nd Battalion, 7th Cavalry, enter Khe Sanh in April 1968, thus ending the long siege of the Marine outpost. Skytroopers assumed perimeter defensive positions, allowing the Marines to conduct operations to the northeast.

mitted to Operation PAUL REVERE II, aimed at stopping an enemy buildup in Pleiku and Kontum provinces. On the first day of the operation Alpha and Bravo Companies came under an early morning attack from an enemy battalion. The Skytroopers resisted three human wave attempts to overrun their positions.

The next day weather conditions were severe, some of the worst flying conditions the division had seen. During a break in the weather the third platoon of Alpha Company assaulted into LZ Pink at 2 p.m. Contact was immediate and heavy. A reinforced NVA company surrounded the 26-man platoon. As the fighting intensified radio contact was lost. The bad weather stymied efforts to relieve the embattled force. Not until 5:30 p.m. did the rest of Alpha Company reach the platoon. For more than three hours the Cavalrymen had held out alone against a much larger force, but in the process 18 had died and the rest had been wounded. The bodies of 16 enemy were found on the battlefield.

The operation continued through the rest of the month, with the battalion conducting search and clear sweeps and serving as the operation headquarters defense unit. A total of 861 enemy were killed during the operation.

On the 25th of August, 1966, the battalion received a new mission and moved that same day some 150 miles to Phan Thiet to commence Operation BYRD. Although most of the fighting during BYRD was between small units in "quick and dirty" encounters, on the 25th of October Company C assaulted two platoons into a Viet Cong position that had been spotted from the air. With close support from aerial rocket artillery (ARA) they accounted for 52 Viet Cong dead in three hours of close-in fighting. Friendly losses were only one killed. This was one of the largest single engagements of Operation BYRD. Throughout Operation BYRD the 2nd Bn, 7th Cav, task force was the only independent American battalion-size force in the country. Operating smoothly and reacting swiftly, the task force set precedents in airmobile operations.

This action, and many others like it, combined to make 1967 and Operation BYRD outstanding successes for the 2nd Bn, 7th Cav, and the 1st Air Cavalry Division.

The beginning of 1968 found the battalion still operating as an independent task force in Operation BYRD in the II Corps Tactical Zone. Pitted against an estimated two Viet Cong battalions, the 2nd Bn, 7th Cav, crushed the insurgents and opened Highway 1, the vital link to Saigon. When the battalion left the location to rejoin the division, convoys could travel from Saigon to Hue without incident for the first time in a decade, and the enemy forces were reduced to the extent that local forces could contain them.

A major force in relieving the Marine bastion at Khe Sanh, the Garry Owen battalion initiated Operation PEGASUS on April 1, air assaulting into the region and gaining control of Highway 9. Beginning a drive toward the beleaguered camp, the Cavalrymen ran into well-fortified NVA trenches and foxholes. Failing to dislodge the enemy with tube artillery and ARA, the unique airmobility of the 1st Cavalry was brought to play.

In May the battalion participated in Operation JEB STUART III, and returned to unfinished business in Houng Dien District and along the "Street without Joy," in what was known to the Cavalrymen as the "Battle of the

Graveyards." In the Lunar New Year Offensive in February, Viet Cong forces overran the northwestern section of the district, a small peninsula in northern I Corps.

The battalion air assaulted into the southern portion of the peninsula and fought its way over the enemy positions, often camping near graveyards, from which the name of the battle was derived. As the enemy infested areas were being cleared out, the battalion was called into the Khe Sanh and A Shau Valley operations, postponing its final victory.

When they returned to the familiar terrain, the 2nd Bn, 7th Cav, evacuated Vietnamese civilians to safe areas, and in a massive effort, organized a sampan flotilla to relocate them. Two thousand tons of enemy and friendly rice were transported in the effort.

Throughout the summer the battalion concentrated its power on finding rice and denying sanctuary along the "Street." Braving numerous booby traps and enemy snipers, the battalion utilized Rome plows, which had proved so successful earlier in the year in Operation BYRD, to expose enemy bunkers and rice and weapons caches, destroying a former Viet Cong haven.

At the end of October the battalion once again assumed the spirit of Khe Sanh and spearheaded the 1st Cavalry drive south to III Corps.

Moving into the unfamiliar territory, the Cavalrymen went to work establishing a firebase and combating enemy forces at the same time.

For the Garry Owen battalion 1969 was a busy year. Engaged in operations to seal off NVA supply routes from Cambodia, the battalion worked out of LZ Jamie, 23 miles northeast of Tay Ninh.

Frustrated by the FIRST TEAM's efforts to shut down their infiltration routes, North Vietnamese regulars launched a desperate attempt to storm LZ Jamie on the 11th of May.

When a trip flare went off near the LZ at 12:45 a.m, no one was surprised. At 1:10 a.m. another trip flare flashed into the night; an observation post reported four individuals lying on the ground. Cavalrymen responded immediately by spraying the area with artillery and small arms fire.

At 2:40 the men at LZ Jamie knew the attack was a determined one. Between then and approximately 3 a.m. some 200 rounds of 107 mm rockets and 60

and 82 mm mortars slammed into the firebase.

In the midst of this deafening mortar and rocket barrage, the crackling of small arms fire was barely audible. From three sides the North Vietnamese poured toward the perimeter. "Just as the mortars were hitting, sappers blew the wire," said Sergeant Vaughn G. Hood, a squad leader with Company D. "We opened up with M-60s, M-16s and claymores, and the artillery fired at Charlie point-blank." The concentrated enemy fire and the holes in the wire, blown by bangalore torpedoes, allowed the NVA to breach the perimeter.

Some of the bunkers had been built with cyclone fence surrounding them. "The fence saved our lives," said Private First Class Larry M. Huff. "The NVA got up to the fence, tried to blow it, but couldn't. We were able to direct mortar fire on the gap in the perimeter wire, and kept on firing all night long."

The NVA did occupy three bunkers,

but not for long. One bunker was decimated by direct 105 mm howitzer fire. "There were enemy swarming all over those bunkers," said Specialist Four John W. Brock, "and the 105 just blew them—and the bunker—away."

Another bunker was retaken by the men of the battalion. "There were still a few NVA soldiers left," according to Master Sergeant David A. Vallee. "They threw frags, and when those didn't do the job we went in and shot them."

With two bunkers in the possession of the enemy attackers and more crossing the perimeter, Captain William Lacey, Jr. organized a counterattack and personally led five volunteers.

Maneuvering against the enemy-held bunkers, CPT Lacey and his men overpowered the enemy on the bunkerline and drove them from the firebase.

Overhead, aerial rocket artillery and

(Continued on P. 264)

Captain Peter J. Conway takes a break during the Cav's blitz drive to relieve the besieged Marine base in 1968. Captain Conway commanded the first U.S. Army ground troops to enter the embattled base. He has doffed his helmet and wrapped a T-shirt about his head to stave off the Vietnam sun.

FIFTH BATTALION SEVENTH CAVALRY

COMMANDERS

LTC Trevor W. Swett, Jr. ....August 1966—December 1966

LTC Charles D. W. Canham II...........December 1966—February 1967

LTC Andrew J. Gatsis ....February 1967—June 1967

LTC John A. Wickham ....June 1967—October 1967

LTC Herlihy T. Long ....October 1967—January 1968

LTC James Vaught ....January 1968—April 1968

LTC Norman Stockton ....April 1968—October 1968

LTC John F. McGraw.......................October 1968—April 1969

LTC Thomas F. Healey.....................April 1969—October 1969

LTC Sanders A. Cortner ....October 1969—

First Lieutenant Bobby Brown calls for aerial rocket artillery (ARA) support while his unit, Company A, 5th Battalion, 7th Cavalry, conducts a search and destroy mission during Operation PERSHING in the Song Re Valley.

The 5th Battalion, 7th Cavalry, joined the 1st Air Cavalry Division on August 21, 1966, and shipped to the Republic of Vietnam from Fort Carson, Colorado, aboard the USNS Gaffey. The battalion landed in Qui Nhon and airlifted to An Khe on August 20. The battalion conducted final training exercises in the vicinity of An Khe, then began a mission nicknamed Road Runner, securing Highway 19.

By the time the month-long operation terminated at the end of September the new "Garry Owens" were ready for full scale operations. In October they made their jungle fighting debut in Operation IRVING. Air assaulting into eastern Binh Dinh Province, they swept east toward the sea while other division elements and Allied units made coordinated sweeps to the north and south. The following week the battalion moved back across Highway 1 to LZ Duz. Operation IRVING was a resounding success with 710 enemy detained and 681 killed. By the end of the operation the enemy units had dissolved and were scattered and hiding.

With November began Operation THAYER II. By mid-morning on November 1, Bravo Company had established contact with the 93rd Battalion of the 2nd VC Regiment in the area between Route 1 and Dam Tra O Lake, south of the Gay Giep Mountains. The company, led by Captain John L. Hitti, killed 43 enemy in the fight that raged on for more than nine hours.

A month later Company B had been hacking its way through densely foliated terrain since daybreak when it got a call that "some other outfit had made contact farther up the valley," First Lieutenant William E. Kail was ordered to take the second platoon to the scene of the action, a small village about 1,000 meters from Phu Huu 2. When they had moved through thick jungle in a little more than an hour, it was 2 p.m. on December 1. The village did not appear to be defended by more than a few snipers so Kail formed his platoon for a quick sweep through. Coming to the edge of the village LT Kail paused to instruct his machinegunners. Specialist Four Dennis Beneditti was placing his machinegun behind a grave mound when an AK-47 opened fire. "Return fire!" LT Kail shouted. The men riddled the hootch to their front, but the fire had been coming from a well-concealed rock bunker next to the house. Staff Sergeant Jeffery B. Neher spotted the bunker when he had crawled within 10 meters of it—he knocked it out with a LAW (Light Antitank Weapon).

Staff Sergeant George Porod took a squad to check out the hootch. As they approached the dwelling a Viet Cong tried to slip out the back door. Porod fired, but the enemy, only wounded, managed to pull himself into the brush. The squad continued, moving forward parallel to a drainage ditch about 10 meters to it left. Crawling they came upon a trail across their front. Just then another VC rifleman jumped from a foxhole just four feet in front of Porod. The sergeant killed him. They began to take fire from the ditch on their left.

LT Kail called Porod on the radio: "There are two hootches to your left. Get inside them." Porod went and the others followed, except for one man whom they did not miss at first.

Private First Class Lewis Albanese, 19, was off on his own, seemingly bent on trying to cover the others with his weapon as they deployed toward the houses.

Porod discovered his absence from the squad and began to call, "Albanese! Albanese!"

There was no answer.

Albanese had discovered that the ditch was really the connecting trench of a series of fortified enemy bunkers. He assaulted the ditch, killing several snipers. He then fixed his bayonet and jumped into the ditch. He began inching his way along the ditch, probing each position along its length and killing six enemy. The men of the platoon heard a prolonged burst of firing from numerous weapons on their left. None of it came toward them. Mingled with the noise of enemy AK-47s was the unmistakable sound of an American M-16.

"It's one hell of a firefight," said SSG Neher, "and I'll bet that's Albanese."

Albanese continued down the trench, firing his weapon ahead of him. He was mortally wounded and out of amunition when he came upon two more Communists. He killed them both in fierce hand to hand combat before he succumbed himself. For his actions, PFC Albanese was awarded the Medal of Honor.

While taking part in Operation PERSHING on February 18, Bravo Company came in contact with an enemy battalion. Delta Company was air assaulted into the area to reinforce Company B and it also made heavy contact. Other Cavalry units set up blocking positions to the south and east of the contact area. At dawn the Skytroopers swept through the area to find that the enemy force had withdrawn, leaving 68 bodies.

Throughout the spring of 1967 the battalion continued to operate in the northern An Lao Valley experiencing light contact almost daily. By the end of June the Garry Owen battalion had chalked up 379 enemy killed.

The battalion moved north in 1968 and took part in the battle of Hue. In mid-February it routed the enemy stronghold in the village of Then Bon Tri near the old imperial capital. The enemy was well dug in in a regimental-sized complex and the infantry was at first unable to get to them. Artillery, air strikes and Naval gunfire were used against the enemy trenches, and the 5th of the 7th slowly pushed into the northwest corner of the hamlet. Three NVA snipers in a concrete bunker, supported

After taking a short break during his platoon's venture through enemy territory on a reconaissance mission, this Skytrooper of the 5th Battalion, 7th Cavalry, prepares to hoist his M-60 machinegun.

by mortar fire, pinned down two platoons in a shallow trench. Private First Class Albert Rocha worked laboriously along the trenchline, stopping once when a sniper's bullet ripped through the handguard of his rifle. He and First Lieutenant Frederick Krupa finally crawled atop the sniper's bunker. While PFC Rocha poured bullets into the hole, LT Krupa and other men from Delta Company worked a satchel charge into the bunker and blew it.

"The snipers were trying to push out the charge," Rocha said, "but the lieutenant held it right there. It went off in their faces. I was almost ready to get up and move out when one of the snipers suddenly appeared in front of me. I killed him."

On February 23 the Garry Owens were airlifted to the north Hue docks to sweep the enemy out of the northern part of the city.

March found them operating from a perimeter seven kilometers northwest of Hue. One evening in early March an ambush squad from Delta Company settled into its position on the south side of Highway 1. Spotting a large number of enemy with weapons the ambushers called in artillery.

Escorted by the Cobra gunship, troops of the 5th Battalion, 7th Cavalry, move toward a landing zone where they will search for the enemy. The infantryman always knows the "snake" will be there if needed.

"The artillery started pounding the woodline," said Specialist Four Willie Calcots, who was watching through his starlight scope, "when 40 enemy with weapons and packs came tearing out of the woodline and went racing down the highway. I counted them through the scope. I saw one round of artillery fall right on one of them."

"We were only about 50 meters from Delta Company," recalled Private First Class Sam Di Polite, who was with the Bravo Company ambush squad nearby, "and artillery was so close that we were getting shrapnel over our heads."

"We started back for our perimeter about 3 a.m.," said Private First Class Gary Cline of Bravo Company. "We were walking along a dike between Highway 1 and some railroad tracks. All at once we heard lots of ducks quacking and heard them flapping their wings. I thought they were quacking because of us. Our front men started dropping to the ground and everybody behind followed, luckily, because about 50 enemy with weapons came running down the road toward Hue. We were 25 meters away from them."

Specialist Four Curtis W. Lantz was walking point on the way back and he was the first man to hit the ground when he spotted the enemy.

"I heard the ducks quacking, at least it sounded like ducks, but the flapping of the wings, I think, was the enemy's sandals flopping against the road," he said. "I looked through the starlight scope and I couldn't see anything until they got about 100 meters away. I motioned for the men in back of me to get down and they passed it back."

"If we had tried to get across the railroad tracks, they would have spotted us against the sky, so we just kept down with our weapons on bushwhack, ready for someone to spot us."

The squads stayed down for 10 minutes, then continued back to their battalion perimeter.

"It was funny in a way," conluded Di Polite afterwards. "They were singing and talking just like GIs do. And there was one straggler, far behind the others, who kept calling to the others like 'Wait for me. Wait for me.' But it wasn't funny when it happened. We were all too afraid one of the stragglers would spot us."

Spring is rice harvest time in I Corps. Peasants had become accustomed to having a large portion of their annual rice supply confiscated by the Com-

A Skytrooper of Company A, 5th Battalion, 7th Cavalry, stops to inspect an enemy footprint as members of his platoon enter a deserted village. They were on a search and destroy mission in the Song Re Valley in II Corps.

munists. The Cavalry set out to change all that.

To protect the farmers' crops the Skytroopers patrolled the area and secured the roads to the government grain storage facilities at Phong Dien by day. They set ambushes at night for the benefit of enemy infiltrators.

Once the harvest was in the 5th of the 7th assaulted into LZ Tiger to begin Operation DELAWARE in the A Shau Valley on April 19. LZ Tiger was ideally situated to command the enemy's supply routes into the valley. Reconnaissance elements captured enemy trucks, supplies and weapons, also destroying bunkers and interdicting roads. As enemy vehicle losses mounted, an estimated platoon struck back, hitting Delta Company on April 25. A ring of flame sprang up around the forward operations base.

The company commander and most of the men with him were wounded. Between them and the rest of the company sat the enemy, entrenched, bunkered and well gunned. In that trenchline were at least two machineguns.

A daylight attempt to breach the enemy line and reach the isolated men was thrown back by a hail of devastating enemy fire. Darkness fell, covering all—Americans and NVA alike—with the blackness that only the jungle can produce. Too impatient to wait for the light of dawn, First Lieutenant James M.

Sprayberry, the Delta Company exec, organized a volunteer night patrol. The plan was to crawl unseen through the blackness to the enemy, blast a hole throught the line and reach the isolated men.

Sprayberry and his volunteers were almost within reach of the enemy line when two machineguns opened up on them, lacing the night with lines of red tracers that danced off the ground around them and shot up into the sky. Sprayberry was furious at being discovered by the enemy. The enemy machinegunners had triggered what was to be a violent, personal vendetta between the lieutenant and the dug-in force.

After placing his men behind cover, Sprayberry scrambled forward in the darkness, half crawling, half running, to the nearest enemy bunker. He pulled a grenade from his belt, pulled the pin and slammed the grenade through the bunker gun port. There was a flurry of movement inside the bunker and then the explosion and flash of the blast spit from the gun port. The bunker was silent.

In a little world of black on black, Sprayberry identified a string of one-man positions in the shadows nearby. He crawled along behind the line, popping grenades into each hole as he went. Behind him, one by one, the holes erupted in the darkness in a moment of grenade flash and blast.

Out of grenades, the lieutenant crawled

back to his men for another load of "frags." As he hooked them to his gear, his volunteers came under more enemy fire. The vendetta was renewed.

Sprayberry charged the source of fire, another bunker, bulleting a frag into it at the end of his run. Another flash and another silent, smoky bunker.

With two men placed to cover him, the lieutenant went forward again to destroy three more bunkers and their occupants with grenades. As the last bunker exploded, and enemy soldier jumped up from his concealed position and raced through the darkness toward Sprayberry, hoping to surprise the Garry Owen officer. Sprayberry heard him, drew his .45 caliber sidearm and shot point blank, blowing the enemy trooper backwards into the night. He then killed the enemy soldiers in another bunker before returning to his men.

The immediate threat to his patrol was eliminated. All was finally quiet. Sprayberry made radio contact with the isolated men on the other side of the now silent bunkerline and guided them toward his position. In a few minutes they were through the line and joined to the volunteers.

Sprayberry organized litter parties and began evacuating the wounded to the rear. For the next several hours Sprayberry and his men moved wounded men through the night.

They were almost finished, there remained but a few wounded with the security men forward, when another enemy machinegun broke the silence

(Continued on P. 261)

The battle won, these 5th Battalion, 7th Cavalry, soldiers proclaim their hard-won victory by posting this sign, welcoming other units to Hue.

Hovering over a newly-established landing zone, a resupply UH-1H Huey helicopter is guided to a touch down. Once down the chopper will become the center of attraction as Skytroopers hustle about to unload its cargo of water, hot food, ammunition and perhaps a little mail.

EIGHTH CAVALRY

The 8th Cavalry Regiment was constituted July 28, 1866, and organized September 21 of that year. Its ranks were filled with hard-fisted miners from the gold fields, restless settlers and adventure-seeking frontiersmen. After outfitting in Fort Concho, Texas, the regiment made a 2,000 mile move by horseback to South Dakota and located its regimental headquarters at Fort Meade. They fought along side the 7th Cavalry against the Sioux and Chief Sitting Bull. The unit became known for its quick striking activities in the trouble spots of the Indian Wars.

The battle honors for that period indicate the unit's mobility. In 1867 they campaigned in Arizona against the Apaches, raced to Oregon in 1867 to fight the Nez Perces, and then back to the plains in 1889 to ride against the Comanches.

In 1898 the regiment moved to Alabama and was staged for overseas movement to Cuba. By 1902 the unit had returned to the border and resumed its patrol missions. It was sent to the Philippines in 1905 and returned to the border in 1907. Many skirmishes developed with Mexican bandits who conducted smuggling operations into the United States. In 1912 the regiment returned to the Philippines and remained for three years. It returned to the States and joined the 5th and 7th Regiments in the Mexican Punitive Expedition. In 1919 it returned to garrison duty at Fort Bliss, Texas, and joined the 1st Cavalry Division on September 13, 1921.

The unit flies campaign streamers for the Indian Wars, World War II (New Guinea, Bismarck Archipelago, with arrowhead, Leyte and Luzon), the Korean War and, of course, Vietnam.

Prior to the Vietnam conflict the unit was decorated with the Presidential Unit

Citation streamer embroidered Luzon; the PUC, streamer embroidered TAEGU; the Philippine Presidential Unit Citation, streamer embroidered October 17, 1944 to July 4, 1945; the Republic of Korea Presidential Unit Citation, streamer embroidered WAEGWAN-TAEGU; the ROKPUC, embroidered KOREA; and the Chryssoun Aristion Andrias (Bravery Gold Medal of Greece), embroidered KOREA.

In Vietnam the 1st Battalion (less

The white horse is officially described as a demi-horse rampant, the forward half of a rearing horse indicating that the horse is untamed and unconquered. The horse denotes the unit's Cavalry origin. The eight stars that appear on the insignia are called mullets, pierced. The mullets resemble rowles from riding spurs, another reference to the unit as Cavalry. The mullets, being eight in number, signify the numerical designation of the unit, the 8th Cavalry. The wording of the scroll is self-explanatory: Honor and courage have always been the hallmark of the 8th Cavalry trooper.

Company A) has been awarded the Presidential Unit Citation for action on June 21 and 22, 1966. Both battalions received the Presidential Unit Citation for the Pleiku Campaign in 1965. Bravo Company of the 2nd Battalion was awarded the division's first Valorous Unit Award for an action on May 16, 1966.

Skytroopers from the 2nd Battalion, 8th Cavalry, move through grass during a reconnaissance patrol in War Zone C.

On August 20, 1965, the 1st Battalion (Airborne), 8th Cavalry, boarded the USNS Geiger at Savannah, Georgia, and sailed for Qui Nhon, Republic of Vietnam, arriving on September 21, 1965. The main body was moved inland by helicopter to the division basecamp north of An Khe in Binh Dinh Province.

There, in the beginning of its years in Vietnam, the battalion occupied a portion of the base perimeter and through October busied itself conducting search and clear operations in the Binh Khe area.

Shortly before midnight on November 3, Alpha Company, co-located at the Duc Co CIDG Camp with the 1st Squadron, 9th Cavalry, was alerted for commitment into an ambush site on the south bank of the Ia Drang River. The men began immediate preparations to move and readied their gear. The south bank had come under repeated enemy assault, and it was there that Alpha Company would meet a battalion of the 66th NVA Regiment.

The landing zone near the river bank would only accommodate five ships at a time, so the beleaguered perimeter was reinforced by platoon echelon. At 12:40 a.m. the first platoon was jumping from the Huey landing skids at its target. They were followed by three other platoons under command of Captain Ted Danielson, and by 2:45 a.m. on November 4 they were all on location. It marked the first time that a perimeter under heavy fire had been relieved at night by heliborne forces—another first for the FIRST TEAM.

From the time they landed until dawn the Cavalrymen fought and threw back NVA attacks, and while they waited in the pitch dark between the running attacks they were subjected to flurries of sniper fire and barrages of grenade attacks. Extraordinary heroism was commonplace that night along the Ia Drang.

Specialist Four Raymond Ortiz distinguished himself with magnificent gallantry there while acting as a medical aidman. He took his first wound early in the fight while exiting the landing helicopter and entered the fray with his left arm shattered and rendered useless by an enemy bullet. But disregarding his wound he moved up to within 30 meters of the enemy firing line to treat and evacuate wounded men from that exposed area. Ortiz moved along the line as if ignoring the deadly enemy grazing fire. Over a distance of some 50 meters

FIRST BATTALION EIGHTH CAVALRY

COMMANDERS

Troops of the 1st Battalion, 8th Cavalry, take a small Vietnamese boat to cross a canal while on a search and destroy mission on the Bong Son Plain.

of open ground and amid the hail of enemy small arms and automatic weapons fire, Ortiz carried six wounded troopers to waiting evacuation helicopters.

He returned a seventh time to seek out a wounded platoon leader who was calling out in the dark. He ignored his comrades' shouts to take cover and moved toward the wounded man's voice, only to be struck in the chest by another bullet and knocked to the ground. Bleeding from the chest wound, he pushed himself to his feet and started off

Skytroopers of Company A, 1st Battalion, 8th Cavalry, move through a small farmyard during a search and destroy mission against the Viet Cong in Phu My Province, northeast of An Khe in I Corps. The mission was part of Operation IRVING, which took place in October 1966.

toward the wounded officer again. Again he was struck by enemy small arms fire and fell to his knees. Then, apparently contemptuous of the enemy fire, he struggled forward with a final effort until he collapsed from loss of blood. He later was presented the Distinguished Service Cross.

In the new year of 1966 the battalion's first move was to "beat the bushes" around LZs Bronc and Stallion in Pleiku Province to ferret out a reluctant enemy force. Hard on the heels of retreating Viet Cong, the battalion stopped just short of inviolable Cambodian territory and established the first prepared landing zone that close to the border in the division's history. Opened on January 8, it was named LZ Cheyenne.

Operation WHITE WING, centered around the city of Bong Son, followed

through to the end of February, resulting in 25 Viet Cong dead, six detained and tons of supplies captured. In mid-March the 1st Bn, 8th Cav, participated in Operation JIM BOWIE, moving in primarily company-sized search and destroy missions with wide sweeps through the Phang Rang and Song Con River valleys. Operations LINCOLN and MOSBY I followed in late March, and on the morning of March 25 the battalion air assaulted directly from An Khe to an LZ near Duc Co—a 78-mile heliborne move of an entire battalion, one of the largest undertaken by the FIRST TEAM. The battalion was again back in the Pleiku area north of the Ia Drang Valley. But this time they came for a reconnaissance in force mission.

On May 20 the battalion again air assaulted into what was euphemistically

The Dong Nai River flows through the center of War Zone D, III Corps, center of the Cav's area of operations in the summer of 1969. The thick triple canopy jungle was the scene of much fierce fighting. The 1st of the 8th was right smack in the middle of that activity.

known as "Happy Valley" in a sector north of LZ Hereford on Operation CRAZY HORSE. Deployed from that location, the battalion's five companies swept back and forth over the "Denver Trail."

It was there that Charlie Company had moved up a steep hill when the Viet Cong, sitting solid in foxholes and bunkers, opened up.

On the left flank of Company C, Captain Roy D. Martin's Bravo Company had meanwhile come up against an impossible situation. The enemy had fortified a steep ridgeline with communications trenches connecting a series of rugged machinegun bunkers, two of which held heavy .50 caliber machineguns. The complex was large enough to hold a battalion of men. At least five .30 caliber and one .50 caliber machineguns opened up on the first platoon's point squad from the heights above, killing six Cavalrymen outright and mortally wounding the platoon leader, Lieutenant Robert H. Crum, Jr. Specialist Four David C. Dolby, a machinegunner, ran to the lieutenant's side and pulled him to cover.

"Take over," the seriously wounded officer ordered. "Get the men out of here."

Dolby immediately took command of what was left of the platoon, directing his comrades to safe positions and covering their movements with fire from his M-60 machinegun as he scrambled from behind rocks to trees. The deep-throated bursts of the enemy .50 caliber followed his movements, chewing branches and chunks of tree trunk into splinters and ripping foot-long furrows in the earth, just missing Dolby's fleet-footed figure. Again and again he set up his machinegun and stitched rounds into one bunker after another with accurate fire.

There was no stopping him. He was everywhere that rainy afternoon, pulling the wounded to safety, placing fire against the enemy bunkers and directing the platoon.

He crawled to within 50 meters of the enemy positions and hurled smoke grenades as far forward toward the bunkers as he could to mark them for aerial rocket artillery (ARA). Minutes

Troops of the 1st Battalion, 8th Cavalry, move cautiously through what appears to be an abandoned village. In fact, however, it is an NVA camp, only recently vacated.

later a Huey beat its way down on the ridge and loosed a salvo of rockets into the enemy line.

According to Private First Class Kenneth Fernadez, Dolby had no regard for his own safety as he moved again and again through the enemy's kill zone to assist the wounded, evacuate them on his back, pop smoke and coordinate fire. "I couldn't believe that a man could move through that fire like Dave Dolby," Fernandez said.

For four hours Dolby carried his one-man war against the entrenched enemy. The men around him said he had silenced each of the enemy machine-guns at least four times with his M-60, but there were replacement gunners to man the guns anew each time. Dolby was ordered to withdraw what was left of his men. He was the last man out of the area, firing a parting burst into two bunkers as he went.

For those several hours of his life as a soldier and a man, Dolby was later presented with the highest honor his country could bestow—the Medal of Honor.

With the approach of summer the battalion moved out on their most important operation of that year, NATHAN

Skytroopers of the 1st Battalion, 8th Cavalry, leap from a 227th Assault Helicopter Battalion lift ship during a combat assault near Xuan Loc in III Corps. The small but effective "instant landing zone" was created by air-bursting a 10,000-pound bomb being lowered by parachute.

Private First Class Paul Oliver, 1st of the 8th Cav, walks hand-in-hand with a friendly village child. His newly-acquired friends, residents of a village in III Corps, followed Oliver and his platoon until the soldiers had walked far outside the village.

A Navy armored troop guides a Cav helicopter in for a landing on their floating helipad during a Navy-Cavalry (NavCav) operation near Saigon in early 1969. The "Jumping Mustang" troopers on board played an essential role in denying the enemy his favorite infiltration route to Saigon. The waterways were no longer for use by the enemy.

A heavily armed Navy gunboat cruises the Vam Co Dong River, carrying the waterborne "Jumping Mustangs" in joint operations with the Navy.

A keen-eyed Cavalryman from Company A, 1st Battalion, 8th Cavalry, is on the watch for enemy movement in a swampy rice field near Quang Tri.

HALE. On June 20 the Skytroopers moved to the vicinity of Tuy Hoa to reinforce the 101st Airborne Division. Linking up with the 2nd Battalion (Airborne), 327th Infantry, the battalion joined an intense battle near Trung Luong and a nameless hill called Hill 258.

On June 22, the enemy launched the most ferocious attack of the campaign. At 5:43 a.m. B Company came under a two-pronged assault on position Eagle. The battle raged on for four bours, often directly and individually on the perimeter. The enemy left 134 of its dead when they broke contact.

Enemy losses during NATHAN HALE were huge. For its exceptional demon-

(Continued on P. 288)

SECOND BATTALION EIGHTH CAVALRY

COMMANDERS

The 2nd Battalion (Airborne), 8th Cavalry, stepped off the USNS Geiger at Qui Nhon, Republic of Vietnam, on September 20, 1965, after 31 days at sea. The following day, CH-47 Chinook helicopters transported the battalion to its already opened base at An Khe.

By October 17, its mission of securing and developing the basecamp had changed, and during late October and early November the unit found itself fully committed to combat operations.

The movement to Camp Holloway on October 23 marked the beginning of the Pleiku Campaign. The battalion air assaulted on the outskirts of the Plei Me Camp on the 27th to "pursue, seek out and destroy the enemy." A series of battalion, company and platoon-size airmobile operations were employed, searching the jungles west of the camp. Significant engagements were made on November 4th and 6th.

The fiercest battle of the period was fought on November 6, when Companies B and C battled a numerically superior force to a standstill. Both companies were conducting platoon-size search operations from separated basecamps. Bravo Company, screening toward the Meur River from high ground about one and one-half kilometers to the east, made contact with a platoon-size enemy force, but by noon the company was engaged with an entrenched enemy who was committing more and more units to the battle.

As the firefight increased in intensity, some elements of B Company were pinned down and the enemy, now in battalion strength, began to encircle them.

Company C wheeled about and made a forced march back to the scene of the fight. Crossing the river, it came under heavy fire. Neither company was able to muster enough firepower from its own position to maneuver decisively. Both sides began to disengage as darkness approached.

The two companies sustained significant casualties, but they had inflicted grievous losses upon the enemy. The

A pair of "Charley-Charlies" barely fit into newly created LZ Wool deep inside the Chu Pong Massif. The 2nd Battalion, 8th Cavalry, had just moved into the area during Operation LINCOLN in April 1966.

after-action report records 77 enemy killed by body count, with an additional 121 estimated killed.

The battalion led off 1966 with Operation MATADOR, moving close to the Cambodian border to block any enemy movement westward.

Operation WHITE WING commenced January 31 for the battalion as it moved to LZ Bird to begin operations in the Crow's Foot and the Bong Son operational areas.

Operation JIM BOWIE was planned as a follow-up to the Bong Son Campaign, as intelligence reports indicated a base area around Kon Truc.

Returning to the scene of the Pleiku Campaign, the battalion began Operation LINCOLN on March 25, terminating April 17.

A suspected enemy build-up east of the Vinh Thanh Valley led the 1st Brigade to request a company-sized reconnaissance operation from the battalion.

The mission was to search and destroy

Bravo Company, 2nd of the 8th, Skytroopers sweep through rice paddies in the Suoi Ca Valley during Operation CRAZY HORSE in May 1966. Working the paddies and surrounding areas called for somewhat different tactics than did moving through heavy jungle.

Troop-carrying helicopters of the 229th Assault Helicopter Battalion transport 2nd Battalion of the 8th Cav soldiers to another location during Operation NATHAN HALE in the central highlands. Multi-battalion lifts were commonplace at this time, as the airmobile concept took root. Perhaps 40 to 60 helicopters would be involved in a single day's move.

in the rugged hill mass between the Suoi Ca and the Vinh Thanh Valleys, in north central Binh Dinh Province.

On May 16, Bravo Company was air assaulted into LZ Hereford on a mountain east of the Vinh Thanh CIDG Camp, moved onto a ridgeline and immediately made contact with a Viet Cong battalion.

When the company commander, Captain J. D. Coleman, heard the terrific brawl his lead platoon was engaged in, he hurriedly put his company in a tight circle, letting the squads of his embattled lead platoon fall into their arc.

The fight went on for four hours without a lull. When the weather broke about 6:30 p.m., aerial rocket artillery (ARA) on station poured round after round in close support of the perimeter. Salvo after salvo, some within just a few feet of the company trace, battered the enemy positions, pinning them down close to the perimeter and holding them there, giving Coleman's troops the edge. The attacks diminished in strength, and by 8 all contact had been broken by the enemy.

With more than 40 wounded personnel, along with 20 others killed, CPT Coleman had little choice but to remain in position and await reinforcements which had landed at nearby LZ Hereford during a brief break in the weather. Bravo Company dug in; the relief force was fed into the perimeter at 10 o'clock.

Members of Company A, 2nd Battalion, 8th Cavalry, (above) jump from a helicopter to begin searching for an enemy bunker complex reportedly seen in the mountainous area some six miles south of Quang Tri. Private First Class Ira Rolston, an RTO for Company B's first platoon (below), tries his hand at blowing a Viet Cong bugle he found while on patrol in the Ia Drang Valley. The men are preparing to move further into the valley.

At 6:15 a.m. the next day, the two companies initiated a "mad minute." Simultaneously, the enemy launched a violent battalion-size attack at all sectors of the perimeter. Enemy soldiers came within a few feet of foxhole positions and the companies' ammunition began to run alarmingly low. Some Skytroopers on the line had already fixed bayonets and were preparing for a last ditch stand when the enemy abruptly broke off the attack, many of their number dead or wounded.

The battle had far-reaching significance. The enemy's intent, according to captured documents, was to direct a regimental attack on the CIDG camp and then to disrupt pacified civilian centers in the valley. After this initial contact, and after the addition later of Skytrooper infantry battalions, the Viet Cong force exfiltrated the area.

For this action, Bravo Company, 2nd Bn, 8th Cav, was awarded the Valorous Unit Citation, the division's first of the Vietnam conflict.

In the months of June and July, Operations NATHAN HALE and HENRY CLAY in Tuy Hoa and Trung Phan Provinces provided further airmobile exercises in finding, fixing and destroying the enemy. In August, search and clear missions in the Tuy Hoa AO were conducted as part of an operation nicknamed John Paul Jones.

THAYER I initiated the first phase of the Binh Dinh Province Pacification Campaign on September 13. Operation IRVING kicked off on October 2, with Companies A, B, C and D air assaulting into the Nui Mieu Mountains at LZs Ebony, Playboy, Adam and Esquire, overlooking a well-populated area near the South China Sea coast. All companies made contact in the next 29 days with a well hidden, well equipped enemy.

On October 8, Captain Charles Getz, commanding Bravo Company, was moving his troops along the coast. A scout helicopter reported the enemy fleeing to a nearby island separated from the mainland by a causeway waist deep under water. Searching toward the area, eight VC were detained. The enemy soldiers informed Bravo Company's CO that others were hiding in caves with entrances beneath the waterline. CPT Getz was an excellent swimmer.

"Who wants to go with me?" he asked the first platoon as he peeled off his webbing and shirt.

Private First Class Louis G. Pom-

A bomb scarred hilltop marks the spot where Company C, 2nd of the 8th Cav, soldiers are to begin patrolling the area near Dak To in Vietnam's central highlands area. They carry boxes of C-rations with them as they depart the relative security of the helicopter.

ponio, a fire team leader, Staff Sergeant Colin K. Hall and Specialist Five Anthony P. Caramda, the platoon medic, all volunteered.

They dived off the rock formation that housed the caves and followed underwater patches of light indicating the cave entrances 20 feet below. The sight of the determined Skytroopers breaking the surface inside the first cave induced the six VC to surrender.

Bravo's aquanauts searched two more caves and captured 11 more VC. Their total at the end of the day was 24 detainees.

Operation THAYER II continued through 1967 with search operations in the central and southern Kim Song Valley. The battalion was headquartered at LZ Santa, air assaulting into the area with Company B to LZ Ho, Charlie to LZ Chi, and D Company to LZ Minh. Alpha Company followed January 6, opening LZ Castro.

THAYER II closed out for the battalion on February 3, and the unit moved to Camp Radcliff to assume responsibility for the An Khe base defense. Its stay was short. Back under the control of the parent 1st Brigade, the battalion began Operation PERSHING I and was to remain in the area until June 18.

Company C discovered three and one-half tons of rice on March 2 in a large bunker complex. Bulldozers were now being used to destroy bunkers and tunnels in the area.

On March 19, Alpha Company approached a hamlet near An Do and LZ Geronimo in the plain area, initiating a three-day battle in which more than 120 NVA were killed.

B Company engaged one individual in a bunker on May 17. He became the FIRST TEAM's 10,000th enemy KIA since the division's arrival in Vietnam.

The 22nd NVA Regiment chose to make contact with elements of the battalion on May 31. Bravo Company was making a sweep west of Highway 1 and was engaged by an NVA company firing from prepared positions in hedge rows and from trees in a hamlet. Three additional companies and a platoon of tanks were directed to the battle area and leveled their firepower at the enemy position. Initially, the tanks provided cover for the engaged companies, enabling them to move into position and

(Continued on P. 291)

TWELFTH CAVALRY

The 12th Cavalry Regiment was constituted on February 2, 1901, in the Regular Army and organized on February 8, 1901, at Fort Sam Houston, Texas, after a Congressional Act provided for an increase in the branch. The 12th was the second of five regiments provided for.

In World War II the regiment participated in the New Guinea, Bismarck Archipelago, Leyte (with arrowhead), and Luzon. The 1st Battalion also earned credit for the Tunisia, Naples-Foggia, Anzio Rome-Arno, North Apennines and Po Valley Campaigns.

The cactus is officially described as a cactus vert. The regiment was organized at Fort Sam Houston, Texas, in 1901, and spent its first two years at that post. The cactus shows the birthplace of the regiment as well as its service on the Mexican border. "**Semper Paratus**" (*Always Ready*), the regimental motto, indicates the unit's willingness to perform any task assigned.

The regiment's decorations include the Presidential Unit Citation (Headquarters and Headquarters Troop cited), streamer embroidered ORMOC VALLEY, LEYTE; the PUC (1st Squadron reinforced cited), streamer embroidered CENTRAL RANGE, LEYTE; and the Philippine Presidential Unit Citation for October 17, 1944, to July 4, 1945. Additionally the 1st Battalion colors carry the French Croix de Guerre with Palm for World War II (81st Cavalry Reconnaissance Squadron cited), streamer embroidered CENTRAL ITALY.

In Vietnam the 1st Battalion has been awarded the Presidential Unit Citation for actions on the 2nd and 3rd of October, 1966. The battalion's Company C won the Valorous Unit Award for heroism during the period May 31 to June 1, 1967, at An Qui.

Troopers of the 2nd Battalion, 12th Cavalry, rest after discovering a series of rice hootches just east of the An Lao Valley during Operation WHITE WING in February 1966. The rice cache was one of the largest found in the war at that date.

On July 28, 1965, the President of the United States, in a message to the nation, alerted and ordered the 1st Air Cavalry Division to duty in the Republic of Vietnam. On the 20th of September the 1st Battalion (Airborne), 12th Cavalry, was disembarking from the USNS Geiger at the harbor of Qui Nhon.

The heaviest battle the battalion fought that year was on October 12 when Companies A and B engaged a VC battalion in the Suoi La Tinh River valley. It was in this critical setting that two men, in particular, personified the spirit of the "Chargers."

The chaplain, Captain Billy Lord, heedless of his own safety, ministered to the wounded, took charge of their evacuation, and carried many of them to safety.

Major Joseph Bellochi, the battalion XO, saw that Medevac helicopters were having difficulty evacuating casualties. He repeatedly flew his own helicopter through intensive small arms and automatic weapons fire helping fly out the wounded. He brought out eight wounded in five trips in his OH-13, a one-passenger helicopter.

The major and the chaplain were subsequently awarded the Distinguished Flying Cross and the Silver Star respectively for their heroism under fire.

The battle lasted until dark. Then the decimated enemy withdrew.

On October 27, 1965, the battalion began Operation ALL THE WAY, the 1st Brigade portion of the Pleiku Campaign. After being airlifted to Pleiku, it air assaulted into several landing zones near the Cambodian border to conduct search and destroy operations. The battalion stayed on the operation 18 days, clearing the area between Plei Me and the border.

November and December were spent operating in and around An Khe, while the New Year found the Chargers operating in search and destroy missions in western Pleiku Province and southern Kontum Province. The battalion participated in Operation MASHER in February and early March in the northeast section of Binh Dinh Province. In late March the battalion was committed to Operation LINCOLN.

On the night of March 30, 1966, the fifth day of LINCOLN, Alpha Company was deployed to assist a scout platoon that had made contact with a large enemy unit in western Pleiku Province near the Cambodian border.

As Alpha Company's Skytroopers

FIRST BATTALION TWELFTH CAVALRY

COMMANDERS

leaped from their assault helicopters they immediately came under fire from all sides.

With the company commander wounded and the company's XO killed, Second Lieutenant Daniel Kapico found himself in command of his company. LT Kapico got the battalion S-3 on the radio and asked for artillery. Night was falling, and with the approach of darkness the enemy would certainly mount a heavy attack.

The enemy kept Alpha Company under constant fire, and the Skytroopers returned the barrage. As the night wore on, the fire from Alpha Company apparently convinced the enemy that he was not going to overpower LT Kapico's command. The enemy withdrew, leaving behind 197 dead.

Infantrymen, even while resting, must still search for the enemy (left): while working (above) he must stay alert, even though his thoughts may be his own. These men are of the 1st Battalion, 12th Cavalry.

During May and June the battalion worked around LZ Hereford in Operation CRAZY HORSE, north of An Khe and Highway 19.

On May 21, 1966, Charlie Company was airlifted to LZ Hereford in the Vinh Thanh Valley. The heavily-burdened troopers of the weapons platoon quickly set up their single mortar in support of the rest of the company hacking through the dense jungle.

Charlie Company swept through the heavily forested area unaware that the enemy had let it pass unmolested in order to attack the mortar platoon on LZ Hereford.

Specialist Four Paul J. Harrison and Specialist Four Charles W. Stuckey, the first members of the platoon to spot the enemy, opened fire on the camouflaged figures moving through the brush and tall grass.

Meanwhile, Captain Don F. Warren spurred Charlie Company on an uphill, dash toward the LZ. When they arrived it was too late. With the exception of a handful of wounded survivors, the weapons platoon had been wiped out. *LOOK* Magazine war correspondent Sam Castan died with them, becoming the only casualty of hundreds of newsmen who have visited the Cav. The enemy, carrying their own dead, had meanwhile vanished into the surrounding jungle.

August found the 1st Bn, 12th Cav, operating once again in Pleiku Province in Operation PAUL REVERE II near the Cambodian border.

Operation IRVING was less than six hours old on the morning of October 2, 1966, when advance scout teams

The "Chargers" of the 1st Battalion, 12th Cavalry, quickly move across open ground after receiving sniper fire while on an operation in the Bong Son Plain during Operation PERSHING. Armored tanks (background) provide a buffer force for the advancing Skytroopers. The tanks are of Company D, 1st Battalion (Mechanized), 50th Infantry.

reported that two helicopters had been shot down near the village of Hoa Hoi. Immediately Company B was air assaulted to the beach east of the village. Moments after insertion, the company began receiving fire from the village. Company A was rushed into the area southwest of the village as soon as helicopters were available.

After Companies A and B had established initial contact with the enemy, they withheld their fire while a psychological operations helicopter circled the village with loudspeakers, directing civilians to move out of the area and imploring enemy soldiers to lay down their arms. During this moratorium, numerous civilians and soldiers did as they were directed by the loudspeaker. When it became evident an hour later that no one else was coming out, The Chargers began moving in.

A and B Companies continued to press the attack from the south while Charlie Company assaulted into the northern outskirts of Hoa Hoi and began moving down to meet them. The battalion command post, with Delta Company in reserve, moved to LZ Irene, a short distance from the village.

At daybreak October 3 Alpha and Bravo braced themselves in blocking positions around the southern half of the village while Company C began to sweep through the enemy positions. The bunkers and an extensive trench system favored the North Vietnamese in their defensive posture and made the Chargers' advance extremely difficult.

Several times Charlie Company was temporarily stopped, but each time the Skytroopers rallied and drove on through the village. By noon that day, after Bravo and Charlie Companies completed their final sweep of the village and began screening the area south of Hoa Hoi, the Chargers had left in their wake 141 enemy dead.

The Chargers detained 35 NVA soldiers and 15 Viet Cong suspects.

The battalion aggressively carried the battle to the enemy, with uncounted incidents of individual gallantry. Friendly casualties were light in comparison with the near total destruction of the entrapped enemy force. For their efforts during the two-day battle, the men of the 1st Bn, 12th Cav, were awarded the Presidential Unit Citation.

On the night of December 26, 1966, the 22nd NVA Regiment, taking advantage of the Christmas cease-fire to mass its troops north of the Kim Son Valley, moved in under the cover of darkness and rain to surround LZ Bird where C Company was defending two artillery batteries.

At 1:05 a.m. the enemy kicked off a savage mortar and ground attack against the 84 defenders at LZ Bird. First Lieutenant Jerald Wallace moved to the point bunker and directed that position's desperate stand against the Communist human wave until he was mortally wounded. The acting company commander, First Lieutenant John Rieke, was seriously wounded early in the battle, leaving First Lieutenant Charles Campanella, the company's forward artillery observer, as the only functioning officer in Charlie Company.

As the defenders were swarmed by the enemy regiment, Staff Sergeant Delbert O. Jennings sprang to his bunker and slowed the enemy wave with machinegun fire, killing at least 12 NVA.

Rejoining his men, Jennings destroyed an enemy demolition crew about to blow up a nearby howitzer and killed three more enemy soldiers. Ordering his men back into a secondary position, he covered their withdrawal, killing one NVA with the butt of his weapon. Observing that some of his comrades were unaware of an enemy force to their rear, he raced through the fire-swept area to warn them.

After helping to repulse the final enemy assaults, he led a group of volunteers through sniper fire and booby traps, recovering eight seriously injured men.

SSG Jennings' heroism and leadership saved the lives of many of his comrades and contributed greatly to Charlie Company's defeat of the numerically superior enemy force. For his action SSG Jennings was later awarded the Medal of Honor.

The 1st Bn, 12th Cav, distinguished itself once again when Charlie Company engaged a battalion-sized force in the village of An Qui. Entering the village with a platoon of tanks on May 31, 1967, the unit immediately received furious raking fire from a heavily-armed enemy force. The Skytroopers and tanks withdrew after killing 25 enemy soldiers. An artillery barrage pounded the village the rest of the morning.

Shortly after noon the Chargers assaulted again. The fighting was at such close quarters that the tanks fired at an average range of 25 yards. The infantrymen attacked individual bunkers and trench systems with grenades and small arms fire.

On the morning of June 1 Charlie Company silenced all remaining enemy fire. An intensive search revealed 96 Communist dead, and a battalion of the 22nd North Vietnamese Army Regiment ceased to exist as a effective fighting force.

Eight members of the company were awarded the Silver Star for their actions during the battle, and Company C was later awarded the Valorous Unit Citation for extraordinary heroism.

The battalion spent the month of June engaged in cordon and search missions of the plains around Binh Di village.

Operation PERSHING lasted from August through November. The Chargers conducted cordon and search operations on the Bong Son Plain and search and clear operations in the An Lao Valley during Operation PERSHING and on through January 1968.

February found the battalion working around Quang Tri City and in the Ba Long Valley. Heavy contact was made throughout the month, during which the Chargers killed more than 100 enemy soldiers.

During the month of April, the 1st Bn, 12th Cav, operated southwest of Khe Sanh then moved to the A Shau Valley.

The Chargers spent the month of June 1968, operating in the Huong Dien, Hai Lang, and Phong Dien Districts. July and August were spent in operations JEB STUART III and COMANCHE FALLS, along the coastal plains northeast of Quang Tri. They continued search and clear operations there through September and October.

The battalion moved to Bien Hoa in February 1969, to thwart enemy movement towards the population centers of South Vietnam's III Corps.

Staff Sergeant Martin A. Manglona, a platoon sergeant in Alpha Company, distinguished himself in a battle on February 10 while defending a forward operations base (FOB) in Bien Hoa Province.

Company A had set up its FOB, sent out ambushes, and settled down for the night. At 3:30 a.m., the stillness of the night was broken by the sudden blasts of enemy mortar rounds. Skytroopers scrambled into their bunkers and waited for the enemy to appear.

"Quite a few men were wounded by the mortars," said First Lieutenant George F. Dove, platoon leader. "Among them were myself and Manglona."

While helping to repulse the ground attack, the platoon sergeant was blinded by shrapnel from a B-40 rocket. Unable to see, SSG Manglona ordered his men to place him in a firing position with his weapon pointed at the NVA. He kept firing at the enemy until all the wounded were evacuated.

"Even after he received reinforcements from the first platoon, he refused to be evacuated until all of his men were safe," said LT Dove.

SSG Manglona was later awarded the Distinguished Service Cross.

In April the Chargers moved to an area south of the "Fishhook" and operated out of Quan Loi. They continued operations there throughout April and into May.

In May the battalion moved to Phuoc Vinh, where it conducted night ambush operations around the village.

On June 13 the 1st Bn, 12th Cav, moved to LZ Grant, 12 miles northeast of Tay Ninh City. The battalion operated in the area, checking Communist infiltration through December.

(**Continued on P. 260**)

SECOND BATTALION TWELFTH CAVALRY

COMMANDERS

Men of the 2nd Battalion, 12th Cavalry, hug the ground behind handy stone walls as they fight their way toward the embattled imperial city of Hue. The battle for Hue saw some of the fiercest fighting of the war.

Major General Harry W.O. Kinnard, 1st Cavalry Division (Airmobile) commander, met the men of the 2nd Battalion, 12th Cavalry, as they left the troop ship USNS Buckner on September 14, 1965, and landed at Qui Nhon, Republic of Vietnam.

From Qui Nhon the 2nd Bn, 12th Cav, flew to the 1st Air Cav's basecamp at An Khe, beginning immediately the job of base defense, and receiving the first taste of combat as snipers harassed perimeter patrols and observation posts.

In late October the FIRST TEAM was given the task of reinforcing ARVN forces in Pleiku Province. The division cranked up Task Force Ingram, the muscle for which was the 2nd Bn, 12th Cav, to secure the provincial capital of Pleiku and to react to developments growing out of the attack on Plei Me CIDG Camp.

On November 1, 1965, came the first important action of the campaign. A rifle platoon of the 1st Squadron, 9th Cavalry, came under heavy enemy fire along the Tae River. Two companies of the 2nd Bn, 12th Cav, relieved the embattled forces. The battalion com-

mander, Lieutenant Colonel Earl Ingram, took charge of the fight on the ground and, in the words of MG Kinnard, "After stopping the last NVA attack cold, he regained the offensive, swept the battle area and established solid positions for the night." A North Vietnamese battalion had been defeated.

On November 11 the battalion moved back to An Khe. For the rest of 1965 it alternated between base and road defense and search and destroy missions. Though contact was generally light, the battalion made significant discoveries of enemy supplies and documents.

January 29, 1966, the battalion air assaulted in the sandy hills north of Bong Son as part of operation MASHER. This was to be the first of many operations in the Binh Dinh coastal area. It had quick results. By February 191 dead enemy and 10 detainees were accounted for. Operation WHITE WING followed. The 2nd Bn, 12th Cav, located and destroyed enemy ammunition and equipment, hundreds of bunkers, 68 tons of rice, and five tons of salt in the hills north of Bong Son.

In March and April base and highway security took most of the battalion's time. In May it participated in Operation LEWIS and CLARK. On May 17, 1966, Operation CRAZY HORSE began in the Vinh Thanh Valley, where the enemy was numerous and well-entrenched. The operation was one of distinction for the fighting battalion. The FIRST TEAM's second Medal of Honor in Vietnam was awarded posthumously to Staff Sergeant Jimmy G. Stewart for his gallantry during the action.

SSG Stewart was a squad leader with Company B. Operating in an area of heavily fortified machinegun bunkers, five men in the squad were wounded, leaving only Stewart unscathed. He refused to abandon his men. Stewart stayed in his position for four hours and fought off three assaults by a Viet Cong platoon, killing at least eight and possibly 23 before he was cut down.

According to the citation, Stewart "fought like a man possessed, emptying magazine after magazine at the determined enemy, and retrieving and throwing back hand grenades." Because of his sacrifice the wounded were safely evacuated. Three years later his son was given the first $1,500 scholarship to be awarded by the newly created Education Foundation of the 1st Cavalry Division Association.

Throughout 1966 the 2nd Bn, 12th

February 1966, found the 2nd of the 12th fighting near the South China Sea coast in Operation MASHER. When not fighting, the Cavalrymen were searching out enemy caches, some of them even built confidently above ground, as is the case of the one this soldier is checking out.

Cav, demonstrated the meaning of airmobility. It switched rapidly from base and highway defense duties in An Khe to search and destroy operations near Cambodia in the Ia Drang Valley and Kontum, back to An Khe, then to the coastal Bong Son hills, then to An Khe, Dam Tra-O Lake, and the Suoi Tem Valley. Soon the battalion had seen nearly every trouble spot in II Corps.

Rapid moves and a variety of operations and assignments also characterized the unit's activities in 1967. From March 14 to June 22 the battalion took part in Operation PERSHING. Initially, the battalion secured three landing zones on the Bong Son plains.

In January 1968 the battalion's Cavalrymen demonstrated American ingenuity. Staff Sergeant John E. Darnell gave this account: "We were sent into the Que Son Valley near Hill 146 to police up five enemy bodies when we ran into a company of North Vietnamese Army regulars.

"They opened fire on us and had us pinned down pretty well. We had some of them trapped in a cave and we were tossing grenades in at them but they started throwing them back.

"Finally we got together and started tossing in five grenades at a time. We had one man pull all the pins and we'd toss in a handful. We wanted to see how fast the enemy was," Darnell smiled, "and we found out that he wasn't fast at all."

Later in January the 2nd Bn, 12th Cav, was in the vanguard of the units that moved from II Corps to I Corps to dislodge the North Vietnamese Army from the ancient imperial capital of Hue.

On January 17 the battalion arrived at LZ El Paso five miles south of Hue. January 27 they moved to Camp Evans northeast of Hue, and on February 2 the battalion airlifted to the headquarters of the 3rd Regiment, 1st ARVN Division. The battalion's mission: "Move toward Hue, make contact with the enemy, fix his location, and destroy him."

Accordingly, at first light February 3 the battalion moved southeast toward Hue on a route south of paralleling Highway 1. At 10 a.m. the battalion reached the first settled, vegetated area before Hue. Moving through it, large numbers of NVA were seen getting in fighting positions 200 meters to the south.

The enemy positions were hit with artillery, ARA and gunships, then the battalion attacked the well-entrenched, fiercely resisting enemy, who put out a withering fire of mortars, small arms and machineguns. The battalion penetrated the enemy positions and pushed the NVA clear of the northern edge of the area, where the battalion established its perimeter for the night. The battalion had damaged an estimated NVA battalion and was now astride one of the major enemy routes to Hue. The next morning an enemy regiment made an all-out effort to eliminate this blockade. They failed.

Lieutenant Colonel Richard L. Sweet, the battalion commander, described the action this way: "By noon we were completely cut off and encircled. We had over 200 mortar rounds land in the perimeter, and the perimeter was only about 150 meters by 200 meters. During the night they had gotten behind us."

As darkness fell, "Instead of pulling out to the rear like we were expected to do, we decided to pull out, make a feint, and go deeper behind the enemy lines . . . We were sure it would work, although we discovered after the battle that nobody else was."

It did work. The entire battalion moved out. Some of the soldiers had concealed their wounds to stay with their buddies and fight. They turned up along the route, a limp here and there revealing a bullet or fragmentation wound, but the only sound the entire night came when an NVA snapped his bolt shut. The Skytroopers were undetected. The next morning the enemy awoke to find their supply and communications route cut. LTC Sweet was awarded the Distinguished Service Cross for the action. Said the colonel, "For my money, the 2nd Bn, 12th Cav, is getting this award. As far as I'm concerned that's what the award is for: the men."

To the men, it was hard-earned. "We went without food and water for a long time," said Specialist Four Frank J. O'Reilly, an RTO in Company A. "We had no water, no water purification tablets, and the rivers were too muddy. The men were eating sugar cane, bananas, and onions. One cigarette might be smoked by 20 people."

Before the unit moved out that night in the ankle-deep water of the rice paddies, said O'Reilly, "the word had gone out just before we left that there would be no smoking. That we didn't have to worry about, because no one had any cigarettes." When the 10-hour night march was completed, "the luckiest men had gotten six hours sleep in the past 48 hours."

From its new position the unit so dominated the area that it successfully interdicted all daylight enemy movement. By February 25 the sweep to Hue was complete. The battalion continued operations in the Hue and Quang Tri area through March.

Hue was clear of the NVA, but on the

A lone 2nd Battalion, 12th Cavalry, trooper walks across one of the few bridges left intact in the battle for Hue. For some of the older soldiers the bridge was reminiscent of Remmagen, and both bridges were known for the fierce fights that raged around them.

other side of I Corps the Marines were still under siege in the Khe Sanh Valley by elements of the NVA 304th and 325th Divisions. The 1st Cav was called upon to break the land blockade that had forced all resupply since January to be by air.

On April 1, Operation PEGASUS began as the 1st Air Cav moved into the area. On April 3 the 2nd Bn, 12th Cav, airlifted into LZ Stud, then moved out to air assault LZ Wharton where the NVA greeted the landing with artillery fire. That evening the landing zone received some 20 rounds of 130 mm artillery fire. On April 4 the battalion began search and destroy operations around the LZ.

By April 6 the battalion airlifted to Hill 471 to relieve Marines at that position. Two companies remained on the hill while two initiated an attack to the south toward Khe Sanh hamlet. Through April 11 operations were continued in the area as the unit located enemy crew-served weapons and ammunition. Only sporadic contact was made, for the bulk of the enemy forces would rather flee than fight a pitched battle with the FIRST TEAM. The battalion was released from the operation and by April 12 had returned to the division's base, Camp Evans.

After a brief respite at Camp Evans, the unit resumed operations in the Quang Tri area near the Demilitarized Zone. In May the battlion participated in Operation JEB STUART III, air assaulting into LZs Merideth and Mooney, making the first deep penetration into Base Area 114 and paving the way for more intensive Allied activity in the area. Throughout the summer they carried out cordon and search operations, ambushes and patrolled extensively generally with light contact.

Light contact—an easy phrase signifying only small actions—but to those involved the phrase can mean hard moments. In one such action Specialist Four Donald Corbin, a squad leader with A Company, was moving to a night ambush position 21 miles south of Quang Tri. The Cavalryman had just propped

his rifle in the crotch of a tree when he heard something hit the side of his foot. "It was dark so I didn't know what it was until I reached down and picked it up."

When he looked closely, Corbin recognized a live Red Chinese grenade. "I dropped it and moved out as fast as I could," recalled Corbin. "I was really scared." Fortunately, the grenade failed to explode.

A few minutes later an NVA ambush struck the company. Shortly after contact A Company pulled back while aerial rocket artillery and machineguns blasted the enemy positions. Related Corbin, "The next morning we returned to the same area and I found the Chicom grenade that hit me."

In November of 1968 the division moved south to the III Corps area along the Cambodian border with the mission to block major Communist infiltration routes to Saigon.

The battalion began its III Corps operations near division headquarters at Phuoc Vinh. By the end of November elements of the battalion were airlifted into an area 35 miles northeast of Quan Loi. As the troops moved out through the hilly area, they came upon a complex of 106 bunkers, three huts and four caves. A short distance away the Sky-troopers discovered 22 enemy bodies.

The men of the 2nd Bn, 12th Cav, were also meeting live enemy. In one firefight 30 miles northwest of Phuoc Vinh Sergeant Charles Dickerson of Alpha Company sought cover in a hole. Said SGT Dickerson, "I discovered I

wasn't alone. Two legs were sticking from under a tree limb that had fallen in the other end. At first I thought the guy must be dead, but just in case, I pointed my M-16 in that direction."

Suddenly the "dead" man jumped up with a Chicom grenade in his hand. SGT Dickerson was about to fire and leap for safety, but the NVA quickly laid the grenade on the ground when he spotted the M-16 leveled at him. "Even so," said Dickerson, "next time I'll look before I leap."

The battalion was operating in the Tay Ninh area at the beginning of 1969. In three days of fighting from January 31 to February 2 the battalion discovered more than 100 tons of rice and numerous bunkers.

The battalion also moved its command post to LZ Grant. LZ Grant would be the site of triumph and tragedy for the unit. Thirty-nine NVA died in the first assault on the base. It was but a token of things to come.

At 12:30 a.m. March 8 the LZ received a heavy rocket and mortar barrage. A 122 mm rocket with a delayed fuse tore through three layers of sandbags atop the battalion tactical operations center (TOC), instantly killing the battalion commander, Lieutenant Colonel Peter Gorvad. Major Billy Brown, the battalion S-3, described the scene as he entered the TOC:

"The colonel was lying just about where I left him, sitting in a chair in front

(Continued on P. 278)

A company of the 2nd Battalion, 12th Cavalry, combat assaults into the tall yellow grass of a jungle clearing near FSB Buttons in Phuoc Long Province, III Corps Tactical Zone.

GRUNTS' WORLD

CAVALRY

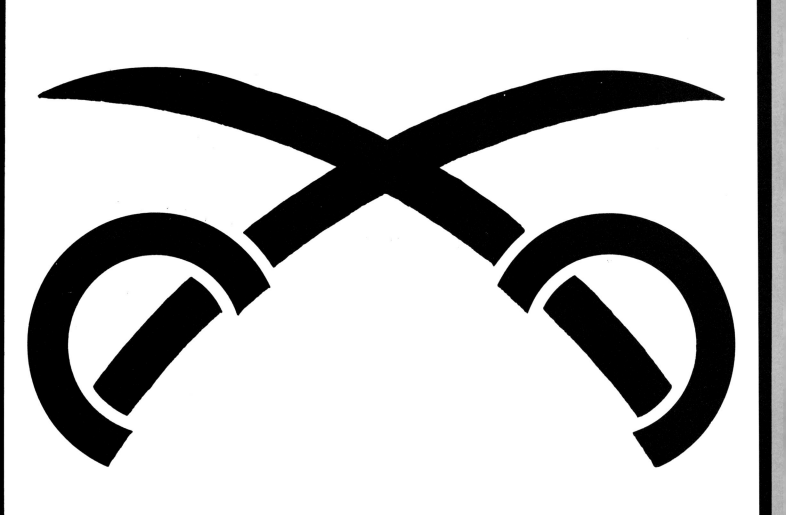

The 1st Squadron, 9th Cavalry, was constituted July 28, 1866, in the Regular Army as Company A, 9th Cavalry, and was organized in October 1866 at Greenville, Louisiana. The unit was officially designated a troop in 1883 as were all other cavalry companies.

The 9th Cavalry was composed of Negro enlisted men and white officers, one of two such regiments whose men won fame as the "Buffalo Soldiers."

In World War II the 1st Squadron, 9th Cavalry, was credited with participation in the European-African-Middle Eastern Theater, New Guinea, Bismarck Archipelago, Leyte and Luzon. The squadron also fought in the Korean War.

In Vietnam the unit has received the PUC, streamer embroidered PLEIKU PROVINCE (1st Squadron cited); PUC, streamer embroidered KIM SON PLAIN (1st Squadron cited); Valorous Unit Award, streamer embroidered PLEI ME (Troop B, 1st Squadron cited).

The distinctive insignia is an Indian in breech cloth and war bonnet, mounted on a galloping pony, brandishing a rifle in his right hand and holding a single rein in his left hand, all in gold, displayed upon a five-bastioned fort in blue edged with gold. The five-bastioned fort was the badge of the Fifth Army Corps in Cuba, of which the 9th Cavalry was a part. The yellow outline is for the Cavalry, and the blue for active service in the Spanish-American War. The mounted Indian represents the Indian campaigns of the regiment.

FIRST SQUADRON NINTH CAVALRY

COMMANDERS

LTC John B. Stockton	July 1965—December 1965
LTC Robert M. Shoemaker	December 1965—May 1966
LTC James C. Smith	May 1966—November 1966
LTC A. T. Pumphrey	November 1966—April 1967
LTC R. W. Nevins	April 1967—December 1967
LTC Richard W. Diller	December 1967—July 1968
LTC William G. Rousse	July 1968—January 1969
LTC James M. Peterson	January 1969—June 1969
LTC James W. Booth	June 1969—August 1969
LTC Edward B. Covington, III	August 1969—September 1969
LTC James W. Booth	September 1969—December 1969
LTC Clark A. Burnett	December 1969—

A 1st Squadron, 9th Cavalry, OH-13 observation helicopter lifts off for a reconnaissance mission near An Khe in the Cav's II Corps area of operations. The OH-13 was later replaced by the faster, more maneuverable OH-6A "Cayuse," better known as the "Loach."

"The Cav of the Cav." That's one of the unique names given to a unique unit, the 1st Squadron, 9th Cavalry, 1st Cavalry Division (Airmobile).

The 1st Sqdn, 9th Cav, is a battalion size unit, 100 percent mobile with organic transport, which includes nearly 100 helicopters. The unit has three air cavalry troops, and each troop has an aero scout platoon, an aero weapons platoon and an aero rifle platoon. Delta Troop is a ground cavalry unit with three platoons mounted on wheeled vehicles.

The mission of the aero scout platoon is to find the enemy. Until 1968 these platoons used OH-13 observation helicopters. By mid-1968 these ships were being replaced by the faster, more maneuverable OH-6A Light Observation

Helicopter (LOH). The scouts skim low over terrain, searching for any sign of enemy movement or activity. The scout platoon is known as the "White" platoon.

The aero weapons, or "Red" platoon, is made up of Huey Cobra (AH-1G) gunships, which replaced UH-1B (Huey) gunships in 1968. Armed with rockets, miniguns and grenade launchers, the "Red" gunships join the "White" LOH to form the "Pink" team, the basic working unit of the 1st Sqdn, 9th Cav. The gunship protects the LOH, and can immediately attack a target.

The aero rifle platoon, the "Blue" platoon, complements the aerial reconnaissance capabilities of the Pink Team by providing ground reconnaissance. Transported by Huey slicks, the Blues can be quickly inserted to check the spottings of the aerial observer, assess the damage inflicted by Cobra or B-52 strikes and pursue enemy elements. Generally only a patrol-size element will be inserted initially, then the rest of the platoon.

Although the 1st Sqdn, 9th Cav, is highly effective in destroying the enemy, its primary mission is to find and fix the enemy. Once it has done that it may call in air strikes, aerial rocket artillery, artillery and infantry rifle units as needed.

The ground cavalry group is designed to perform reconnaissance and surveil-

A Cobra gunship from Troop C, 1st of the 9th, rides shotgun over the jungle terrain of III Corps, waiting for enemy activity. Should NVA or VC forces make the mistake of conspicuous movement, the Cobra "snake" will dive with fangs bared and rockets, mini-gun and 40 mm cannon blazing.

lance operations, provide security, and engage the enemy as an economy of force unit. It may secure a road, escort a convoy, or collect information with roving patrols through hamlets and villages.

Although most of the 1st Sqdn, 9th Cav, did not arrive in Vietnam until mid-September 1965 when the USNS Darby docked at Qui Nhon, an ad-

vance party had landed in August to begin the search for the enemy. On August 17, 1965, Major Donald G. Radcliff, the squadron's executive officer, became the 1st Air Cavalry Division's first casualty. He was killed in action on an aviation mission. The division basecamp at An Khe was later named in his honor.

The first major operation the squadron participated in was SHINY BAYONET in October 1965. Contact was constant, but involved mainly small bands of Viet Cong who were engaged with air to ground fire.

In late October the squadron moved to Pleiku Province, where the Pleiku Campaign was beginning. The squadron became the first unit in the division to capture any North Vietnamese soldiers when Charlie Troop took three NVA prisoners on October 30 near Pleiku.

On the morning of November 1 Bravo Troop scouts spotted eight enemy hiding in foxholes and in nearby trees. Soon Charlie Troop scouts spotted 34 more NVA in the area. An hour after the first sighting the Bravo Troop rifles were on the ground and in contact.

As the battle intensified, the squad-

The "Blues," men of Troop C's Blue Platoon, jump from the skids of Headhunter Three-Six during an air assault into the Bong Son Plain. The action was part of Operation PERSHING. With their quick-strike capability and constant standby readiness, the three Blue Platoons of the 1st of the 9th were responsible for many of the Cav's initiated contacts.

Bravo Troop's "Blues" assault onto a mountaintop overlooking the A Shau Valley. As a ready-reaction force, the Blues usually average more than one mission a day.

ron's other rifle platoons were committed. The greatly outnumbered Blues fought off enemy counterattacks and refused to yield to enemy mortars and snipers, even though the closeness of the contact excluded the use of artillery or aerial rocket support. After fighting 10 hours, the Blues were extracted and the task of finishing off the remaining enemy given to the 2nd Battalion, 12th Cavalry. The operation cost the 3rd NVA Regiment its aid station, $40,000 worth of medical supplies and 99 killed.

Two nights later the squadron again drew blood. The evening was clear and brightly lit by a full moon. The squadron had established a patrol-ambush base near the Ia Drang River and had set out ambushes. Charlie Troop Blues, manning the southernmost site, spotted a large, heavily laden NVA unit of company size. The enemy paused to take a rest break just outside the killing zone. As the NVA smoked and joked for an hour and a half, the Blues quietly sweated it out. Finally the NVA unit moved noisily

along the trail. The lead element was allowed to pass, then the trap was sprung.

Eight claymore mines simultaneously detonated, and the ambushers opened up with their M-16s. The enemy's lead element was blasted by three claymores and rifle fire from the flank security element. No fire was returned.

Deciding that the ambushed unit was probably the vanguard of a larger force, the platoon leader, Captain Charles Knowlen, quickly withdrew to the patrol-ambush base. He was right. At 10:20 p.m. a battalion-size enemy force hit the base. When attempts to overrun the base failed, the NVA had snipers firing from trees, using the bright moonlight to their advantage.

It was some time before enough space was established between defenders and and attackers to permit gunships to blow the snipers from the trees. Daring night helicopter landings on the tiny LZ carried the squadron's wounded to safety and brought them reinforcements.

The ambush marked two significant

firsts for the 1st Cav Division and the 1st Squadron. It was the first heliborne reinforcement at night of a unit in contact, and the first time that ARA had been employed at night in such close support—within 50 meters of friendly troops. Ninety-eight NVA were killed and 10 detained, and more than 120,000 rounds of 7.62 ammunition evacuated or destroyed.

The squadron continued to find and fix enemy elements throughout 1965, initiating most of the division's contacts. Christmas was celebrated in real airmobile style. As the squadron's helicopters buzzed the village of An Khe, the men threw toys to the children below.

Operation MASHER/WHITE WING was launched on January 25, 1966, in Binh Dinh Province near the Vietnamese coast. As it began the squadron operated with excessive activity away from the true target areas for deception purposes, As the campaign picked up momentum, the squadron operated in earnest locating numerous targets and

Bravo Troop "Blues" gather before moving out in pursuit of a suspected enemy into force. If they make contact, the Blues are more than capable of holding their own until regular reinforcements can be assaulted the fight. Once relieved in the action, the Blues are taken out and returned to their base of operations to wait for another shot at the enemy.

nflicting many casualties. The unit also performed its own operation, nicknamed "Kidnap," as Charlie Troop swooped into the An Lao Valley to detain two residents for questioning about enemy activity. As the suspects were extracted heavy enemy fire was received from the area, and the pair proved to be VC cadre.

The squadron was operating near the Chu Pong Massiff on the Cambodian border when on March 30 Bravo Troop scouts sighted 32 enemy in well entrenched positions. Squadron gunships raked the area and the Air Force hit it with napalm. Alpha Troop's Blue platoon assaulted and took a prisoner, who informed them that there were 1,000 enemy in the area. The platoon started to withdraw to the LZ for extraction when it came under fire from enemy troops in foxholes and bunkers.

The platoon continued to move in dispersed elements toward the LZ while squadron gunships provided fire support. As the gunships exhausted their ammunition the crews resorted to M-16s and side arms to keep the pressure off their comrades on the ground. The Blues were relieved by the 1st Battalion, 12th Cavalry, but the squadron's extraction was marred by the crash of two lift ships. The Viet Cong left 197 bodies on the field of battle, and some 200 more were estimated killed.

In the summer of 1966 the squadron played a major role in the division's search and clear operations, providing road security and gaining intelligence.

Bravo Troop moved with the 2nd and 3rd Brigades back to the Pleiku area in August for Operation PAUL REVERE II. Once again the division smashed enemy activities in the Chu Pong-Ia Drang area. Bravo Troop was at the forefront of the fighting, earning a Valorous Unit Citation for its actions from August 9 to August 16 near Plei Me. According to the citation the men of Bravo Troop "not only engaged hostile forces with lightning-like strikes, but also exposed themselves to extreme danger in locating and capturing numerous enemy soldiers." The troop took credit for a large number of the 861 enemy killed in the action.

On October 2 the squadron made the division's first contact in Operation IRVING. A scout team saw seven men in green and tan uniforms carrying packs on Hung Lac Penninsula near Hoa Hoi Village. The Alpha Troop commander was on the scene almost immediately, drawing enemy fire to determine their precise location. Racing through the enemy bullets he made a gun run, killing three VC, then hovered his ship 20 feet above the rice paddies to kill five more VC.

Alpha Troop's infantry platoon was inserted with the mission of passing through the village and searching it. Within minutes of landing the Blues made contact. The rifle platoon moved toward the village under heavy fire. In a daring display of courage, Private First Class John F. Wiegart, a grenadier with the third squad, expended all his grenades attempting to knock out two

Delta Troop—better known as "The Rat Patrol"—makes a sweep through clearings and jungle in the area surrounding Phuoc Vinh, the division's III Corps headquarters.

Travelling "light to fight" (carrying only weapons, ammo and water), Bravo Troop's Blues prepare to move out on a sweep through the An Lao Valley on July 28, 1967. Their commander (center) is Lieutenant Billy Johnson. At that time the Blues sported blue and white neck scarves.

.50 caliber machinegun positions, then charged one with his .45 caliber pistol, killing the two man NVA crew. Out of .45 ammo, he grabbed one of the dead soldiers' AK-47 rifles and continued the firefight.

The second enemy machinegun was firing directly into the main body of the platoon and was well covered by automatic rifles. Having returned from refueling his gunship, the troop commander hovered 20 to 30 feet above the enemy while Specialist Five Larry Wright and Private First Class Robert Andrews climbed out onto the Huey's skids to pour machinegun and M-79 fire into the enemy position, killing more than 30 NVA.

As the Blues continued their advance they found that every courtyard and field in and around the village was encircled by trenches and hedgerows two and three deep in which well-armed NVA in squad sized groups were either hiding, delivering fire on the platoon or crawling to the west to escape. At one point, the troop aircraft placed their fire three feet in front of friendlies to eliminate two machineguns.

Private First Class Lynn Gaylord was moving with his squad of Blues toward the village when he spotted a machinegun no one else had seen. To warn the others, Gaylord stood up and ran from position to position until he drew fire, an enemy round ripping into his shoulder. His action enabled his fellow riflemen to spot the gun and destroy it with 18 hand grenades. Gaylord later received the Silver Star.

While the rest of the platoon had advanced toward the village, the fifth squad had been pinned down. Two weapons teams brought their ships to the squad's aid, raking the enemy positions with rockets and miniguns. The troop commander flew his aircraft to the squad and hovered between it and the enemy, hoping to draw fire long enough to permit the squad to break contact and withdraw to the LZ. Because of its casualties the squad could not withdraw, but did move to a covered position.

The troop commander had his ship touch down to pick up the squad's seriously wounded medic, although by this time the crew had exhausted all the ammunition for its organic weapons. As the crew chief dismounted to retrieve the medic, the ship's pilot, First Lieutenant Patrick Haley, saw an NVA approaching from the rear. The pilot raised the Huey and swung the tail rotor into the NVA, killing him.

In a hail of enemy fire the Huey lifted off. Enemy rounds splatted into the fuel cell, the hydraulic and transmission lines. The wounded bird limped the 150 meters to the LZ where the medic was evacuated by another bird and the lieutenant called in for a new aircraft.

The squadron had fulfilled its mission of locating and fixing the enemy, and units of the 1st Bn, 12th Cav, were moving to the village to engage the NVA. As they did so, they also came under enemy fire. A scout team located two enemy machinegun positions. Despite serious damage to the bird from the enemy fire, the crew destroyed one by dropping grenades and marked the other for the gunships. With both positions out of commission the scout aircraft made a forced landing next to the downed command helicopter.

By 11:05 a.m. Alpha Troop Blues were ready for extraction. Alpha Troop aircraft continued to support friendly elements in the area for the rest of the

On convoy escort in the An Lao Valley in July 1967, a recoilless rifle jeep of Troop D hits a suspected enemy position with a 106 mm round. Staff Sergeant David Gonzales is the gunner.

day. When the action was over, the enemy had sustained 233 confirmed KIAs.

For this and other actions in October 1966 the 1st Sqdn, 9th Cav, was awarded the Presidential Unit Citation for "unparalleled application of exceptional imagination, fearless courage and unrelenting determination."

The squadron maintained a high level of activity for the rest of 1966. The division was sweeping the Kim Son Valley on November 30 when squadron scout ships spotted movement in the hamlet of Phu Huu. Charlie Troop Blues were inserted and spent the night. When the infantrymen began to move forward in the morning they were pinned down by automatic and semi-automatic weapons fire. The squadron having made the initial contact, additional troops were piled on. By the time the squadron withdrew, 40 dead enemy were accounted for.

Operation THAYER II, which began in 1966, carried over to 1967 as the division continued search and destroy operations in the Binh Dinh Province. Troops Alpha and Bravo participated until the operation's end in February.

THAYER II was succeeded by Operation PERSHING, the division's longest operation, which continued until early

While a Bravo Troop Blue (top) keeps his eyes and M-60 machinegun on the jungle, another man enters an enemy bunker armed with his .45 caliber pistol, the best weapon for tight places. Motorcycle tracks (right) in the mud trail approaching a bamboo bridge on the Jolley Trail in III Corps get a close inspection from a Blue Platoon RTO to see how recently they had been made. The NVA infiltration route, complete with bamboo bridges and tunnels, was found by Bravo Troop and named for the troop commander, Major Charles Jolley. A Charlie Troop Cobra (below left) flies in to provide air cover over a 1st of the 9th salvage crew (below right), which is working to lift out a damaged LOH (light observation helicopter).

A 1st of the 9th Cobra comes home late from a mission (above). Another Cobra pilot is seen in a cockpit mirror as he scans the terrain for the enemy (right), and a Pink Team, one Red Platoon Cobra gunship and one White Platoon LOH, entice the enemy for their special one-two punch.

1968 from Qui Nhon to Quang Ngai.

Impetuous enemy riflemen touched off the first major engagement of PERSHING when they fired on a squadron gunship the morning of March 6. A squadron infantry platoon was air assaulted into the area and immediately made heavy contact. Other units moved in to block escape routes. Seventy-six enemy were killed before the fighting stopped.

In April 1967 Bravo Troop deployed from the PERSHING area of operations to LZ Montezuma at Duc Pho to support the division's 2nd Brigade in Operation LEJEUNE. Although the division's infantry units returned to Operation PEGASUS on April 22, the troop remained until June supporting the 25th Infantry Division. When the troop returned it had killed 471 enemy and detained 2,100 suspects. The 3rd Brigade, 25th Infantry Division, commander said of Bravo Troop, "I have seen 'Can Do' units and 'Will Do' units but you are the first 'Do Do' unit I have ever seen."

After LEJEUNE, Bravo Troop joined other squadron units in continuing to compile an outstanding record in Operation PERSHING. In June the squadron

started five battalion size battles and accounted for more than 300 enemy dead. Probably the highest point for the squadron in PERSHING came in October of 1967. The squadron's actions were concentrated in the An Lao Valley-Bong Son Plain area and the Que Son Valley, although Bravo Troop made important contacts in the Chu Lai vicinity as a part of Operation WALLOWA.

Among the major actions of the month was one on October 10 when squadron elements located an enemy infiltration group and destroyed 54 NVA soldiers. On October 20 gunships killed 51 NVA from a sapper battalion. Squadron troops in the PERSHING AO killed a total of 514 enemy in October, the highest for any month since the squadron arrived in Vietnam, and that was only a partial count, for B Troop accounted for 350 enemy while working with the Americal Division.

Bravo Troop made a significant intelligence find on December 5, 1967. A few kilometers from a firebase, the troop commander's gunship cut down four khaki-clad NVA. More NVA popped up and the troop eliminated 13 more. The Blue platoon went into the area to investigate. They reported something unusual: nine of the enemy soldiers were armed with pistols and had numerous documents and maps in their packs. They were rushed back to brigade headquarters where a read-out revealed that the gunships had slain the commander of the 3rd Regiment, 2nd NVA Division, the political officer (a full colonel) of the division, the division intelligence officer and the operations officer. The documents further revealed a battle plan, fully detailed with maps and operations orders for an attack on the 1st Cav Division's bases in the area. The warning of the squadron was instrumental in turning back the NVA attack when it came a month later.

The day after that find the squadron was responsible for starting one of PERSHING'S biggest battles. On the afternoon of December 6 squadron scout ships noticed antennas protruding from huts on the lush Bong Son Plain at the village of Dai Dong. A Blue platoon airlifted into the area was quickly in heavy contact, as was another Blue platoon sent to reinforce them. They were fighting the 3rd NVA Division's

(Continued on P. 272)

110

ARTILLERY

DIVISION ARTILLERY

COMMANDERS

COL William A. Becker .... July 1965—January 1966

COL William F. Brand .... January 1966—March 1967

COL George W. Putnam, Jr. .... March 1967—September 1967

COL Richard M. Winfield, Jr. .... September 1967—March 1968

COL William R. Wolfe .... March 1968—February 1969

COL James A. Munson .... February 1969—October 1969

COL Morris J. Brady .... October 1969—

The Division Artillery (DIVARTY shield is the same shape as the division', shoulder patch. The background i. yellow and a black horse's head is in the upper right hand corner, a black cannon in the lower right and a yellow rocket is located in the red band. The golden-yellow background and the horse indicate that the unit is part of the 1st Cavalry Division. The band of red symbolizes the traditional artillery color and the rocket and cannon, of course, denote the weapons used. The motto "First and Foremost" across the top of the shield depicts the unit's pride and desire for excellence.

Headquarters and Headquarters Battery earned the Presidential Unit Citation for the Pleiku Campaign. In addition, the battery has been awarded the Meritorious Unit Commendation for the period September 13, 1966, to July 31, 1967.

The "Redlegs" of Division Artillery (DIVARTY) sailed to Vietnam aboard the USS Upshur, arriving at Qui Nhon September 5, 1965. Their last two weeks in September were spent setting up unit headquarters at Camp Radcliff, the then division basecamp at An Khe.

Under DIVARTY control artillery units participated in their first major actions during the month of October. That operation was called SHINY BAYONET. DIVARTY's role, as it would be in all division operations, was to coordinate tube artillery, aerial rocket artillery, air strikes and artillery forward observers to provide "accurate, fast and massive firepower."

They shifted a forward element to the Catecka Tea Plantation some 14 kilometers south of Pleiku in late November. Then began the Pleiku Campaign, one for which the division would eventually win the Presidential Unit Citation. DIVARTY's fire support was instrumental in breaking up enemy efforts to

A cannoneer shields his face from dust, dirt and small stones flying in the 100-mile-an-hour rotor wash of a huge Chinook helicopter as it slings in a 105 mm howitzer for Bravo Battery, 1st Battalion, 77th Artillery, on the Bong Son Plain.

overrun several FIRST TEAM landing zones. The enemy learned quickly that to appear in force in the open was to risk heavy bombardment, and in the end, high casualties.

The headquarters was still located at An Khe in December, and the first year of Vietnam operations had already seen the development and perfection of many techniques, then unique to the 1st Cav, but which have since been adopted by other American divisions. The division's artillery batteries had proven their ability to move rapidly by air to provide a blanket of protection wherever and whenever the infantry needed. In a matter of hours if needed an entire battery could be moved to a new location, set up and be providing combat support to infantry troops.

Operation MASHER/WHITE WING was conducted in northern Binh Dinh Province from January 4 to March 6, 1966. Here DIVARTY moved its forward command post from Camp Radcliff to the Bong Son CIDG Camp.

There were two significant firsts for artillery during this campaign. A special sling was devised that allowed the displacement of the 155 mm howitzer by CH-54A "Flying Crane" helicopters. This permitted the 155s to be placed in firing positions that would otherwise have been inaccessible. The 1st Cav

Division had taken another step forward in airmobility. The other historical "first" was the successful firing of the combination SS-11 missile/2.75 inch rocket system on February 2. Designed by 1st Cav Warrant Officer Robert W. Maxwell, the weapons system was the first that allowed Cav aerial rocket helicopters to carry both the SS-11 and the 2.75 inch rocket at the same time.

From March 25, 1966, to April 8, 1966, DIVARTY participated in Operation LINCOLN in the central highlands southwest of Pleiku, centered in the Chu Pong Massiff—Ia Drang River area. Artillery accounted for more than 200 enemy killed during the operation. Operations later in May resulted in little contact, but provided valuable training in employment and movement of the 105 mm howitzer, Model 102.

DIVARTY saw action in numerous other areas throughout 1966. By the end of the year it had participated in 14 major combat operations from the South China Sea to the Cambodian border. On November 11, 1966, DIVARTY personnel were present at the firing of the one millionth artillery round in support of the division's Vietnam operations.

The year had also marked the initiation of successful civic action programs by the unit's S-5. The surgeon and

members of the Headquarters Battery medical section conducted sick call twice a week in the resettlement village of Tu Luong. The communications section established wire communications for the village to the district headquarters. Other battery members contributed time and energy to teaching English language classes, helping the people with construction projects and distributing items such as soap and other sundries.

In 1967 DIVARTY participated in Operation PERSHING, operations of the division primarily concentrated in the area from the South China Sea west to Vinh Than Valley in Binh Dinh Province, and from the Binh Dinh-Quang Ngai Province boundary in the north to Phu Cat in the south. Forward elements of the artillery headquarters shifted with the combat operations, but an element always remained at Camp Radcliff to perform the vital missions of providing counter mortar coverage, survey and metro support, and coordination for defensive fires.

The unit's civic action program continued to aid Tu Luong. A medical dispensary in the village was completed and furnished with supplies. The artillerymen also helped in the construction of a school and supplied surplus fruit

(Continued on P. 270)

2nd BATTALION 19th ARTILLERY

COMMANDERS

LTC Francis J. Bush ....July 1965—July 1966
LTC Wilbur H. Vinson, Jr. ....July 1966—December 1966
LTC James F. Culp. ....December 1966—June 1967
MAJ Vernon W. Gillespie ....June 1967—December 1967
LTC Arnold L. Boykin ....December 1967—August 1968
LTC Robert C. Morrison ....August 1968—March 1969
LTC Edward M. Knoff, Jr. ....March 1969—July 1969
LTC Leo J. Fitzgerald ....July 1969—January 1970
LTC Thomas E. Gernon ....January 1970—

The eagle in the upper right hand corner of the shield is the eagle of Amnedes, one of the 19th Artillery's major battles in World War I. The crown on the eagle's head is the crown of the king of battle. The red bar is for service. The diamond in the lower left corner represents the 5th Infantry Division shoulder patch. The regiment served with the 5th Infantry in World War I. The gold background is the secondary color of the artillery. Red is the artillery's primary color.

personnel and equipment) from Korea to Fort Benning, Georgia, on July 1, 1965, and reorganized as part of the 1st Cavalry Division (Airmobile).

The 19th Artillery participated in the campaigns of St. Mihiel and Lorraine (1918) in World War I, and Normandy, Northern France, Rhineland, Ardennes-Alsace, and Central Europe in World War II.

With the rest of the 1st Cavalry Division (Airmobile), the battalion received the Presidential Unit Citation for the Pleiku Province Campaign in 1965. A 13 man detachment won the Presidential Unit Citation (First Oak Leaf Cluster) for actions in October 1966. Battery B won a PUC for action on LZ Bird in December 1966.

The 19th Artillery was constituted on June 3, 1916, in the Regular Army as the 19th Field Artillery. It was organized June 1, 1917, at Camp Wilson, Texas. On December 12, 1917, the regiment was assigned to the 5th Division (later 5th Infantry Division). The unit was inactivated on September 6, 1921, at Camp Bragg, North Carolina.

The 19th Field Artillery was activated October 5, 1939, at Fort Knox, Kentucky. It was reorganized and redesignated October 1, 1940, as the 19th Field Artillery Battalion.

The battalion was redesignated on October 15, 1957, as the 2nd Howitzer Battalion, 19th Artillery, and activated and assigned to the 1st Cavalry Division in Korea (concurrently, organic elements were constituted and activated). On September 1, 1963, the unit was redesignated 2nd Battalion, 19th Artillery. The battalion was transferred (less

As the gunner checks his aim, another artilleryman prepares to yank the lanyard that will start the 105 mm howitzer's 38-pound high explosive shell on its way.

The USNS Geiger steamed into the harbor at Qui Nhon, Vietnam, on September 19, 1965, carrying the 2nd Battalion (Airborne), 19th Artillery, 1st Cav Division (Airmobile). At the time the battalion was not only airmobile, but airborne, the only artillery battalion in the Army to share those designations.

The battalion's batteries were soon in place in the vicinity of the division's Camp Radcliff basecamp at An Khe. Their first missions were harassment and interdiction fires and fires at suspected Viet Cong locations.

On October 23 the battalion received a warning order to be prepared to move to the vicinity of Pleiku near the Cambodian border. The Pleiku Campaign, for which the division would win a Presidential Unit Citation, had begun. The battalion's batteries moved to firing positions on Highway 14. An ARVN column was rolling down the highway toward the beleaguered Plei Me Special Forces Camp. When the column was ambushed, Bravo Battery provided close-in defensive fires that assisted the armored vehicles in beating off the Viet Cong.

In November elements of the 2nd Battalion, 8th Cavalry, attacked an NVA staging area. Charlie Battery's RTO with the infantry unit, Private First Class Joseph G. Brown, called very close artillery fire to smash the enemy; he called it so close, in fact, that the rounds were bursting around him. The enemy retreated leaving 30 dead.

The battalion returned to the An Khe area in mid-November. The battles at Pleiku had given the batteries valuable combat experience and improved their methods of operations. Lessons such as the importance of sling loading ammunition and equipment, rather than loading it internally, had been learned and would be put into effective use in the future.

The first day of the new year saw the battalion leave Camp Radcliff for Pleiku to support 1st Brigade operations in search of the enemy. Light contact characterized the action and the battalion was back at An Khe on January 20, 1966.

After supporting several 1st Brigade operations in the east, the battalion went to Pleiku once more for Operation LINCOLN in late March. There was continuous contact with squad size units by the brigade's infantry, and the battalion's supporting fires caused 68 NVA casualties.

In April the battalion was equipped with the M102 howitzer. They soon put them to use in Operation CRAZY HORSE, an action marked by the heaviest use of artillery up to that time. Routes of enemy movement in the Vinh Thanh Valley were continually sealed by artillery interdiction. The operation lasted from mid-May to June 5. The battalion fired more than 37,000 rounds of ammunition and was credited with 75 Viet Cong killed.

For action on October 2 and 3 a 13 man detachment of the battalion, elements of the 1st Battalion, 5th Cavalry, and the entire 1st Battalion, 12th Cavalry, won the Presidential Unit Citation. The artillerymen were observers with the infantry companies as they battled well-entrenched enemy in Hoa Hoi village. The citation praised the Skytroopers for "determination and extraordinary courage."

In December Bravo Battery won more fame for the battalion when LZ Bird in the Kim Son Valley was attacked. The attack from the east surprised First Lieutenant Charles R. Campanella, a forward observer for the battalion. But he reacted quickly taking command

In October 1968, artillerymen of the 2nd Battalion, 19th Artillery, were sitting astride the rolling and forested terrain of LZ Davis in the rugged foothills near Dak To. They were there to provide fire support for infantrymen in Operation COMANCHE FALLS.

of the LZ's rifle company when all its officers were either killed or wounded. Before the night was over he had won the Silver Star.

Bravo Battery's Captain Leonard L. Schlenker was asleep but fully clothed when the attack started. As he scrambled outside "a line of red tracers went between me and the FDC (fire direction center)." When the fire broke off for a moment Schlenker dashed to the FDC tent and called for supporting fires. Seconds later the radio was knocked out. The captain headed for his guns. He, too, won the Silver Star.

Specialist Four Charles S. Tournage, a medic for the battery, was hit by white phosphorous from an ammo bunker that had taken a direct mortar hit. When his clothes started to smoke, Tournage stripped them off as he wallowed in a mud puddle to stop the smoldering. Later, the unclad mud-covered medic was mistaken for an NVA by an NVA leader who started waving and giving him directions. Tournage shot him point-blank with an M-79 shotgun round.

Perched on a windblown mountaintop landing zone called Laramie, the gun crews (above) of "Boom Boom" wait for final word on target coordinates during a fire mission in support of Operation

PERSHING. A 228th ASHB Chinook (below) hovers in to deliver a sling load of artillery ammunition atop LZ Laramie for the men and guns of the 2nd of the 19th.

Then he turned to treating the wounded, ignoring the enemy forces swarming through the camp. Tournage was another Silver Star winner.

First Lieutenant John D. Piper was helping man number two 105 howitzer when he decided to use a Bee Hive round—a cannister of steel darts designed to be fired at massed infantry at close range. The battery executive officer and Staff Sergeant Robert L. Underwood loaded the round and pointed his gun toward a 155 position now overrun by some 150 NVA. Lacking a flare to alert friendlies of the firing of the round, the lieutenant screamed "Bee Hive! Bee Hive!" Cavalrymen between the 105 and the 155 laid flat and the Bee Hive flew over them, sounding, said one, "Like a million whips being whirled over my head." The lieutenant fired one more Bee Hive and the enemy advance in that section of the LZ came to a dead stop.

Throughout the LZ the "Redlegs" used everything from M-14s to 45s to keep the enemy from destroying their guns, and in the face of impossible odds they kept several of the howitzers firing. With the help of aerial rocket artillery and a thousand supporting rounds fired by the battalion from other LZs, the enemy attack was broken. By the time the pursuit of the enemy was finished 266 enemy had died as a result of the unsuccessful assault and the battery ultimately was awarded the Presidential Unit Citation.

In 1967 the battalion continued to support 1st Brigade operations throughout the II Corps area, primarily in the division's longest action, Operation PERSHING, aimed at clearing the Bong Son Plains and An Lao Valley near the Vietnamese coast of the enemy. The battalion fired its 500,000th round in Vietnam in September of 1967.

As 1968 began, the battalion continued to support the 1st Brigade's search and clear operations in the An Lao Valley and Bong Son Plain. In the latter part of January the division moved to the I Corps Tactical Zone. The battalion made eight moves, fired 1,470 missions and 27,812 rounds from January 18 to January 31.

Throughout this period and the month of February the city of Quang Tri was threatened by five NVA regiments. Three of the regiments in succession tried to take the city, but the combination of 1st Brigade infantry and battalion howitzers crushed their efforts. In April

and May the battalion provided artillery fire as division elements entered the enemy's longtime sanctuary in the A Shau Valley. The operation was characterized by light to heavy fighting requiring continuous artillery support.

In October and November the division and the 2nd Bn, 19th Arty, left Vietnam's northernmost provinces for the III Corps Tactical Zone, with the assignment of interdicting the enemy infiltration routes that led from Cambodia toward Saigon. The battalion's new home was Tay Ninh.

In March the battalion fired its one

(Continued on P. 294)

Sergeant Jesse Thomas, a gunner with Battery A, 2nd of the 19th, brings steel on steel as he stakes in a 105 mm howitzer shortly after arriving at the battery's new temporary home, LZ Carolyn. The landing zone is located in III Corps.

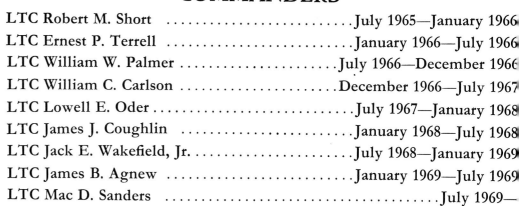

1st BATTALION 21st ARTILLERY

COMMANDERS

The shield of the 1st Battalion, 21st Artillery, is silver divided by a red band. In the upper corner is a gold demi-sun charged with an Aztec banner. In the lower corner is an eagle with closed wings and a collar. The red band denotes that this is an artillery unit. The sun and banner were symbols of the 3rd Field Artillery, from which the 21st was formed. The eagle is one of the supporters of the arms of St. Mihiel, site of the most important World War I engagement in which the regiment participated.

Cav cannoneers (right) move to clear the area as a CH-47 Chinook brings in a 105 mm howitzer and a load of ammo for a new 1st Battalion, 21st Artillery, gun emplacement and landing zone. Another 1st of the 21st artillery crew (opposite page) readies its howitzer for a sling out and move from FSB Jerri, located in III Corps.

The 1st Battalion, 21st Artillery, was organized June 1, 1917, in the Regular Army at Camp Wilson Texas, as Battery A, 21st Field Artillery. The unit was assigned to the 5th Division on December 12, 1917. The battery was relieved from assignment to the 5th Division on November 4, 1920, and inactivated at Camp Bragg, North Carolina, on September 23, 1921.

The unit was assigned to the 9th Division on March 24, 1923. It was relieved from this assignment on January 1, 1930, and assigned to the 5th Division (later 5th Infantry Division). The battery was activated on October 6, 1939, at Fort Knox, Kentucky. On October 1, 1940, the unit was reorganized and redesignated as Battery A, 21st Field Artillery Battalion.

The battery was inactivated June 1, 1957, at Fort Ord, California, and relieved from assignment to the 5th Division. Concurrently it was reorganized and redesignated 1st Battalion, 21st Artillery, and assigned to the 1st Cavalry Division and activated in Korea. Organic elements were simultaneously constituted and activated. In July 1965, the battalion became part of the 1st Cav Division (Airmobile).

In World War I the battalion participated in the St. Mihiel and Lorraine (1918) campaigns. In World War II the battalion was at Normandy, Northern France, Rhineland, Ardennes-Alsace and Central Europe.

In Vietnam the battalion was decorated with the Presidential Unit Citation (streamer embroidered PLEIKU PROVINCE) and with the Meritorious Unit Citation (streamer embroidered VIETNAM 1967). Bravo Battery received the Valorous Unit Award (streamer embroidered QUANG NAM) for extraordinary heroism in defense of LZ Leslie in January 1968.

The 1st Battalion, 21st Artillery, landed in Vietnam at Qui Nhon in 1965. The battalion's 105 mm howitzers were soon firing in support of the 1st Cav Division's infantry operations, specifically those of the 3rd (Garry Owen) Brigade.

In late October the 3rd Brigade was given the assignment of relieving enemy pressure on ARVN and Special Forces bases in the Pleiku-Ia Drang area. This, the Pleiku Campaign, was the division's first major campaign, one for which the entire division would win the Presidential Unit Citation.

The most important battles of the Pleiku action came at LZ s Albany and X-Ray in mid-November. The 1st Bn, 21st Arty, fired artillery support for both, its batteries pumping out more than 4,400 high explosive rounds from their position at LZ Falcon to protect the embattled Skytroopers at LZ X-Ray on the night of November 14.

The battalion also participated in the last major action of 1965, Operation CLEAN HOUSE, in which the 3rd Brigade swept a valley northeast of Binh Khe in Binh Dinh Province. Operation MASHER/WHITE WING was the battalion's first important action in 1966. The battalion fired 27,920 rounds in close support of 3rd Brigade maneuver elements, and was given credit for part of the 806 enemy killed in the operation.

The next significant operation for the battalion was DAVY CROCKETT. The operation began on May 4 and was concluded on May 16. The 21st Artillery was credited with 64 KIA.

On Operation NATHAN HALE/HENRY CLAY in late June 3rd Brigade elements made heavy contact with VC forces. Continuous artillery fire was provided until contact was broken. Of the 131 VC KIA, 34 died from artillery fire, and it was estimated that 43 more died as a result of artillery inflicted wounds. The battalion fired 21,594 rounds during the 10 day operation.

As a result of heavy contact in the

Cannoneers of Battery C, 1st of the 21st, await the word to fire as the battery is set to fire a high angle mission from LZ Two Bits, in support of Operation PERSHING.

vicinity of the Catecka Tea Plantation between the U.S. 25th Division and the 630th NVA Division, the 3rd Brigade was committed to LZ Oasis with the battalion for support. Thus began Operation PAUL REVERE II, which lasted from August 1 to August 25, 1966, with a net result of 687 NVA KIA and 78 NVA detained.

One of the artillery highlights of the operation occurred on August 8. Company A, 1st Battalion, 7th Cavalry, came under heavy fire in the vicinity of LZ Juliet. Charlie Battery quickly answered an urgent call for artillery support, delivering 1,408 high explosive rounds in two hours that eliminated 98 NVA.

Through the rest of 1966 the battalion alternated between base defense of division headquarters at Camp Radcliff and support for 3rd Brigade search and clear operations throughout the division's II Corps AO.

The battalion began 1967 on base defense. In mid-February it departed Camp Radcliff for the Bong Son Plains and Operation PERSHING, which would continue until January of 1969. The battalion would participate in PERSHING until September of 1968. The battalion supported the operations of the 3rd Brigade, which were mainly centered in the An Lao Valley.

In mid-June the battalion temporarily moved to the area north of Kontum for Operation GREELEY. There was only limited contact, and in July the battalion returned to the PERSHING AO.

In late September 1967 the 3rd Brigade and the 1st Bn, 21st Arty, moved into the I Corps Tactical Zone to relieve the 5th Marine Regiment at Hill 63, which Skytrooper units renamed LZ Baldy. This was Operation WALLOWA,

The heavy firing done by the 1st of the 21st during Operation WALLOWA built a sea of 105 mm cannisters at LZ Baldy.

the principal opponents being the 3rd and 21st NVA regiments.

On the morning of October 10, 1967, Charlie Battery at LZ Colt was attacked by sappers who broke through the perimeter wires and attempted to destroy the battery. Continuous self-illumination and direct fire by the battery during the four hour attack were instrumental in turning back the enemy.

For its operations in the period from February 1 to October 31 of 1967, the 1st Bn, 21st Arty, was awarded the Meritorious Unit Citation. The citation praised the battalion for highly responsive and effective artillery support that contributed immeasurably to the success of 3rd Brigade operations. The unit was cited for detecting and engaging well-concealed targets and consequently disrupting enemy plans and inflicting numerous casualties.

Intelligence information indicated the presence of three NVA regiments in the Hiep Duc area in November, prompting an air assault by the battalion's batteries on November 6. The battalion gave close support to the infantry in several clashes. In December intelligence reports indicated the enemy planned attacks on 3rd Brigade bases.

The intelligence was right. Early in the morning of January 2, 1968, LZ Leslie, location of Bravo Battery, was hit by 82 mm mortars, 122 mm rockets and an NVA ground attack. Alpha Battery blasted the enemy with direct fire. By dawn the Communists gave up and retreated, leaving 58 bodies behind.

LZ Leslie was attacked again later in the month. The enemy again was repulsed. For its part in stopping the NVA

The request for artillery fire has been received and fire direction center (FDC) personnel work to plot the fire mission. An FDC artilleryman used the field artillery digital computer to produce and double check the fire mission data. The information is then radioed to the battery which has been picked to deliver the high explosive support to ground troops in contact with the enemy.

attack, Bravo Battery received a Presidential Unit Citation. According to the citation, the men of the battery "exhibited profound discipline under fire, exemplary courage and a determination to defend their position regardless of personal risk." The citation said the battery's direct fire was instrumental in halting the enemy onslaught and praised the artillerymen for not seeking shelter during the attack. Those who were not manning the guns used their

rifles to pick off enemy soldiers approaching the battery's perimeter.

The Communists began their all-out Tet Offensive in January of 1968. The battalion moved to I Corps and the area around Hue in February, where its task was to support the 3rd Brigade in the liberation of Hue.

The drive into Hue was characterized by fierce, close contact. With the guns almost as exposed as the infantry, the 1st Bn, 21st Arty, continued to make things uncomfortable for the enemy.

By the time Hue was captured at the end of February the battalion had fired 52,171 rounds to support the brigade's advance.

In late October the battalion received word that it was going south. The divi-

(Continued on P. 269)

A gun crew commander talks to his firebase FDC over the radio while the gunner makes his sightings and another crewman rams a shell into the breech. The 1st of the 21st gun crew is about to fire in support of the Cav's 3rd Brigade fighting in Que Son Province.

COMMANDERS

Editor's note: List of commanders begins at the approximate time that the battalion commenced close and continuous support of the 1st Air Cavalry Division.

The shield of the 1st Battalion, 30th Artillery, has a red background, the traditional color of the artillery. The star at the top of the shield symbolizes the North Star and the regiment's World War II service in the Aleutian Islands. The two wavy lines, called "barrulets," are for the Pacific and Atlantic Ocean, indicating that the unit has seen action in lands bordering both. The dragon ("Lindwurm passant") at the bottom of the shield stands for the unit's World War II service in Germany. "Striving to the Highest" is the regiment's motto, indicating its desire to excel.

The unit was organized August 10, 1918, in the Regular Army at Camp Funston, Kansas, as Battery A, 30th Field Artillery, an element of the 10th Division. The unit was demobilized on February 5, 1919, at Camp Funston.

The battalion was reconstituted March 24, 1923, in the Regular Army. It was activated June 4, 1941, at Camp Roberts, California. On May 18, 1944, the unit was reorganized and redesignated Battery A, 521st Field Artillery Battalion. The unit was redesignated Battery A, 30th Field Artillery Battalion, on May 1, 1945. The battery was inactivated February 9, 1949, at Fort Bragg, North Carolina. It was activated February 22, 1950 at Fort Bragg.

The battalion was attached to the 23rd Artillery at Fort Lewis, Washington October 2, 1963. The battalion was attached to the 1st Cav Division February 10, 1968, and assigned to the division June 1, 1968.

The battalion participated in the Aleutian Islands, Rhineland and Central Europe Campaigns of World War II. It received the Meritorious Unit Commendation for Vietnam actions from October 1966 to September 1967, and another MUC for actions from January to September 1968. Bravo Battery won a Presidential Unit Citation for actions in Dak To in 1966.

1st BATTALION 30th ARTILLERY

A CH-54 "Flying Crane," for the first time in actual combat, lifts a 155mm medium howitzer into a fight. The gun belonged to Bravo Battalion, 30th Artillery, and the gun was being moved to LZ Brass during Operation MASHER/WHITE WING. LZ Brass was "an isolated outpost" atop a ridgeline between the An Lao Valley and the Bong Son Plain. The date was January 25, 1966.

The men and 155 mm howitzers of the 1st Battalion, 30th Artillery, left Oakland, California, on the USNS Sultan in early November 1965. On November 26 the battalion landed in the Republic of Vietnam.

In 1965 and 1966 the battalion, organic to the I Field Force, was opcon to several units. In February 1966, while working with the 1st Air Cavalry in operation MASHER/WHITE WING, the unit made history when howitzers from Bravo Battery were airlifted by CH-54 "Sky-cranes" to a mountaintop firing position, the first time that a 155 mm towed howitzer was transported by helicopter to a combat position. In 1967 the battalion was committed to the support of the division in Operation PERSHING, the longest Skytrooper action of the war. While the battalion would not become organic to the division until June 1, 1968, from PERSHING forward the two units consistently worked together.

During PERSHING the battalion fired more than 300,000 rounds, supporting the division in actions from the Bong Son Plains and the An Lao Valley to Duc Pho. Observed fires showed some 300 enemy killed by the battalion's batteries, and that was only part of the destruction of enemy personnel, positions and supplies wrought by the battalion.

For its part in Operation PERSHING, and for Charlie Battery's earlier role in Operation PAUL REVERE IV, where it accounted for 81 enemy dead when it blasted apart an NVA ambush near Cambodia, the battalion received the Meritorious Unit Citation. The battalion was praised in the citation for its efficiency in making numerous moves, for the accuracy of its fires, and for a civic action program that provided medical and dental care and hygiene training to 6,000 Vietnamese citizens.

On January 28, 1968, the battalion displaced from the II Corps Tactical Zone to I Corps and the division's new headquarters, Camp Evans. The battalion's operations were concentrated in the Hue-Phu Bai area. Alpha and Bravo Batteries landed inside the walls of Hue on February 19, and churned out 51,000 rounds in direct support of the division's 3rd Brigade as it drove the enemy from their strongholds in and around the imperial city.

The division launched Operation PEGASUS in March, aimed at relieving the beleaguered Marine base at Khe Sanh. The battalion headquarters moved to LZ Stud on March 25 with Charlie

On Thanksgiving Day 1969, the cannoneers of Charlie Battery, 1st of the 30th, were in the middle of their meal when called for a fire mission in support of infantry troops who had made contact with the enemy—as usual, the war did not observe the holiday. Old Glory, flying from an engineer stake near one of the battery's 155 mm guns, shudders in the breeze and muzzle blast put out by the hefty cannon.

pleted their operations in May.

For its performance during the Hue, Khe Sanh and A Shau operations the battalion was awarded a second Meritorious Unit Citation. The citation praised the men of the battalion for their knowledge, skill and fast accurate firepower, which "inflicted heavy losses on enemy infantry, destroyed enemy havens and supply installations and gave vital support" to maneuver elements.

In June Charlie Battery's guns combined with those of a 105 mm battery to fire on two NVA companies moving along a river west of Camp Evans. An aerial observer counted the bodies of 25 enemy.

Just before the division left I Corps for its new area of operations the battalion fired its 750,000th round since arriving in Vietnam. Charlie Battery launched the projectile from LZ Jack at an enemy bunker complex.

By November 10, 1968, all elements of the battalion had arrived in Vietnam's III Corps Tactical Zone. The batteries would now support the division as it operated north of Saigon near Cambodia, interdicting major enemy supply routes. Charlie Battery was located at Quan Loi, Bravo at LZ Rita, Alpha at Tay Ninh

Battery, which soon was blasting enemy anti-aircraft positions on route to the valley. Alpha and Bravo batteries followed in April, firing ground preparations for combat assaults of the division. In three weeks the battalion's batteries moved 10 times by air and ground and fired 20,000 rounds.

The division's next major operation was DELAWARE, the invasion of the NVA's longtime sanctuary in the A Shau Valley on the Laotian Border. Once again the 1st Bn, 30th Arty, was there. Despite frequent shellings by enemy 130 mm artillery, the battalion's Bravo and Charlie Batteries continued to provide covering fire until the maneuver battalions com-

The one millionth round to be fired in action by 1st of the 30th gunners in Vietnam stands ready for loading (above), painted and decorated for the occasion. Weighing at least 96 pounds each, one million rounds of 155 mm ammo represent some 48,000 tons of ordnance thrown against the enemy—a good portion of it fired with the heavy 155s turned down to fire point blank into attacking enemy soldiers at isolated Cav firebases. Less decorative and more businesslike shells (right) stand fused and ready for action.

and Headquarters and Headquarters Battery at Camp Gorvad, the division basecamp at Phuoc Vinh.

The battalion's first major operation in the new AO was TOAN THANG II. The 155 batteries expended more than 54,000 rounds and were credited with 75 observed enemy dead.

This period from Frebruary on would see the men of the battalion repel a number of enemy ground attacks. The first came on February 23 to Alpha Battery on LZ Grant. The battery fired 595 rounds of direct fire and killed at least 13 of the attacking enemy. Grant was hit by a bigger atack on March 8. Alpha Battery again lowered its tubes straight at the onrushing enemy. This withering fire helped account for the 39 NVA killed by artillery in the attack.

LZ Carolyn, a firebase north of Tay Ninh, came under attack on May 6,

A newly emplaced 155 mm howitzer of the 1st of the 30th sits ready to lend high explosive support from a firebase north of Tay Ninh City in III Corps, while its crew works to improve the gunpit. Bulldozers of the 8th Engineer Battalion have pushed a protective mound of dirt up around the gunpit, a circle of earth that will serve both as protection against shrapnel from enemy rockets and mortars that strike close to the gun, and also as a fighting wall where the gun crew can defend its position and howitzer should the enemy penetrate the firebase.

1969. Shortly after midnight a trip flare went off and a B-40 rocket slammed into the perimeter. The explosion was followed by many more B-40 and 107 mm rockets, then heavy small arms and automatic weapons fire as the enemy tried to overrun the LZ and succeeded in occupying six bunkers.

"There were several NVA in the bunker 10 feet to the front of our gun position," said Private First Class Jerry Peck, assistant gunner with Bravo Battery's Section 6. "Four of them began to jump over our berm, and throw satchel charges into the pit. But I killed three of them before they could make it.

"(Specialist Four Thomas D.) Pullen kept 'Charlie' off our backs with his M-16 so we could continue to pump rounds from our 155 howitzer," added Peck. The next day the PFC received the Silver Star from Major General E.B. Roberts, 1st Cav Division commander. The battery fired 597 rounds of direct fire, killing 25 of the 170 enemy who died in the attack.

On May 12 LZ Grant was attacked again, this time by an elite NVA sapper battalion. Alpha Battery's Sergeant First Class Norman A. Wilfong exposed himself

(Continued on P. 270)

A mammoth CH-54 Flying Crane begins to lift out one of Battery C's howitzers in a move from FSB Wescott to FSB Vivian to keep up with the spearheading 3rd Brigade infantry in November 1969.

Aerial view of the fortified firing position for the 105 mm howitzers of Battery B, 1st Battalion 77th Artillery, at Camp Gorvad, the 1st Cav's division basecamp in III Corps.

On the 77th Artillery insignia are five gold "fleur-de-lis" on a red background. Above is a green, prickly pear cactus on a golden-yellow background. Below is the regimental motto, "En Garde" (On Guard). The shield is red for artillery. The golden-yellow symbolizes the formation of the organization from cavalry. The cactus indicates service as cavalry on the Mexican border. The fleur-de-lis signify the five major engagements of the unit as artillery in France (WWI).

The 1st Battalion, 77th Artillery, was organized June 11, 1917, in the Regular Army as Troops A and B, 19th Cavalry, at Fort Ethan Allen, Vermont. The unit was converted, consolidated, reorganized and redesignated as Battery A, 77th Field Artillery on November 1, 1917, and assigned on November 19, 1917, to the 4th Division. The battalion was inactivated on September 21, 1921, at Camp Lewis, Washington. The unit was relieved from assignment to the 4th Division and assigned to the 7th Division on March 24, 1923.

The battalion was redesignated on July 1, 1960, as the 1st Howitzer Battalion (105/155 mm: Self-propelled), 77th Arty. The unit was assigned to the 1st Cavalry Division and activated in Korea. On September 1, 1963, the unit was reorganized and redesignated as the 1st Battalion, 77th Artillery. In July of 1965 the battalion was transferred less personnel and equipment and assigned to the newly organized 1st Cavalry Division (Airmobile).

The battalion participated in five European campaigns of World War I. In World War II the battalion had campaign credit for Sicily (with arrowhead), Naples-Foggia, Anzio, Rome-Arno, Southern France (with arrowhead), North Ardennes, Ardennes-Alsace, Rhineland, Central Europe and the Po Valley.

With the rest of the 1st Cavalry Division (Airmobile) the 1st Bn, 77th Arty, received the Presidential Unit Citation (streamer embroidered PLEIKU PROVINCE) for action in the Ia Drang Valley in 1965. Battery A's Forward Observer Section and the battalion's 3rd Liaison Section received the Valorous Unit Citation for action in March of 1967.

1st BATTALION 77th ARTILLEY

COMMANDERS

LTC Harold C. Smith . . . . .July 1965—August 1966

LTC Arthur L. Kelly . . . . .August 1966—May 1967

MAJ George P. Dawson . . . . .May 1967—November 1967

LTC James White . . . . .November 1967—June 1968

LTC Richard Thompson .June 1968—December 1968

LTC James K. Bamberry .December 1968—June 1969

LTC William J. Harrison .June 1969—December 1969

LTC Thomas J. P. Jones . . . . .December 1969—

The 1st Battalion, 77th Artillery, sailed to Vietnam on the USNS Buckner, leaving Charleston, South Carolina, in August 1965 and coming ashore at Qui Nhon, Vietnam, on September 13.

The "On Guard" battalion's first assignment in Vietnam was direct support of the 2nd Brigade in defense of the division's An Khe basecamp. Bravo Battery became the battalion's first battery to fire in support of combat operations in Vietnam when it supported offensive operations of the 101st Airborne Division in September.

In October and November of 1965 the battalion was fully committed to extended combat operations. Alpha Battery kicked off October with an air assault to support a CIDG camp, and Charlie Battery followed to support a relief-in-position.

The 77th Artillery moved out by road convoy on October 8 for what was to become a 42-day operation. The destination was Vinh Thanh Valley; the mission to aid 2nd Brigade in clearing the valley to permit reestablishment of a Special Forces camp. The combination of infantry and artillery soon drove the enemy from the valley and the camp was reestablished. The On Guard battalion also helped clear an area nearby for a base for the Republic of Korea's Tiger Division.

To the west the battle for the Ia Drang Valley in the Pleiku area had begun and the 2nd Brigade was assigned to assist the 3rd. On November 21, the 1st Bn, 77th Arty, moved to the Pleiku area of operations. Approximately 500 missions and 4,400 rounds later, enemy resistance was broken and the unit returned to An Khe on November 28 to resume base defense.

The unit's batteries spent much of December supporting the 2nd Brigade as it worked to clear the northwest sector of the division AO. It closed the year on base defense at An Khe.

The year had just begun when, on January 4, 1966, the battalion moved out in support of the 2nd Brigade's Operation MATADOR I, an eight-day operation in which the base area for the 3rd Brigade, 25th Infantry Division, was secured at Pleiku. MATADOR II began on January 12 when the 77th Artillery assaulted into two LZs west of Kontum to assist search and destroy operations along the Cambodian border.

The battalion was involved in February in its heaviest fighting to that time, when the action switched to the Bong Son area and Operation MASHER/WHITE WING. The 77th Artillery would spend over a month in this operation. Before it was over the battalion would be responsible for direct support of five infantry battalions. Not only did the unit fire 2,012 missions and 20,433 rounds, but it coordinated the reinforcing fires of 155 mm, 175 mm, 8-inch and aerial rocket artillery. During the An Lao Valley phase of the campaign the battalion fired Division Artillery's 200,000th round in Vietnam.

Through July the 77th Artillery batteries alternated between base defense and operations characterized by light contact. Increased enemy activity southeast of Pleiku in early August signaled the beginning of Operation PAUL REVERE II. The battalion was immediately deployed to western Pleiku Province to

A 1st of the 77th cannoneer quickly dispatches the slightly warm cannister from a 105 mm round just fired during a high angle mission.

A CH-47 Chinook settles into a new firebase (above) with a 105 mm howitzer for men of the 1st of the 77th "somewhere in I Corps." Radio static and ringing telephones fill the air as men (at right) in the fire direction center (FDC) handle the urgent artillery needs of troops in contact.

support the 2nd Brigade in a major campaign against the 630th NVA Division. The brigade hit heavy contact when it assaulted into the Chu Pong Massiff on the Cambodian border. The battalion fired steadily in ground assault preparations, suppressive fire, and harassment and interdiction fire. By the end of August the enemy fled across the border.

The 1st Cav Division's longest operation began in February 1967 and would last until January 1968 as Skytroopers worked in Operation PERSHING to clear the enemy from the coastal areas of II Corps, the terrain ranging from rugged hills to valleys and sandy plains. On more than half a dozen LZs south of the Bong Son River in the Phu My District the guns of the 1st Bn, 77th Arty, boomed their support for 2nd Brigade operations.

In March the battalion's 3rd Liaison Section and its forward observer section, working with the 2nd Battalion, 5th Cavalry, won the Valorous Unit Citation. The infantry battalion made heavy contact March 11 on the Bong Son

Plain. In a vicious firefight lasting throughout the night, skillfull employment of artillery enabled the wounded to be evacuated and helped reduce two NVA battalions to ineffectiveness.

While other battalion units continued their support of Operation PERSHING, Charlie Battery moved out of the PERSHING AO in September to support the 3rd Brigade in Operation WALLOWA.

In early January 1968, both Alpha and Charlie Battery were operationally controlled by the 3rd Brigade at LZ Ross. On January 2 the NVA blasted Ross with 200 82 mm mortars and 20 122 mm rockets, then launched a ground attack. The batteries decimated the enemy with direct counter-mortar fire. After the NVA retreated, 143 enemy bodies were found around the perimeter.

Later in January the Communists launched their all-out bid for power, the Tet Offensive. In February, as the 1st Cav's infantry units moved toward Hue to drive the enemy from that important city, the 2nd Battalion, 12th Cavalry, ran into stiff resistance. The unit desperately needed artillery support, therefore two howitzers from the 77th Artillery were airlifted to an ARVN camp within

range of the firefight. Although the enemy hit the camp with mortars 14 times that day, the "Redlegs" kept pumping out their rounds at the NVA.

The battalion moved to LZ Stud in April to prepare for movement to firebases south of Khe Sanh, where the batteries supported the division's drive to relieve the besieged Marine base. For those two weeks in May the battalion shifted its operations to the Dong Ha area, then moved to LZ Jane to support the 2nd Brigade in rice denial operations in the vicinity of the "Street without Joy" on Highway 1.

In June an aerial observer spotted two NVA companies in a dense jungle. Alpha Battery, combined with air strikes, poured heavy fire into the area, accounting for 25 NVA killed, The observer estimated the number of dead "perhaps closer to 80 or even 100. The ones we found were floating in the river. The others had been carried away."

Through the summer and fall of 1968 the battalion supported operation JEB STUART III, firing a total of 155,094 rounds. In October Charlie Battery moved to the III Corps AO and the rest of the battalion followed in November.

The unit's Headquarters Battery began

1969 in Quan Loi, then the 2nd Brigade basecamp. The battalion's firing battery at Quan Loi fired an average of 10 missions nightly.

Charlie Battery, stationed at LZ Grant, played a vital role in February and March in repulsing several ground attacks against the small LZ.

The worst attack came March 8. Shortly after midnight a barrage of rockets and mortars hit the base; simultaneously, two reinforced NVA battalions began their assault.

Enemy rockets, mortars, recoilless rifle and machinegun fire fell throughout the base as the NVA reached LZ Grant's barbed wire. The artillerymen cranked their howitzers down and fired point blank. Several NVA broke through the wire. Charlie Battery, firing with short fuses timed to tenths of a second, shot airbursts just above the wire. The battle rocked back and forth until first light. When it was over, 157 NVA were dead.

(Continued on P. 283)

This 1st of the 77th battery has just been landing on a mountain top near Quang Tri and is immediately called upon to shell the slopes beneath it.

ECHO BATTERY 82nd ARTILLERY

The red background of the shield of Battery E, 82nd Artillery, is the traditional color of the artillery. The dragon in the upper left box comes from the arms of the 1st Cavalry Division, the regiment's parent organization. The black projectile on the wavy bar symbolizes the shell fired by the regiment across the Rio Grande River in clearing Juarez of Villaistas on June 15, 1919. It was the regiment's first hostile shot.

COMMANDERS

MAJ David L. Carson ....July 1965—January 196•
LTC Ralph O. Benefield ....July 1966—January 196ʺ
MAJ Stuart G. McLennan ....January 1967—June 196ʺ
MAJ Edward E. Lee ....June 1967—July 196:
MAJ James H. Brown ....July 1967—December 196ʺ
MAJ Thomas J. Denny ....December 1967—April 196£
MAJ William E. Horton, Jr. ....April 1968—August 196£
MAJ D. Grieshop ....August 1968—January 196(
MAJ James R. Spears ....January 1969—May 196(
CPT Lance K. Hiltbrand ....May 1969—June 196(
MAJ Robert N. Tredway ....June 1969—July 196(
MAJ Joseph S. Davis...........................July 1969—January 197(
MAJ Chesley F. Harriman ....January 1970—

The battery was organized June 5, 1917, in the Regular Army at Fort D. A. Russell, Wyoming, as Troops I and K, 24th Cavalry. The unit was consolidated, converted, reorganized and redesignated November 1, 1917, as Battery E, 82nd Field Artillery, and concurrently assigned to the 15th Cavalry Division.

The battery was absorbed by Battery B, 82nd Field Artillery Battalion, on January 3, 1941. Battery E was reconstituted June 1, 1958. It is entitled to share history and honors of Battery B, 82nd Field Artillery Battalion, for the period from January 3, 1941, to June 1, 1958. The battery was redesignated July 31, 1959, as Headquarters and Headquarters Battery, 5th Battalion, 82nd Artillery.

Headquarters, Headquarters and Service Battery, 5th Battalion, 82nd Artillery, was reorganized and redesignated Battery E, 82nd Artillery, and concurrently transferred (less personnel and equipment) on July 1, 1965, from Korea to Fort Benning, Georgia, reorganized and assigned to the new 1st Cavalry Division (Airmobile).

The battery participated in the New Guinea, Bismarck Archipelago, Leyte (with arrowhead) and the Luzon Campaigns of World War II. In Korea the battery participated in the UN Defensive, UN Offensive, CCF Intervention, First UN Counteroffensive, CCF Spring Offensive, UN Summer-Fall Offensive and Second Korean Winter Campaigns.

The battery has been decorated with the Philippine Presidential Unit Citation (streamer embroidered OCTOBER 1944 to JULY 1945), the Republic of Korea Presidential Unit Citation (streamer embroidered WAEGWAN-TAEGU), the Chryssoun Aristion Andrias (Bravery Gold Medal of Greece) (streamer embroidered KOREA), the Presidential Unit Citation (streamer embroidered PLEIKU PROVINCE) and the Meritorious Unit Commendation (streamer embroidered VIETNAM, 1966–1967).

A light observation helicopter (LOH) of Battery E, 82nd Artillery, is silhouetted in the sun as it searches for signs of the enemy in the jungle below. The maneuverable LOH—almost like a hummingbird in its aerial actions—can often use the sun to its advantage in avoiding enemy fire. The darting LOH is hard enough to draw a bead upon, even when the sun isn't in the enemy's eyes. The battery's aircraft are used for Division Artillery reconnaissance missions.

Another of the 82nd's aircraft, the U-6 Beaver, wings off from Camp Gorvad on a cloudy day for a mission of observation. The four-seater monoplane is also used to transport personnel in the business of conducting the artillery war. Along with the Cav's OV-1 Mohawk (twin engine observation and radar aircraft) and the O-1 Bird Dog (single engine observation and spotter aircraft), the Beaver is one of the minority of fixed-wing aircraft in the primarily helicopter populated skies over "Cav Country."

The mission of Battery E (Aviation), 82nd Artillery, is to provide aerial reconnaissance, adjustment of artillery fire and command liaison for the 1st Cavalry Division (Airmobile), with secondary functions of aerial surveillance, limited resupply of artillery elements, personnel lift and medical evacuation. The battery is organic to Division Artillery (DIVARTY).

Elements of the battery began to arrive in Vietnam in August 1965. By September 30 Echo Battery pilots had logged 359 hours in 382 missions. At the time the battery's main aircraft was the OH-13 observation helicopter. The unit also had four Huey UH-1B helicopters.

Throughout the rest of 1965 the battery provided observation helicopters to support the division's artillery units in various operations. The helicopters enabled effective reconnaissance and location of targets and aerial adjustment of fires.

The most important action in 1965 was in Pleiku Province near the Cambodian border. This operation would win the entire 1st Cavalry Division the Presidential Unit Citation. During the campaign the battery's aircraft flew 1,234 hours and 2,489 sorties.

In the early days of the 82nd Artillery's deployment in Vietnam, the OH-13 helicopter served as the main observation platform for the unit's fire missions. The OH-13 first saw combat action in the Korean War, and the familiar ''Egg Beater'' filled a vital role in the Vietnam conflict before being replaced by the OH-6A ''Cayuse.''

Operation CLEAN HOUSE, a brigade-size operation in the Binh Khe area began on December 18. The operation marked the battery's first use of airplanes to supplement its mission capability. The added flexibility led the battery to request permanent assignment of fixed wing aircraft to the unit.

As 1965 ended the aviation battery had participated in three major combat operations and innumerable small unit actions. In three and a half months in the Republic, Echo Battery flew 3,076 missions, 3,564 hours and 6,737 sorties. Enemy fire damaged eight aircraft, forcing two down. Only one slight wound from enemy action was received by a member of the battery.

In 1966 the battery continued to serve as the eyes of the artillery, and to provide transportation for DIVARTY and battalion officers. The unit's request for airplanes was met with the assignment of 0-1 "Bird Dogs" giving the battery new capabilities.

The battery supported all the division's major operations in 1966, including MASHER/WHITE WING, LINCOLN, PAUL REVERE, THAYER and CRAZY HORSE.

At the commencement of Operation PERSHING on February 12, 1967, the battery moved from LZ Hammond to LZ Two Bits. During PERSHING, the longest operation in the division's Vietnam history, the battery was responsible for several of the enemy's losses on the Bong Son Plains as the aviators

With a Cav patch painted on its rudder, an 82nd Artillery 0-1 Bird Dog flies over III Corps jungle, as a high and well-forward observer, to adjust the strike of distant artillery guns.

carried out their mission of direct support for three artillery batteries and DIVARTY.

The battery also reconned in front of advancing division elements and brought DIVARTY personnel to the head of the action so better command and control would be maintained. For its performance of these assignments from November 1966 to April 1967 the aviation battery received the Meritorious Unit Commendation. The citation praised the men of the unit for their untiring devotion to duty and to the crucial role their observations played in assessing enemy strength and permitting accurate artillery fires.

During the first month of PERSHING Second Lieutenant Geoffrey Birchard won a Distinguished Flying Cross. In a fierce fight between American and NVA troops Birchard hovered and zigzagged his unarmed OH-13 over enemy positions so his observer could direct artillery fire. His helicopter was hit 11 times by enemy bullets and he and his observer were wounded but he kept flying until artillery was on target.

In the middle of June Echo Battery provided a Huey for support of the Aerial Auto Tape Survey System (AATSS) being tested by DIVARTY. The test was essential to the eventual successful use of the system.

On October 1 the 3rd Brigade was put

Both doorgunners, armed with M-60 machineguns, lean well out of their LOH, looking for enemy action as the two 82nd Artillery pilots are "tree topping it" in search of the enemy. The gunners are there primarily to protect the helicopter from enemy ground fire—a hazard particularly dangerous at such low altitudes—but they are often credited with taking on and defeating enemy ground forces which decide to engage the little and harmless looking LOH.

under the operational control of the American Division in the Chu Lai area. Echo Battery sent a direct support section of OH-13s and one Huey to work with the 1st Battalion, 21st Artillery, in Operation WALLOWA.

Operation PERSHING ended in January 1968, and the division moved to a new AO, I Corps. Echo Battery headquarters arrived at the new division basecamp, Camp Evans, on January 22. The battery's first mission in the new AO was to provide surveillance for the drive to force the enemy out of dug-in positions in and surrounding the enemy-held city of Hue.

February 28 was the day five OH-6A aircraft were received by the battery. The OH-6A, Light Observation Helicopter (LOH), with advantages in speed and maneuverabilty, would be the unit's main aircraft by the end of the year.

On October 26, 1968, the aviation battery sent its advance party south to III Corps to prepare for the battery's movement there. The main body of

Echo Battery departed Camp Evans on November 2, arriving at the division's new basecamp in III Corps, Phouc Vinh, on November 3.

Operation SHERIDAN SABRE began on November 8, 1968, to interdict movement of major enemy forces using the division's area of operations as an infiltration route. LOH sections were located in Tay Ninh, Ton le Chan and Quan Loi in support of 2nd Battalion, 19th Artillery, 1st Battalion, 77th Artillery, and 1st Bn, 21st Arty, respectively. The general support section, now consisting of four Hueys, eight LOHs and the fixed wing section, remained at Phuoc Vinh.

During the last two months of the year Echo Battery was engaged in general logistics support and aerial reconnaissance in the northwestern sector of III Corps. This action continued into early 1969, as all sections engaged in continuous flight and aerial reconnaissance south of the Cambodian border.

The battery developed a new technique

in 1969 with the "Blue Pecker" team, in which an ARA Cobra from the 2nd Battalion, 20th Artillery, combined with a battery LOH. The LOH added close observation capabilities to the Cobra's quick strike firepower. The team derived its name from the Cobra's "Blue Max" and the LOH's "Woodpecker" nicknames.

Throughout the rest of the year, the battery's efforts were concentrated in the northern part of III Corps near Cambodia. The area was one of thick jungle covering numerous bunker complexes, caches and infiltration trails. The planes and helicopters of the battery were invaluable in spotting targets and adjusting artillery fire on them with maximum effectiveness. They also enabled artillery battalion and DIVARTY officers to make frequent visits and thus keep in close personal contact with artillery batteries at firebases scattered through the combat zone.

Utilizing the aircraft of two units with entirely different missions, a LOH of E Battery, 82nd Artillery, and an aerial rocket artillery (ARA) Cobra of the 2nd Battalion, 20th Artillery, give Echo Battery its own hunter-killer teams. Nicknamed "Blue Pecker," the combination flies daily patrols against enemy infiltration along numerous trails in the III Corps jungle.

The 20th Artillery insignia shows a red background crossed diagonally by a gold bar. On the bar is a red diamond. At the bottom of the shield is a scroll with the battalion motto, "Duty Not Reward." The red is the traditional color of the artillery. The 20th Artillery won the right to bear the golden bar on the shield for its part in breaching the Hindenberg Line in 1918. The red diamond is the same design as the shoulder patch of World War I's 5th Division, to which the 20th Artillery was organic. The motto typifies the spirit of the artilleryman.

The 20th Artillery was constituted June 3, 1916, as the 20th Field Artillery in the Regular Army. The regiment was organized June 1, 1917, at Fort Sam Houston, Texas, as an element of the 5th Division. On September 5, 1921, the unit was inactivated at Camp Bragg, North Carolina.

The 20th Field Artillery was relieved from its assignment to the 5th Division on October 16, 1939, and activated June 1, 1940, at Fort Benning, Georgia, and concurrently assigned to the 4th Division (later the 4th Infantry Division). The unit was reorganized and redesignated as the 20th Field Artillery Battalion on October 1, 1940. The battalion was inactivated February 13, 1946, at Camp Butner, North Carolina.

The battalion was activated October 15, 1957, in Korea and concurrently assigned to the 1st Cavalry Division. The unit was redesignated the 2nd Rocket Howitzer Battalion, 20th Artillery, on July 1, 1960. It was redesignated 2nd Battalion, 20th Artillery, on September 1, 1963. On July 1, 1965, the battalion was transferred (less personnel and equipment) from Korea to Fort Benning, Georgia, and reorganized.

The battalion has campaign participation credit for St. Mihiel and Lorraine (1918) in World War I and for Normandy (with arrowhead), Northern France, Rhineland, Ardennes-Alsace and Central Europe in World War II.

The battalion received the Belgian Fourragere, 1940, for action in Belgium (cited in the Order of the Day for the Belgian Army) and for action in the Ardennes (cited in the Order of the Day for the Belgian Army). In Vietnam the unit received the Presidential Unit Citation (streamer embroidered PLEIKU PROVINCE) and the Valorous Unit Citation (streamer embroidered TAM QUAN).

2nd BATTALION 20th ARTILLERY

COMMANDERS

LTC Nelson A. Mahone, Jr. .... July 1965—April 1966

LTC Morris J. Brady .... April 1966—October 1966

LTC Lester C. Farwell .... October 1966—April 1967

LTC Robert B. Knowles .... April 1967—November 1967

LTC Robert M. Tyson .... November 1967—July 1968

LTC Charles Franklin .... July 1968—January 1969

LTC John H. Schnibben, Jr. .... January 1969—July 1969

LTC Jerry M. Bunyard .... July 1969—January 1970

LTC Hubert Morris .... January 1970—

The men of the world's only aerial rocket artillery battalion stepped ashore at Qui Nhon, Republic of Vietnam, on September 15, 1965. Two days later they flew their first combat mission, as Charlie Battery fired 2.75 inch rockets in support of elements of the 101st Airborne Division. Sixty-four Viet Cong were killed.

That was the enemy's first taste of the rockets of the 2nd Battalion (Aerial Artillery), 20th Artillery. At that time the rockets of this unique unit were mounted on UH-1B Huey helicopters. The battalion had the ability to provide

In the early, pre-Cobra days of aerial rocket artillery (ARA), the always paired rocket ships of the 2nd of the 20th were UH-1 Hueys.

immediate artillery fire support to airmobile units, often operating beyond the range of conventional artillery. Because the aerial artillery pilot was at the target site, his fire could be quickly adjusted for maximum accuracy and could provide extremely close fire support.

On September 18 the battalion demonstrated another new technique, the "light ship," a Huey mounted with seven landing lights. The illumination the ship provided proved extremely effective as a tool for base security. On October 3 the battalion fired the first SS-11 guided missle to be used in combat, destroying a villa and the 10 Viet Cong inside. In all, from September 17 to October 20 the battalion flew 78 missions, expended 2,870 rounds of rockets and killed 411 Viet Cong.

In late October the battalion was called upon to provide support in the Pleiku Campaign, for which the division would win the Presidential Unit Citation.

Alpha Battery saw the first major action in the campaign when Plei Me came under attack the night of October 29-30. By the light of flares dropped by the Air Force, battery pilots bombarded enemy forces assaulting and mortaring the camp. As one platoon expended its ordnance another would take its place.

The action continued until 4:30 a.m., with rockets fired within 100 meters of the friendly forces.

Charlie Battery was positioned for the campaign on a small strip on a tea plantation south of Pleiku City. On the night of November 12-13 the enemy attacked the position in battalion strength. As the first mortars hit the camp, pilots dashed to their helicopters and quickly had them all in the air, the first instance in Vietnam when all aircraft evacuated without loss from an airstrip under attack. Despite wounds, battery operations officer Captain Charlie D. Hooks and operations NCO Sergeant First Class Francis L. MaGill directed the ARA fire against the VC, who withdrew under the battery's counterattack.

Bravo Battery flew a unique mission

is the closing days of the campaign when on November 28, Special Forces requested that the battery destroy the gates of a fortified VC village. The gate's heavy timbers were protected by booby traps and weapons positions from which the enemy delivered withering fire. Three well-aimed SS-11 wire-guided missiles blasted the gates open.

In December the battalion was engaged in supporting operations from the Cambodian border to the South China Sea. Charlie Battery destroyed 56 enemy and numerous weapons emplacements on December 18, and over the next 10 days accounted for an additional 313 enemy casualties, killing 75 VC on December 22 alone.

The first major campaign of 1966 was Operation MASHER/WHITE WING

in the plains and foothills around Bong Son. The operation marked the first successful firing of the combination SS-11 missle/2.75 inch rocket weapon by Warrant Officer Robert W. Maxwell of Bravo Battery. Before, the battery's helicopters had carried one rocket or the other. By enabling the helicopters to carry both simultaneously, the new system combined the pinpoint accuracy of the SS-11 missle and the area fire superiority of the 2.75 inch rockets. This flexible and responsive system added greatly to ARA capability.

The battalion fought numerous engagements during the MASHER/WHITE WING operation. During the period from January 26 to January 31, low ceilings and reduced visibility forced the aircraft to fly at extremely low altitudes and reduced speed. Often the Hueys were at 50 feet or less. Despite their vulnerability they continued to seek out the enemy, and were credited with 100 VC killed.

Information was received on February 12 that a Viet Cong heavy machinegun was holding up the advance of infantry near Bong Son. Major Roger J. Bartholomew, Charlie Battery commander, located the 12.7 mm anti-aircraft gun, attacked it with rockets and killed all six crewmen. He then landed and captured the weapon to prevent the enemy from putting it back into service.

By the time the campaign in the Bong Son area ended, ARA inflicted 574 casualties on the VC and destroyed 157 enemy fortified positions.

Operation LINCOLN took place in March near the Chu Pong Massif on the Cambodian border. Several company-size units of the division were in heavy contact in the area where both extraction and reinforcement were difficult. At 5 p.m. ARA was committed. There were solid layers of fog and haze up to 5,000 feet, but the aircraft remained on station until 7:30 the next morning, firing 1,250 rockets to support the hard pressed troops. ARA fire killed 138 enemy in the campaign.

The battalion also began a major civil affairs program in early 1966, donating clothing, toys and sundries to villagers in the hamlet of Tu Luong, near Camp Radcliff. The program proved its effectiveness in February when a battalion helicopter crashed in the mountains south of An Khe. The villagers volunteered to search the VC-infested hills for the aircraft and its crew, and successfully located it in time to save two

The call for Cobra gunship support from troops in the field brings immediate response from the pilots of the 2nd Battalion, 20th Artillery. These pilots race to their ship and within minutes will be on station with their deadly ordnance.

seriously injured crewmen.

On May 16 the battalion commander, Lieutenant Colonel Morris Brady, and MAJ Bartholomew, the Charlie Battery commander, volunteered to fly two ARA birds in support of a company in contact and in danger of being overrun by a large VC force. They inched their aircraft through fog, rain and darkness up the slopes of a mountain peak east of An Khe, until they were hovering directly over the beleaguered company; then, directed by the artillery forward observer below, they unleashed ripple after ripple of rockets into an enemy assault force. Their timely fire support was credited by the ground commander with stablizing an extremely grave situation.

On May 22, 1966, the battalion fired its 100,000th rocket in Vietnam. The rocket was fired in support of Operation CRAZY HORSE, aimed at clearing the area around east of An Khe of VC elements planning attacks on newly pacified areas. Despite heavy anti-aircraft fire from the enemy, ARA killed 202.

Captain Frederick S. Beck of Alpha Battery was operating in the Kontum area June 11 when two 12.7 mm anti-aircraft machineguns opened fire and four armor piercing rounds tore into the helicopter, setting the rocket pods on the right side on fire. Disregarding the natural inclination to jettison the burning rockets, the irate CPT Beck swung his aircraft sharply around and emptied his remaining 41 rockets into the enemy positions, silencing them.

The battalion continued to support division operations through the summer and fall of 1966. The battalion demon-strated just how much the enemy feared its weapons on October 9. Alpha Battery received a fire mission against an enemy bunker that could not be effectively engaged with 2.75 inch rockets. Two SS-11 guided missiles were fired at the bunker; the first exploded a foot away from the one by six foot aperture. The second entered the aperture and exploded inside, destroying it. The 55 VC in the adjoining bunker decided not to test the pilot's accuracy. They laid down their arms.

At 1:05 a.m. December 27, LZ Bird was attacked by the 18th NVA Regiment and Alpha Battery responded to the call for support. Despite the night, fog and heavy rain the battery delivered a withering fire on the attacking enemy half an hour after the battle began. Charlie Battery soon joined the fight, and the aircraft stayed on station until the attack was repelled and the enemy force destroyed.

In 1967 the battalion continued a vigorous civic action program with emphasis on schools, medical aid and long range civic improvement programs. This was a joint effort with the communities providing the labor and those materials within their resources and battalion providing material and technical support.

Operation PERSHING, which was to be the division's longest operation, began in February. Its aim was to root out the enemy forces in the Bong Son Plain, An Lao Valley and the mountains adjacent to An Lao. The battalion moved its command post, with Alpha and Charlie Batteries, to LZ Two Bits.

During this period the battalion had added to its arsenal CH-47s, Chinooks armed with grenade launchers, two pods of rockets and two .50 caliber machineguns. In March a five man recon team on the ground came under heavy automatic weapons fire. Lift ships wouldn't make an extraction of the team from a sharp ridgeline obscured by clouds, so a CH-47 hovered near the ledge, which was too small to allow a landing, set its rear wheels on the ground and took the men aboard. Enemy fire made several hits but the extraction was completed successfully without injury.

The battalion continued to support Operation PERSHING actions through-out 1967. During the year the unit added the mortar aerial delivery system to its arsenal. The 81 mm mortars were used on interdiction targets with canopy cover. By the end of the year the battalion had fired 500,000 rockets since arriving

A cluster of 17-pound rocket warheads stick out of the portside pod of an ARA rocket and gunship Cobra, ready for flight.

The rockets are on their way to any enemy position (below) as the ARA Cobra, "The Blue Max," streaks down on its target at 180 knots. The target area (lower right) jumps under the rapid succession of bursting warheads.

in Vietnam.

For actions from December 6-10, 1967, the battalion won the Valorous Unit Citation. According to the citation, "the officers and men of the battalion displayed extraordinary valor in accomplishing all assigned tasks in the face of almost certain death." The battalion's aircraft flew at ground level between the division's forces and the enemy, providing a screen for the Skytroopers to withdraw so heavy artillery could destroy the enemy bunkers.

The division moved from II Corps to I Corps in 1968, meeting the enemy head on in the battle for Hue, Khe Sanh and the A Shau Valley. In numerous close firefights aerial rocket artillery blasted the enemy, foiling his plans for victory. The deadly accuracy of the SS-11 missile penetrated his bunkers and fortifications. Psychological operations leaflets used pictures of ARA aircraft to frighten enemy soldiers into surrendering.

Men of the battalion pulled off a daring rescue of surrounded Cavalrymen east of Khe Sanh during the operation to relieve the Marine base. Crew members of Captain Charles D. Dorr's ship spotted two wounded men on the ground. Despite the presence of the enemy CPT Dorr salvoed all his rockets to make his ship lighter, and set his helicopter on the edge of a bomb crater. The crew dragged the wounded men to the helicopter and took off, while supporting rocket fire hit within 30 meters of the

aircraft. All three members of the crew received the Silver Star for their action.

During the assault into the A Shau Valley in May another ARA pilot earned the Silver Star. Warrant Officer Clint Stanley was flying in support of a unit being airlifted into the valley when his chopper came under intense enemy fire. Several times anti-aircraft explosions rocked the helicopter as it made firing runs on the enemy. After expending all his ammunition Mr. Stanley continued flying over the area, making low level dummy passes that kept the enemy pinned down, enabling the Skytroopers to be successfully airlifted.

Later in May, Alpha Company, 2nd Battalion, 7th Cavalry, forces were only a short distance from wounded men, but unable to reach them because of an overwhelming barrage of enemy automatic weapons fire. Because of the close proximity of the enemy troops to the American forces, the ARA ships of Captain David J. Whitlinh and Major Daniel J. Delaney flew at a much lower than normal altitude, laying down a heavy volume of rockets that permitted the evacuation of the wounded.

During 1968 the battalion made the transition between Huey ARA ships and the AH-1G Cobra. Unlike the Huey, the Cobra was specifically designed for fire support, and carried firepower equivalent to that of three conventional

(Continued on P. 281)

AVIATION

11th GENERAL SUPPORT COMPANY

The 11th General Support Aviation Company was constituted and activated on March 1, 1957, in Germany as the 11th Aviation Company, an element of the 11th Airborne Division.

It was inactivated on July 1, 1958, in Germany and transferred to the control of the Department of the Army.

On February 1, 1963, it was redesignated as the 11th General Support Company and assigned as an organic element of the 11th Air Assault Division.

The next day the unit was activated at Fort Huachuca, Arizona.

On July 1, 1965, the company was released from its assignment to the 11th Air Assault Division and assigned to the 1st Cavalry Division (Airmobile).

The 11th General Support Aviation Company received a Meritorious Unit Commendation for the period September 1965 to November 1966.

On August 19, 1965, the advance party of the 11th General Support Aviation Company landed at Nha Trang, Republic of Vietnam. It moved to An Khe and began clearing the area in preparation for the rest of the company, which was to arrive at Qui Nhon on September 17.

On September 18, a UH-1D Huey flown by Captain Gerald Burns and Chief Warrant Officer Gilbert D. Scheff made the first combat assault mission of the division, to relieve an American force pinned down by heavy enemy fire.

The company, with 509 assigned personnel, fullfills an important mission in the division, "providing aviation support for the division headquarters, 11th Aviation Group Headquarters, DISCOM and other units without organic aircraft." What that means is that 11th GS

cranks up at least seven Hueys daily to ferry around the division's skies such personages as the division commander, the two assistant division commanders, the aviation group commander, the DISCOM commander, not to mention the division's chief of staff and his G-2 and G-3.

And that's just the part played by the UH-1H folks. The light observation helicopter pilots handle such diverse tasks as carrying the division liaison officers from the division to corps headquarters and back; transport visitors for the protocol and information offices and generally make themselves handy to anyone who wants or needs a bird.

For its outstanding performance of duty from September 1965 to November 1966, the 11th GS Company received the Meritorious Unit Commendation.

Until late summer of 1969, 11th GS was the parent unit for the Aerial Surveillance and Target Acquisition Platoon (ASTA), which consisted of several OV-1B/C Mohawks. The "Hawks" were transferred by theater order to Vung Tau, where they now support the Cav on the same basis as do the Flying Cranes. The transfer was, in reality, a paper transaction, because ever since the Cav arrived in III Corps, the flying portion of the ASTA platoon had been stationed in Vung Tau.

During Operation PERSHING, the ASTA platoon was brought forward to Bong Son, and when the Cav moved to I Corps in February 1968, it moved along, too, and, for a period, was reasonably close to the division's main area.

But then came the move to III Corps and a gradual divorcement of the platoon from the company.

The 11th General Support Aviation Company now, as always, is devoting itself to providing the best aviation support possible. And they have done just that. The devotion to duty and efficiency of the officers and men of the unit has made the "Angry Hornets" a respected name throughout the 1st Air Cavalry Division.

One of the many helicopters supplied and maintained for the 1st Cav Division by its 11th General Support Company is this UH-1H Huey, the division commanding general's personal "command and control" helicopter.

SPECIAL PURPOSE AIRCRAFT

A Nighthawk team (above) takes off at dusk to begin its night mission around Camp Gorvad. The special Huey is armed with a minigun and a powerful night-probing searchlight, and is backed up by the rocket artillery of the accompanying "Blue Max" Cobra from 2nd of the 20th. A closer view of the special Huey (right) shows Specialist Four Harold W. Boatz manning the 50,000 watt searchlight and starlight scope with the minigun (operated by another gunner) to his right. Another special purpose aircraft operated by the 11th GSC (below right) is the Iroquois Night Fighter and Night Tracker (INFANT). The INFANT's rotating miniguns and fixed rocket pods are aimed through infrared cameras which give the pilot a daylight-like television picture of the terrain—and the enemy—in the dark of night. At lower left is one of the two identical weapons mounts on the INFANT: infrared camera, minigun and rocket pod. The camera swings with the minigun to pick up the jungle area "illuminated" by the infrared searchlights mounted on the ship's nose.

The crest of the 227th Assault Helicopter Battalion pictures a tern against the background of a red arrowhead. The tern, one of the fastest flying birds, denotes the speed of the battalion's attack; and the arrowhead is representative of the accuracy of the attack.

At the bottom of the crest is the battalion's motto, "Pouvoir," meaning "Able To."

227th ASSAULT HELICOPTER BATTALION

COMMANDERS

LTC Jack Cranford .... July 1965—July 1966

LTC A. T. Pumphrey .... July 1966—November 1966

LTC James F. Hamlett .... November 1966—June 1967

LTC George C. Horton .... June 1967—November 1967

LTC Willie F. Dixon .... November 1967—June 1968

LTC George R. Thayer .... June 1968—December 1968

LTC Edward Couington III .... December 1968—June 1969

LTC Willard M. Bennett, Jr. .... June 1969—December 1969

LTC David Johnson , ... December 1969—

Originally the 31st Transportation Company, the unit was enlarged and redesignated the 227th Assault Helicopter Battalion, an element of the 11th Air Assault Division, in 1963.

On July 1, 1965, the battalion was reorganized, relieved from assignment to the 11th Air Assault Division and reassigned to the 1st Cavalry Division (Airmobile).

The battalion was awarded the Presidential Unit Citation in the Republic of Vietnam for the Pleiku Campaign. It also earned a Meritorious Unit Commendation for the period October 1965 to November 1966.

The aircraft carrier Boxer had special cargo aboard as it neared Qu Nhon in September 1965. Among the aircraft aboard were the helicopters o the 227th Assault Helicopter Battalion the world's first such unit.

The "Pouvoir" (Able To) men soo cleared a landing area out of the dens jungle growth near An Khe in the centra highlands of the Republic of Vietnam and helped establish the world's larges heliport.

The battalion had arrived in Vietnam —soon to write new chapters in the his tory of the FIRST TEAM, the Army' first airmobile division.

The 227th is divided into four com panies. Company D's gunships fl support for the lift ships of the other thre companies, as well as special missions such as "Nighthawk."

Throughout such operations as th Pleiku Campaign, NATHAN HALE PAUL REVERE, THAYER and BYRD the 227th proved that airmobility is a vital factor in the success of the Army' most successful division in Vietnam, th 1st Cavalry.

In fall of 1965 the battalion parti cipated in the Pleiku Campaign, airliftin troops into the rugged province nea Cambodia, often in the face of heav enemy resistance.

During the campaign, the 227th air lifted the equivalent of 65 infantry com panies, flying a total of 6,066 sorties With the rest of the division, the bat talion received a Presidential Uni Citation for this operation.

Throughout 1965 and 1966 the bat talion provided integral support an

Lift ships of Company C, 227th Assault Helicopter Battalion, carry Skytroopers of Bravo Company, 2nd Battalion, 12th Cavalry, into a landing zone during Operation NATHAN HALE in July 1966.

Company C, 227th lift ships drop 1st Battalion, 5th Cavalry, troopers into the An Lao Valley (left) during Operation MASHER in February 1966.

A Cobra gunship pilot (center left) checks the sky above him as he lifts off from an airstrip while departing on a support mission.

A 227th lift ship heads in for a jungle clearing on a combat assault (below center) as a white phosphorous artillery shell explodes ahead, signalling the end of the artillery prep of the landing zone.

transportation for the division, developing new techniques and perfecting old ones to meet the challenging conditions in the Republic of Vietnam. For its outstanding air support the battalion received the Meritorious Unit Commendation.

No one who has been to Vietnam need be told that war and combat is a serious business that wears and grinds both body and mind. But like everything else, it has its moments of humor, relief and counterpoint—sorely needed moments. So it was that the Great Helicopter Race took

Delta Company's Cobra gunships serve as escort for the Huey lift ships enroute to a combat assault, flying in flanking formation (bottom), and then dive ahead to strafe and rocket the landing zone as the troop-laden Hueys descend to the assault. The Cobras and their firepower fill the gap between the end of the artillery prep and the actual Huey lift birds' touch down. And they also provide cover for the assaulting troops after the Hueys lift out.

place while Lieutenant Colonel Jack Cranford, a master Army aviator, was commanding the 227th. It was mid-March 1966.

In those pre-Cobra days of combat assault, the UH-1 Huey filled the role of gunship escort, fitted with rocket pods and front-firing 7.62 mm machineguns. As an escort gunship the Huey had but one drawback; it could fly no faster than the Huey slicks it was escorting and could therefore make only one or two gun passes on the LZ as the troop-carrying Hueys dipped in to land.

To boost the Huey gunships' speed, the Army had the ships fitted with new, extra-width rotor blades designed to take a bigger bite out of the air and add speed with the same engine power. The change worked well. The gunship Hueys were significantly faster than before.

Pleased with his high-speed Hueys, LTC Cranford offered a challenge to Lieutenant Colonel Max Clark, then commander of the 228th Assault Support Helicopter Battalion, the Cav's fleet of mighty CH-47 Chinook helicopters.

The Chinooks (then known as Max's Mobile Homes), big and ungainly looking aircraft, give an appearance that belies their speed. LTC Clark, proud of his ships and his pilots, duly accepted the gauntlet from Cranford.

The race was set over a 10-mile course, a straight flight between Mang Yang Pass in the mountains west of An Khe and the flight control tower at the An Khe airstrip. It would be a race against the clock with one of LTC Cranford's modified, speedy Hueys getting first

With the landing zone of a combat assault secured and declared "green," a Skytrooper guides in the birds of the secondary lifts. Soldiers on the chopper stand on the skids ready to hop off as soon as the chopper nears the ground. Why? Because a "green" LZ can quickly turn into a "hot" one, so the helicopters are not unnecessarily risked by allowing them to linger on the ground in unfriendly territory.

Whipping up a small gale, lift ships of the 227th arrive at a firebase to take on a load of infantrymen for a combat assault into the III Corps jungle. Another mission begins.

crack at the course. Men were stationed at the mountain pass, including an Army radio reporter who gave the auspicious event live coverage through the radio station at An Khe.

There was more at stake than a contest between aircraft. Unit pride was, of course, involved, and a rumor had it that the two commanders had also made a wager on the race—the loser to buy a round of beer for the winner's battalion. That was a lot of suds. Attention was high.

Both colonels were at the An Khe tower, and each had a stopwatch in his hands. A third clock was kept by Colonel Al Burdett, 11th Group commander. As the Huey lifted off from the pass and nosed over into a high-speed profile toward An Khe, the clocks were started by word from an RTO atop the pass. The unseen Huey became a speck in the distance, grew quickly and then flashed by the tower. Three colonels mashed their watch buttons and marked the time. It was a good time; a fast, classified time.

At Mang Yang Pass the Chinook cranked its rotors and lifted into the mountain sky, all noise and wind. The Huey hare had run. What looked like a city bus was taking off.

The pilot pointed the Chinook's nose for An Khe and opened up with everything the Chinook had in her. As he barrelled down on what he thought was An Khe, the Chinook pilot knew his

time would be good, very good. The colonels sat immobile, watching the approaching Chinook speck grow larger. The radio commentator filled air time with words about the two aircraft while he, too, watched for the Chinook.

At first, no one noticed it, but it was soon apparent that the distant dot of the Chinook was not getting any bigger at all. It was, in fact, getting smaller. The pilot was lost. He was not headed anywhere near An Khe.

After a few long seconds spent frantically checking his map against terrain features, the pilot quickly discovered his navigational error and swung the pounding Chinook back toward An Khe and the awaiting colonels.

The Chinook lumbered on, drew near and big and finally thundered past the tower. LTC Clark smiled. LTC Cranford grunted.

The Chinook had bettered the Huey's time by "a significant number of seconds," even though the pilot had lost time in wandering off course.

LTC Clark and his Chinook crew professed to be possessed by a great thirst. The Great Helicopter Race was over.

Operation PERSHING in 1967 presented new problems to the airmobile division as it rooted out the enemy from Binh Dinh Province. But the Cav and the 227th didn't expect to go where the going was easy.

The mountainous terrain surrounding the plain, with its inherent clouds and heavy rainfall, made low-level flying through the valleys a necessity. Ceiling and visibility were often reduced to zero.

"It was a different war then," said Major Edward Colburn, deputy commander of the 11th Aviation Group, who commanded Company B of the 227th Assault Helicopter Battalion during his first tour in Vietnam with the Cav. "There were more enemy, more contact and more aircraft shot at and hit; and all of these problems were compounded many times over by the weather conditions."

In those days airmobile operations were generally large. "I once led a 64-aircraft lift going into the Bong Son," reminisced MAJ Colburn, "but you don't see anything like that anymore."

On January 31, 1968, a member of the 227th distinguished himself under heavy enemy fire. Chief Warrant Officer Frederick E. Ferguson, commander of a resupply helicopter, monitored an emergency call from the wounded passengers and crew of a downed helicopter under heavy attack within the enemy-held imperial city of Hue. He unhesitatingly volunteered to go in and attempt evacuation. Despite warnings for all aircraft to stay away from the area due to heavy anti-aircraft fire, Mr. Ferguson headed in.

He began a low level flight at maximum speed along the Perfume River toward the tiny, isolated South Vietnamese Army compound in which the crash survivors had taken refuge. Coolly and skillfully maintaining his course in the face of intense, short-range fire from enemy occupied buildings and boats, he displayed superior flying skill and courage by landing his craft in an extremely confined area under heavy mortar and small arms fire.

Although the helicopter was severely damaged by mortar fragments during the loading of the wounded, Mr. Ferguson disregarded the damage, and, taking off through the continuing hail of mortar fire, he flew his crippled ship on the return route through the rain of fire that he had experienced earlier and returned his passengers to friendly control.

For his gallantry, Mr. Ferguson received an interim award of the Silver Star, and, one year later, became the first Army aviator to win the Medal of Honor.

Operation DELAWARE brought the 1st Cav into the A Shau Valley, a slit in the mountains near the Laotian border which the NVA considered as a sanctuary. No Allied forces had penetrated the valley since 1966, when a Special Forces camp closed.

Much of the success of the operation was due to the men of the "Garry Owen" Brigade. And they, in turn, owed a large debt of thanks to the men of the 227th Assault Helicopter Battalion.

Entering the A Shau brought many, but not unexpected, problems to the pilots of the 227th's helicopters. With a large concentration of enemy troops in the area, a large volume of ground to air fire was expected. The NVA had 37 mm anti-aircraft guns, capable of hitting an aircraft at 25,000 feet. Numerous .50 caliber machinegun emplacements added a wall of red tracers for the helicopters to penetrate.

Aside from the enemy there were other problems. The valley, nestled among the high peaks, was constantly overcast with heavy cloud cover, and rain and heavy fog were commonplace.

To counter these hazards the pilots adopted new flight tactics. Contour flying became the rule of the day. A dangerous maneuver, the low-level flight tested and proved the skill of the pilots.

The same tactics proved worthwhile

(Continued on P. 269)

As Skytroopers file off the Company B lift bird, the doorgunner watches the debarkation to be sure everyone is safely clear of the helicopter before telling the pilot he is "clear" to take off. Since neither pilot is in a position to see to the rear of his ship, both doorgunners on the bird's flanks must act as their pilot's eyes, telling him when the tail rotor is dangerously near trees or jungle growth in a tight LZ.

228th ASSAULT SUPPORT HELICOPTER BATTALION

On April 26, 1966, the United States Institute of Heraldry granted the 228th Battalion its blazon, based on an original crest designed by Captain David L. Boivin in January of 1964.

The crest depicts Pegasus, the winged horse of Greek mythology, a symbol of the strength and stamina of the battalion. It is placed between four silver stars on a field of blue. The four stars are indicative of the unit's world wide deployment.

LTC Benjamin S. Silver .... July 1965—November 1965
LTC Max. A. Clark .... November 1965—July 1966
LTC Robert A. Michelson..................... July 1966—February 1967
LTC Frank W. Nadeau, Jr. .... February 1967—August 1967
LTC Robert C. Kerner .... August 1967—January 1968
LTC Richard Speedman .... January 1968—June 1968
LTC Dean R. Paquette .... June 1968—December 1968
LTC David D. Dukes .... December 1968—June 1969
LTC Emory W. Bush .... June 1969—November 1969
LTC Lawrence C. Davis .... November 1969—December 1969
LTC Francis J. Toner .... December 1969—

A 228th Chinook lifts into a late afternoon sky (top). A sister ship stirs up a dust storm delivering an artillery piece in the field (above), and a third "hook" is gently settled into a hover over riggers (left) to take on a sling load of ammo.

A 228th Chinook hitches a ride (above) aboard an aircraft carrier in the division's move from I to III Corps in December 1968. The big Chinook sports a full bank of instruments (right) and keeps pilots busy. Despite its great bulk, the Chinook mission demands precision flying skills to gently bring the cargo hook within reach of a ground rigger (center left) without knocking him over. The Chinook crew chief oversees maintenance on the ground, and in flight he serves to keep an eye peeled on the sling loads (two center) through "the hole." A waist gunner (center right), one of two on each "hook" watches dawn paint III Corps with a promise of heat. Both gunners must have sharp eyes and quick reactions to out-gun enemy anti-aircraft gunners who would, given the chance, down the hook. When not delivering artillery or supplies (bottom right), the big hooks also ferry full platoons of infantry (bottom left) to the fighting.

The 228th Assault Support Battalion was constituted on February 1, 1963, as part of the 11th Air Assault Division.

On July 1, 1965, the battalion was again reorganized and relieved from assignment to the 11th Air Assault Division and assigned to the 1st Cavalry Division (Airmobile).

The cargo and troop transport helicopters of the 228th Assault Support Helicopter Battalion—the CH-47 Chinooks —are the workhorses of the 1st Air Cavalry Division. Major General John Norton, former commanding general of the division, said, "We move with the 'hooks.' The hooks are the key to our mobility of firepower. They can do anything."

The mighty CH-47 Chinooks seemingly can do anything; but it can never be forgotten that nothing they do would be possible without the hard work and devotion to duty so characteristic of the men of the battalion.

The first Chinook departed the USNS Boxer on September 11, 1965. Sixty-nine hours later the last Chinook on board departed, and the airlift from Qui Nhon to the division's new base at An Khe had started.

During the month of October the battalion supported the division in Operation SHINY BAYONET.

During the Pleiku Campaign the Chinooks lifted the equivalent of 67 artillery batteries. The 28th flew a total of 7,692 sorties, delivering 6,852 tons of supplies into forward LZs.

During their first three and one-half months in the Republic of Vietnam, the men of the battalion were awarded 772 Air Medals, proof of the long hours and dedication of the "Winged Warriors."

General William C. Westmoreland visited the 228th during the Christmas holidays and praised the men for their hard work. "The Chinook has added a new dimension to the battlefield heretofore unthought of in Vietnam. To be able to move an entire artillery battalion by air was a tremendous stride in defeating the VC."

The first six months of 1966 were ones of experience and innovation, and the last half of the year was one of industry and refinement. During this period the artillery raid was born. A standardized procedure for downed aircraft was conceived and infusion and exchange programs came into being.

The artillery raid technique marked a

departure from tactical and terrain limitations on artillery support that had fettered field commanders in the American Civil War and the Korean War alike. In both of those conflicts, despite the vast differences in technology they represented, commanders knew that they could not rely on close artillery support for their troops unless there were good roads in the battle area over which they could tow the ponderous guns. When the 228th began operations in Vietnam with the Chinook it broke that age-old restriction; roads were no longer needed because light and medium artillery, the latter moved by CH-54 Flying Cranes, could go virtually anywhere the airmobile foot soldier could go. And it could get there with the speed of flight. Artillery was no longer ground-bound.

Beginning in March 1966 the Chinooks were also used in an innovative technique of making combat assaults into the extremely thick jungles of Bong Son. The technique required much coordination. First the chosen spot was heavily bombed by tactical air support jets. A small team then rappelled from Hueys to the jungle floor through the small opening in the canopy left by the air strikes. When the team had secured

As 8th Engineer Battalion soldier-engineers guide a new bridge span into place, the Chinook—at the hands of a pilot with surgeon-like precision—lowers the bridge onto its abutments. The Chinook has saved countless man hours of labor in construction and repair.

Cavalrymen about to board a 228th Chinook for transport turn their heads away from the maelstrom of dust and dirt stirred by the the 100-knot wind which descends from the hook's huge rotors. The troops are about to go into action near An Khe.

the area the Chinooks of the 228th arrived, hovered just above the jungle opening and lowered ladders to the ground. The queue of combat laden troops flapped in the breeze of the Chinook rotors, clinging to the rungs of the flexible ladder as they descended to the ground.

The "hook ladder," an invention of the 1st Brigade's deputy commander, Lieutenant Colonel Harlow Clark, was found to be a successful technique and was used by elements throughout the Cav wherever the terrain was appropriate.

During the latter half of 1966, the battalion was called upon to participate in civic action projects. Many strange loads resulted. Cattle and horses were rounded up and corraled in the Chinooks. Tons of rice and grain were transported. Refugees were moved. On one occasion, due to an impending attack on a Vietnamese village, a record of 162 refugees were transported in one sortie—by one Chinook—out of the danger area.

In recognition for the outstanding job done by the battalion since its arrival in the Republic of Vietnam, the 228th Assault Support Helicopter Battalion received the Meritorious Unit Commendation for the period September 1, 1965, to October 31, 1966.

The battalion's work load for the year speaks for itself in the grand totals column. More than 150,000 passengers were carried, more than 75,000 tons of cargo delivered and better than 64,000 sorties were flown with nearly 22,000 flight hours on the birds.

Firmly established as the movers of the division, the 228th continued its outstanding service through the next years, Even though the battalion was flying long hours under all weather conditions, it repeatedly set safety records. Time and again the battalion recorded more than 20,000 flying hours without an accident.

In 1968 the division fought many important battles, at Hue, Khe Sanh and the A Shau Valley. Chief Warrant Officer Frederic L. Wilken, a pilot with 228th Assault Helicopter Battalion in 1969, was also in Vietnam during March-November 1968.

During the siege of Khe Sanh, Mr. Wilken was one of many 228th pilots who flew into the embattled base to haul out Marine Corps supplies and equipment in preparation for the Marine evacuation. Stopping at Khe Sanh even for a momentary hover brought enemy 175 mm artillery shells whistling in from across the DMZ. "When we went in to pick up a sling load the shelling would start," said Wilken, "so we had to sling the loads ourselves—the crew chief would hop out, attach the sling to our hook and then hop back inside. The Marines couldn't be standing around on the hook pad when we came in because we always brought enemy artillery fire with us, so the Marines prepared the sling loads and then stayed in the bunkers—which was sensible."

In October 1968 the battalion moved with the rest of the division to the III Corps Tactical Zone, where the 1st Cav was given the mission of blocking enemy infiltration routes.

In August of 1969, Lieutenant Colonel Emory W. Bush, battalion commander, received an award from the Boeing Corporation, makers of the CH-47 Chinook, for the unit's completion of 100,000 flying hours in Vietnam. The 228th was the first battalion to reach this mark.

Just two months later the battalion

(Continued on P. 268)

149

The 229th Assault Helicopter Battalion was constituted on March 18, 1964, and activated the next day as part of the 11th Air Assault Division (Test) at Fort Benning, Georgia.

The battalion was reorganized on July 1, 1965, concurrently relieved from assignment to the 11th Air Assault Division and reassigned to the 1st Cavalry Division (Airmobile).

In Vietnam, the battalion received a Presidential Unit Citation for the Pleiku Campaign, and the Meritorious Unit Commendation for the period September 1965 to November 1966.

"Stacking the deck" in a card game usually results in a winning hand. The same is true with the 1st Air Cavalry Division's "Stacked Deck" battalion— the 229th Assault Helicopter Battalion. Due to its performance, the battalion is constantly dealing itself a winning combination.

The first aircraft of the 229th landed on Vietnamese soil at Qui Nhon on September 13, 1965. The next day they began the move to An Khe, where an advance party had already been clearing land in preparation for the building of the battalion area.

Although the unit had not planned or packed to immediately conduct combat operations upon its arrival in Vietnam, a warning order was received on September 18 to assemble available aircraft, which consisted of 13 UH-1Ds and two UH-1Bs, to support operations of the 1st Brigade, 101st Airborne Divison, in the area northwest of Qui Nhon.

Very little protective equipment was available to the crews. Gunners had not yet been assigned for lift ships—cooks, clerks and communications personnel were being used—newly assigned pilots were not adequately trained in formation flying and operations in and out of relatively confined areas. However, the battalion made three lifts on the 18th and 19th of September into the combat area carrying personnel and ammunition. All the aircraft returned safely with no casualties.

The battalion was soon operating to full capacity and realizing its missions of providing tactical mobility for combat troops and transporting supplies and equipment to units of the division during airmobile combat operations. The battalion proved able to provide continuous support (day and night) during

229th ASSAULT HELICOPTER BATTALION

WINGED ASSAULT

The insignia of the 229th Assault Helicopter Battalion is dominated by a lightning bolt, indicative of the swiftness of the strike capabilities of the unit. The lightning bolt travels from upper left to lower right, showing the association of the unit with the 1st Cavalry Division.

In the lower left, against a blue background, is a silver sword, denoting combat.

At the bottom of the crest is the battalion motto, "Winged Assault."

LTC Robert S. Keller	July 1965—July 1966
LTC Leo D. Turner	July 1966—December 1966
LTC John M. Blair	December 1966—May 1967
LTC John E. Bell	May 1967—May 1968
LTC Gene E. Brown	May 1968—June 1968
LTC Charles A. Dawdy	June 1968—December 1968
LTC Quay C. Snyder	December 1968—August 1969
LTC Arthur F. W. Liebel	August 1969—

A Company D Cobra pilot heads back toward Tay Ninh and the Black Virgin Mountain at mission's end (top left). With the troops off-loaded and clear (top right), a Company C, 229th pilot pulls pitch to lift off and out of the way of following birds. On ships of the 229th flying in staggered double column formation (above center), another combat assault goes into the III Corps jungle. One of the most comforting of sights for a "grunt," or infantryman, is the heavily armed Cobra (above left), flying over his jungle position. Another lift bird off-loads infantrymen in a clearing, an action repeated several times a day, seven days a week, in what has been called "the most advanced form of combat assault" for jungle warfare.

marginal visual and weather conditions.

As more aircraft became available and more crews were trained, the battalion increased its combat operations in the An Khe area and the Song Con "Happy Valley," to the east. By the beginning of October 1965, brigade-size operations were becoming common with all the resources of the 229th in support. The first combined operation began on October 10, Operation SHINY BAYONET, with the battalion in support of the 3rd Brigade. The battalion flew a total of 2,405 sorties, lifted 3,655 troops and 81 tons of cargo.

The Pleiku Campaign began on October 23, 1965, and proved to be a severe test of the battalion's capabilities. The battalion assumed the mission of directly supporting the division's commitment of brigades in the Plei Me tactical zone and remained in direct support until November 26. During that period the 229th airlifted the equivalent of 128 infantry companies. A total of 10,840 sorties were flown and, although 14 aircraft were hit by hostile fire and two shot down none were lost permanently. During the heavy fighting of November 14-18 the battalion's lift ships provided the bulk of medical evacuation under heavy enemy fire.

In mid-December 1965 the 229th battalion was called upon to air assault division infantry units into the vicinity of Binh Khe, Binh Dinh Province. The assault was typical of battalion operations. On the basis of maps, photos and aerial reconnaissance, the sites for the assault were chosen. For the 1st Battalion, 8th Cavalry, one of the units the 229th would carry, the objective was a small hill rising 50 feet above the surrounding rice paddies. Two LZs were chosen in the area immediately north of the objective.

The 229th brought the first infantry company in on schedule. When a gunship covering the assault was shot down south of the objective, the lift ships changed LZs and brought the second company in near the gunship to enable the rescue of the crew. Enemy fire was heavy, and almost every helicopter was hit at least once, but none was put out of action. Lieutenant Colonel Robert Kellar, 229th commander, brought his ship down to pick up the injured crew. The third infantry company was landed at the pre-planned LZ. Despite periodic heavy rain, and unexpected change in plans and heavy enemy fire, the 229th had performed in an outstanding

manner. According to the infantry battalion commander, it "was an excellent example of the flexibility of airmobility, in execution and in the mental agility of its commanders."

In the beginning of 1966 the 1st Air Cavalry was underway at full throttle in its fight against the Communist forces in the highlands. The helicopter pilots soon learned during Operations MASHER and WHITE WING that carrying troops into low areas resulted in receiving much ground to air fire. The division soon changed its tactics, dropping the Cavalrymen on the high ground to avoid enemy gunners.

Throughout 1966 the 229th Assault Helicopter Battalion supported the division, and especially the 1st Brigade, in such operations as NATHAN HALE, PAUL REVERE and BYRD. The battalion performed in an outstanding manner, flying thousands of sorties to carry troops and supplies to the battle zones.

Daily combat assaults became numerous, with Company C setting a record of 40 "Charlie Alphas" during one week of Operation BYRD.

In 1967 the battalion supported Operation PERSHING, aimed at clearing the enemy from populous eastern Binh Dinh Province. Ground to air fire was

frequent from enemy occupying well-entrenched positions.

In November 1967 one of the battalion's Huey crews came to the rescue of a stranded Chinook. The Chinook was out of fuel on the west end of Dak To airfield during a mass mortar and ground attack.

Another Chinook had gone in ahead to drop a bladder of fuel. "I was carrying the pump," said Warrant Officer Marian F. Clemens, "and as I landed the mortars were being walked toward us. I told the Chinook to get out, and as he left the mortars started walking back the other way." An ammo dump had been hit and there were explosions all around.

"It took us about 25 minutes to pump all the fuel out of the bladder," said Clemens, "but the Chinook got out without a scratch." Mr. Clemens received the Distinguished Flying Cross and his three crew members Bronze Stars with "V" device.

The year 1968 brought two severe tests to the men of the 1st Air Cavalry. In February, the enemy's Tet Offensive began. Then came the operations in the A Shau Valley, a known enemy stronghold.

During these campaigns Skytroopers exacted huge losses on the enemy, and the 229th was no exception. During the

period of February through June, 112 men of Company B alone were recommended for heroism awards.

In early 1968 battalion Hueys flew Marines in their first air assault in "skids" ships. In a hair-raising ride the helicopters of Bravo Company whizzed in at treetop level and zig-zagged in between trees to avoid enemy ground fire. "It was pretty wild," said one Marine sergeant. Others marvelled at the hot food the 229th flew them daily. "I think I'm joining the Army," said one squad leader.

The flying methods of the battalion may have seemed unusual to the Marines, but they didn't prevent the battalion from setting a record of 17,000 acident free hours flown from April 16, 1967, to March 31, 1968, in combat assaults and combat support operations.

Throughout its history the 229th Assault Helicopter Battalion has flown missions other than the normal troop carrying and logistical resupply missions. Among these are sniffer, cordon, nighthawk and "lightning bug."

The lightning bug mission was used to great success in the Cav's area of operations in the highlands and I Corps.

It was developed to prevent the enemy from using the many rivers and streams in the area as a means of infiltration. As one aircraft flew at high level, dropping flares over the rivers, a low bird with a .50 caliber machinegun flew at low level, skimming over the water and trees, looking for enemy soldiers exposed in the bright light of the flares.

The lightning bug missions developed into the Nighthawk mission of III Corps. Heavily armed UH-1H Hueys, with powerful searchlights and special starlight scopes, search for the enemy in the dense jungle of the III Corps area. Supported by an AH-1G Cobra, these missions proved again the advantages of airmobility.

With the "exodus" to III Corps complete in late 1968, the division found new tactics were necessary to engage and destroy the enemy. Whereas the enemy often worked in large groups in the highlands, Cavalrymen soon discovered that the enemy moved and fought in smaller units in the bamboo jungles of III Corps.

In III Corps several battalion helicopters were assigned a new task, psychological operations. The main PSYOPs "weapons" were leaflets and 1,000 watt loudspeakers, audible at 2,500 feet. The leaflets and speakers urged the enemy to switch sides and villagers in VC territory to flee to the government. The PSYOPs choppers were central to the 2nd Brigade's success in attracting several hundred ralliers in Phuoc Long Province.

First Lieutenant Samuel R. Manning, Jr., of 229th's Company A, was flying a command and control helicopter near Song Be when he saw a LOH, riddled by enemy fire, go down in hostile territory. In the face of a hail of fire from enemy guns LT Manning brought his ship down to pick up the LOH's crew and the men from a second downed LOH. A blanket of M-60 fire from doorgunners Private First Class Thomas Perkins and Specialist Four Thomas C. Dixon provided the necessary cover to make the rescues successful. The two doorgunners and the pilot received valor awards for the action.

Throughout 1969 the battalion provided support for the division's 1st Brigade in Tay Ninh Province and shared with the 227th battalion responsibility for supporting the 2nd Brigade in Phuoc Long Province.

ELEVENTH AVIATION GROUP

The crest of the 11th Aviation Group pictures a silver hawk, symbolic of courage and aggressiveness. Pictured on the hawk's wings are two red arrows, denoting the unit's swift firepower. The hawk is pictured against a blue background, representing the sky and the function of the unit, aviation.

At the bottom of the crest is the unit's motto, "We Make the Difference." The unit does indeed make the difference, as it is the source of a great share of the division's airmobility.

However, the crest worn more often by 11th Aviation Group troopers is one which omits the arrows and motto. This unofficial crest is the one pictured above.

COMMANDERS

COL Allen M. Burdette, Jr. . . . . July 1965—June 1966

COL Howard I. Lukens . . . . June 1966—July 1967

COL Joseph L. Gude . . . . July 1967—May 1968

COL J. Elmore Swenson . . . . May 1968—December 1968

COL Foy Rich . . . . December 1968—July 1969

COL Leo F. Soucek . . . . July 1969—January 1970

COL Kenneth Mertel . . . . January 1970—

The 1st Air Cavalry Division is Army aviation in action; the helicopter being the lifeblood of the Army's first airmobile division.

There are three aviation battalions organic to the division, and together they comprise the 11th Aviation Group. Also a part of the 11th Aviation Group is the 11th General Support Aviation Company, which supplies support aircraft to the division headquarters, 11th Group headquarters, and to other units without organic aviation.

The air support is normally distributed as follows: The 227th Assault Helicopter Battalion supports the 3rd Brigade, the 229th Assault Helicopter Battalion services the 1st Brigade and the two jointly assist the 2nd Brigade. The 228th Assault Support Helicopter Battalion, which flies the mighty CH-47 Chinooks, has its companies spread throughout the division's area of operations to support the entire division.

As command and control headquarters, the 11th Group is chiefly respon-

The 11th Aviation Group consists of the 227th and 229th Assault Helicopter Battalions, the 228th Assault Support Helicopter Battalion, the 11th General Support Aviation Company, and Headquarters and Headquarters Company, 11th Aviation Group.

Constituted on February 1, 1963, as Headquarters, Headquarters Company, 11th Air Assault Aviation Group, the unit was organic to the 11th Air Assault Division. Four days later the unit was

activated at Fort Benning.

On July 1, 1965, the unit was reorganized and redesignated Headquarters and Headquarters Company, 11th Aviation Group, and assigned to the 1st Air Cavalry Division.

The 11th Aviation Group was awarded the Presidential Unit Citation for the Pleiku Campaign of 1965, and the Meritorious Unit Commendation for the period September 1965 to November 1966.

(Continued on P. 268)

This photograph, taken in early 1969 at the Quan Loi airstrip in northern III Corps, shows some of the aircraft then organic to the 11th Aviation Group. In the foreground an OH-6A LOH hovers before takeoff while an AH-1G Cobra (far right) and a UH-1H Huey (center) refuel. These three craft are organic to the 11th Group. At center left an OV-1 Mohawk observation and radar craft taxis to the runway, and, above it in the distance already airborne, a C-7A Caribou wings skyward. Both the OV-1 and C-7A were also once organic to the 11th Aviation Group.

DISCOM

DIVISION SUPPORT COMMAND (DISCOM)

COMMANDERS

COL John J. Hennessey .... July 1965—March 1966
LTC James E. Smith .... March 1966—May 1966
LTC Benjamin S. Silver .... May 1966—July 1966
COL Jonathan R. Burton .... July 1966—December 1966
COL Charles D. Daniel .... December 1966—June 1967
COL Hubert S. Campbell .... June 1967—November 1967
LTC Robert Vaughn .... November 1967—January 1968
COL Conrad L. Stansberry .... January 1968—April 1968
LTC Grady R. Poole .... April 1968—May 1968
COL William Dysinger .... May 1968—May 1969
COL Richard G. Beckner .... May 1969—November 1969
COL Tom M. Nicholson .... November 1969—

The Division Support Command traces its heritage to Headquarters and Headquarters Company Band, Support Command, which was organized on September 1, 1963. Two units of the 1st Cavalry Division were combined to form this unit: Headquarters and Headquarters Detachment and the 1st Cavalry Division Trains and Band.

The division band is one of the oldest of Cavalry units, dating back to March 3, 1855, when it was constituted as the 2nd Cavalry Regiment Band. Slightly more than a year later, the band was organized at Camp Verde, Texas.

In August 1861, the musicians were disbanded and reorganized as the 5th Cavalry Regiment Band. It supported the regiment throughout the Civil War, then was disbanded in 1866.

In 1869 the band was reorganized again as part of the 5th Cavalry. It remained with the unit until 1945, when it was placed under command of the 1st Cavalry Division, then stationed at Camp Drake, Japan.

Throughout its long history the band has received various honors and campaign awards. Among these are 11 Indian War campaigns, 17 Civil War campaigns, the Mexican Expedition, four World War II campaigns (Luzon, Leyte, Bismarck Archipelago and New Guinea), and seven Korean War campaigns.

It received a Distinguished Unit Citation at Los Negros Island, a Meritorious Unit Commendation in Korea and the Philippine Presidential Unit Citation for the period October 17, 1944, to July 4, 1945.

In Vietnam, DISCOM and its support units were decorated with the Presidential Unit Citation for the Pleiku Campaign and the Meritorious Unit Citation for the period June 1, 1967, to May 31, 1968.

The Division Support Command DISCOM) has one of the broadest and most important jobs in the division. The mission of the support command is to supply the man in the field with the food, clothing, ammunition and transportation that he needs to do the job.

DISCOM units include the 15th Medical Battalion; the 15th Transportation Corps Battalion, responsible for aircraft maintenance; the 15th Supply and Service Battalion, which provides 1st Air Cavalrymen with everything from toothpicks to gasoline; the 27th Maintenance Battalion, which pulls maintenance for the division's vehicles and weapons; and Headquarters, Headquarters Company and Band.

DISCOM sent its three forward service support elements (FSSE) throughout the Cav's area of operations in support of Operations CRAZY HORSE, PAUL REVERE and THAYER in 1966.

The third forward service support element set a record for continuous support in a single location, as it remained at Phan Thiet in support of the 2nd Battalion, 7th Cavalry, throughout 1967. Eighty tons of supplies were delivered daily to the task force, located 200 air miles from the division base at An Khe.

Due to the large commitment of the division's numerous battalions in the central highlands, DISCOM began operations with four forward service supply elements in July. By November, a fifth FSSE had been added.

The year 1967 ended with the FSSE's

A 15th Medical Battalion Medevac medic raises a bottle of life-saving plasma to an overhead hook after administering first aid to a wounded trooper. The Medevac chopper is speeding across the jungle to a hospital—a familiar scene in history's fastest and most daring medical evacuation system.

The 1st Air Cavalry Division band gives one of its frequent firebase concerts designed to give some variety and entertainment to the otherwise repetitive days on jungle outposts. The musicians are also soldiers. One afternoon in November 1969, the band members had to drop their instruments and take up their M-16s when they were fired upon during a concert in a small Vietnamese village.

supporting Operation WALLOWA at LZ Baldy, Operation PERSHING at LZs English and Uplift and Operation BYRD at Phan Thiet.

In January 1968, a new dimension in support was initiated by DISCOM. In mid-month all subordinate units began air, land and sealift movements to the Hue-Phu Bai area in northern I Corps in preparation for immediate military operations in support of the 3rd Marine Amphibious Force.

For their accomplishments, DISCOM and its assigned units were awarded the Meritorious Unit Citation for their performance from June 1, 1967, to May 31, 1968.

The remainder of 1968 saw DISCOM continue its service and supply missions in an outstanding manner. The biggest task was yet to come.

The move south to III Corps brought new problems to the support command, whose task was two-fold. It would not only have to move its own equipment and personnel, but would also need to ensure other elements of the division would still receive their supplies during the move.

As the move was completed, DISCOM set up its rear area and headquarters in Bien Hoa. Forward service support elements were also sent to Tay Ninh, Quan Loi and Phouc Vinh.

The 15th Transportation Corps Battalion (Aircraft Maintenance and Supply) insignia is a shield, picturing a winged dragon on a blue background. Inscribed along the bottom on a scroll is the battalion's motto: "Over The Best."

15th TRANSPORTATION CORPS BATTALION

COMMANDERS

LTC Charles McQueary . . . . .July 1965—July 19

LTC Keith J. Bauer . . . . .July 1966—July 19

LTC Vaughn C. Emerson . . . . .July 1967—May 19

LTC Albert W. Schlim .May 1968—November 19

LTC William E. Cornwell . . . . .November 1968—May 19

LTC Harold E. Cook . . . . .May 1969—December 19

LTC Bently J. Herbert . . . . .December 1969

The 15th Transportation Corps Battalion was constituted on October 15, 1957, as the 15th Aviation Company, 1st Cavalry Division, and was activated in Korea.

In September 1963, the unit was reorganized and redesignated Headquarters and Headquarters Company, 15th Aviation Battalion; and its organic elements were constituted and activated concurrently.

The battalion was redesignated and converted to the 15th Transportation Corps Battalion as part of the 1st Cavalry Division (Airmobile) on July 1, 1965.

The battalion deployed to the Republ of Vietnam with the division in Septembe 1965.

It recieved the Presidential Unit Cita tion for the Pleiku Campaign, Octobe 23 to November 25, 1965.

Balancing on a Huey rotor blade, a 15th Transportation Corps mechanic makes necessary adjustments. The Hueys and other helicopters are good aircraft, but they need constant and diligent maintenance.

Ask any aeronautical engineer what keeps a helicopter airborne and more than likely you will receive a 30-minute lecture on the principles and dynamics of aerial flight. Ask a 1st Air Cavalry aviator the same question and chances are his answer would be the 15th Transportation Corps Battalion.

Whether a bullet hole needs patching or the 1,180 pound engine of a Chinook needs replacing, the task falls to the men of the 15th TC (Aircraft Maintenance and Supply).

Each month, 90 to 120 tons of repair parts are bolted, welded and fitted by the maintenance men to service Cav birds. The well-oiled, computerized parts order system shoots the full spectrum of parts to the men at places like Bearcat, Phuoc Vinh, Tay Ninh or Quan Loi.

The battalion's shops are equipped to handle any electrical, hydraulics or avionics problem. The damaged helicopter may need the skills of the men

Almost dwarfed by the large tail rotor assembly of a CH-47 Chinook, a mechanic performs the required 100 flying hours inspection and maintenance. Every 1,800 hours of flight, the giant Chinooks are completely torn down and rebuilt, making sure that every part functions perfectly.

Mechanics of 15th TC overhaul an OH-13 helicopter (above) at the An Khe airstrip in August 1968. Another engine specialist works on the maze of hydraulic tubing and wiring (right) inside a Cobra gunship.

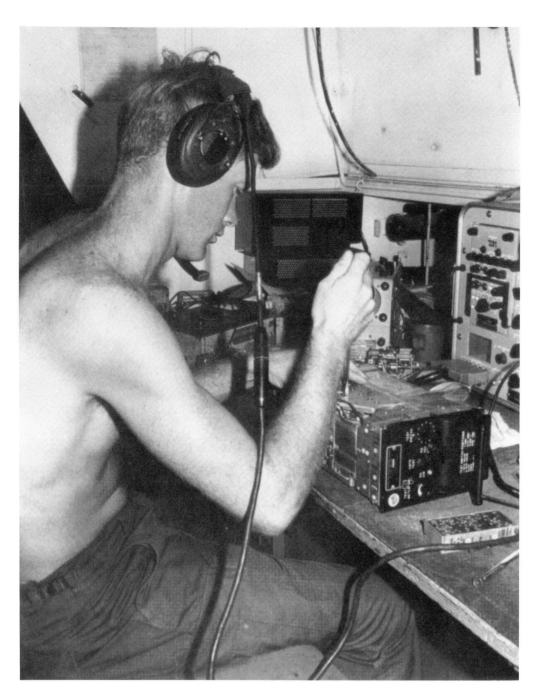

in the sheet metal, engine, or prop and rotor shops. The jobs call for specialization; whether the need exists for a specially machined part or an intricate adjustment of the armament on a deadly Huey-Cobra, there is a shop to fit the mission.

Interim inspections are held for every 25 hours of flying time, and comprehensive inspections are carried out after 100 hours. The Cav's helicopters perhaps take more punishment than those of any other division, and therefore are overhauled more often. The mighty Chinooks, the primary movers of the division, are completely overhauled after 1,800 flying hours.

After the aircraft is rolled out of the repair shops it is given a thorough test fligh' before being released for service. Since their arrival in the Republic of Vietnam in 1965, the men of the battalion have seen to it that 1st Cav ships stay in the air.

Because of the large number of helicopters organic to the airmobile division, the 15th TC Battalion from 1965 to 1969 was one of the largest battalions in the Army, having more than 1.300 people assigned. With so many men available the battalion was able to provide maintenance detachments throughout the area in which the division

A 15th TC radio specialist cures the ills that constantly plague radios that must submit to rough handling inside helicopters. The persistent vibration in helicopters adds to combat damage in radios, keeping these specialists working long hours.

A 2nd Battalion, 20th Artillery, "Blue Max" Cobra gets torn down for a complete overhaul under the hot Vietnamese sun. But because of need for operational Cobras, Chinooks, Hueys and LOHs, the men of the 15th TC find themselves doing as much work at night as during the day.

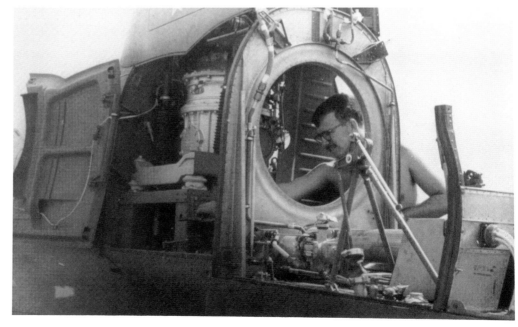

A temperamental Cobra gets its fuel cell checked in one of a score of regular maintenance checks. Because a helicopter, unlike fixed-wing aircraft, has both its thrust source and lift surface combined in one element, the rotor and engine, "preventive maintenance" is doubly important. Failures must be caught and corrected before they occur. If a fixed-wing pilot loses power at 4,000 feet, he's in trouble, but he has time to pick a landing place and glide in. When a helicopter pilot loses power at 4,000 feet, he's in serious trouble. Auto-rotation is a tricky maneuver, at best.

operated; Cav helicopters were never far from a maintenance team.

When the division made the move south to III Corps in late 1968, the battalion proved its excellence. The men worked overtime, preparing virtually all of the division's helicopters for the immense work load they would be carrying.

The move was made, and the effort of the men of the battalion paid off. As they arrived in the Air Cavalry Division's new AO, they quickly set up their operation, and the outstanding service they provided was not delayed a moment longer than necessary.

Then in mid-1969, the battalion underwent a massive change, one which altered its operation greatly.

The unit's strength was greatly reduced, from four to two companies, dropping personnel levels to about 600. In turn, separate maintenance detachments were assigned to each company-sized aviation unit in the division.

This was done to provide even better service to the aviation units. In the past, the four companies of the battalion had not been co-located with the aviation units, and time and distance factors sometimes precluded instant service.

Although their job has changed since their arrival in Vietnam, the men of the 15th Transportation Corps Battalion are constantly providing the best in service and support for the division. They're keeping the airmobile division "in the air."

The black diagonal *bar* of the *15th Supply and Service Battalion crest is suggestive of the 1st Cavalry Division shoulder insignia, indicative of the long association of the two units.*

The red upper portion of the crest is the color of the Transportation Corps. The buff color below the red is indicative of the Quartermaster Corps.

The six points of the medallion are representative of the six citations won by the unit during World War II and the Korean War.

The 15th Supply and Service Battalion was originally organized as the 675th Motor Transport Company in February 1919, at Camp Henry Knox, Kentucky.

Prior to the Vietnam conflict the unit was decorated with two Meritorious Unit Citations (MUC), streamer embroidered PACIFIC THEATER; the MUC, streamer embroidered KOREA; the Philippine Presidential Unit Citation (October 17, 1944, to July 4, 1945); the Republic of Korea Presidential Unit Citation, streamer embroidered TAEGU-WAEGWAN; and the Chryssoun Aristion Andrias (Bravery Gold Medal of Greece).

In Vietnam the battalion, along with other units of the division, received the Presidential Unit Citation for the Pleiku Campaign.

15th SUPPLY AND SERVICES BATTALION

LTC Frederick Osterhout	July 1965—July 1966
LTC Harry L. Corkill, Jr.	July 1966—June 1967
LTC Robert D, Vaughn	June 1967—November 1967
LTC Clarence Metz	November 1967—June 1968
LTC Grady R. Poole	June 1968—September 1968
LTC Leroy Jorgenson	September 1968—May 1969
LTC Perry W. Broaddus	May 1969—September 1969
LTC Lloyd H. Manjeot	September 1969—

Combat is the heart of war. The engagement with, and destruction of an enemy force is the end toward which all soldiers strive. But few people outside of the military know the workings of war, what goes into fighting a battle or just day-to-day survival. What people see and hear of war is mainly combat; but combat may be likened to an iceburg cap, a top that only faintly bespeaks the mass of effort beneath it.

Among many others, a large portion of that sub-surface mass is the supply and service corps, the people who keep those on the front lines in supply with what they need to meet and defeat the enemy.

In the airmobile division, these are the

There is little glory in the war of supply, but it remains the heart of victory. Without the many tons of bread and bullets needed, the best crack division in the Army would falter on its course. For the 15th Supply and Services Battalion "supply" means providing everything the 21,000 1st Cav soldiers eat, wear or shoot. And added to this is the fact that they must supply to an area some 4,000 square miles large, approximately the size of the State of Connecticut. Here tons of supplies (right) await transportation from Bien Hoa to the forward areas.

A Redhat, one of the 15th S&S men who rig and hook sling loads for Chinook and Flying Crane transportation, steps away from a load of empty water blivets before they swing free of the ground.

people of the 15th Supply and Service Battalion. They provide nearly everything soldiers eat, wear, build or shoot. This is their job they have done in an outstanding manner since arriving in the Republic of Vietnam with the 1st Air Cavalry Division in 1965.

The primary functions of the battalion are two-fold, the first being services. The unit aids the FIRST TEAM by furnishing or coordinating such services as laundry facilities, ice cream plants and the explosive ordnance disposal team.

The second function is supply, which involves supporting the division with all classes of material.

The battalion uses ground and air

Redhats stand ready to hook a load to an incoming CH-47 Chinook.

While the greater bulk of supply materiel is moved by air, the 15th S&S system is significantly augmented by truck convoys, which in the latter part of 1969 became common, as northern III Corps roads became more secure against the enemy's ambushes. These convoys help ease the strain on air transports.

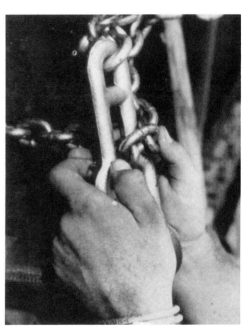

transportation to move supplies from depots in Saigon or Long Binh to Bien Hoa or the forward areas. Convoys depart Bien Hoa for Tay Ninh, Song Be and Quan Loi, the heavily laden trucks supported by armored vehicles and helicopter gunships.

Rations are handled by "Class I" supply. These include "A" rations, or fresh food, which is mostly brought from the United States, but also includes such items as bananas cut from the Vietnamese jungle and tomatoes from Japan; "B" rations or canned food; "C" rations or canned meals; and "LRRPs," the dehydrated meals so often sought after by infantrymen.

Boots, clothing, field gear, plastic

With goggles on to protect his eyes from flying dirt and pebbles, a soldier waits for just the right moment to thrust the heavy "dough-nut" onto the nearing hook of a huge CH-54 Flying Crane (above) that will lift the D-6 tractor off to a new firebase for construction work. For the most part, 15th S&S work is hard labor, labor done by hundreds of hands like those putting lift chains (above right) through a slip ring to prepare a sling load for helicopter flight.

The work is heavy work. Artillery shells, for example, can weigh between 36 and 140 pounds. When not being moved singly, heavy equipment moves in to shift the shells' location. Here some 700 pounds of 105 mm artillery shells are positioned for sling out rigging.

spoons, sandbags and a multitude of other gear are handled by "Class II" and "IV". Since the move south in the final months of 1968, more than four million sandbags have been flown to Cav firebases, along with millions of board-feet of two by fours.

One large storage yard at the battalion's headquarters in Bien Hoa contains a FIRST TEAM invention, the firebase kit. The kit contains everything needed to construct a firebase: concertina wire, timbers, support steel, culverts for hootches and thousands of sandbags, all packaged and ready for shipment at a moment's notice.

An example of the large job done by the men of the 15th S & S Battalion was the Cav's operation in the A Shau Valley. During this period, 15,000 gallons of fuel per day were slung into a refuel point set in the valley.

Ammunition for the division is handled "Class V" supply. Class V provides technical assistance to the division, insuring that, among other things, every unit has the proper amount of ammunition, a long and never-ending job.

The third branch of the battalion is aerial equipment supply, whose respon-

In late 1969 the 15th S&S riggers took part in a facet of Vietnamization, the Dong Tien or "Forward Together" program, when they taught ARVN troops, notably of the 1st ARVN Airborne Division, how to rig and sling out artillery pieces when using the CH-54 Flying Crane. While the ARVN student (top) holds the "doughnut," a 1st Cav Redhat at left keeps his hand forward to catch and ward off the approaching hook, a swinging hazzard in the gale-force rotor wash of the giant helicopter.

sibility it is to technically supervise the rigging of sling loads and to pack parachutes used by the Path Finders.

The riggers, or "Redhats," are scattered throughout "Cav Country." Their job is most important, for there is not a minute of the day when one of the mighty Chinooks is not in the air, carrying a load of lifesaving cargo to a Cav firebase.

The men of the 15th Supply and Service Battalion have made a distinguished record for those who follow. Although the men are individuals, they have one thing in common: They work long and hard to see that those doing the fighting get what they need, when they need it.

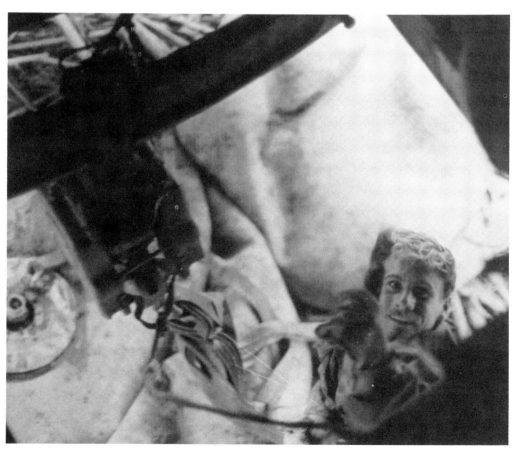

A Redhat (above), who has just slammed the "doughnut" home onto the CH-47's hook, turns upward to give the traditional "thumbs up" signal to the ship's crew chief. At right another of the increasingly frequent supply convoys between Phuoc Vinh and Song Be winds its way north in December 1969.

EX ANIMO

27th MAINTENANCE BATTALION

Crimson and yellow are the colors of the Ordnance Corps, and they are dominant in the 27th Maintenance Battalion's crest. The colors yellow and black and the horseshoe and hammers in the center of the crest represent long association with the cavalry and the transition from mounted to mechanized cavalry. The sea shells in the upper right and lower left corners represent the four battalion honors won by the battalion in the Pacific during World War II. At the bottom of the crest are the words, "Ex Animo," meaning "Willingly."

Since the original activation of the unit on September 20, 1921, it has undergone a series of reorganizations and redesignations. Throughout this entire period, however, the battalion has remained assigned to the 1st Cavalry Division. Prior to coming to Vietnam with the airmobile division, the battalion saw duty overseas in the Pacific and Korea.

Throughout its history the 27th Maintenance Battalion has received honors and decorations for outstanding service. Four Meritorious Unit Commendations have been won by the unit, two in the Pacific, one in Korea and one in Vietnam (October 22, 1965, to April 6, 1966). The battalion has also received the Philippine and Korean Presidential Unit Citations as well as the Bravery Gold Medal of Greece.

In Vietnam it earned the Presidential Unit Citation for the Pleiku Campaign.

COMMANDERS

LTC Granville M. Stagg .... July 1965—May 1966

LTC Shreve D. Squires .... May 1966—May 1967

MAJ William H. Creed .... May 1967—April 1968

LTC Frank Ragano .... April 1968—March 1969

LTC Robert C. Hawlk .... March 1969—

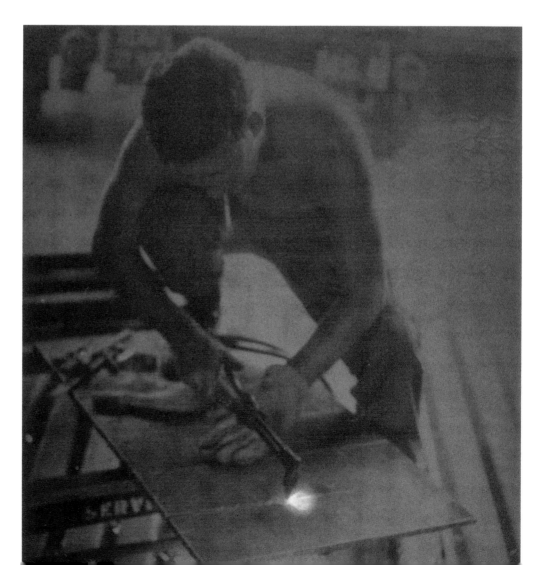

A 27th Maintenance Battalion mechanic gets well into the bowels of a five-ton truck (right) as he remedies the gradual damage done by wear and tear in the Vietnamese climate and dust. Another specialist, expert in the maintenance of electronics, repairs a teletype machine (below) to be returned to part of an important link with higher headquarters.

On September 15, 1965, the 27th Maintenance Battalion arrived in the Republic of Vietnam after a 30-day voyage from Savannah, Georgia, aboard the USNS Upshur. Disembarking at Qui Nhon, the battalion was transported to An Khe by helicopter to begin it role in division support.

The months of September and October were spent receiving equipment and establishing semi-permanent bases throughout the division's area of operations.

With the month of November came the division's first extensive operations, and the men of the 27th Maintenance provided full support. At the same time they continued to make improvements in their own work areas. At the end of

the year the Skytroopers were thus permanently located.

During 1966, the battalion continued to give direct support to the division. Not only working out of the basecamp at An Khe, the battalion sent detachments and contact teams out with each forward support element on all operations in which the division participated.

For its outstanding work the battalion received the Meritorious Unit Commendation for the period October 1965 to April 1966.

Throughout the year the battalion sent detachments to forward areas in support of the division in operations such as NATHAN HALE, PAUL REVERE II and THAYER II.

During 1966 the battalion also completed more than 22,000 maintenance jobs. Some of the most important of these were done on the 105 mm howitzers. The guns' "searing surfaces" were found to be wearing at an above normal rate, and

One of the 27th's most important missions is that of keeping more than a thousand division vehicles in working order. Here a mechanic closes a small shrapnel hole in a jeep radiator.

Three 27th Maintenance men install a new rear axle and differential for a 20-ton truck.

battalion suffered a critical shortage of manpower. This was due to a large number of rotations and the fact that replacements were held to authorized limitations. Even with the shortage of personnel, the battalion maintained its high level of performance and continued to support the division in an outstanding manner.

On Christmas Day, 1968, the men of the battalion distributed more than 700 Christmas packages to the children of the Dong Chi Refugee Camp, located east of An Khe.

The ever-increasing efficiency of the battalion was evidenced in the large number of maintenance jobs completed during the year, numbering nearly 68,000.

The big story of 1968 was the move south to III Corps. On October 27 the battalion received word of the move, and by November 15 all units had been moved and were operational in their new areas of operations.

Throughout 1969, as in previous years, the battalion supported the division in an exemplary fashion. It proved its ability to perform any mission, no matter how difficult. The battalion's motto "Anywhere—Anytime," truly described the unit's mobility and ability.

A mechanic from the 27th gives preventive maintenance to one of many diesel generators (above) operating in the Cav to provide electrical power—one of the uses of that electricity is to light spotlights surrounding major and permanent Cav base areas to discourage enemy ground attacks. Two other mechanics lend the all-important repairman's ear to the sound of a running engine (right), as they begin their diagnosis.

the work of the dedicated repairmen kept the infantry supplied with necessary fire support.

The battalion initiated and maintained a policy of training its personnel in certain MOS categories before sending them to the forward detachments during 1967. This was done primarily with those skills associated with unique airmobile divsion equipment, since many people had no prior experience with these particular items.

The battalion initiated a 20-hour course in maintenance to motor officers and NCOs in all the units of the division. In turn, these students taught their personnel the course, which aided greatly in keeping vehicles rolling throughout the division.

During the last months of the year the

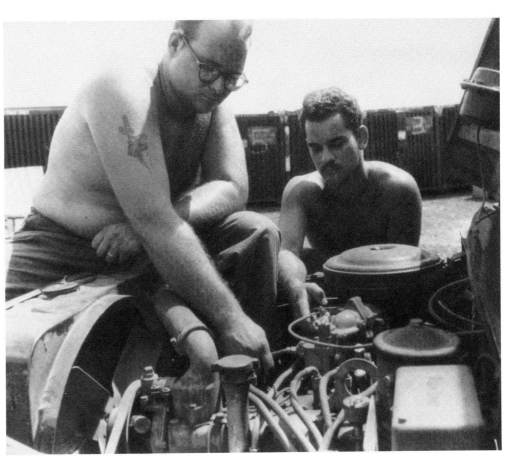

15th MEDICAL BATTALION

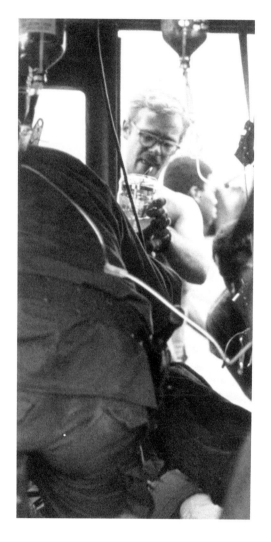

The crest of the 15th Medical Battalion is a shield, maroon and white, the colors of the medical corps. In the upper right is a bluebonnet, the Texas state flower, signifying the unit's place of origin.

COMMANDERS

LTC Jueri J. Svaginstev	July 1965—November 1965
CPT Charles Greenhouse	November 1965—December 1965
LTC Jueri J. Svaginstev	December 1965—January 1966
CPT Charles Greenhouse	January 1966—February 1966
LTC Jueri J. Svaginstev	February 1966—June 1966
LTC Kenneth E. Guenter	June 1966
LTC Jueri J. Svagintev	June 1966—August 1966
LTC J. W. Rasone	August 1966
LTC Henry A. Leighton	August 1966—June 1967
LTC W. Rex Davis	June 1967—July 1968
LTC Guthrie Turner	July 1968—June 1969
LTC Joseph W. McNaney	June 1969—

The 15th Medical Battalion, as it is now known, was organized in 1926 at Fort Bliss, Texas, and designated the 1st Medical Squadron.

The unit travelled with the 1st Cavalry Division throughout World War II campaigns in the South Pacific. The unit entered Tokyo with the Cav in 1945, and was stationed at Camp Drake, where in 1949, it was redesignated the 15th Medical Battalion.

In June, 1965, at Fort Benning, Georgia, the 11th Medical Battalion, 11th Air Assault Division, was deactivated and the 15th Medical Battalion became the first airmobile medical battalion in the Army.

In World War II the unit participated in campaigns in New Guinea, the Bismarck Archipelago (with Arrowhead), Leyte (with Arrowhead), and Luzon. Seven campaign stars were earned in Korea.

The 15th Medical Battalion was decorated in World War II with Meritorious Unit Citation, streamer embroidered PACIFIC THEATER (three awards) and the Presidential Unit Citation, streamer embroidered LOS NEGROS ISLAND.

Additionally, three platoons were cited for actions at Leyte, Luzon and Manila for actions July 1950 to January 1951. Both the Ambulance and Clearing Companies earned Meritorious Unit Commendations in Korea.

In Vietnam the Valorous Unit Award was presented to Company B for heroism on June 6, 1967, during Operation PERSHING. The battalion received a streamer embroidered PLEIKU PROVINCE for its part in the historic Pleiku Campaign.

day the Cardinal departed Vietnam for Okinawa. As he began his visit to the Army hospital there, he was surprised and amazed to meet and talk with the same young Skytrooper he had talked with the previous day. The soldier had been wounded that afternoon and evacuated in less than 24 hours to a modern hospital thousands of miles from the battle zone.

Medical Battalion personnel were proving themselves under fire time and again.

On the night of February 16, 1967, Private First Class James H. Monroe, serving as a medic with the first platoon, Company C, 1st Battalion, 8th Cavalry, distinguished himself in action through the supreme sacrifice.

While in an ambush position, his

A 15th Med medic prepares to lower the jungle penetrator (left), a device designed to slip down through towering and thick jungle trees and growth to rescue wounded from locations which do not permit landing. The Medevac pilot must hover his helicopter (below) with little or no movement until all wounded (below left) are winched aboard.

Providing medical support to an airmobile division requires a special type of medical unit. In the 1st Air Cavalry Division, this unit is the 15th Medical Battalion.

The men of the medical battalion take great pride in the accomplishments of their unit. This pride was summed up by a former aviation platoon leader: "The wounded man on the ground deserves the best. He has done his job and then it becomes our job. He deserves to be taken care of."

Just how effective is an airmobile medical battalion? During Cardinal Spellman's Christmas visit to Vietnam in 1967, he met and talked with a 1st Air Cavalryman in the field. The next

In 1965, the 15th Medical Battalion was deployed to the Republic of Vietnam with the 1st Cavalry Division. The battalion headquarters was quickly set up at An Khe, as the companies were assigned to forward areas. As Cavalrymen quickly underwent their baptism of fire, the advantages of aero-medical evacuation became more and more evident. In fact among the first Skytroopers killed in action was a Medevac pilot.

Throughout the division's operations in the mountainous jungles of the central Vietnamese highlands, the personal devotion to duty and bravery of the men of the battalion became written in the history of warfare as examples for all who follow.

From the Medevac helicopter pilot, who goes into a landing zone under heavy enemy fire, to the most basic medical unit, the combat medic, 15th

unit came under heavy enemy fire. While treating several men, PFC Monroe saw a grenade land near his position and immediately jumped on it, absorbing the explosion with his body. He was awarded the Medal of Honor, posthumously, in 1968.

Just one month later, Specialist Four Charles C. Hagemeister, serving as a medic with Company A, 1st Battalion, 5th Cavalry, distinguished himself in action and received the Medal of Honor. SP4 Hagemeister repeatedly gave treatment and words of encouragement to the wounded members of his platoon during heavy fighting in Binh Dinh Province. Killing four enemy soldiers and silencing a machinegun during the battle, he raced through a fusillade of enemy fire to secure help from a nearby platoon. His actions, at the risk of his own life, saved the lives of many of his comrades, and helped inspire them to repel the enemy attack.

The personal bravery of these two men was in the highest traditions of the medical corps, men who are ready and willing to go when the hurt cry out for help.

These incidents of personal bravery are not exceptions. The night of June 6, 1967, the battalion's Company B distinguished itself when its base came under a heavy mortar attack. Enemy mortars landed in the ammunition storage area, which contained 1,250 tons of explosives. The medical personnel repeatedly evacuated patients and personnel from the area, resulting in no loss of life. The company was awarded the Valorous Unit Citation for its actions.

A major part of the 15th Medical Battalion's efforts has been spent working in civic action programs. Thus, the MEDCAP (Medical Civic Action Program) was initiated. Medical personnel visit villages and hamlets, treating the local nationals for everything from a toothache to starvation.

The medical personnel created a hospital in An Khe for the treatment of the 70,000 people of the An Tuc District in Binh Dinh Province. Thousands of patients were treated at the hospital, and hundreds of babies were delivered. The medical personnel soon received the trust and gratitude of the Vietnamese people. Their job has been described as "one

A combat medic (above), one of the most revered men in the history and tradition of the infantry, moves out after off-loading from a combat assault. He is loaded down with his field gear and has an extra medical kit bag hanging from his left shoulder. This particular medic is not carrying a weapon, an option afforded only to field medics and chaplains. In almost every field company the medics are also known by their hallmark—unfailing courage in the face of fire. When a buddy is wounded every man will pitch in to help, because he knows that others would do the same for him. A radio telephone operator (RTO) and three other men (right) race across a paddie in February 1968, to get a wounded man to an incoming Medevac chopper (right bottom). The wounded man was under expert medical care at a forward field hospital 11 minutes after he tripped a Viet Cong booby trap in the field.

part medicine, two parts compassion."

The move south to III Corps in 1968 brought about many changes in methods of operation for many Skytroopers, but not for the medical battalion personnel. Their job remained the same; help those in need. Help they did.

The Headquarters Service Company, located in Phuoc Vinh, conducts daily sick call, runs a dental clinic and administers to local nationals.

The battalion's companies are located at the division's three brigade headquarters, as well, where they can administer aid to the men stationed in those forward areas.

Yet the men of the battalion are dedicated to their foremost task. When the word goes out for help, Medevac ship crews scramble, for theirs is also a mission of mercy and compassion. The injured in the field receives medical attention within a matter of minutes.

Since its arrival in the Republic of Vietnam in 1965, the 15th Medical Battalion has rendered top-notch medical support to the FIRST TEAM: New chapters have been written in the unit's history: Happy Valley, Ia Drang Valley, Bong Son, Plei Mei and War Zone C. Wherever the tide of battle takes the 1st Air Cavalry Division, the 15th Med will be there ... conserving the fighting strength.

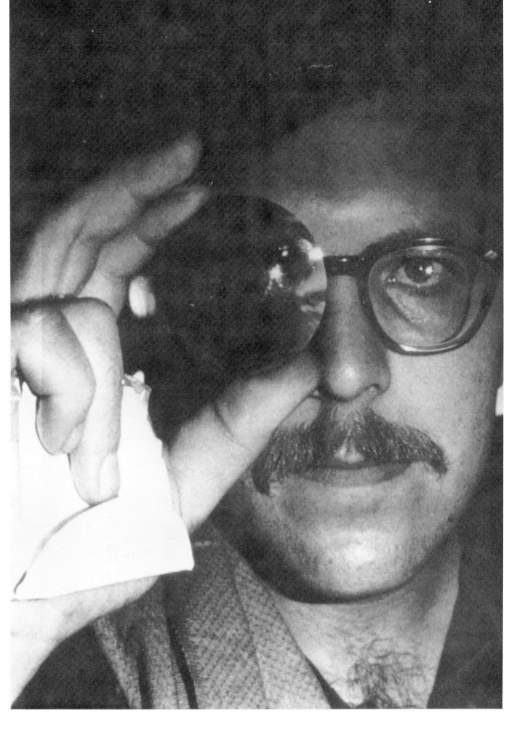

Behind the pilots and crews of Medevac, the combat medics in the field and the doctors at forward field hospitals, there stands a thorough and efficient medical organization in the 15th Medical Battalion. The battalion offers a full range of medical care, even beyond that needed for combat wounds. A medical specialist inspects a lens (top right) to be ground for use in spectacles for 1st Cav troopers. Specialist Four Jerry W. Heger fills a patient's prescription (left) at the 15th Med pharmacy at Phuoc Vinh, and Dr. Daniel Kozlowski gives dental work to a Skytrooper (right) in a bunkered dental clinic, located on a firebase.

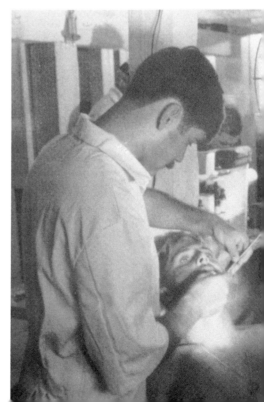

medevac ✚

There is a mystique about Medevac.

So much has been written of the courage, the dedication and esprit de corps of the men in Medevac that today they live with legend.

"It's why I joined the Army," said Medvac pilot Warrant Officer Richard Leonard. "There's something about saving a life—and the way Medevac does it, defying the odds—that makes it appealing."

"I've never seen a mission aborted," said Specialist Four Dick Gamester, who monitors Medevac Control at Phuoc Vinh. "I've seen missions delayed by weather and suppressive fire, but never called off. There are nights when the only birds in the sky are Medevac."

The esprit de corps touches everyone. You can't get into the program unless you volunteer, and even then the competition is tough.

Specialist Four Mike Vineyard, a helicopter mechanic at 15th Med, worked in a maintenance shop before he got a shot at a crew chief position in Medevac. "I frequently flew doorgunner when we'd go after a downed bird," he said.

"You just do it," he said. "When a bird goes down, everyone heads for the pad. It's like a brotherhood."

That startling routine response to a call that seems beyond that of duty is part of the mystique of Medevac. Yet there is another side.

"It gets to be a little hairy at times," said Medevac pilot Captain Ernest Bayford. "But I wouldn't say there's excessive strain on anyone."

He's right, of course. Medevac teams lead a very comfortable life when the going is slow. Half their time is free. Even at the brigade field hospitals, where the teams are on call 24 hours a day, they have no duties until suddenly, though routinely, they are called to scramble.

"Downed aircraft, let's go!" CPT Bayford shouted from the doorway of the crew quarters. It was 2:21 p.m. and the scramble was on. The crew reached the chopper at full stride; in minutes it was airborne, hitting 100 knots at treetop level. The bird climbed to 2,000 feet; then nine minutes after the call and 10 miles northeast of Quan Loi, the descent

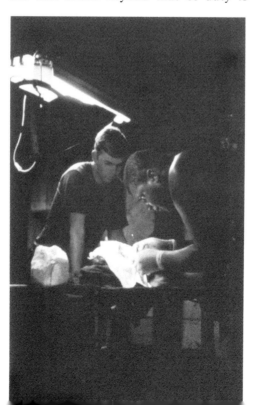

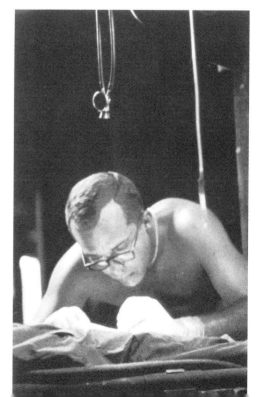

began.

They circled once at 300 feet as a Cobra gunship pulled in behind. The downed aircraft was somewhere in the thick green foliage below. A light observation helicopter (LOH), flying as low as it could, finally spotted the wreckage and marked it with purple smoke.

Aircraft commander Bayford banked the ship to the left and hovered over the now visible downed helicopter. its slender tail protruding through the bamboo.

It was 2:33 when Specialist Five William Meeks attached the yellow, torpedo-like jungle penetrator to the cable hoist and lowered it to the bamboo below.

On the ground a man grasped at it and, shielding his face from the entangling bush, rode the cable skyward. He looked straight up at the chopper with a strained smile, drawing closer, closer until he could touch the skid, grab the medic's hand and pull himself aboard.

"We've got to get the pilot out! We've got to, got to!" he said again and again, breathing hard as he lay against the cabin wall.

The whine of the hoist started up again, bringing the rescued doorgunner to the side of the ship and inside. He clutched at the medic-crew chief. It was 2:35.

"He's trapped. I couldn't budge him. He waved me away," the man blurted out. "We've got to get him out, we've got to," said the doorgunner.

"They will. They will," answered the medic.

The ship gained altitude slowly, banked to the left and circled again at 300 feet. It was up to the Blues now—the crack infantry element of the 1st Squadron, 9th Cavalry, already airlifted into the area an maneuvering toward the downed aircraft and its pinned pilot.

The Medevac chopper circled above. SP5 Meeks turned at once to his patients, wrapping and taping the crushed toes of the doorgunner.

(Continued on P. 287)

SEPARATE BATTALIONS AND COMPANIES

15th ADMINISTRATION COMPANY

The unit was consituted September 6, 1921, and organized at Fort Bliss, Texas, as the 1st Cavalry Division Quartermaster Train later that month. After a series of reorganizations and redesignations, and an inactivation in 1947, the unit became the 15th Administration Company October, 15, 1957.

The company has campaign participation credit for World War II (New Guinea, Bismarck Archipelago, Leyte and Luzon), and Korea.

The unit had been honored with three Meritorious Unit Citations; two streamers embroidered KOREA; the Philippine Presidential Unit Citation; the Republic of Korea PUC; and the Bravery Gold Medal of Greece.

In Vietnam, the company was awarded the Presidential Unit Citation for the Pleiku Campaign.

In late October 1965, Lieutenant Colonel Malcolm Baer, the adjutant general of the 1st Air Cav, stepped out of his tent and surveyed a chunk of real estate on the southwest corner of the "golf course," the 1st Cav base at An Khe. What he saw was a gaggle of tents and hootches that represented the whole of the administrative backbone of the division—the 15th Administration Company.

It was the last time the company ever served together in one geographical location.

A strict definition of the TO & E places all the elements of a division's administrative services unit in one location and under the operational control of the adjutant general. And so it was when the division closed on the An Khe base in mid-September, the elements of the 15th Admin Company parked their bags and pitched their tents in one location.

But the TOE never envisioned an airmobile division launching strike forces some 150 miles distant from its main base.

So when the Pleiku Campaign got well under way in late October, elements of the company were displaced westward to co-locate with the forward command post of the division. The first elements to move were from the information office and the casualty reporting section of the AG shop.

Back at Camp Radcliff the offices of the inspector general, staff judge advocate, division chaplain and finance continued to operate as a whole.

Finance and AG, in particular, were

A 15th Administration Company clerk is pictured (above) handling part of the tons of paper work required to run a division of 21,000 men. One of the most important morale factors in the Vietnam War—as in any war—is fast and complete mail service. Mailmen (below) prepare several tons of mail for helicopter shipment to forward areas and to the men in the field.

putting down roots—big machine records kind of roots—which precluded their moving anywhere.

As the division's forward or "jump" command post increased in size, so did a proportionate slice of the admin company that followed. AG classified and reproduction moved a sizable shop forward to Bong Son to support Operation MASHER/WHITE WING. The information office again displaced a larger force to support the brigades and thus was born the concept of putting information teams with each committed brigade.

The division chaplains moved forward, too, as did finance contact teams.

In late 1966 and during 1967, the division, for all intents and purposes, had abandoned Camp Radcliff as an operational base. Elements of the 15th Administration Company reorganized under AG to become a personnel services battalion. An Khe still was the focal point of all admin services. Pay and personnel records were maintained there, and Camp Radcliff became the Skytrooper's first and last stop in the Cav.

When the division made its great leap northward from the Bong Son Plain to I Corps and Camp Evans, the forward command post that had grown into becoming, in reality, the division main

(Continued on P. 287)

The division training center at Bien Hoa is managed by the 15th Admin Company. This involves the processing and training of hundreds of replacement soldiers every week. One of the training periods new Cavalrymen receive at the FIRST TERM Academy (FTA) is that of rappelling from helicopters. The training center employs a 45-foot tower where men get their first taste of the art of rappelling (above). During his 12-month tour with the 1st Cav, the average soldier will probably rappel into combat from helicopters at least once.

1st Cav artist, Specialist Five Ron Doss, portrayed another 15th Admin clerk at his inglorious, but most essential job, in the paper war.

179

8th ENGINEER BATTALION

COMMANDERS

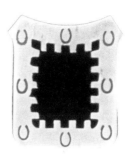

LTC Robert J. Malley . . . . July 1965—June 1966

LTC Charles G. Olentine . . . . June 1966—May 1967

LTC Edwin S. Townsley . . . . May 1967—May 1968

LTC Francis J. Walter Jr. . . . . May 1968—May 1969

LTC Andre G. Broumas . . . . May 1969—September 1969

LTC Scott B. Smith . . . . September 1969—

This shield is red with a white border, the colors of the Corps of Engineers. The eight horseshoes indicate the numerical designation of the organization and its mounted service.

The battalion was constituted on June 30, 1916, in the Regular Army as the 1st Battalion Mounted Engineers. On July 29, 1917, the battalion was redesignated as the 8th Engineer Battalion (Mounted).

The 8th Engineer Battalion participated in the World War II campaigns at New Guinea, Bismarck Archipelago, Leyte, and Luzon. During the Korean War it participated in the UN Defensive, the UN Offensive, the CCF Intervention, the First UN Counteroffensive, the CCF Spring Offensive, the UN Summer-Fall Offensive, the Second Korean Winter, and Korea Summer-Fall 1952.

The 8th Engineer Battalion has been presented with the Meritorious Unit Commendation, streamer embroidered ASIATIC-PACIFIC THEATER, the Philippine Presidential Unit Citation, (October 17, 1944 to July 4, 1945), the Republic of Korea Presidential Unit Citation, streamer embroidered WAEGWAN-TAEGU, the Republic of Korea Presidential Unit Citation, streamer embroidered KOREA, the Chrysson Aristion Andrias (Bravery Gold Medal of Greece), streamer embroidered LOS NEGROS ISLAND.

In Vietnam, like other units of the division, the battalion earned the Presidential Unit Citation for the Pleiku Campaign. The Meritorious Unit Commendation, Second Oak Leaf Cluster for the period October 1965 to August 1966, and Third Oak Leaf Cluster for the period September 1, 1966, to August 31, 1967, also is proudly displayed by the battalion.

Imagine that you are a workman with a large construction firm which contracts the building of airstrips, roads and suburban housing developments, and whose schedules require the completion of these projects in a minimal amount of time.

Add to this situation the fact that all your work is done in a tropical country where either a blazing sun bakes the back of your neck or the gush of monsoon rain buries your equipment in two feet of mud.

Having their work complicated by exactly these circumstances, the "Skybeavers", the airmobile engineers of the 8th Engineer Battalion, operate when and where things need building or improvement.

The battalion's expedient workmanship gives the division the required, bare necessities for tactical operation. The airstrips the engineers build keep supplies flowing by Air Force fixed wing and their roads move the sustenance for battle. In the case of the Cav's engineers, the civilian housing project becomes a firebase, an airmobile division's landing zone.

But perhaps the most important mission of the Cav's "private construction company" is that of building LZs. These mobile tactical locations are used for varying lengths of time, ranging from only a few hours to several months, based on the tactical situation. This fact of life makes the mission of the Skybeavers a very important one, indeed.

Seemingly impregnable, Cav firebases serve a necessary function in that they give the infantry battalion the latitude needed for finding the enemy in his own habitat, the triple canopy jungle. While the infantrymen meet the opposition on the battlefield, engineers fight a different war, one against nature and her elements.

Any engineer's parched lips, tired muscles, tanned back and dirty fatigues tell the story of a Skybeaver engineer's

An 8th Engineer Battalion soldier gets into the thick of it in trying to free his road grader (above) from the persistent and clinging Vietnam mud.

way of life. Whether he is a surveyor, drives an earth mover or a backhoe, carries steel, constructs bunkers, or fills one of a thousand sandbags, the engineer is the Cav's I-beam, the backbone of the division's comfort and tactical mobility.

He is a FIRST TEAM engineer.

On August 16, 1965, the first unit of the 8th Engineer Battalion landed in Vietnam as the first squad of the first platoon of Charlie Company stepped off a C-130 at Nha Trang. By August 21 the remainder of the advance party had arrived and Major Thomas M. McClelland flew in from Saigon to assume over-all command.

The engineers of Charlie Company had hardly pitched their tents in An Khe when they found themselves besieged by enough work for a battalion. They were charged with the mission of preparing An Khe for the rest of the division that was already on its way.

On September 12 the USNS Darby dropped anchor in Qui Nhon Harbor, completing a 28-day journey with the main body of the battalion. As the members of the unit greeted each other after the month's separation they found themselves facing the same problem Company C had—but on a larger scale. There was now enough work for an engineer group.

The men of the 8th Engineer Battalion are, of course, builders of firebases, roads and jungle airfields, but they are also soldiers. This engineer keeps his M-16 rifle loaded and handy as he takes sightings in the construction of another remote firebase.

It seemed as if everyone needed a road into their area, a rice paddy drained or an anthill knocked down. Faced with so much work, the battalion could only answer the most urgent requests for aid and, in order to answer these, frequently worked around the clock. The most pressing project was the leveling of the top of Hon Cong Mountain, a massive rock-tipped mountain just to the west of the basecamp, to be used as a signal complex.

In October units of the battalion participated in their first tactical operations. Company C was first as it supported the 3rd Brigade on Operation SHINY BAYONET. Bravo Company swung into action even before Charlie Company returned by supporting the 2nd Brigade in an operation in the Vinh Thanh "Happy Valley." Both companies worked primarily on route maintenance.

These operations set the pattern for tactical employment of engineers in 1966. Normally, companies, reinforced by equipment and medics, were attached to the brigades. The platoons were further attached to infantry battalions, and two or three-man demolitions teams were attached to infantry companies. It was these demolition teams that were to see the most action and suffer the most casualties.

Beginning in late January the battalion launched a new phase in its combat engineer support of the division. In addition to what had become normal engineer support missions, the 8th Engineer Battalion initiated an extensive airfield construction program which saw seven new airfields constructed before the end of June. Two other airfields were lengthened to twice their previous size, and the extensive repair and modification of numerous other airfields was undertaken during this same six month period.

During Operation MASHER, which began on January 24, the battalion was given the mission of construction of an airfield at Position Dog, a few kilometers north of Bong Son. Alpha Company, with the second equipment platoon from Headquarters Company attached, moved overland from An Khe to Position

Dog. The men and equipment arrived on the site on January 28 and began work the same day. Their mission was completed on the 31st, after working around the clock for 70 hours. In what was to become characteristic of the men of the 8th, they did not stop work but continued on their own initiative for another day until the airstrip was capable of handling C-123 aircraft. This field was named English Airfield in honor of Specialist Five Carver J. English who was killed in the crash of a CH-54 "Flying Crane" on January 5.

On February 22, Headquarters Company began work on a C-130 airfield six kilometers north of Phu Cat. In addition to the required runway of 3,200 feet, which was completed in 120 hours, a parking apron for 10 aircraft and three kilometers of access and service roads were built. The entire project was completed on March 5. The airfield was named Hammond Airfield in honor of Sergeant First Class Russell E. Hammond who had been killed in action a few months before. The security for the work force was provided by Company B.

While a portion of the battalion's resources were being used to construct these two airfields, the larger portion of the battalion's effort was directed to support of the brigades in Operations MASHER, WHITE WING, EAGLE'S CLAW, BLACKHORSE and SITTING BULL.

During Operation LINCOLN, which lasted from March 25 to April 8, Company A had no sooner finished an airfield at Position Oasis when the battalion requested and obtained permission to construct a 3,500 foot C-130 airfield at the same location. Work began immediately. The field was constructed with bulldozers, tractor-scrapers, graders and self-propelled rubber-tired rollers.

In August the Skybeavers participated in Operation PAUL REVERE II, which witnessed the heaviest commitment of the battalion in any single operation to that date. After studying the division's disposition and planned operations, Lieutenant Colonel Charles G. Olentine decided to also move the battalion headquarters to a forward area in order to better support the division effort and control engineer resources. This was the first time since the arrival of the 8th Engineer Battalion in Vietnam that the battalion headquarters operated outside of Camp Radcliff. All of Company B, Company C and Headquarters Company moved to Tuttle Airfield at

A huge CH-54 Flying Crane lowers a steel and plank bridge span into place as the 8th Engineers reopen another section of Highway 9—the only ground route into the besieged Marine base at Khe Sanh—during Operation PEGASUS, the relief of Khe Sanh.

Position Oasis. Since it was during the monsoon season, all of the battalion's resources and skills were fully required during the month-long operation.

The most unusual mission in Operation IRVING was conducted by Company C in support of the 3rd Brigade. On October 5 the third platoon assumed control of three ARVN light tactical raft half-pontoons with motors and used them to ferry confiscated rice to a secure area. The first platoon of Company C used four pontoons and one pneumatic assault boat, all with outboard motors, to patrol the rivers in its area on the 5th and 10th of October. The normal

demolition missions of the company in IRVING resulted in 212 military and 383 civilian bunkers being destroyed along with 18 caves and two tunnel systems.

Two other operations were in progress in the last five months of 1966 which were supported by the 8th Engineer Battalion. A task force from the 2nd Battalion, 7th Cavalry, was supported by the second platoon of Charlie Company in Operation BYRD near Phan Thiet in the southeast corner of the II Corps area. The "lonesome end" platoon left for Phan Thiet on the 1st of August and was still there on the last day of 1966.

Numerous landing zones had been cleared and several forward bases established by the platoon. Under the leadership of First Lieutenant James S. Rawlings, the second platoon earned the reputation of being the hardest working platoon in the task force.

The New Year 1967 found the entire battalion still in Binh Dinh Province participating in Operation THAYER II, but at the same time it marked the climax many trying experiences. Hammond Army Airfield had survived the devastating effects of a severe monsoon season only because of the never-tiring efforts of the Skybeaver battalion. Charlie Company had a platoon in direct support at this time, and it nursed each new wound in the airfield promptly and professionally. Headquarters Company continued to maintain and rebuild the road network, which periodically washed out.

Operation THAYER II came to a close on the 12th of February and Operation PERSHING began shifting two brigades and division headquarters to the Bong Son area. Thus started the longest single operation in the history of the 1st Air Cavalry Division centered in the Bong Son Plain. With this new operation, Company A moved from LZ Pony to LZ English with the 1st Brigade. It immediately began clearing battalion-size firebases and destroying enemy bunkers and tunnel systems.

Lieutenant Colonel Edwin S. Townsley had hardly assumed command when the battalion received its first major mission since his arrival—to open the road from Gia Huu to Sa Huynh. The road to Sa Huynh is actually an eight kilometer section of Highway QL-1 extending northward from the boundary between Binh Dinh and Quang Ngai Provinces to the Task Force Oregon boundary. This section of Highway 1 and not been used for commercial traffic since 1962 when the Viet Cong destroyed nearly all the bridges, dug deep, wide trenches across the roadway and installed many barricades to limit its usage and extract tolls. In addition, each rainy season continued to carve into the roadway where the roadbed had been weakened.

This was the scene that confronted Lieutenant Hartford Bennerman of the first platoon of Company A on the 4th of June, after LTC Townsley directed that Company A open the road with equipment support from Headquarters Company. It was no easy task and one that had to be completed within four days. Within two days the work parties joined forces without any sign of enemy activity. It was hot, hard work with the temperatures well above 100 degrees throughout the operation. Approximately 2,500 cubic yards of fill were dumped or dozed alongside the bridges and 354 feet of culvert were emplaced to construct bypasses for the flow of future military and civilian traffic.

During August the division expanded its area of operation in a new phase of Operation PERSHING and this intensified the combat support requirements of all the Skybeaver companies. Emphasis was placed on the preparation and establishment of new landing zones and artillery firebases. Construction engineering tasks continued as the battalion improved lines of communication, began construction on a new airfield and progressed rapidly toward the completion of the new LZ English munitions storage area.

One of the major projects in August involved the construction of a 1,400 by 60 foot airstrip at LZ Pony by First Lieutenant Thomas Howard's first equipment platoon.

During the first week of October nomadic Charlie Company, in support of the 3rd Brigade, again picked up its belongings in true airmobile fashion and moved to a place named Hill 63. When Company C departed LZ English, it also took along one platoon from Bravo Company and one heavy equipment platoon from Headquarters Company. Most of the engineer effort during the first few days of October was expended on preparing its own company area, constructing a brigade briefing room and improving the existing barrier. Operation WALLOWA began on October 4 and continued through the end of 1967 and the early part of 1968.

Early in the month of December the 1st Brigade established contact with an estimated two NVA battalions of the 22nd NVA Regiment near Tam Quan. Alpha Company provided direct support to the operation by sending the first and third platoons into the contact area. The two platoons supported the infantry by destroying bunkers, directing the clearing of LZs and filling trenches. The battle of Tam Quan was a real test of the Skybeavers ability to assume their secondary mission as infantrymen. In the first 40 hours of the contact, they advanced alongside or in front of the infantry killing 10 NVA and allowing the infantry to capture 10 weapons.

Again in the year 1968 the Skybeavers proved themselves a match for their motto: "No one else can do so much."

In 1968 the 8th Engineer Battalion deployed to the II Corps Tactical Zone. Operations PERSHING, WALLOWA and BYRD were soon to be terminated and the extension of the runway at LZ Baldy was completed prior to the move north to I Corps.

As the FIRST TEAM became the

As builders and soldiers both, the 8th Engineers wear two hats and often perform both jobs at the same time. Here a platoon of engineers climb down the Chinook ladder to secure a jungle area and begin blowing out trees so that future helicopters can land. The Chinook ladder is safe— providing you're not getting shot at right then—but with a full pack and equipment the ladder descent is tricky and hard work.

The engineers get the job done. And if a ladder isn't handy, they improvise. Here two 8th Engineers secure A-frame joists in building a "hootch" for one of the more permanent Cav base areas.

U.S. Army's northernmost division, the 8th Engineer Battalion was among the first units to begin operations in the JEB STEWART AO. One battalion of the 1st Brigade, supported by First Lieutenant Gary V. Diers' third platoon of Company A, led the division into LZ El Paso, near Hue, on January 17. There they were joined two days later by the first platoon. Working with organic and borrowed heavy engineer equipment, maximum effort was expended to open the division's forward basecamp.

Company A devoted the first week of May to preparation for the final phase of Operation DELAWARE in the A Shau Valley. Begining May 8 groups of five to six engineers accompanied the infantry units as far as LZ Stallion with a mission of area denial operations.

Still in the A Shau on June 5, the third platoon, Charlie Company, moved to LZ Mooney to begin construction of the new firebase. In four days the men completed a supply helipad, 12 gun emplacements, a tactical operations center, an aid station and an ammunitiion bunker.

Early in August Company B began preparations for the arrival of the

2nd Brigade by rebuilding LZ Nancy. Shortly after midnight on August 16 mortar and rocket rounds rained in on the landing zone, followed by a heavy ground attack along the south side of the perimeter. At several points the perimeter was breached and enemy sappers rushed onto the firebase. Due to a fine defense and the valorous acts of many of its men, Bravo Company repulsed the attack from its sector. The two 'hour battle took its toll, one Skybeaver was killed and six wounded. Nine valor awards were won by members of the company for their actions during the fight.

On October 27, 1968, the division was alerted to move to the III Corps Tactical Zone. Immediately all construction work ceased and effort was directed toward preparing for the move. Within 36 hours after notification, elements of C Company had closed on III Corps, constructing the first of 10 landing zones they were to build in the next 60 days. The completed move relocated Company A at Tay Ninh, Charlie Company at Quan Loi and Headquarters and Bravo Companies at Phouc Vinh. On March 12

One of the most often used pieces of 8th Engineer equipment is the backhoe, used primarily after airlift via helicopter, to dig underground tactical operations centers (TOC) at firebases.

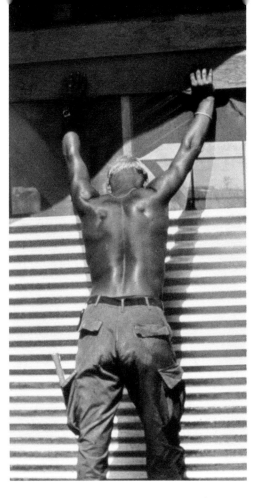

A soldier-engineer puts his back into the job in throwing up the always needed hootches that house rear echelon workers. In addition to their pay, most engineers usually get a free suntan, courtesy of the Vietnam climate.

Bravo Company moved to Lai Khe with the 2nd Brigade.

On April 1, 1969, one platoon of Bravo Company moved to Bien Hoa to aid in the construction of the division training center, which was completed on April 22. On April 17 a platoon from Bravo Company moved to Phouc Vinh to become the general support platoon for the division.

Each company in the 1st Cav has its commanding officer, executive officer and platoon leaders. But Company A, 8th Engineers, has something unique—a rice officer. When the Cavalrymen from the 2nd Battalion, 12th Cavalry, began discovering the white staple, First Lieutenant Stephen Dacey was assigned as the company's rice officer.

"Division headquarters had decided that each engineer company would handle the rice for its brigade," said Lieutenant George M. Walker, executive officer for the company. "We were to store the rice we found until we had enough to send to the Montagnard village near Song Be."

The discovery of more than 100 tons of rice on the 7th of February came as a surprise to many people, including the ice officer.

Moving the rice initially by truck and Chinook helicopter, the engineers had a crew waiting to load the staple on pallets and transport it to the Tay Ninh airstrip to be carried to Song Be on C-7A Caribou aircraft.

"The Viet Cong tried to stop us from moving the rice by blowing up the bridge between LZ Grant and Tay Ninh", said LT Dacey. "But we were able to finish the moving by Chinook."

The Skybeavers diligently worked to move the rice. Chinook after Chinook landed beside the dusty LZ and lifted the rice-laden slings to Tay Ninh.

After delivering 20 tons of rice to Song Be, the engineers turned the distribution of the remaining rice—some 80 tons—to the brigade civil affairs officer. He in turn distributed it to local villagers.

Throughout the period May to August the Skybeavers performed their missions of building and upgrading firebases and giving minesweep and demolition support to the infantry battalions.

At Bu Dop the Skybeavers fought and won a different kind of battle—one with monsoon season rain and mud—when they set to work in September resurfacing and expanding the vital Bu Dop airstrip. It was during a flight from Quan Loi to Bu Dop that the chopper carrying Lieutenant Colonel Andre Broumas and a Skybeaver planning staff was shot down, killing all aboard.

The platoon of heavy equipment operators from Headquarters Company had to cope with "rain that would make any engineer company throw up its hands and quit," said Command Ser-

During construction of airfields, the engineers often have to yield to arriving and departing aircraft using the runway even before it is completed. They also have to contend with enemy mortar crews who try to stop progress of the runway.

geant Major Henry Salazar. "But we worked with what we had, and rain was something we had plenty of."

The other problem that hampered construction of the airstrip was enemy mortar fire. Not only would the engineers have to run for cover when the rounds crashed into the runway, but they also had to repair the craters that began to pockmark the strip.

"It took my men three days to fill some of these craters because most of the work had to be done by hand," said First Lieutenant Thurston McDaniels, officer in charge of the project. "We could have gotten the job done in a couple of weeks if it hadn't been for the bad weather and enemy mortar fire."

During the runway lengthening, rubber trees had to be blown down tree by tree. With 400 more feet of runway and clear view for take-offs and landings, pilots found Bu Dop a little easier to

use for flights into the area.

Company A once again remained in support of the 1st Brigade at Tay Ninh through the end of October. LZ Ike was reopened on August 8 and LZ Becky was closed on August 11.

Alpha Company used September to upgrade the defensive posture of LZs Jamie and Grant, and to provide combat support for the infantry. One platoon was deployed to Camp Gorvad to take over base development projects from September 8 to October 17.

Bravo Company remained in support of the 2nd Brigade at Lai Khe until the middle of August when the airmobile engineers moved with the brigade to FSB Buttons. From August to the end of October, Bravo Company opened firebases Caldwell, Mary, Don, and Alvarado, while FSB Judie was reopened.

Charlie Company spent the time from August to November based in Quan Loi in support of the 3rd Brigade. In August C Company closed LZs Vivian and Ellen and built FSB Eagle I.

FSB Eagle I was closed in September and firebases Jerri and Ann were built. Vivian was reopened on the 1st of October and Ellen was reopened later in the month.

Other construction in support of the brigade included the upgrading of the Quan Loi greenline and the building of the Special Forces Camp at Bu Dop.

So the year went, and once again in 1969, as in all the years before, the 8th Engineer Battalion Skybeavers proved that "No One Else Can Do So Much."

Private First Class Jarom Mitchell straps tape explosives to a cluster of jungle trees as he prepares to blow them to clear a new firebase.

COMMANDERS

13th SIGNAL BATTALION

Orange and white are the traditional colors used for the Signal Corps. The mountains are symbolic of the mountainous areas of the Pacific in which the unit provided communications for the 1st Cavalry Division during World War II. They also represent the invasions of Bismarck Archipelago and Leyte. The arms grasping the lightning flashes allude to the mission of the unit enabling information and orders to be sent and received. The seven lightning flashes commemorate the seven decorations awarded the unit for services in World War II and Korea. The temple refers to action in Korea during the Korean War.

Signalmen work midway up the tall communications tower at the division headquarters in Phuoc Vinh, Camp Gorvad. The commanding general and his staff must be assured of instant and clear radio contact with the division elements spread over 4,000 square miles.

The 13th Signal Battalion was formed on June 7, 1917, as the 7th Field Signal Battalion.

From 1921 to the time the unit went into combat in World War II, signal equipment and procedures were drastically changed. The old pack radios and telegraph fell by the wayside. Modern equipment came into universal use, and the flags and torch were relegated to nothing more than collar insignia.

When the 1st Cavalry Division moved into the battle areas of the Southwest Pacific, the 13th Signal moved right with it. Lorengau and Mamote in the Admiralty Islands were among the first campaigns in which the 13th Signal participated. From there the unit moved right with the division until the Japanese surrendered. Actions in the Pacific earned for it three Meritorious Unit Streamers.

The unit saw combat again in 1950 when the 1st Cavalry moved into Korea at the outbreak of hostilities. For its commendable action, it received a Meritorious Unit Commendation.

The 13th Signal was relieved from the scene of fighting and returned to Hokkaido with other units of the division. It returned to Korea in 1957, when the 24th Division was inactivated and redesignated the 1st Cavalry Division.

In Vietnam the battalion received the Presidential Unit Citation for the Pleiku Campaign.

The 13th Signal Battalion has provided telephone, radio, teletype and cryptographic services to an airmobile combat division spread over an area of operations approximately the size of Connecticut. They did all of this with the smallest signal battalion in the Army, and with the least and lightest equipment. The equipment had been cut down, transistorized and compacted to fit into a one-quarter ton trailer or to be slung under a Chinook.

By necessity the number of men in the battalion had been drastically reduced. They had to be ready to move into a different area at a moment's notice; to wherever the FIRST TEAM happened to be fighting. "Voice of Command" is the slogan of the battalion. These professional communicators lived this sobriquet from the beginning.

The 13th Signal Battalion arrived in Qui Nhon, Republic of Vietnam, in mid-September 1965 and moved its personnel, vehicles and equipment overland on Route 19 west to the division basecamp at An Khe. They spent the remainder of the year helping to develop the basecamp and meeting the division's tactical communications requirements. They also established the Hon Cong Mountain signal facility which became the communications hub of the northern half of the republic.

The battalion teamed up with the

The division headquarters, the three brigade basecamps and some of the Cav's firebases, are also connected by telephone communications. The around-the-clock business of war demands that switchboards (above) be manned constantly. But the bulk of combat communications is carried on the radio waves, from the single platoon radio to what often looks like a small and thin forest of antennas (right) at headquarter areas.

187

information office to provide AFRS radio programming to Skytroopers at Camp Radcliff. Since the AM signal from the Qui Nhon booster station could not be heard in the An Khe Valley, a transmitter and tower were obtained from AFRS in Saigon. The battalion loaned Sergeant Keith A. Shiley to the information office as technical advisor. SGT Shiley, using surplus materials, built a console, wired in four tape decks on loan, and, in early December, AFRS-An Khe, broadcasting at 1300 kilocycles, signed on the air. The basic network signal was brought in by a VHF link from Qui Nhon. Later, SGT Shiley built an FM transmitter and was experimenting with a stereo rig when he departed the battalion on rotation.

The battalion's basic signal systems were given their first full scale combat test in the Plei Me Campaign that took place in the Ia Drang Valley in October and November of 1965. The advance communications center was located at the division forward command post at

Specialist Four Paul R. Beavcage of the 13th Signal Battalion nears the end of a 12-hour shift at the 2nd Brigade communications switchboard at Lai Khe in early 1969—beard coming out and voice not a little hoarse from hours at the board. "Working, sir?"

A 13th Signalman checks basecamp phone lines looking for the cause of a breakdown in "commo."

Pleiku which, in turn, was in a personnel pod carried by a Flying Crane. All communications equipment and personnel at the forward command post were provided by the signal battalion. This center was operational 24 hours per day for the duration of the entire operation.

Particularly outstanding and very effective was the airborne relay. This flying communications van was credited with saving the lives of many who would otherwise have been unable to communicate their needs or distress. The unit consisted of a fixed wing aircraft equipped with two powerful FM radios. The craft would fly an orbit, 10,000 feet above the widely dispersed combat units to pick up and retransmit messages among units which would not otherwise be able to communicate.

During the early part of 1965 a VHF teletype circuit was instituted between the division forward and the division base command post. The installation vastly improved security and reliability of command and control.

The communication demands of Operation PAUL PEVERE II precipitated the creation of a rear operations

The Signal Corps in the airmobile 1st Cav must also learn to be airmobile. The 13th Signal Battalion worked to re-design radio and other communications equipment so it could be transported with greater speed and efficiency. Here two signalmen unload their radios after a move to another base area.

A cameraman with an artist's eye caught this signalman high on a commo pole, as he worked to string more telephone wire in an ever increasing communications network.

support platoon. The element was formed from all parts of the signal battalion in order to support the division forward command post.

Another systems innovation was initiated in the summer of 1966. The plan was to standardize the prewiring of the forward switchboard and to produce a telephone directory prior to an operation, thus eliminating much of the confusion previously associated with a move of the division foward command post.

An air courier was required to meet the needs of Operation THAYER. A UH-1 helicopter was maintained with a dependable schedule throughout the autumnal campaign. Operation PAUL REVERE IV ran concurrently with Operation THAYER II. In order to meet the needs of the dual situation several distinct duplicate nets had to be be created.

As an example of how widely dispersed the 13th was during 1967, at one time it was providing communications teams at Bong Son, An Khe, Kontum, LZ Uplift, LZ English, Duc Pho, LZ Sandra, Qui Nhon, Bagi, Saigon and Phan Tiet. The teams also operated at times during 1967 from Pleiku, Plateau Gi, Tuy Hoa and Chu Lai.

(Continued on P. 277)

The insignia of Headquarters and Headquarters Company, 1st Cavalry Division (Airmobile), and of all non-color bearing units in the division, is identical to the division patch, with the exception of two gold stars on the black band.

HHC

A division at war is a remarkable thing—flexible, vital, and powerful. The response to changes of conditions in Vietnam required extraordinary discipline and initiative from Headquarters and Headquarters Company (HHC), the division nerve center.

The history of HHC is a microcosm of the story of the entire division. The preoccupations of the division as a whole were those of HHC.

HHC was, by its definition, a hodge-podge of differing elements. It was home for legions of clerks, lexicographers, supply personnel, intelligence and personnel specialists. It contained the division command structure, including the commanding general and his staff, aide, and direct subordinates.

The manpower strength of HHC was greater than a maneuver battalion. Its disparate membership, the clerks, cooks, draftsmen, security platoon members, RTOs, supply sergeants, all linked into a vast network of command, coordination, and creativity reaching out to firebases and rear areas, pilots and infantrymen.

The division's analogy to a brain, HHC had to fulfill its precise and exacting function under the adverse conditions faced by an airmobile division on the move in Vietnam.

HHC had a bearing on nearly everything affecting the Cavalryman. Planning concerning pay; distribution of R&R allotments; granting of leave; delivery of food, ammunition, and construction materials; determination of when a new firebase was to be built; selection of battlefield tactics; gathering, analysis and storage of intelligence; supervision of pacification programs; the leadership of the whole division, all came through HHC.

And below the top echelon, as always, were the junior officers and enlisted men toiling at the thankless and crucial tasks involved in organizing and maintaining the division's command structure.

Maps had to be up to date, someone had to keep the files and records and print up the reports working under pressure for deadlines and accuracy far more exacting than in the most hectic metropolitan newspapers.

People had to be on the phones and radios 24 hours a day in the DTOC.

The giant Cav patch leaves no question as to who occupies the summit of Hon Cong Mountain, the site of a heavy VC mortar and ground attack on February 19, 1966.

which at times appeared to be nothing more than a tangle of organized chaos buried in tents and bunkers.

The RTO in the DTOC worked 12 hours a day. That meant several men doing nothing but waiting on radios, listening for reports from the brigades and units in the field, prepared to ensure the fastest distillation and proper disposition of all information coming in.

Only in this way would the general staff know what was happening, when it was happening. Everything had to be recorded, distributed and filed.

The success of the airmobility concept in Vietnam can be largely credited to the creation of a command system able to respond to its special demands. HHC was a vital and integral part of that command system.

Specialist Four Edward Morley double checks information over the phone as the war room hums with its average day cacophony of ringing phones and rasping radio boxes. At night, when both the Cavalrymen and the enemy settle into their positions, the action usually drops off. But even so, with both sides setting nightly ambushes, the electric sign lettered "Troops in Contact," which hangs over the war board, will begin flashing three or four times a night, and the radios and phones once again begin their racket.

Lieutenant Colonel George Stotser (center), 1st Cav G-3, and Lieutenant Colonel Richard Wood, his predecessor, check the Division Tactical Operations Center (DTOC) war map as Specialist Four Reuben Gonzales points out a "troops in contact" position. The DTOC war room is the nerve center of combat operations in the Cav AO, and it is manned 24 hours a day by men of Headquarters Company.

545th MILITARY POLICE COMPANY

In July 1965 the 545th Military Police (MP) Company was alerted, reorganized and packed to move into combat. When the main body of the company arrived in Vietnam it joined the advance party at An Khe and began to expedite the flow of traffic. By mid-October an MP desk with traffic and criminal investigation division (CID) sections was estáblished in the division base area. A second MP desk was operated in the village of An Khe where a conex container had to be modified to serve as a "drunk tank." A vice squad worked in An Khe while patrols and gate guards controlled and expedited the flow of traffic in the division base area as command post (CP) security was provided for the operations area.

The MPs were operating roadblocks by the end of 1965 with the assistance of the Vietnamese National Police.

The 545th MP Company supported Operations MASHER/WHITE WING beginning January 25, 1966. They provided guards for captured materials and weapons and operated an inclosure for detaining VC suspects.

The MPs aided military intelligence teams whenever they became involved in sweeps of populated areas—guarding, searching, detaining, protecting and detecting. MPs regularly accompanied civil affairs personnel to secure ·them while they operated in the division's tactical area of operations.

It was also necessary to use patrols and checkpoints to control the flow of refugees.

In late March, during Operations LINCOLN and MOSBY, the first platoon provided convoy escorts from An Khe to the 1st Brigade's forward CP. Additionally, the company provided guards for the MACV compound in Pleiku.

In October 1966 forward collection

Private First Class Craig Albertson of the 545th MP Company signals oncoming traffic to stop as he directs traffic in the center of the 1st Cav's division basecamp at Camp Gorvad, Phuoc Vinh.

points were set up in the areas where brigades were operating. All military-age males and enemy detainees were sent by the maneuver battalions to the collection point supporting its brigade. There confirmed enemy were interrogated for immediate tactical information then evacuated through regular prisoner of war channels. Other detainees were held at forward collection points for questioning by military intelligence, the national police or hamlet cadre in order to classify them as friend or foe. Innocent civilians were released and allowed to return to their homes. Those who turned out to be refugees were evacuated to a central collection point where they were helped to resettle in a refugee center. This screening during Operation IRVING virtually destroyed the Viet Cong infrastructure, placing the district under government control for the first time in several years.

The MPs launched into operations with the Police Field Force (NPFF) in June 1967. These were combined operations, mainly with the Vietnamese 222nd Battalion, Combat National Police. The plan was to cordon a village during the night, followed by a combined sweep through the village at dawn. The Vietnamese police searched houses and questioned people as they moved through. They often returned repeatedly to the same hamlets.

Ever try to outrun a grenade? On another sweep of a hamlet on the Bong Son Plain in August 1967, an MP spotted a hole ahead of him, just as an arm reached out and tossed a hand grenade. The MP turned and ran out of range. Another frag followed and he ran still further. Finally, when the VC poked his head up to lob a third one, one of the other MPs shot him, leaving the specialist still running, but unhurt.

Later, the team flushed out several Viet Cong and a firefight broke out. Specialist Four Joe Ferraro, a former schoolteacher from Boston, was hit in

A roving MP-patrol jeep receives a call to investigate an incident—another daily item of the police work required in any community of 21,000 men.

the chest and his weapon was knocked away from him as he fell. He lay still as the fight raged on around him. Suddenly, one of the enemy soldiers jumped up and ran, trying to escape into the nearby jungle. He was charging right past Ferraro when the wounded MP leaped to his feet with a brick in his hand and killed the startled VC with a single blow before the enemy could raise his rifle.

When the division moved north to I Corps in 1968 the MPs had to surmount the problems of having to secure multiple and constantly mobile tactical operations centers. They continued to process prisoners and detainees even though they were always on the move. When they finally settled down for the summer of 1968 at Camp Evans, the company built a POW collection camp. The "cage" became a model for the handling of hostiles throughout Vietnam. An International Red Cross inspection team gave the facility a maximum rating for complying with the highest standards of treatment.

After the 1st Cavalry Division moved south to III Corps, the MPs continued their missions of TOC security and convoy control. They also began com-

(Continued on P 283)

Two MPs and a member of the Vietnamese National Police Force stop to talk with a "mama-san" at her fruit stand. The 1st Cav MPs team with National Police and ARVN MPs to make up patrols that then have the authority to deal with any situation, whether it involves Vietnamese, Americans or both.

Since its arrival in Vietnam, the 1st Cavalry Division has relied exclusively on the men of Division Chemical, a special staff section which works in cooperation with the G-3 (plans and operations), for the use of chemical material in all of its aspects.

In turn, the 26th Chemical Detachment aids Division Chemical in accomplishing its mission and acts as a ready reserve for the chemical platoon.

The 184th Direct Support Platoon is under the operational control of Division Chemical; its operations section being primarily responsible for all "flame" operations within the division.

It is this operations section which constructs, installs and maintains all the fougasse barrels around 1st Cav basecamps and fire support bases. The fougasse charges have proven invaluable in base defense, especially when used against attacking enemy, who have a particular dislike for the simple weapon.

The platoon also installs "Husch Flares," a type of flame field expedient used in base perimeter defense, illuminating an area for up to six hours.

The direct support maintenance-section of the platoon inspects all chemical equipment in the division and performs maintenance when necessary.

Items of primary maintenance concern for the platoon are protective masks and flamethrowers. While the enemy has not frequently used gas agents in combat, the possibility of its use requires that division personnel have access to functional protective masks.

One of the platoon's specialties is operation and maintenance of the airborne personnel detector. Better known as the "people sniffer," the sensitive instrument is operated from a low flying helicopter and has the ability to detect enemy activity or lack of it in the areas over flown.

All sections of the 1st Cav's chemical complex are consistently researching methods of improving chemical support. They are constantly involved in testing new developments and have contributed numerous innovations.

One such innovation is the BURB, an example of the platoon's chemical ingenuity that has come to be expected. In early 1969 Master Sergeant Jack Watts developed the Bunker Use Restriction Bomb (BURB), a device made from discarded ammunition cannisters which is detonated inside an enemy bunker, contaminating its interior with persistent CS.

DIVISION CHEMICAL UNITS

As 1969 drew to a close, Division Chemical was also doing its part to help in Vietnamization of the war, contributing its knowledge and experience to ARVN troops under the Dong Tien (Forward Together) Program. Along with the 1st ARVN Airborne Division troopers, the chemical men of the 1st Cav conducted combined chemical operations, including a series of one-week training courses at Phuoc Vinh where the ARVN soldiers were familiarized with all phases of chemical operations. The graduates of these courses served apprenticeship terms in the field with the contact teams before returning to their own units as instructors and chemical team leaders.

As a unit attached to the 1st Air Cav in October, 1965, the 26th Chemical Detachment is entitled to share the Presidential Unit Citation earned by the division during the Pleiku Campaign.

A member of the Cav Chemical detachment prepares a Bunker Use Restriction Bomb (BURB). An invention of the chemical men of the Cav, the BURB contains an explosive device and several pounds of CS powder. It is used to contaminate—and thus render useless—any enemy bunkers or caves found in the field.

191st MILITARY INTELLIGENCE

The 191st Military Intelligence Company (MIC) has the mission to perform all specialized intelligence and counter-intelligence functions requiring the employment of special skills or foreign languages.

Consisting of a company headquarters and four functionally organized operations sections—Order of Battle (OB), Interrogation of Prisoners of War (IPW), Imagery Interpretation (II), and Counter-Intelligence (CI)—the company provides tactical commanders at all levels with timely intelligence to meet the changing situations created by the 1st Cav's mobility.

The unit was first constituted in September 1950 and participated with the Cav through six campaigns in the Korean War.

The detachment went to the Republic of Vietnam in September 1965 and there provided intelligence for the division leading up to and throughout the Pleiku Campaign, October 23 to November 26, 1965.

Intelligence networks require time to develop. That network and the 191st's surveillance of enemy activity continued to expand the wealth of intelligence throughout 1966.

Early in 1968, when the Skytroopers

moved to the Northern I Corps, the 191st had its work cut out—all commanders had to be familiarized with the new situation. Within two days after the division headquarters made the move a comprehensive Order of Battle book of some 100 pages and a distribution of more than 300 copies was made. This was the first Order of Battle handbook published on the Northern I Corps area for use by U.S. forces.

One of the intelligence specialists' primary sources of information was the Imagery Interpretation section. This section interpreted photos and data from missions flown by reconnaissance aircraft. The imagery interpretators identified numerous enemy targets from aerial photographs. The enemy bunkers and trenches detected were reported to the combat arms for "appropriate action." The analysts also have the capability to interpret infrared and side-looking airborne radar.

During 1969 the interrogation section supported every major operation undertaken by the 1st Cavalry Division and in July 1969 the debriefing of a Hoi Chanh furnished the division with information on an enemy plan to attack the Quan Loi basecamp. A complete interrogation provided the 1st Cav with the routes of attack, enemy units involved, time of the attack and routes of withdrawal. The information proved to be reliable and the Skytroopers took advantage of the forewarning to crush the attack.

While the interrogation teams were questioning hundreds of prisoners, Hoi Chanhs, and civilians each month in their quest for information, the Counter-Intelligence (CI) section was out to prevent subversion of the FIRST TEAM by the enemy.

The CI section performed security inspections, validated security clearances and established an internal net for early warning collection.

In November 1969, members of the 2nd ARVN military intelligence were assigned duties with the special operations branch of the CI section, and there received on-the-job training in intelligence activities.

A member of the 191st Military Intelligence Company studies aerial reconnaissance photographs to locate new enemy concentrations, movement or caches.

The insignia of Company H (Ranger), 75th Infantry (Airborne), originally was worn by members of the 5307th Composite Unit, Provisional. Nicknamed Merrill's Marauders for Brigadier General Frank D. Merrill, the first commander, the unit made deep penetrations behind enemy lines in the China and Burma jungles in 1944. It was a fitting forerunner of today's rangers. The star in the upper left corner is the symbol of the Republic of China, whose troops worked with the unit. The star in the lower right corner comes from the American flag.

COMPANY H, (RANGER) 75th INFANTRY (AIRBORNE)

On February 2, 1967, the 1st Air Cavalry Division organized its first division-operated Long Range Reconnaissance Patrol (LRRPs). Attached to 191st Military Intelligence Company, the LRRPs were composed of two patrols of six men each. The men were all hand picked volunteers who had successfully passed a grueling 12 day training course.

In April of 1967 the LRRPs were attached to Headquarters and Headquarters Company of the 1st Air Cavalry Division under the operational control of the G-2 section. As before their mission was to find the enemy.

On December 20, 1967, the LRRPs were reorganized as Company E, 52nd Infantry. They continued to provide the division with valuable intelligence about enemy activity. They proved throughout III Corps that the fewer aircraft used to make an insertion into enemy occupied territory, the more certain they could be of remaining undetected. Using their special operational procedure, they proved to be invaluable to the division.

On January 5, 1969, one team from Company E, 52nd Infantry, commanded by Captain George A. Paccerelli, made contact with an enemy force northwest of Phouc Vinh that outnumbered it by 20 to one. For two hours the men were pinned down by enemy fire.

As a result of their action two men were awarded Silver Stars and three received Bronze Stars with "V" devices.

Staff Sergeant Ronald J. Bitticks, 24, and Sergeant Howard Fatzinger III, 19, both received Silver Stars and were promoted to their present ranks. Sergeant Edward Moline, 21, Sergeant John Geiger, 21, and Staff Sergeant Guy McConnell, 23, were awarded the Bronze Stars.

This is their story as told by their team leader, SSG Bitticks:

"We were inserted by helicopter shortly after dawn and began moving through the thick bamboo. Our mission was to try and locate enemy elements believed to be operating in the area. We hadn't been on the ground too long when SGT Geiger, our medic, spotted some commo wire running along the ground. I called in and reported it and received instructions to check out the area.

"We spotted a trail that was so well-used it was difficult trying to determine how many individuals had used it. While I was examining the trail, SGT Moline, the front scout, spotted two enemy soldiers wearing light-colored uniforms and carrying AK-47s moving down the trail some 50 feet away. They were approaching rapidly and afforded us no opportunity to set up an ambush.

"A second part of our mission involves detaining suspects when possible. Thinking that this might give us the opportunity to complete that part of the mission, I jumped out on the trail 10 to 15 feet from the NVA and yelled 'Chieu Hoi!'

"It was evident by the surprised expressions upon their faces that they didn't believe what they saw. For a few seconds they just stared; then they went for their weapons. I opened up with my M-16, killing one while the other managed to escape into the bamboo.

"By 3 p.m. we had moved only 300 meters from the contact area. We were forced to move slowly through the thick growth in order to keep noise at a minimum. The trail off to our right flank made a sharp bend, and coming around the bend about 50 meters away we spotted a group of enemy soldiers.

"We counted over 42 enemy. It was like watching the ducks at Coney Island come on line in the shooting gallery. I thought the line would never end.

"We figured the enemy hadn't spotted us so we tried to signal the gunship which had arrived on station without giving our position away by using a mirror. Nevertheless three of the enemy advanced towards our position."

"They got to within 20 feet of us. Realizing they would soon spot us, we opened up, killing all three. This gave our our position away and we began receiving a heavy volume of fire from three sides.

"This went on for over two hours. If it hadn't been for the gunship we never would have got out alive. At 5:15 p.m. we were extracted. The gunships again hit the area followed by an Air Force jet strike. A scout team counted 32 confirmed enemy dead from the air.

"When we got back to the company emotions took over. The scene was one as though we hadn't seen one another for years. Tears flowed freely."

On February 1, 1969, Company E, 52nd Infantry, was reorganized as Company H (Ranger), 75th Infantry (Airborne).

Upon joining the 75th Infantry, each Ranger goes through a 12-day training period where he is qualified to perform the duties of a radio-telephone operator, medic and scout. Other courses offered in the school are combat intelligence, map reading, use of ropes, and escape

Men of the 75th Ranger Company swing beneath a UH-1H Huey (opposite page) after practicing an emergency jungle extraction with the "McGuire rigging." Another ranger rappels from a Huey frequent practice jumps. Rappelling is one means the rangers use to get into thick jungle.

and evasion. By the time a man completes the course he is fully qualified to call in artillery on enemy locations or treat the wounded as are most artillery and medical specialists.

At one time or another most Rangers travel to Nha Trang for a special course in long range patrols. The school is operated by the 5th Special Forces, lasts three weeks, and goes deeper into the art of jungle patroling.

Company H (Ranger), 75th Infantry (Airborne), is attached to the 1st Squadron, 9th Cavalry, and is supported by it. The company operates with 12 patrol teams, with an average of five men per team.

One typical mission, Team 32 was inserted by Troop C, 1st of the 9th, into the jungle near Song Be. "We went out on visual reconnaissance with the 9th Cav and trekked through triple canopy jungle after our drop," said Sergeant Stanley D. Edwards.

Moving out from its landing zone, the team came across a recently used footpath leading to a trail which had been used by an NVA company. Communication was now essential, and the Rangers raised their long whip antenna to make contact with FSB Buttons. After a quiet night, the Rangers' patience was rewarded when seven NVA in khakis and carrying AK-47s wandered up the trail.

"We were sitting about eight meters off the trail," said SGT Edwards, "but we were well camouflaged and were trying to look like part of the trees."

A call from Charlie Troop, 1st of the 9th scout team, alerted the Rangers to a bunker complex about 600 meters down the trail. Carefully timing the NVA move toward the bunkers, the Rangers called in 155 mm howitzer fire from Buttons at the moment the enemy reached the bunkers.

Fifteen minutes later, three NVA staggered down the trail, one of them wounded by shrapnel. The Rangers quickly ambushed the trio, killing all three and capturing three AK-47 rifles.

The Blues from Troop C, 1st of the 9th, combat assaulted into the bunker complex to give the Rangers reinforcement. Five AK-47s and a collection of documents rewarded their search. Its work done, Ranger Team 32 headed back to Buttons.

The Rangers from Buttons played a crucial role again when on November 4,

(Continued on P. 257)

This ranger, his face camouflaged before going on a mission, carries the CAR-15, a favorite ranger weapon because of its short metal stock and fast rate of fire.

The ranger way is the way of stealth. Though the rangers often make contact with the enemy, when faced with an enemy battalion the four-man ranger team must use discretion, back-off, and call in the big guns.

OTHER UNITS

SCOUT DOGS & COMBAT TRACKERS

You won't find their names in the division roster, but anyone contending that Bruno and Tux and King and Duke are not Skytroopers of the first order would get a good argument from members of the 25th and 34th Infantry Platoons (Scout Dog) and the men they work with.

The two platoons supply scout dogs and handlers to company size units in the 1st Air Cavalry. The sign on a handler's locker reads, "Don't worry, Mom. I'll be right back. I'm just out

walking the dog." The sign's simplicity belies the important mission the handler and his canine perform.

The four-footed pointman makes good use of his extra-keen senses and animal instincts as he guides troops through enemy territory.

Having spent months developing a close, pitcher-catcher rapport with his particular dog, the handler walks point with the dog, devoting his complete and concentrated attention to the dog alone, not the jungle around him. The handler waits and watches his dog for some sign of an "alert." It may be a perking of the ears, a tense position, a jerking of the head or a subtle move, but the skilled handler is taught to recognize the indicator immediately.

The handler will rely solely on his dog to warn him of an approaching enemy or of an enemy ambush, because the dog will detect the enemy's presence long before human sense could detect him. Some dogs have been known to "blow the whistle" on an enemy force as far as 750 meters distant.

Employing the tracker dog in their operations, the four highly autonomous tracker teams in the division are usually inserted into a combat area following heavy contact or after another unit has sprung an ambush and some of the enemy have fled. Though they pack plenty of fire support to take care of themselves, their job is to track the enemy, not make contact with him.

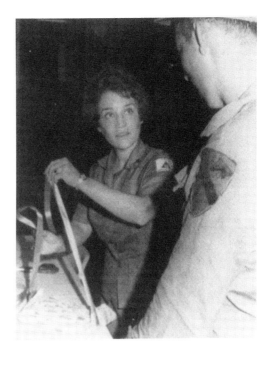

RED CROSS SERVICES

They see as much of Cav Country as any Skytrooper, these energetic Donut Dollies. She doesn't really need a white uniform—a striking contrast to the universal olive drab of Vietnam—to stand out in the crowd. Her good looks and charm and the memories she jogs of the sweetheart back home are enough to serve as conversational starting points with Air Cavalrymen.

The girls are part of the American Red Cross organization, which, in Vietnam just as in the states, helps soldiers coordinate confirmation of emergencies back home and obtain leaves whenever necessary. This work is done by a unit of field directors who live and work with staff of the FIRST TEAM. But the frosting on the Red Cross cake for GIs is the Donut Dolly.

RADAR DETACHMENTS

The 268th and 273rd Radar Detachments, along with an additional radar section, scan Cav Country with sophisticated electronic equipment in search of the enemy. Under the control of Division Artillery, the detachments employ $35,000 radar systems mobile enough to be lifted by Chinook helicopter to any area where they are needed. The operation of the system is basically a simple

one. While an electrical wave sweeps across a field or search and is reflected on an oscilloscope screen, an operator watches for the telltale blip indicating troop or vehicle movement. An audio system helps confirm the spottings.

The radar section, consisting of smaller, less powerful systems, is spread throughout the division at basecamps and firebases and is used in ground surveillance and in counter-mortar and rocket attacks.

SERVICE CLUBS

An important part of the Army's effort to keep morale among the troops at a healthy level is played by the Service Clubs in the division. Operated by civilian, professional and military personnel of the Special Services Branch, the clubs involve themselves in a myriad range of activities geared to "assisting in the development of the efficiency and morale of enlisted personnel," in their military mission. The clubs stage floor shows, coffee calls, hail and farewell parties, birthday celebrations and tournaments for would-be pool, chess and pingpong champions.

Keeping in tune with the Cav's pacification and Vietnamization programs, the clubs employ Vietnamese nationals who devote their time and efforts toward acquainting Skytroopers with a greater knowledge, and, therefore, greater understanding of the people they seek to befriend and aid.

AIR FORCE FACS & WEATHER

They belong to another branch of the military—the United States Air Force (USAF)—but the Cav patch they wear on their left shoulder makes them unmistakable members of the FIRST TEAM.

Most glamourous of the two Air Force units working with the division is part of the 19th Tactical Air Support Squadron—the men who fly the two-seat, turbo-prop OV-10 Bronco fixed wing aircraft. With forward air control (FAC) parties supporting each of the division's brigades, the Air Force pilots' primary missions are to provide visual reconnaissance, control and mark Air Force air strikes and adjust artillery.

Operating Location 2 of the Air Force's 5th Weather Squadron provides 1st Cav ground troops and helicopter pilots with weather forecasts and observations on a twice-daily basis. Drawing on field reports from their own teams as well as Path Finders at forward areas, the ob-

servers play a key role in allowing commanders to consider potential weather threats before completing tactical plans.

An Air Force OV-10 "Bronco" slips into a steep, banking dive on a rocket marking run against an enemy position in III Corps.

UNITS WHICH ONCE WORE THE 'BLANKET'

The following units were attached to the division at various times in its history. They played an important and valuable role in the operations of the FIRST TEAM, and Skytroopers are as thankful for their contributions as these units were proud to serve with the 1st Cavalry Division.

ARTILLERY

The 6th Battalion, 14th Artillery, was attached to the division on October 29, 1965. Its 175 mm self-propelled guns provided heavy support for the 1st Cavalry in the division's early operations. The battalion was detached in February of 1966.

The eight-inch self-propelled howitzers of the 3rd Battalion, 18th Artillery, were attached to the division from October 29, 1965, to February 1, 1966, and took part in Operation SHINY BAYONET, one of the division's first operations.

The 2nd Platoon (Searchlight), B Battery, 29th Artillery, served with the division from October 23, 1965, until early 1968. The platoon's searchlights

This mighty eight-inch self-propelled howitzer, "Cherry Buster," was one of the 3rd Battalion, 18th Artillery's guns which assisted the Cav during the division's early months in Vietnam.

sliced the darkness around division basecamps to detect enemy movements and attempts to breach the wire. It also shares the Pleiku Campaign PUC.

In spring of 1966, C Battery, 6th Battalion, 16th Artillery, was attached to the division. The 155 mm howitzers of the battery were at LZ Bird in December 1966 when the LZ was attacked by three battalions of NVA. The Redlegs helped hurl back the attack, which cost the enemy 200 dead. The battery was detached from the division in early 1967.

Charlie Battery, 4th Battalion, 60th Artillery, provided Quad-50, (truck-mounted .50 caliber machineguns), Dust-

Until 1969 the 478th Aviation Company (Heavy Helicopters) was an integral part of the division's operations. The huge CH-54 Flying Cranes, at the time organic to the Cav, made the first combat lift of 155 mm howitzers in 1966.

ers (truck-mounted 40 mm cannon) and jeep-mounted searchlight support to the division in 1968 and 1969. The 5th Battalion, 2nd Artillery, replaced the unit in December of 1969. These units generally operated to beef up basecamp perimeter defense.

AVIATION

From September 1965 through October 1966, the 17th Aviation Company was attached to the FIRST TEAM, its Caribous providing instantly responsive fixed-wing cargo support.

The CH-54A Flying Cranes of the 478th Aviation Company (Heavy Helicopters) were an integral part of the division's operations from September 1965 until 1969, when the 478th was replaced by the 273rd Aviation Company (Heavy Helicopters). The 478th made the first combat lifts of 155 mm howitzers in 1966, flying batteries to firing positions that would otherwise be inaccessible. Without the heavy hauling capabilities of the CH-54A the division's airmobility would be severely limited.

Both aviation units earned a share of the Pleiku Campaign PUC.

The 241th Signal Detachment (Avionics) supported the 478th Flying Crane company from fall of 1966 through early 1968.

CIVIL AFFAIRS

Several elements of the 41st Civil Affairs Company were attached to the division from January 1967 through early 1968. The company carried out various civic action programs to improve the lot of the Vietnamese people and strengthen their allegiance to the Vietnamese government.

INFANTRY

From September 1965 until detached January 17, 1968, the 54th Infantry Detachment (Ground Surveillance) swept the perimeters of the division's firebases with its radar, searching for enemy movement and firing positions. It often brought a quick halt to mortar attacks by discovering their source and calling in counterfire. Organic units replaced the 54th.

From August 1967 through April 1968, the 1st Battalion, 50th Mechanized

Tanks of the 1st Battalion, 50th Infantry (Mechanized), move inland from the northern coastline in support of Cav troops from 1st Battalion, 12th Cavalry. It was early 1967.

The M-42 self-propelled track, better known as a "Duster," moves along the road in support of division operation operations in Quang Tri Province. This I Field Force weapon lent the support of its imposing twin, 40 mm cannon to Cav ground operations.

Infantry, provided tanks and armored personnel carriers to the division for operations against fortified enemy positions.

The 7th and 8th Combat Tracker Teams were attached to the division in 1968. Four teams from the 62nd Infantry served with the division in 1969. The tracker dogs of the team sniff out enemy personnel who may have escaped from an ambush, firefight or probe on a firebase.

RADIO RESEARCH

The 10th Radio Research unit was attached to the division from September 1965 through January 1967. The 371st Radio Research Company replaced it and was still attached to the division as of January 1970.

SIGNAL

Detachment 1, 54th Signal Battalion, was attached to the division from October 1965 through spring 1966. The 586th Signal Company (Support) was attached to the division from September 1965 through January 1967.

WEATHER

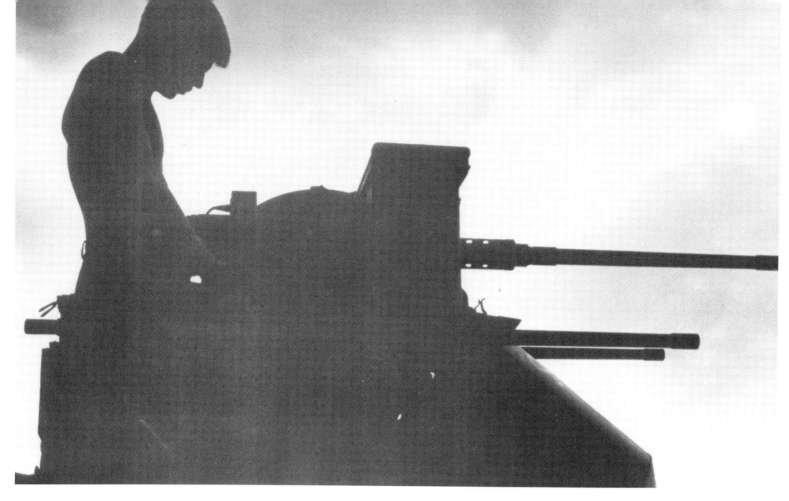

A member of the 4th Battalion, 60th Artillery, and his "Quad-50" (four .50 caliber machine-guns mounted together), are silhouetted against the darkening sky as night falls over Vietnam.

The 30th Air Force Weather Squadron provided information on weather conditions in the Cav's AO, information vital to the division's operations. It was attached in October 1965. In November 1966 it was replaced by the 24th Detachment of the 5th Weather Squadron. In 1968 that unit left the Cav and the 31st Detachment, 5th Weather Squadron, replaced it.

Any unit, assigned, attached or under the FIRST TEAM's operational control shared in the Pleiku Campaign Presidential Unit Citation. This included the 34th Quartermaster Battalion DS/GS, and the 70th Engineer Battalion, both working at An Khe, as well as the smaller units listed above.

The long barrel of a big 175 mm self-propelled gun bespeaks of the weapon's long reach. The gun belongs to the 6th Battalion, 27th Artillery, which provides heavy fire support for the troops near Camp Gorvad, Phuoc Vinh.

MAJOR COMBAT ACTION

— 1965 —

MAJOR OPERATIONS IN WHICH SKYTROOPERS TOOK PART OR COMPLETED

Name	Date	Units	Enemy KIA	Location
Pleiku Campaign	Oct. 19-Nov. 26	Division	3,561	Pleiku Province
Clean House	Dec. 17-31	3rd Bde	137	Suoi Ca Valley, II Corps

MAJOR BATTLES

(BASED ON 50 OR MORE ENEMY KIA TO A SINGLE, IDENTIFIABLE ACTION)

Battle	Date	Units	Enemy KIA	Location	Map Key
Battle of Duc Co	Nov. 4	1/8, 1/9	110	South Bank of Ia Drang River	A-Plt I
Battle at LZ X-Ray	Nov. 14-16	1/7, 2/7, 2/5	2,049	Chu Pong Massif, Pleiku Province	B-Plt I
Battle at LZ Albany	Nov. 17	2/7, 1/5	503	Chu Pong Massif, Pleiku Province	C-Plt I
Battle on the Tae River	Nov. 1	1/9, 2/12	282	North bank of the Tae River	a-Plt I
Battle at LZ Wing	Nov. 6	2/8	198	West of Plei Me	b-Plt I

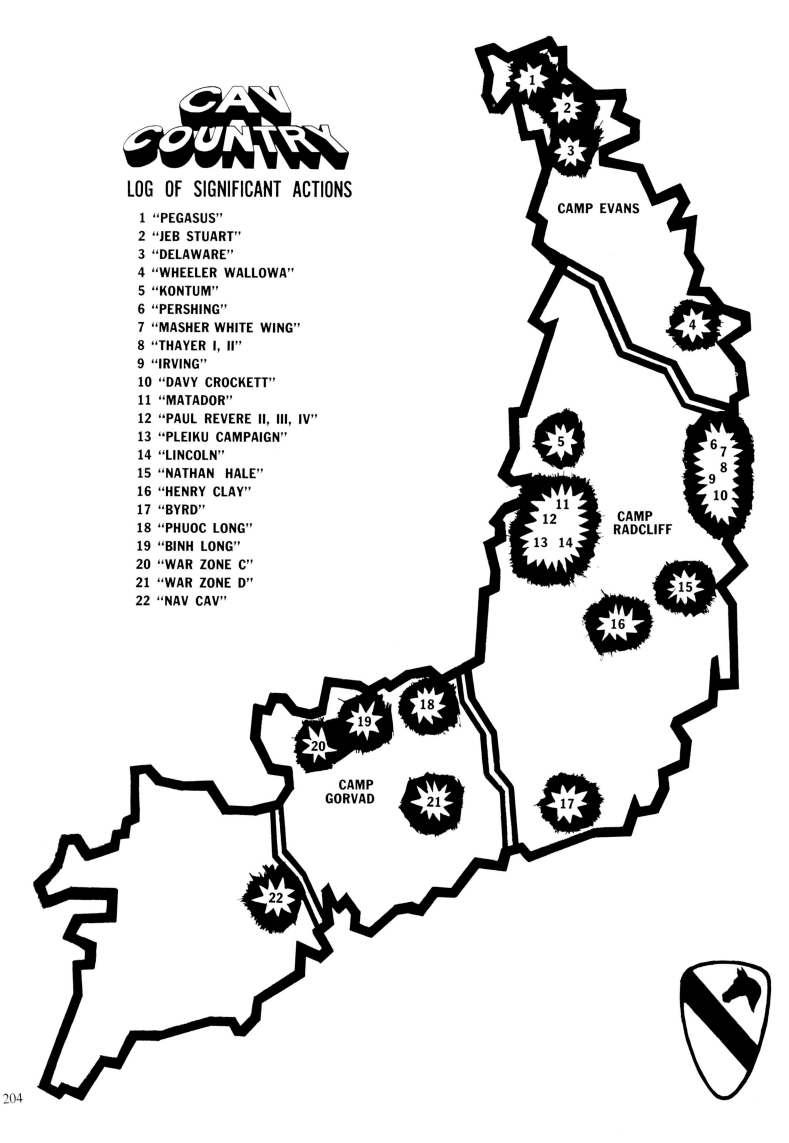

CAV COUNTRY

LOG OF SIGNIFICANT ACTIONS

1 "PEGASUS"
2 "JEB STUART"
3 "DELAWARE"
4 "WHEELER WALLOWA"
5 "KONTUM"
6 "PERSHING"
7 "MASHER WHITE WING"
8 "THAYER I, II"
9 "IRVING"
10 "DAVY CROCKETT"
11 "MATADOR"
12 "PAUL REVERE II, III, IV"
13 "PLEIKU CAMPAIGN"
14 "LINCOLN"
15 "NATHAN HALE"
16 "HENRY CLAY"
17 "BYRD"
18 "PHUOC LONG"
19 "BINH LONG"
20 "WAR ZONE C"
21 "WAR ZONE D"
22 "NAV CAV"

CAMP EVANS

CAMP RADCLIFF

CAMP GORVAD

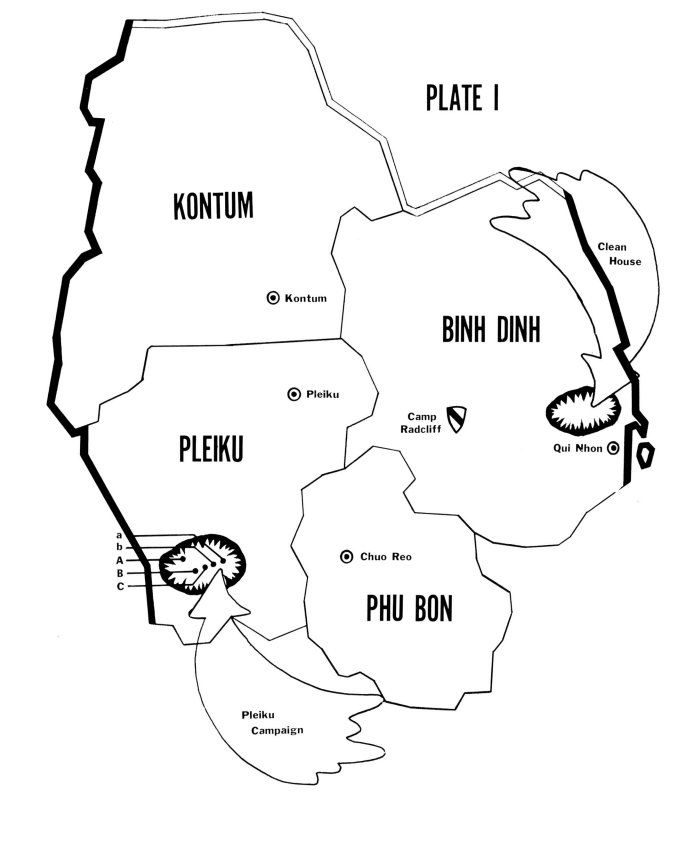

PLATE I

KONTUM

⊙ Kontum

BINH DINH

Clean House

⊙ Pleiku

PLEIKU

Camp Radcliff

Qui Nhon ⊙

a
b
A
B
C

⊙ Chuo Reo

PHU BON

Pleiku Campaign

PLEIKU

1966

MAJOR OPERATIONS IN WHICH SKYTROOPERS TOOK PART OR COMPLETED

Name	Date	Units	Enemy KIA	Location
Masher/White Wing	Jan. 25 Mar. 6	Division, III Marine Task Force, 22nd ARVN Div, ARVN Abn, ROK Capital Div.	1,744	Binh Dinh Province
Lincoln	Mar. 25 Apr. 8	1st & 3rd Bdes 25th Inf Div 3rd Bde	453	Chu Pong Massif, II Corps
Davy Crockett	May 4-10	3rd Bde	374	Northeastern Binh Dinh Province
Crazy Horse	May 16 June 5	1st Bde, 4th ARVN TF	501	Area between Vinh Thanh and Suoi Ca Valleys
Nathan Hale	June 19 July 1	1st & 3rd Bdes	459	Phu Yen Province
Paul Revere II	Aug. 1-25	2nd & 3rd Bdes	809	Ia Drang-Chu Pong area
Byrd	Aug. 25 Jan. 30	TF, 2/7	849	Binh Thuan and Phan Thiet
Thayer I	Sep. 13 Oct. 1	1st & 2nd Bdes	231	Kim Son Valley
Irving	Oct. 2-24	1st & 3rd Bdes	681	South China Sea Coast, Binh Dinh Province
Thayer II	Oct. 25 Feb. 12	Division	1,757	Bong Son, eastern Binh Dinh Province
Paul Revere IV	Oct. 31 Dec. 27	2nd Bde, 4th Inf Div	977	Ia Drang-Chu Pong area

MAJOR BATTLES

(BASED ON 50 OR MORE ENEMY KIA KEYED TO A SINGLE, IDENTIFIABLE ACTION)

Battle	Date	Units	Enemy KIA	Location	Map Key
Battle with the Quyet Tan Regiment	Jan. 29-30	2/7	81	Binh Dinh Province	E-Plt II
Battle of the An Lao Assault	Feb. 7	2/7	57	An Lao Valley	F-Plt II
Battle of the Iron Triangle	Feb. 18-21	2nd Bde	312	12 miles south of Bong Son	G-Plt II
Battle near Chu Pong Massif	Mar. 30-31	A/1/9, 1/12	197	Chu Pong Massif	H-Plt III
First Battle of Crazy Horse	May 16-17	B/2/8, A/1/12	132	Vinh Thanh Mountains	I-Plt II
Battle at Position Eagle	June 22	1/8	134	Tuy Hoa Vicinity, Phu Yen Province	J-Plt II
Battle in Darlac Province	Aug. 8	1/7, 1/12	106	Ia Drang Valley, Darlac Province	K-Plt III
Battle of Hill 534	Aug. 14-15	1/5, 2/5	138	Chu Pong Massif	L-Plt III
Battle of Hoa Hoi	Oct. 2-3	1/12, 1/9, 1/5	233	Hoa Hoi Village, An Lac Peninsula	M-Plt IV
Battle of Phan Thiet	Oct. 25	2/7	52	Phan Thiet	OO-Plt VI
Battle of Charlie, 1st of the 5th	Nov. 21	C/1/5	145	Chu Pong Massif	N-Plt III
Battle in 506 Valley	Dec. 17-19	1/8, 1/12, 1/9	95	Highway 506	O-Plt IV
Battle of LZ Bird	Dec. 27-31	1/12, C/6/16 Arty, B/2/19 Arty	266	Kim Son Valley	P-Plt IV

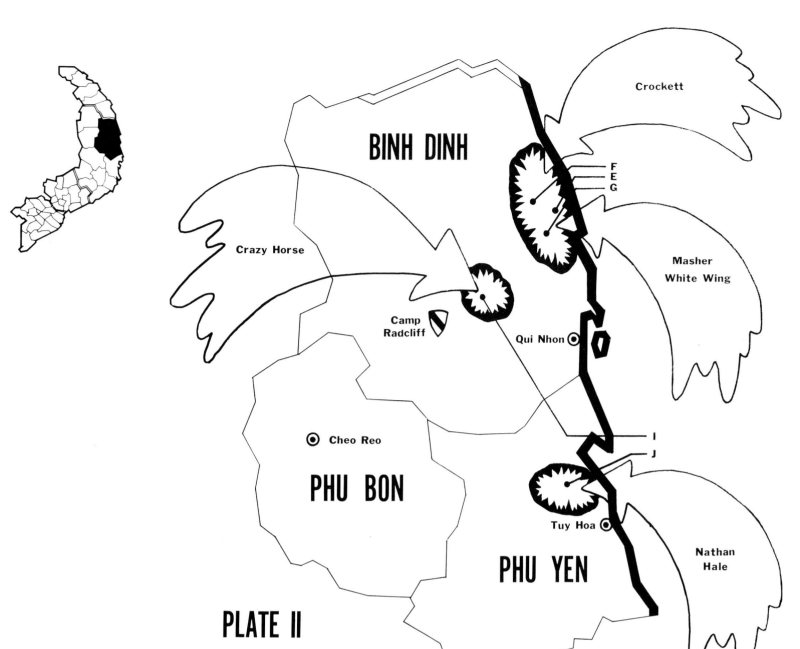

BINH DINH

Crockett

Crazy Horse

F
E
G

Masher
White Wing

Camp
Radcliff

Qui Nhon ◉

◉ Cheo Reo

PHU BON

Tuy Hoa ◉

PHU YEN

Nathan
Hale

PLATE II

BONG SON

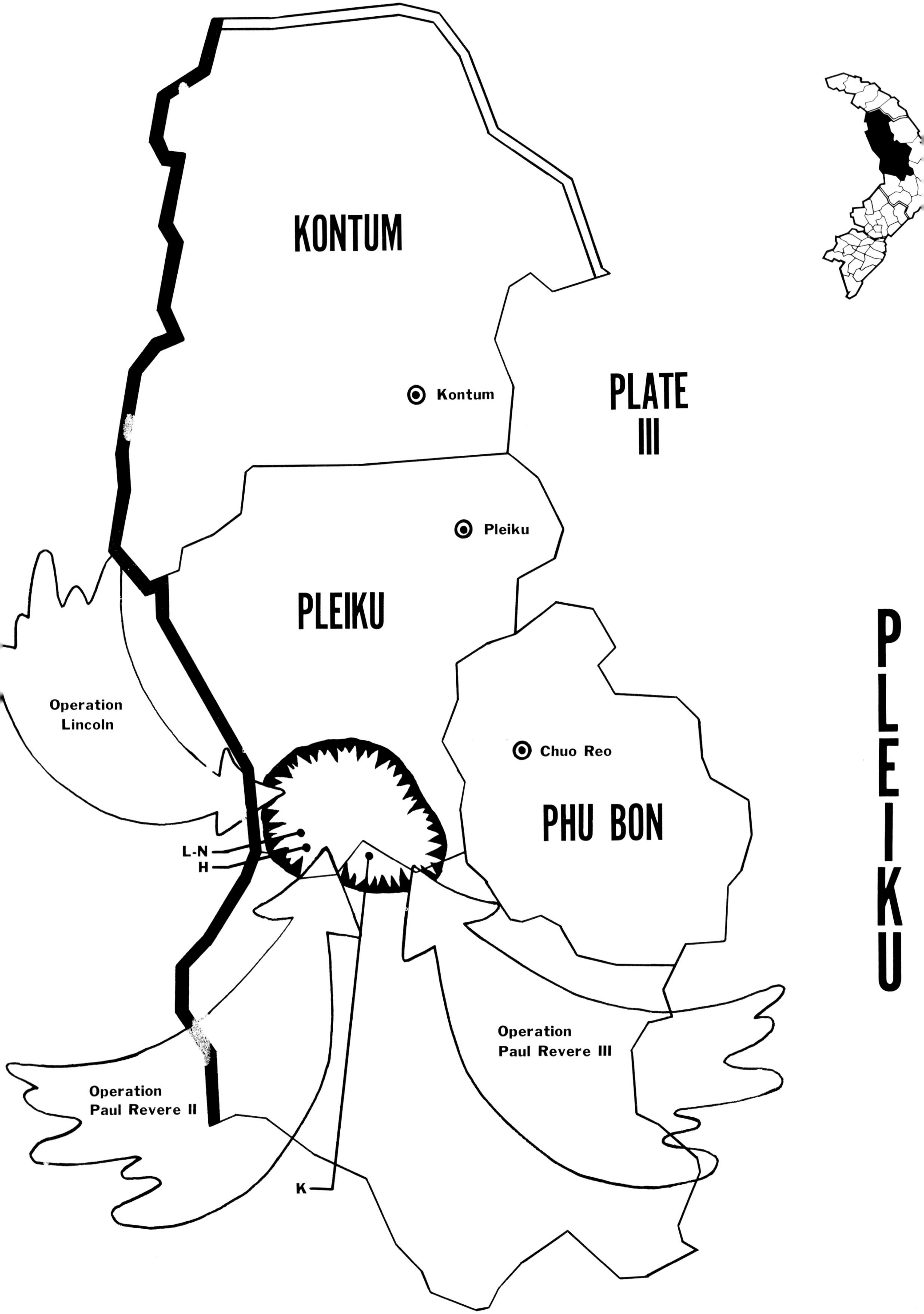

KONTUM

⊙ Kontum

PLATE
III

⊙ Pleiku

PLEIKU

Operation
Lincoln

⊙ Chuo Reo

PHU BON

L-N
H

Operation
Paul Revere III

Operation
Paul Revere II

K

P
L
E
I
K
U

1967

MAJOR OPERATIONS IN WHICH SKYTROOPERS TOOK PART OR COMPLETED

Name	Date	Units	Enemy KIA	Location
Pershing	Feb. 12 Jan. 21	Division	5,401	Eastern Binh Dinh Province
LeJeune	Apr. 7-22	2nd Bde	181	Quang Ngai Province
Song Re	Aug. 1-20	3rd Bde	149	Song Re Valley, Quang Ngai Province
Wheeler/Wallowa	Oct. 2 Jan. 25	3rd Bde	3,188	Que Son Valley, Quang Ngai Province

MAJOR BATTLES

(BASED ON 50 OR MORE ENEMY KIA KEYED TO A SINGLE, IDENTIFIABLE ACTION)

Battle	Date	Units	Enemy KIA	Location	Map Key
Battle east of Bong Son	Jan. 27	2/12	72	Bong Son Plain	Q-Plt IV
Battle of Bullseye V	Jan. 30	2/12, 1/5, 1/9	104	Northeast Bong Son Plain	R-Plt IV
1st Battle of Tuy Au	Feb. 18-19	1st Bde	68	Western Bong Son Plain	S-Plt IV
Battle of Hoa Tanh (1)	Mar. 6-7	2/5, 1/9	81	Hoa Tanh (i) Village, Binh Dinh Province	T-Plt IV
1st Battle of Tam Quan	Mar. 19-21	1st & 2nd Bdes	121	Tam Quan, Bong Son Plain	U-Plt IV
Battle in An Lao Valley	Apr. 4	3rd Bde	78	An Lao Valley	V-Plt IV
Battle of An Qui	May 30-June 1	1/8, 1/9, 1/12	96	An Qui, Bong Son Plain	W-Plt IV
Battle near Highway 1	May 31	2/8	90	West of Highway 1, Binh Dinh Province	X-Plt IV
Battle of Dam Tra-O	June 21	1/5, 2/5	84	Dam Tra-O Lake	Z-Plt IV
2nd Battle of Tuy Au	Jul. 2-3	1/8	86	Western Bong Son	AA-Plt V
Battle of LZ Pat	Aug. 9	2/8, 1/9	73	Song Re Valley	BB-Plt V
2nd Battle of Tam Quan	Dec. 6-20	1st Bde, 20th ARVN Regt.	650	Tam Quan, Bong Son Plain	CC-Plt V

PLATE IV

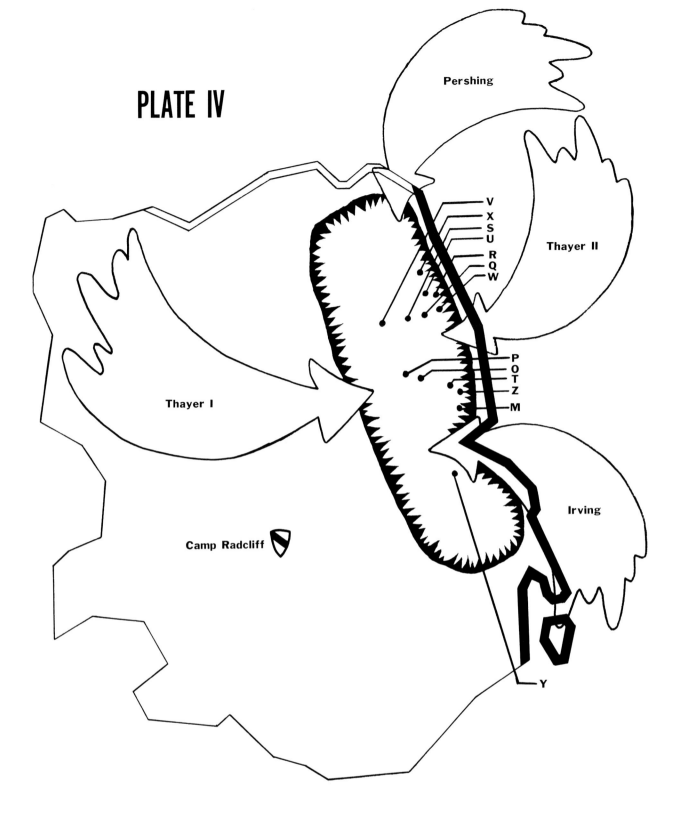

Pershing

Thayer II

V
X
S
U R
Q W

P
O
T
Z
M

Thayer I

Irving

Camp Radcliff

Y

BONG SON

1968

MAJOR OPERATIONS IN WHICH SKYTROOPERS TOOK PART OR COMPLETED

Battle	Date	Units	Enemy KIA	Location
Jeb Stuart	Jan 22 Mar. 31	1st & 3rd Bdes 3rd Bde, 101 Abn	3,288	Quang Tri & Thua Thien Provinces
Pershing II	Jan 22 Feb. 18	2nd Bde	614	Eastern Binh Dinh Province
Pegasus/Lamson 207	Apr. 1-15	Division, 1st & 26th Marine Regts ARVN Abn TF	1,259	Khe Sanh
Delaware/Lam Son 216	Apr. 19 May 17	1st & 3rd Bdes	739	A Shau Valley
Concordia Square	May 8-17	2nd Bde	347	Quang Tri Province
Jeb Stuart III	May 17 Nov. 3	Division	3,288	Quang Tri and Thua Thien Provinces
Comanche Falls	Sept. 11 Nov. 7	2nd Bde	107	Southern Quang Tri Province
Toan Thang II	Nov. 12 Feb. 16	Division	3,324	Northern III Corps

MAJOR BATTLES

(BASED ON 50 OR MORE ENEMY KIA KEYED TO A SINGLE, IDENTIFIABLE ACTION)

Battle	Date	Units	Enemy KIA	Location	Map Key
Battle of An Lac Hamlet	Jan. 2-4	1/5, 2/5, 1/9, 1/50 Mech Inf	97	East of Dam Tra-O Lake	EE-Plt V
Battle for LZs Ross and Leslie	Jan. 3	3rd Bde	289	Que Son Valley	FF-Plt VI
Battle of Quang Tri	Jan 31 Feb. 6	1st Bde, 9th ARVN Abn Bn, 1st ARVN Regt.	553	Quang Tri City	GG-Plt VI
Battle of Hue	Feb. 2-25	3rd Bde, 1/9	404	Hue and environs	HH-Plt VI
Battle of Dong Ha	Feb. 7	C/1/9	53	Dong Ha	II-Plt VI
Battle of Thon Xuan Duong Hamlet	Mar. 25	1/8, 1/9	276	Thon Xuan Ouong Hamlet	JJ-Plt VI
Battle of April 5	Apr. 5	A/1/9	53	Khe Sanh Valley	KK-Plt VI
Battle of Gia Dang III	May 27-30	1st Bde	108	Gia Dang III, Quang Tri Province	LL-Plt VI
Battle of Binh An	Jun. 27-30	2nd Bde	233	North of Quang Tri City	MM-Plt VI
Battle near Quang Tri	Aug. 20-23	1/8, 1/9	144	Northeast of Quang Tri City	NN-Plt VI

QUANG NGAI

Song   Re

BB

PLATE V

Pershing

AA

CC

BINH DINH

EE

BONG SON

212

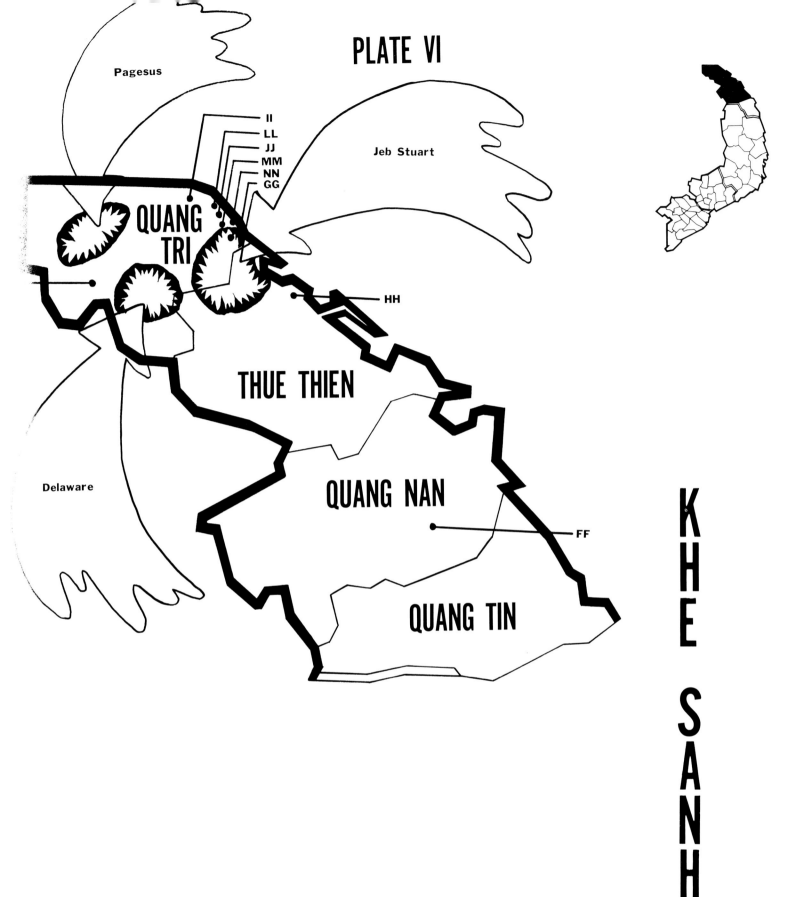

PLATE VI

Pagesus

II
LL
JJ
MM
NN
GG

Jeb Stuart

QUANG TRI

HH

THUE THIEN

Delaware

QUANG NAN

FF

QUANG TIN

KHE SANH

I CORPS

1969

MAJOR OPERATIONS IN WHICH SKYTROOPERS TOOK PART OR COMPLETED

Battle	Date	Units	Enemy KIA	Location	Map Key
Toan Thang III	Feb. 17	Division	11,205*	Northern III Corps	
Comanche	May 14	3rd Bde	132	Southern III Corps	
Warrior/Creek II	June 1				

*Editor's Note: Operation Toan Thang III was continuing as this book went to press. Casualty figures cover the period from Feb. 17 to Dec. 31, 1969.

MAJOR BATTLES

(BASED ON 50 OR MORE ENEMY KIA KEYED TO A SINGLE, IDENTIFIABLE ACTION)

Battle	Date	Units	Enemy KIA	Location	Map Key
Battle at LZ Grant	Mar. 8	2/12, 1/30 Arty, C/1/77 Arty	157	LZ Grant,	PP-Plt VII
2nd Battle at LZ Grant	Mar. 11	2/12, A/1/30 Arty, C/1/77 Arty	62	LZ Grant, War Zone C	PP-Plt VII
Battle at LZ Carolyn	May 6	2/8, A/2/19 Arty, B/1/30 Arty	198	LZ Carolyn, Tay Ninh Province	QQ-Plt VII
Battle on May 10	May 10	A/1/9	55	III Corps	RR-Plt VII
Battle at LZ Jamie	May 12	2/7, B/2/19 Arty	70	LZ Jamie, War Zone C	SS-Plt VII
Battle of Dong Nai	June 2	1/8	54	North of Dong Nai River, III Corps	TT-Plt VII
1st Battle at LZ Ike	June 20	2/5	90	LZ Ike, Tay Ninh Province	UU-Plt VII
Battle of Binh Long Province	July 25 Aug. 12	3rd Bde	460	Binh Long Province	VV-Plt VII
Battle at FSB Becky	Aug. 12	2/8, A/1/30 Arty	101	FSB Becky, War Zone C	WW-Plt VII
Battle of Quan Loi	Aug. 12	3rd Bde	54	Quan Loi area, Binh Long Province	XX-Plt VII
Battle of Phuoc Long	Nov. 3-4	2nd Bde, B/1/9	153	Song Be area, Phuoc Long Province	YY-Plt VII
2nd Battle at FSB Ike	Nov. 4	2/5, A/1/9	98	FSB Ike and vicinity, Tay Ninh Province	ZZ-Plt VII

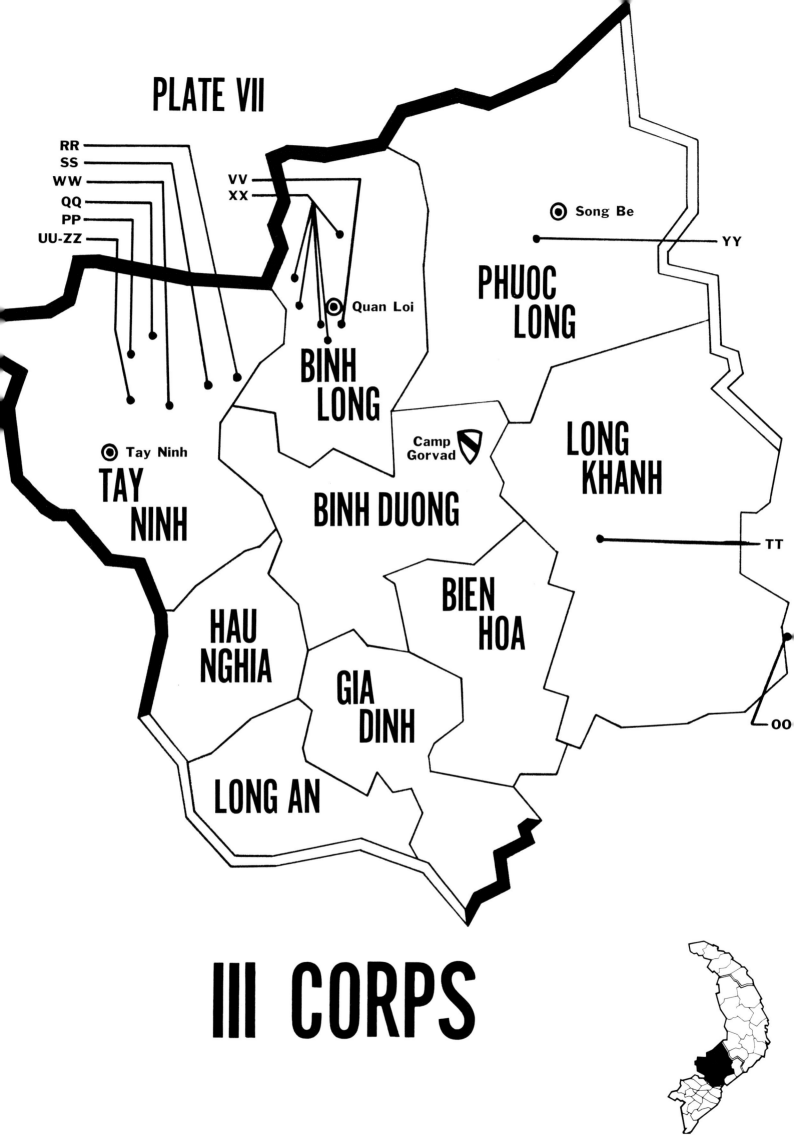

PLATE VII

RR
SS
WW
QQ
PP
UU-ZZ

VV
XX

◎ Song Be

YY

PHUOC
LONG

◎ Quan Loi

BINH
LONG

◎ Tay Ninh

Camp
Gorvad

LONG
KHANH

TAY
NINH

BINH DUONG

TT

HAU
NGHIA

BIEN
HOA

GIA
DINH

OO

LONG AN

III CORPS

Cavalry Faces

The personable Major General Harry W. O. Kinnard, steering force in the development of the airmobile concept, commander of the experimental 11th Air Assault Division and first commander of the 1st Air Cavalry Division, infused the revolutionary division with his own style and elan when he first took it into combat. After the division surgeon prescribed an eye patch for the general's slight eye injury, MG Kinnard added the insignia of his division. Hardcore . . . and with style.

Even in combat there is time for a smile as this member of the Cav shows on his way back to camp following a hard day on patrol.

He who laughs last, laughs best, and Specialist Four Robert R. Gorgensen is all smiles after he stumbled over a 12-foot python while on a mission with Company D, 2nd of the 12th. Gorgensen bagged the considerably dangerous reptile with his M-16. It was an enemy infiltrator.

For a "grunt" in the field, happiness is a bath (above), and this soldier has the South China Sea for his bathtub. Any C-ration chef worth his beans knows that the best gift from home is a bottle of meat sauce (below left) to spark his field gourmet efforts. First Sergeant Hollis Stephens of Company B, 2nd of the 12th, "taking five" during Operation PERSHING (below right), has the set jaw and hard face that belongs to an old soldier—and a look that bespeaks of a thousand tales of war.

...Just

Manila ... Pyongyang ... Vietnam ... the faces change but the look is the same. This one (above) belongs to Private First Class Richard Coleman of the 5th Battalion, 7th Cavalry. Specialist Four Mack A. Hassler (right) pours water from a helmet over Private First Class Lee A. Bilbrey, who is getting his first bath in 22 days, after his unit was pulled back from the front line for a rest during Operation MASHER in January 1966.

A Cavalry officer finds a perch in a small hilltop tree to scan the distance with field glasses (above), looking for signs of the enemy on the move in hills near Quang Tri. While a machinegun crew sends rapid grazing fire into the enemy's treeline position (left) another Cav trooper sprints forward, "cultivating a low, running profile," toward the action. The firefight took place northeast of Tay Ninh in January 1970.

Airmobile or not, the soldier's age-old plague —thick, deep, grabbing, tiring, impeding, heavy mud—was always a problem in Vietnam (below), especially in the long months of the monsoons. Much of the Cav's fighting in III Corps was done in the rubber plantations (right) that sprawl over the central and northern parts of the Corps area. This Skytrooper runs for cover as sniper fire breaks out in the rubber east of Quan Loi.

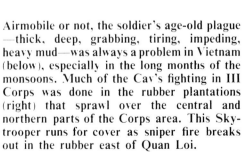

Pictures...

While waiting to board choppers for a combat assault (above), this trooper takes the opportunity to catch some more sleep, a commodity always in short supply for the "grunt." One welcome by-product of the fighting was large bomb craters that filled with rainwater (below) and that became handy, if not really clear, bathing pools.

A Montagnard woman in Vietnam—a witness of many wars—reflects (top center) on the latest conflict raging over her homeland. It was hot and it was usually wet. If there weren't rice paddies to cross and it wasn't pouring out of the monsoon sky, there would surely be one of a thousand streams and rivers to cross (top right) which served to get the trooper thoroughly soaked. A special breed of the enemy was the NVA sapper (below), a soldier who underwent 18 months of training in North Vietnam to learn how to penetrate American firebases and basecamps expertly and silently with his load of TNT charges. This man rallied to the southern cause and showed Cav soldiers how he would penetrate their defenses if they were unwary.

One of the best times in the field for a "grunt" comes when a "care package" from home arrives. Getting a good mouthful of candy while on a mission near Song Be with Company D, 2nd of the 12th, is Private First Class Dennis E. Sullivan.

Let there be no mistake: the war, the combat, they were always an ugly business. Sergeant Donald Scott comforts a wounded member of his squad (below), a victim of one of the horrors prominent in the Vietnam War, a VC booby trap.

Terrain

On the edge of a Cav installation atop Nui Ba Ra Mountain a few flowers survive to belie the war that washes back and forth across the plains below, where—secured by the 1st Cav and saved from enemy attack in August 1969—the capital of Phuoc Long Province, the village-city of Song Be, flourishes as best it can during the war.

With the helicopter as much to the Cav as the rifle to the infantryman, the airmobile Cav is, as MG Kinnard said, "freed forever from the tyranny of terrain." But if no longer a tyrant for the airmobile division, terrain still serves as a heavy cloak of secrecy for enemy infiltrators and basecamps. When discovered by the Cav—and if they are of sufficient size to warrant the measure—enemy basecamps are treated to the specialty of a B-52 bomb strike (above) turning the area into a void.

With varying intensity, warfare has continued in Vietnam since the end of World War II. The older scars of artillery barrages and bomb strikes gradually sink and fill as nature heals her wounds (below); in time they will all disappear.

Any "grunt" would say that the best way to see the often beautiful fields of rice paddies (above) is from a helicopter, a nice dry helicopter. When sites for a new firebase are considered by headquarters commanders, preference is naturally given to open, semi-clear ground; but the tactical need is the greater dictator and, if need be, the jungle forest is sliced open for a new base (below) that sits like an oasis in the wilds.

The manner in which "the tyranny of terrain" was ended can be seen from this UH-1H Huey, as it, and others, circle the target landing zone just before banking in for the assault. Artillery shells slam into the assault area as a Huey smoke bird lays down a screen to obscure the enemy's vision.

DONG TIEN
(FORWARD TOGETHER)

They carried everything from AK-47s to M-16s, wore tennis shoes and a variety of uniforms (including black pajamas), and they folowed two Viet Cong veterans to a basecamp hidden in the thick bamboo rain forest.

Several hundred meters behind, a company of 1st Air Cavalrymen followed in hot pursuit.

But this scenario of war is not what it seems. The mission of Company C, 2nd Battalion, 12th Cavalry, was to support, not attack, the lead element of Vietnamese Regional Forces troops from Phuoc Long Province in search of a weapons cache.

The two Viet Cong veterans with them had rallied to the Republic of Vietnam under the Chieu Hoi program several days before and were walking point for the combined force operation. The target was a secluded Viet Cong basecamp where the Hoi Chanhs had lived for two years.

Combined operations of this type are common throughout Cav Country and especially numerous in northern Phuoc Long Province where the defense of Song Be has been given top priority. In a typical operation 24 hours earlier, an ARVN company made a combat assault with 1st Cav helicopters, while a company of Air Cavalrymen on APCs of the 11th Armored Cavalry Regiment broke through a thick forest to meet

When the 1st ARVN Airborne Division received its first 155 mm howitzers, the first such guns its unit ever had, a facet of "Dong Tien" moved into play with men of the 1st Battalion, 30th Artillery, showing the ARVN soldiers how to rig and sling out the medium range guns and their ammo (right) using the giant CH-54 Flying Cranes. In the more informal aspect of Dong Tien, Cav troopers and ARVN Airborne soldiers (above) pass idle time like all soldiers do—shooting the breeze.

them, hoping to trap the enemy in the vise.

"We're glad to have the ARVNs working with us, especially in this populated area," said Lieutenant Colonel Thomas Healy, commander of a 1st Cav battalion at Song Be. "It's hard for the Vietnamese—and impossible for us—to tell a peaceful farmer from a hard core Viet Cong.

"We treat the ARVN units like our own here, even when they operate alone."

The Hoi Chanhs, followed by AK-carrying locals, walked swiftly toward the VC camp along well-used trails. The Americans moved more cautiously, cutting their own path to the objective.

But the Regional Force troopers saw nothing strange in their methods. "They're not going to ambush friends who are leading Vietnamese with AK-47s," said Sergeant First Class Phan Hong Thanh, an interpreter with the unit.

There was no ambush. The campsite of elaborate bamboo hootches was deserted. The Hoi Chanhs did, however, lead the unit to the promised weapons hidden in the river bed.

With growing emphasis on "Vietnamization" of the war, the 1st Air Cavalry has swung into high gear with its "Dong Tien" (Forward Together) program. Combined operations are an everyday occurrence throughout Cav Country.

Throughout the Cav's campaigns in II and I Corps the ARVN forces in the area played a vital role. From Plei Me to Khe Sanh Vietnamese forces have fought alongside Americans.

The airmobile division, with its in-

stantly available artillery and gunship support, is an ideal component for a combined operation. The ARVN forces, often lacking their own tube artillery 'and air support, are highly effective fighters when given the aid of the Cav's mobility and firepower. Prior to the advent of vast combined operations in the III Corps Tactical Zone, the 1st Cav made preparations for the coming missions. A major part of the preparation was spent in teaching Vietnamese soldiers the "how to's" of a combat assault, the Cav's "thing."

A very representative part of the training took place in August—September 1969 at LZ Alvarado, then home of the 2nd Bn, 12th Cav.

Regular classes on how to dismount a helicopter were given by Major Anthony J. Andrews, commander of Company A,

A newly trained ARVN Airborne Division rigger keeps a cautious eye on the approaching CH-54 Flying Crane (below left), and especially the Crane's nosewheel, which will pass directly over him.

First Lieutenant Steven A. Young (below right), an artillery forward observer, watches the firing procedure of ARVN soldiers undergoing "Dong Tien" training.

227th Assault Helicopter Battalion, and Captain Calvin C. Jones, Jr., the company operations officer.

The first of these classes was presented to 50 members of a 334th Regional Forces (RF) Company, part of the force of Phuoc Long Province. Ranging in age from 15 to 60 years old, the men of the RF company were preparing to conduct future combat assaults with elements of the division's 2nd Brigade.

The class was conducted through an interpreter provided by the province chief. The RFs were eager students and learned quickly. At the end of the class was a practical exercise—a combat assault.

Ten enthusiastic Vietnamese soldiers piled into each chopper and lifted off. When the trip was over, several excited RFs pointed to their shoulder patches, then to the patches on the shoulders of nearby Skytroopers: "Same, same," they exclaimed.

Some combined operations have been going on throughout III Corps for years. One of these has been taken over by 1st Air Cavalrymen since their arrival in Phuoc Vinh.

Defending the Song Be Bridge, a vital link between Saigon and northern III Corps, is the mission of a combined Vietnamese, 1st Air Cavalry Division force.

Combined U.S.—Regional Force patrols comb the surrounding area daily. Ambushes are set up at night. Riverine operations search for infiltrators. A class in small arms proficiency is given to both 1st Cav and RF soldiers. "This is the first chance my men have had to meet the Vietnamese without the pressure of battle," said Captain Leigh Fairbank, commander of Company E, 2nd Battalion, 5th Cavalry. "In the field you're too busy fighting." Security is tight around the bridge. Vietnamese guards stand ready to inspect every vehicle before it is allowed to pass. Individuals must present their ID cards.

"Working together helps establish confidence in each other," said CPT Fairbank.

With Cav units rotating back to the field, and new units taking over the security mission, the operation allows many Skytroopers to become more familiar with the RF soldiers.

"I've been standing guard with the Vietnamese for a month now," said Private First Class Charles Hespell. "My understanding of Vietnam, its

A joint operation conducted by the 1st Cav's 545th Military Police Company and a company of Vietnamese National Police (above) begins with a cordon and search operation in a village near Phuoc Vinh. As early as mid-1968, the 1st Cav was conducting joint operations with ARVN troops, as when the two forces combined (below) for a sweep 20 miles north of Hue That operation ended in five VC killed and two captured.

The overall planning for the joint operation, between 1st Cav troops and members of Phuoc Long Province's Popular Force units, was carried out by the high-ranking representatives from both the American and Vietnamese sides. The three-day mission was conducted north of FSB Buttons, the 2nd Brigade headquarters.

A 1st Cav soldier (above) goes over the platoon-level details of a joint operation with his Vietnamese Popular Force counterparts. Emphasis is placed on the units—whether of company or squad size—operating as a single unit rather than having them act separately, with one or the other eventually winding up as observers. As the troops prepare to move out, the two commanders (below), American and Vietnamese, go over final plans and check map coordinates for final objectives.

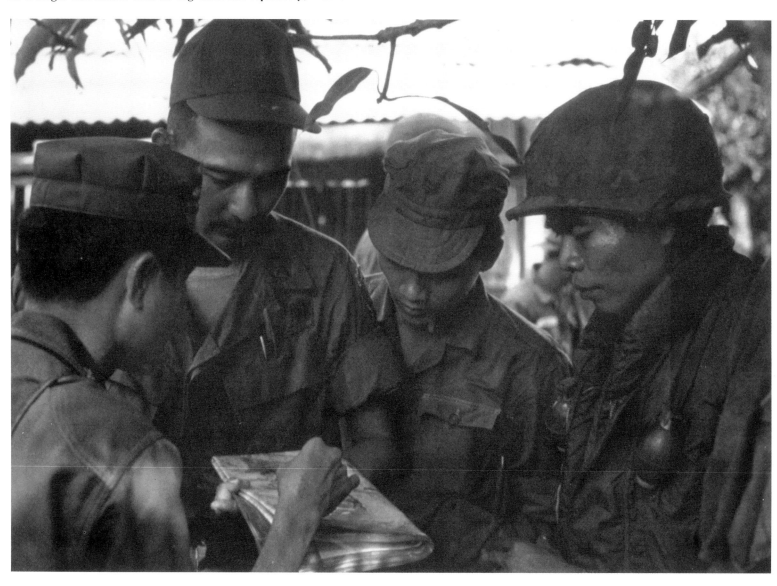

people and language has increased immensely. It's quite a change of pace from the field."

Late 1969 found elements of the 1st ARVN Airborne Division moving into Cav Country, especially the 1st Brigade's area of operations.

Airmobility was just a vague concept to a battalion of men from the 2nd ARVN Airborne Brigade when it was airlifted to an isolated clearing 22 miles northeast of Tay Ninh.

Within 48 hours they had established a firebase and moved against the enemy with the same group tactics and air support used by every line company in the airmobile 1st Cavalry.

"This is completely new to us," said Major Dudley McIver, senior advisor to the 3rd ARVN Airborne Battalion. "Previously we had to move in a mass. When you don't have much artillery and air support you need a large number of troops for firepower. Of course, you lose the element of surprise."

The paratroopers now have that support: an ARVN 105 mm battery at the battalion's firebase. 1st Cav helicopter gunships, aerial rocket artillery ships and artillery at nearby firebases are committed to the battalion's ground activity.

1st Cav Hueys and Chinooks brought in food, water and building machines. The division's 8th Engineers arrived the first day with bulldozers and other heavy equipment.

"We're here to build the TOC, the aid station and the berm," said Private First Class George Coles, one of the 50 combat engineers at the firebase. "After that it's their baby. We're showing them how to set up the wire and clear the area, but they're doing most of the work. The next time they'll be on their own."

At times the firebase looked like an outdoor classroom. Infantry, artillery, logistics, communications and engineer officers from the Cav's 1st Brigade met their ARVN counterparts in informal discussions throughout the first day.

"These guys can really work," said Private First Class Wayne Boss, who was demonstrating to several ARVN s the proper way to set up concertina wire.

Vietnamization of the war, at least in this part of the Cav's area of operations, was proceeding smoothly.

One of the best examples of combined operations in Cav history has been taking place in the Bo Duc—Bu Dop area of northern III Corps in Phuoc Long Province. Throughout the area, the scene of heavy enemy activity in the late months of 1969, 1st Air Cavalrymen and Vietnamese soldiers worked and fought side by side.

FSB Jerri, located three miles south of Bu Dop, was the scene of much activity throughout November and December. Incoming rounds were a daily occurrence. The 3rd Mobile Strike Force, consisting of Civilian Irregular Defense Group (CIDG) soldiers and American advisors, patrolled the area around the firebase, searching for the enemy's rocket and mortar launching points.

As Allied control over the area increased, the 1st Cav turned the firebase over to the Vietnamese troops, adding it to the many Vietnamese controlled firebases throughout Cav Country.

The Vietnamese have secured the area, refusing the NVA one of their major infiltration routes from Cambodia.

In mid-December 1969, Skytroopers from Company D, 2nd Battalion, 7th Cavalry, combined with Civilian Irregular Defense Group troops to kill 100 NVA in a four day battle near FSB Jamie.

Combat assaulting into the area to reinforce the aerial rifle platoon (Blues) of Troop A, 1st Squadron, 9th Cavalry,

ARVN Airborne Division riggers go it alone after learning rigging techniques from 1st Cav troops.

(Continued on P. 277)

CIVIC ACTION AND PACIFICATION

A 1st Cav trooper, one of those many who worked at the Cav's An Tuc dispensary in I Corps, makes a friend in a little Vietnamese girl who had been treated at the dispensary.

Pacification is the process of organizing the people for their own self-defense, self-government and self-development with the ultimate objective of securing their political support to the national cause of defeating the enemy.

A necessary precondition to pacification is that a sufficient level of sustained and credible security is first established by the regular forces to enable the territorial security forces to protect the people from undue harassment.

Pacification seeks to elicit popular commitment to the national effort by involving the people in that effort at a level meaningful to them and by developing a sense of common participation toward common goals. It involves every agency of the Government of the Republic of Vietnam and potentially every man, woman and child in the nation.

The 1st Air Cavalry Division has continuously . strived to promote the pacification programs of the Republic of Vietnam. Through civic action programs, personnel of the division have worked to aid the people of Vietnam in their struggle for peace and freedom.

One of the most important and dramatic programs initiated by the Government of Vietnam (GVN) is the "Chieu Hoi" or "Open Arms" program. It offers amnesty to the enemy and persuades them to rally to the side of the GVN. It offers them a chance to start a new life within GVN society and to help in the economic and political development of the nation.

The success of this program is dependent upon the treatment the individual receives after he has rallied. Security and human treatment are guaranteed the rallier by the Government of South Vietnam and Free World Military Forces. This guarantee is printed on safe-conduct passes distributed in enemy areas by various means. While the safe-conduct pass facilitates the act of rallying, it is not a prerequisite.

The FIRST TEAM, like other American units in the Republic of Vietnam, takes special care to comply with the provisions of the Chieu Hoi program. If the rallier needs medical care, food or clothing, he gets it. The individual is searched, of course, and security is maintained, but the Hoi Chanh's dignity is preserved, a most vital part of processing and orienting the individual into the GVN society.

Through the use of PSYOP (Psychological Operations) broadcasts from helicopters and jungle clearings and the dropping of leaflets, the civil affairs sections of the division have brought many people back to the safety and support of the South Vietnamese government.

An excellent example of the success of the program was the tide of ralliers turning themselves in to 1st Cav firebases in the 2nd Brigade AO during the months of September to November 1969. In a period of two months, 546 civilians and former enemy soldiers responded to 1st Cav PSYOPs broadcasts and rallied to the Government of the Republic of Vietnam.

With them the people brought tales of horror, of years of living under the watchful eyes of Viet Cong and North Vietnamese soldiers. When ARVN or American troops would approach the often unmapped hamlets, the enemy would force the people off into the jungle at gunpoint.

The villagers spent their days working in fields, growing food for the Viet Cong. In return for their work, they would receive as little as one-half potato per day to survive on. Many villagers reported burning elephant grass and eating the ashes as a salt substitute.

Night brought added terror to the villagers. Sleeping in holes, they would listen as American planes and helicopters fired on the enemy in the nearby jungle. They wondered when the American bombs would land on them, knowing the Allies were unaware of their presence and captivity.

Through the efforts of the PSYOPs personnel, the villagers were made aware of a new life of security and freedom. They began sneaking out of their villages during the night, a few people at a time, to turn themselves in at a nearby firebase in the morning. Often the desire for freedom was so great that families would be separated, but such was their desire to be rid of the Viet Cong.

Observing the Cav's pacification efforts and the resulting successes, the Viet Cong and North Vietnamese started their own "counter-pacification" program.

The enemy attempted to convince the people that the Americans were lying, that "Saigon is in ruins." They repeatedly held forced indoctrination sessions during which the people were informed that the Saigon government was defeated and the Communists would soon be in power.

The villagers questioned the FIRST TEAM's pacification workers about the Communist claims. The civil affairs people came up with an excellent idea to convince the villagers that the enemy had been lying.

Visits to Saigon were arranged for the children of the local villages and hamlets. They were taken on sight-seeing tours of the city and shown that the bustling capital was its normal self. Such attractions as the zoo were shown the children, who went back to their villages and told their parents of the wonders of the big city. The enemy was once again defeated.

Cav engineers construct a playground for Vietnamese children (above), one of frequent gestures of friendship and compassion that yielded the best, if least, tangible results in Cav pacification efforts.

A Skytrooper chats with two young girls (above) during a break while on patrol near Phuoc Vinh.

A Vietnamese farmer receives modern equipment from the 1st Cav civic action program; he is then taught how to use it along with other modern agricultural tools and techniques. He does the work himself, retaining both dignity and pride.

Two Cav medics of Company A, 1st Battalion, 8th Cavalry, rush a 12-year-old Vietnamese boy to a Medevac helicopter. The boy was brought to a civic action sick call with a severe case of malaria.

A Delta Company, 2nd Battalion, 7th Cavalry, soldier and a Popular Forces soldier help Vietnamese villagers move their cut wood into waiting sampans in relocating a village threatened by Viet Cong recruiters and tax collectors. The people of the village asked to be moved to a safer area rather than continue playing a dangerous game with the VC.

The history of the Cav in Vietnam is filled with stories of the division's efforts to help local people develop a better and more meaningful life.

"Nha thuong" is the traditional Vietnamese expression for hospital and means "house of love." The 1st Air Cavalry's 15th Medical Battalion, over a three-year period, created such a refuge for the ill in the An Khe area.

Shortly after the Cav deployed to Vietnam in 1965, a Medical Civic Action Project (MEDCAP) was set up to minister to the needs of the 70,000 people of the An Tuc District, part of Binh Dinh Province.

Many came to be healed, and in the spring of 1966 the program was put on a permanent basis. An old stone house furnished operating and waiting rooms while division engineers erected wards and the medical battalion selected men to guide the venture.

Local help was quickly enlisted, since many Vietnamese were eager for the regular salary offered. Yet out of the toil and trials born together and joys commonly shared grew bonds of friendship, and those who stayed on became the beginning of a family.

A distraught mother brought her afflicted child to the dispensary and, when the child recovered, stayed on in gratitude to help with the cleaning chores.

The dispensary maintained 76 sickbeds and with 10 more in a separate maternity section. In 1967, more than 2,000 patients were given care and 350 babies were delivered. Nearly 27,000 people, about one-third of the district's population, came for treatment ranging from ointments to innoculations.

Staff Sergeant John D. Rozzell extended time and again to work with the clinic staff, and it was he who was most responsible for the project's success. "We help anyone who comes here without regard to his background or politics. We are here to serve," he said.

The division's policy of treating all Vietnamese regardless of political beliefs proved salutary in some unexpected ways. Eliminating politics helped overcome the doubts of many Vietnamese. For example, following one instance in 1968 when the dispensary was hit by rockets, word filtered back that the Viet Cong had apologized for the incident.

The dispensary was more than simply a clinic and place for the sick. It sponsored several children in school. It offered first aid training and instruction in hygiene and basic English. It even began an experimental program in modern agricultural methods.

Since its founding, however, it was

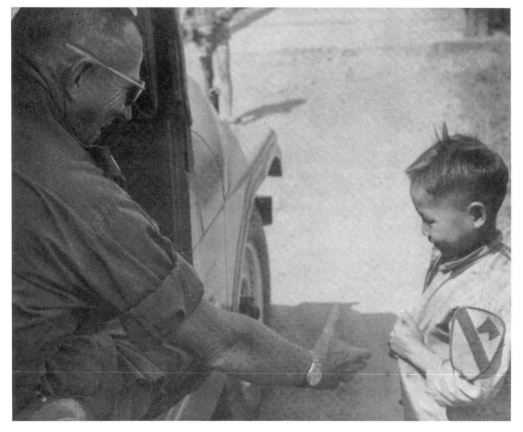

Major General George I. Forsythe, former commanding general of the 1st Cav, extends a hand of friendship to a young Montagnard refugee who proudly sports a Cav patch given to him by Skytroopers.

understood that one day the dispensary should be given to the Vietnamese people for whom it was built. On April 3, 1969, that goal was realized when Lieutenant Colonel Guthrie L. Turner, Jr., division surgeon and commanding officer of the 15th Medical Battalion, presented the facilities to the deputy chief of Binh Dinh Province at dedication ceremonies.

When the FIRST TEAM's rear detachment moved to Bien Hoa in April, the 4th Division assumed the responsibility for providing any further assistance that might be required by the dispensary. But the people of the An Tuc District never will forget the efforts of the men of the 1st Air Cavalry Division. Theirs was a mission of mercy: one part medicine and two parts compassion.

The building of the hospital at An Khe represented only a small fraction of the division's medical aid to the civilian population. MEDCAPs continue to be the largest medical programs, and they are very successful.

By going out to the people the doctors and medics of the Cav are able to win the people's confidence, as well as sparing them the trip to the sometimes distant Cav base.

In one average three-month period,

A young resident of the Phuoc Vinh orphanage reaches out in appeal to Cav MEDCAP personnel (right). Arriving in true airmobile, modern Santa style, civilian S. Claus (below) has donned an honorary Cav patch for his visit to the children of a village near Phuoc Vinh. Though oriental children are not traditionally acquainted with Santa Claus, the Western custom is firmly entrenched after one visit.

A Cav infantry captain seems to get as much enjoyment out of the little girl's reaction as she does out of the new toy. This is civic action at the grass roots.

the division held 575 MEDCAPs during which 27,550 patients were treated.

With the Cav securely located in III Corps, new problems were to be solved. A main focus of interest has been in Phuoc Long Province, part of the 2nd Brigade's AO—an area of low economic development.

As part of the continuing efforts to aid the economy of Phuoc Long Province the Cav's 2nd Brigade civil affairs section (S-5) has repeatedly initiated self-help projects for the people in the area.

Animal husbandry has taken a front seat in the 2nd Brigade's efforts. By providing the people with animals, the Cav not only supplies needed meat sources, but the reproductive capabilities of the animals make the programs self-sustaining.

Most of the programs worked, but some didn't; but the failures provided valuable lessons learned to Skytroopers and villagers alike. One such lesson was that some types of poultry do not adapt readily to environmental changes.

A case in point was when the brigade supplied 230 ducklings to the people of An Luong and Thuan Khiem 4, two hamlets in the province.

According to Captain Michael W. Griffith, the brigade civil affairs officer, the program was to be self-sustained. The district chief told the recipients

Specialist Four Herbert Marchese helps a Montagnard woman settle down in her new home after the Cav relocated the tribe's village.

A 15th Medical Battalion lab technician checks blood samples at the An Tuc Dispensary lab, part of the facility constructed by the Cav for the people of the An Khe area.

Staff Sergeant John D. Rozzell, the man primarily responsible for the great success of the An Tuc Dispensary, comforts one of the many Vietnamese children born at the dispensary under his care.

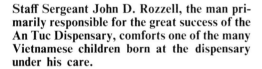

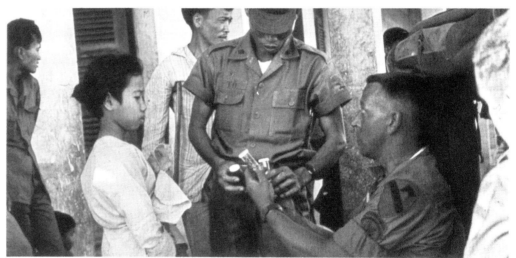

A Cav medic, working through an intepreter prescribes medication for a Vietnamese woman seeking aid during a Medical Civic Action Project (MEDCAP). FSB Buttons, headquarters of the Cav's 2nd Brigade and located next the provincial capital of Song Be, was the scene of a special Christmas party as children of the city were brought into the base to receive Christmas packages from the Skytroopers stationed there.

that after a period of time, he would require that 230 ducklings be produced so that they could be passed on to other villagers.

Unfortunately the young birds, unused to the environment of the Song Be area, didn't survive long enough to reproduce.

On the other hand, rabbits, a source of food and fur for all culture throughout history, are not fazed by mere changes in scenery and climate.

The brigade S-5 section purchased 20 rabbits and distributed them to five families in the area. The program has developed into one of the most successful of the division's efforts.

Another project brought seven cows, 750 baby chicks, 20 pigs and seven goats to Phuoc Long Province for distribution among Montagnard refugees at Don Luan and Bo Duc.

The refugees, forced to flee their homes due to Communist aggression, have been settled in other parts of the province. The program is designed to give them the means to start a new life, a life not dependent on the government.

The animals have brought about a new life for these people. They are able to grow crops to feed themselves and their livestock, and they will soon be fully established in their new homes.

One of the biggest problems for many villagers in Vietnam presents itself at harvest time. As the rice crops are picked, the Viet Cong arrive to take the

Medical treatment was not the only service available (above) at the An Tuc Dispensary. Dental care, general hygiene, agricultural methods and simple things, like the use of a sewing machine, were taught to the people. Vietnamese children surround a Cav doctor on a MEDCAP mission in Phuoc Vinh village (below), shortly after the Cav moved to III Corps.

A Vietnamese woman and her newborn baby—another born at the An Tuc Dispensary—receive the warm attention (below left) of a dispensary staffer. A 15th Medical Battalion member (below right) of the An Tuc Dispensary staff takes the pulse of an ill Montagnard child.

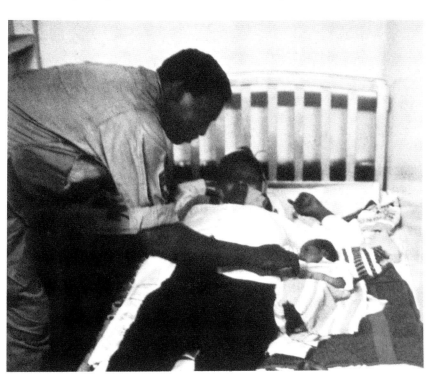

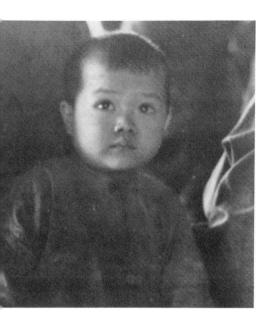

1st Cav civic action touches all ages, from the little Vietnamese boy (above), who is too young to really understand what is going on, to the very old (below), like this elderly woman listening to the 1st Cav band playing at Song Be.

Lieutenant Truman Arnett of Battery C, 1st Battalion, 77th Artillery, presents a portion of a shipment of seeds to a member of Hoi An village. The seeds were provided by the Division Artillery chaplain.

While a Vietnamese priest looks over progress on reconstruction of a village, the children clamor over a Cav engineer advisor at right. The village was located near An Khe.

food from the people, leaving them to starve. It is a vicious, ugly part of the war, as any Skytrooper who has seen the bloated stomach of a young child suffering from malnutrition will admit.

To counter the loss of crops in the Phuoc Long Province area, the 2nd Brigade civil affairs section shipped some 80 tons of rice to the villages of Bo Duc and Duc Phang during a three-week period in October 1969.

The rice was also a vital factor in aiding the resettlement of hundreds of refugees recently moved to the areas. With food available, they were able to immediately go to work to build homes for themselves and get their own rice crops sown.

Aiding the refugees in building homes was a shipment of four tons of tool kits, sent along with the rice. The Cav's airmobility was a vital factor in supplying the people with the essentials for the beginning of their new lives. With no roads available to allow motor convoys access to the villages, the mighty CH-47 Chinooks of the FIRST TEAM took over the supply mission, and accomplished it in the usual dispatch of the 1st Cavalry Division.

One shipment of rice is not news in itself. But the sharp-eyed Skytroopers of the division have been finding huge enemy rice and salt caches since their

(Continued on P. 271)

AWARDS AND DECORATIONS

Presidental Unit Citation

In the White House Rose Garden, the President of the United States, Lyndon B. Johnson, attaches the Presidential Unit Citation streamer to the 1st Air Cavalry Division colors, held by Division Sergeant Major C. K. Westervelt. Lieutenant General Harry W. O. Kinnard, Army deputy chief of staff and first commander of the 1st Air Cav, looks on. The division won the award, the first in Vietnam, for its outstanding accomplishments in the Pleiku Province campaign. After making the presentation, President Johnson read the citation below:

By virtue of the authority vested in me as President of the United States and as Commander in Chief of the Armed Forces of the United States, I have today awarded the Presidential Unit Citation (Army) for extraordinary heroism to the 1st Cavalry Division (Airmobile) and attached units.

The 1st Cavalry Division (Airmobile) and attached units distinguished themselves by outstanding performance of duty and extraordinary heroism in action against an armed enemy in the Republic of Vietnam during the period 23 October 1965 to 26 November 1965. Following the attack on a Special Forces camp at Plei Me, in Pleiku Province, on 19 October 1965 by regular units of the Army of North Vietnam, the 1st Cavalry Division (Airmobile) was committed to action. The division was initially assigned the mission of protecting the key communications center of Pleiku, in addition to providing fire support both for an Army of the Republic of Vietnam (ARVN) armored column dispatched to the relief of the besieged camp, and for the camp itself. Using air assault techniques, the division deployed artillery batteries into firing positions deep within enemy-held territory and provided the vital fire support needed by the ARVN forces to accomplish the relief of the Special Forces camp. By 27 October,

the tactical and strategic impact of the presence of a North Vietnamese regular army division in Pleiku Province necessitated a change in missions for the 1st Cavalry Division. The division was given an unlimited offensive role to seek out and destroy the enemy force. With bold thrusts, elements of the division pursued the North Vietnamese regiments across the dense and trackless jungles of the west-central highlands, seeking the enemy out in his previously secure sanctuaries and giving him no quarter.

The superb training, unflinching devotion to duty, and unsurpassed gallantry and intrepidity of the Cavalrymen, individually and collectively, resulted in numerous victories and succeeded in driving the invading North Vietnamese division back from its positions at Plei Me to the foot of the Chu Pong Massif. There, in the valley of the Ia Drang, the enemy was reinforced by a fresh regiment and undertook preparations for more attacks into Pleiku Province.

The 1st Cavalry Division deployed its men and weapons by air to launch an attack on this enemy staging area, which was 35 kilometers from the nearest road and 50 kilometers from the nearest logistical base. Fully utilizing airmobility in applying their combat power in a series of offensive blows, the men of the division completely defeated the numerically superior enemy. When the enemy finally withdrew his broken forces from the battlefield, the offensive capability of the North Vietnamese Army in the II Corps Tactical Zone had been blunted. The outstanding performance and extradinary heroism of the members of the 1st Cavalry Division (Airmobile) and attached units, under the most hazardous and adverse conditions, reflect great credit upon themselves, the United States Army, and the Armed Forces of the United States.

Signed by President Lyndon B. Johnson on 19 August 1967.

The Medal of Honor Recipients

2LT WALTER J. MARM, JR.,
1st Battalion, 7th Cavalry, November 14, 1965

*SGT JIMMY G. STEWART,
2nd Battalion, 12th Cavalry, May 18, 1966

SP4 DAVID C. DOLBY,
1st Battalion, 8th Cavalry, May 21, 1966

*PFC LEWIS ALBANESE,
5th Battalion, 7th Cavalry, November 14, 1966

SP4 CHARLES C. HAGEMEISTER,
1st Battalion, 5th Cavalry, March 20, 1967

*PFC BILLY LANE LAUFFER,
2nd Battalion, 5th Cavalry, September 21, 1966

SSG DELBERT O. JENNINGS,
1st Battalion, 12th Cavalry, December 27, 1966

*PFC JAMES H. MONROE,
1st Battalion, 8th Cavalry, February 16, 1967

*SP4 GEORGE A. INGALLS,
2nd Battalion, 5th Cavalry, April 16, 1967

*SP4 CARMEL B. HARVEY, JR.,
1st Battalion, 5th Cavalry, June 21, 1967

*SP5 EDGAR L. McWETHY, JR.,
1st Battalion, 5th Cavalry, June 21, 1967

CW2 FREDERICK E. FERGUSON,
227th Aviation Battalion, January 31, 1968

1LT JAMES M. SPRAYBERRY,
5th Battalion, 7th Cavalry, April 25, 1968

* Awarded posthumously.

234

For Valor and Outstanding Service in Vietnam: These medals were awarded to Skytroopers

Editor's Note: The number below each medal represents the number of 1st Cavalry Skytroopers to earn that medal for valor in Vietnam. With the exception of the Medal of Honor, awards and decoration figures below are for 1966–1969 inclusively. Figures for 1965 were not available.

DISTINGUISHED
SERVICE CROSS
99

SILVER STAR
2,766

DISTINGUISHED
FLYING CROSS
2,697

SOLDIER'S MEDAL
540

BRONZE STAR
FOR VALOR
8,408

AIR MEDAL
FOR VALOR
2,910

ARMY COMMENDATION
MEDAL FOR VALOR
5,328

PURPLE HEART
16,123

235

The Vietnamese Cross of Gallantry Citation

The Cross of Gallantry with Palm has been awarded by the Government of the Republic of Vietnam for outstanding service during the period 9 August 1965 through 19 April 1969 to the 1st Cavalry Division (Airmobile).

The 1st Cavalry Division (Airmobile) arrived in Vietnam on 7 August, 1965, and participated in successive military operations in Pleiku, Phan Thiet, Binh Dinh, Quang Nam, A Shau, Khe Sanh and Thua Thien, frustrating the Communists many times. In particular, during the period it was stationed in the III Corps Tactical Zone from 26 October 1968 to the present time, the 1st United States Cavalry Division has been under the command of Major General George I. Forsythe and has been on constant alert and participated in clashes over the entire battlefield. Disregarding unfavorable terrain, as well as modern and intense anti-aircraft fire from well-fortified enemy trenches, the men of this unit have gallantly engaged in bloody battles in Phuoc Long, Binh Long, Tay Ninh, Hau Nghia and Bien Hoa Provinces, blocking infiltration by the North Vietnamese regular forces through the Cambodian-Vietnamese border in a timely and effective manner. Furthermore, this unit also intervened and repulsed enemy attacks against friendly forces, smashed many large-scale troop movements designed to shell and attack the capital city of Saigon during the Viet Cong Winter-Spring Campaign of 1968–1969, and neutralized the enemy military potential in secret zones, inflicting continuous personnel casualties and weapons losses upon the enemy. With the above-mentioned outstanding achievements, the 1st Cavalry Division has effectively assisted the Republic of Vietnam in the fight against the Communists to preserve peace and freedom.

Lieutenant General Do Cao Tri, ARVN III Corps commanding general, affixes the Vietnamese Cross of Gallantry streamer to the 1st Air Cavalry Division colors during ceremonies at Camp Gorvad, Phuoc Vinh, South Vietnam, on April 19, 1969. Major General George I. Forsythe, then Cav commanding general, stands at salute just behind LTG Tri and the colors.

Mother Dorcy and the Patch

In September 1921 the War Department authorized the establishment of the 1st Cavalry Division. A directive was published requesting submission of a design for the "shoulder sleeve" of the new unit's uniform.

The message required that the new insignia satisfy three principles: that it bind men together in a common devotion; be an easily recognizable sign by which men could reassemble after battle; and be a word picture which would inspire the men of the division. Additionally, postwar conditions limited the use of colors to two for economy production.

The design selected for the FIRST TEAM patch was submitted by Colonel and Mrs. Ben Dorcy. The colonel was then the commander of the 7th Cavalry Regiment at Fort Bliss, Texas, with the newly activated division.

Mrs. Dorcy relates that the combination of the golden sunset at Fort Bliss and the traditional cavalry colors of blue and gold were a great influence in the selection of the background color of the insignia. The bright yellow inner liner of one of the colonel's old dress capes became the cloth on which the first design was drawn.

The choice of the horse's head for the design was made by the Dorcys after they observed a mounted trooper ride by their home on a beautiful blue-black thoroughbred.

The shape of the patch represents the shield carried by knights in battle. The bar, or slash, across the yellow shield also finds its origin in heraldry and is always shown on a coat of arms diagonally from left to right. It represents a scaling ladder used by the knights of old to breach castle walls. The ladder and horse occupy equal places of honor since both were necessary to meet with the enemy.

As time went by the blue of the patch was changed to black, otherwise the patch has not changed from its original design and shape.

The shoulder patch of the 1st Cavalry Division is the largest of all U.S. Army division insignias. Mrs. Dorcy explained: "The patch had to be large enough to be seen through the dust and sand at Fort Bliss, and we made it that way because it's worn by big men who do big things."

The patch, like the division, had a proud and noble heritage. Mother Dorcy has maintained her love for the FIRST TEAM as evidenced by her dedicated correspondence with the officers and men in the unit today.

Mrs. Ben H. (Mother) Dorcy, wife of the late Colonel Ben H. Dorcy, looks at the 1st Cavalry Division flag, whose primary feature, the Cav patch, was designed by Colonel and Mrs. Dorcy. Mrs. Dorcy was visiting the Institute of Heraldry at Cameron Station, Alexandria, Virginia.

Father (LTC) McGrath and Chaplain (LTC) Webb (above) stand behind the altar of the 1st Cav's Division Chapel at An Khe. Members of Company B, 8th Engineer Battalion, sit in silence (lower left) while a chaplain conducts a memorial service for a fallen comrade.

CHAPLAINS' ACTIVITIES

He can't match the Division Artillery or ARA for firepower, but the support the chaplain provides to the 1st Air Cavalryman is sometimes the most vital offered in the war zone.

The chaplain is in Vietnam to give the soldier strength in his faith and spiritual guidance, to provide counsel and aid him in worship. To accomplish his mission the Army chaplain often goes to extraordinary lengths, reaching the combat soldier in the most remote areas, providing a hand for those who need one.

There are 24 chaplains in the 1st Air Cavalry Division and the American fighting man has always had access to these men who know and understand a soldier's spiritual needs.

The following vignettes are meant to illustrate the FIRST TEAM chaplains' work in Vietnam.

—Not many priests "back in the world" serve a parish covering some 3,500 square miles, but Chaplain (CPT) James J. Brennen does. Like other Skytrooper chaplains Father Brennen serves men located some distance apart with the 1st and 5th Battalions, 7th Cavalry, and he travels a great deal. He's a modern version of the legendary "circuit rider" of days gone by; he uses a helicopter in place of the horse and buggy.

"The guys out there come to know themselves," Father Brennen said. "When they start analyzing what they have they come to appreciate things more and they share with one another what little they have because they rely on each other so much."

—When Company A, 2nd Battalion, 8th Cavalry, made the division's first combat assault into III Corps, Chaplain (CPT) G. L. Gogl was with them. "The company had no services recently," he said. "It was the only way I could get to them."

—Sergeant Anthony Minotti, a squad leader with Company B, 1st Battalion, 8th Cavalry, carried with him a Bible printed by the American Bible Society in 1844 that had been in his family for more than 100 years. It was first carried to the Civil War and spent two years and six months in a Confederate prison. The same Bible was carried by men of faith during World Wars I and II, the Korean War and a tour of the Philippines. The inscription inside reads, "Carry it with you and I'm sure its wisdom will guide and keep you as it did me."

—"The church is more accessible in

Vietnam than it is in the States, particularly in the Cav, where we can travel anywhere to teach our people," said Chaplain (CPT) Henry C. Hilliard. The Division Artillery chaplain had more than 500 field worship services under his belt, merits several Air Medals, wears two Bronze Star Medals for valor under fire, and a Soldier's Medal for pulling an injured pilot from a burning helicopter. And he has the Purple Heart.

—On FSB Mary the chapel is named for the patron saint of the artillery, Saint Barbara. Once it consisted of a single cross carved from a brass 105 mm cannister. It had grown to include a row of pews, a picket fence and an altar for the cross. Made from "walnut stained" ammo boxes (the "walnut stain" is tar paper coated in gasoline) it is the pride of Battery A, 1st Battalion, 21st Artillery, a mutual effort of men of all faiths to have a place to worship.

—Being an Army chaplain in Vietnam involves a lot more than conducting Sunday worship services and holding spiritual counseling sessions. It is a 24-hours-a-day, seven-days-a-week job that caters to not only the spiritual needs of men, but to their intellectual and physical needs as well.

"There men deserve the best we can give them," said Chaplain (CPT) John E. Snider of the 1st Battalion, 5th Cavalry. To Chaplain Snider this includes chapel dayrooms, dry socks, Kool-Aid, pens and paper and nightly movies. One night he stood guard on the perimeter so that the man whose post he took could run the movie projector at the battalion chapel that night.

—Villagers in the southern coastal farming hamlet of Nhut Dong were forced to flee their homes and rice crops when the Viet Cong "liberated" the area. Their Catholic church, a twin-spiraled Gothic structure, was ransacked.

Months later as the villagers returned to the area to harvest their rice under the protection of the 2nd Battalion, 7th Cavalry, Chaplain (CPT) James Ware was approached by an elder. "The people miss the bells," the old man said.

"They were beautiful," Chaplain Ware said. "One was French, one was cast in Hue and the third was a Buddhist bell of traditional pattern."

A special helicopter was dispatched and the bells were airlifted to Huong Dien where the villagers had been relocated.

The Cavalry chaplain, a modern-day circuit rider, goes where the troops are in need of service. Conducting services at stark landing zones or in the center of combat zones, these men must make-do with what is at their disposal, whether it be a rock, log or ammunition boxes when preparing their altars.

No matter where he may be, the Skytrooper (above) has services made available to him. The sacraments and religious messages are brought anywhere, anytime by the chaplains, some 24 in all. The bell (below) was hung in the Division Chapel at An Khe and was given by citizens of Phoenix, Arizona. The bell, along with the chapel, were dedicated on Easter Sunday 1967.

Before he left, Chaplain Ware, a Protestant, conducted a service for the harvesters in their old church. The Vietnamese, all Catholic, said this didn't make any difference. "All right service, same-same Jesus," approved one man.

—On World Communion Sunday all Christian faiths are united in their common observance of a rededication and spiritual renewal.

Chaplain (CPT) W. Richard Waddle of the 5th Battalion, 7th Cavalry, traveled daily to individual companies but this was a day he hoped to reach them all. He held seven services that day in a span of 14 hours. One company was in contact and he was unable to land. "The day went pretty well," he said. "Maybe I can get to that other company tomorrow."

—"For God and Country," by Chaplain (CPT) Claude Newby, 1st Squadron, 9th Cavalry, chaplain:

"As a chaplain on my second tour with the 1st Cav, I am often asked if I volunteered to return to Vietnam and if I asked to return to the Cav. To my affirmative answers to both questions, there is often a strange period of silence.

"Sometimes the questioner will walk away silently shaking his head. I can almost 'hear him mumbling, 'Why, you'd never know it just by looking at him. He almost looks normal.'

"Traditionally, men entering the military service receive this advice, 'Never volunteer for anything,' from relatives, fellow recruits and old veterans. The sanity of one who too easily volunteers is immediately suspect. In fact, being a volunteer can actually be embarrassing.

"Few volunteers will simply answer, 'Yes, I volunteered,' and leave it at that. Most, with some slight or strong embarrassment, will attempt to explain why they felt justified in volunteering as a defense to their mental reputation. However, in the heat of actual combat, the volunteer comes into his own.

"I recall a day when I lay exposed only about 70 feet from an enemy bunker. The terrain was open. Enemy fire was coming from the bunker and from many points along our front and flanks. As I lay there, trying to crawl under my belt buckle, I witnessed a fellow soldier take a serious hit just about 25 feet from me.

"It only took me a moment to convince myself that I had to go forward and help the wounded man. Just as I started to move, a medic slithered past me and told me to stay put. He then crawled forward and gave the wounded soldier aid. Because that medic had volunteered for a very dangerous task, I was able to sigh with relief.

"How thankful I felt for that volunteer being there. In combat the volunteer comes into his own.

"Our Savior, Jesus Christ, was a volunteer. He volunteered for the most dangerous mission the world had ever seen. He volunteered to take upon himself the greatest suffering the world has ever known or shall know.

"He volunteered to suffer such horrible suffering of spirit that it would suffice to meet the requirements of justice for all who would accept the payment by accepting the Christ, and taking His way of life.

"Because the Savior accomplished His voluntary 'suicide' mission, both physical and spiritual death is overcome—all mankind can sigh with relief because a volunteer paid the price for the "big DEROS" to our Father in Heaven.

"Let us thank God for Jesus Christ, the volunteer; and for the many other volunteers who have followed His example in their lives to care for us."

Veteran performers George Gobel, Bob Hope and George Jessel visited "Cav Country" in 1969, bringing a little bit of home to members of the division.

SPECIAL SERVICES

Dancer Suzanne Charney made a tremendous hit with Skytroopers as she toured Vietnam with Mr. Hope's show in 1969.

Theresa Graves, one of the cast in television's "Laugh-In," toured Vietnam with Bob Hope's Christmas Show, entertaining Skytroopers at Lai Khe, Cu Chi and Long Binh.

The call came over the radio, "You're getting a Uniform Sierra Oscar tomorrow." At 1 p.m. the next day a Chinook landed and immediately drew a large crowd of bare-chested men volunteering to help unload its precious cargo.

Unlike the usual supply missions that the Chinook flew into the remote little village cut from the jungle when one or two men helped the crew chief carry off the cargo, two dozen men stood in the hot blast of the engines and swirling wind behind the hook to help the cargo safely off. The musicians, huge amplifiers and instruments in large cases, trunks of clothes, then the girls, clad in brightly colored miniskirts, emerged from the waiting hook.

In a few minutes all but the most essential activity had ceased at the re-

Cav Sergeant Bill Ellis toured firebases, entertaining Skytroopers with his songs about the life of an infantryman. Those who heard them, "Grunt," "Firefight" and the others, know they were songs about their everyday life . . . not a pleasant life, but one not soon to be forgotten.

The Jefferson Helicopter, (below), composed of men from various units of the division, spent 60 days TDY to Special Services and toured Cav firebases and basecamps. Bob Hope and Connie Stevens (right) teamed up to entertain Skytroopers in 1969. Cavalrymen were flown to three available sites to see the performers.

Cavalrymen (below left) watch Bob Hope's Christmas Show (below right) at Long Binh. The Golddiggers, a group of 13 beautiful, round-eyed reminders of home, brought the house down with each number.

mote outpost and the booming sounds of rock music echoed through the jungle, replacing the usual thunder of howitzers. A USO (United Services Organization) show had come to the lonely Skytroopers—arranged by the Cav's Special Services.

In the Cav, even the Special Services are airmobile. Hundreds of USO shows from Ron "Tarzan" Ely's one man tour to large shows like the Christy Minstrels have toured the Cav since 1965, all by air.

One of the Special Services' main jobs is to prepare a touring show to be transported to 1st Cav firebases.

When the show is too massive to be taken to the troops, the troops are taken to the show. Special Services arranged for a flotilla of fixed wing and helicopter craft to transport 2,000 Skytroopers to each of three Bob Hope Christmas Show locations in 1969.

Besides arranging for transportation and schedules for travelling shows, Special Services often produce their own. Talented Cavalrymen are chosen at auditions to go on temporary duty as entertainers, touring the 1st Cav firebases and often also touring all of Vietnam.

One of these talented Skytroopers, Sergeant Bill Ellis, became the unofficial Cav troubador in 1969 by singing the songs of the grunts in the field. An ex-infantryman, SGT Ellis composed songs, including "First Team" and "Firefight."

Special Serices also entertain the men with Service Clubs sprinkled throughout the area of operations. The girls who run the Service Clubs entertain soldiers with a wide variety of games, activities and hobbies—from playing ping pong to reading, drinking coffee or just sitting back in a comfortable chair and relaxing for a few precious moments.

Miss World, Eva Reuber-Staier, a dazzling beauty from Austria, and Bob Hope team up (below) to entertain at Long Binh.

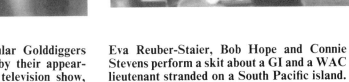

A member of the now-popular Golddiggers group, made more popular by their appearances on the Dean Martin television show, performs for the men.

Eva Reuber-Staier, Bob Hope and Connie Stevens perform a skit about a GI and a WAC lieutenant stranded on a South Pacific island.

The third anniversary of the Phuoc Vinh Service Club was highlighted by a cake baking contest between the mess halls at Camp Gorvad. After a lengthy deliberation by the judges, the cake (below) of Headquarters and Headquarters Battery, Division Artillery, won first place.

The entire Hope Christmas Show cast, Connie Stevens, Suzanne Charney, Bob Hope, Eva Reuber-Staier, Theresa Graves and the Golddiggers, close the show at Long Binh with the singing of "Silent Night."

Santa Claus made an unexpected visit to "Cav Country" in 1969. Arriving in true airmobile fashion, he rappelled into the Phuoc Vinh helipad at one point, carrying his bag of goodies.

Personnel recuperating at the 93rd Evacuation Hospital in Long Binh managed to get out to see the Christmas Show.

DISTINGUISHED VISITORS

Major General Harry W. O. Kinnard, 1st Air Cav commanding general (far right), points out enemy weapons captured during fighting in the Ia Drang Valley. His visitors are (from left to right) General Earl Wheeler, chairman of the Joint Chiefs of Staff, John McNaughton, Department of Defense official, and Secretary of Defense Robert McNamara. The date: November 27, 1965.

Secretary of Defense Robert McNanara, Lieutenant General Vinh Loc, ARVN II Corps commanding general, and General William Westmoreland, commander of U.S. Forces in Vietnam, are escorted by Major General John J. Tolson, 1st Cav commanding general, on a tour of Cav firebases in the II Corps Tactical Zone in 1967.

Even in combat the visitors came to see and marvel. Without question, the Cav has been the most thoroughly visited unit in Vietnam. On these pages are just a few of the distinguished visitors who came calling—from the Ia Drang to I Corps to War Zone C, in basecamps, on remote mountaintops and muddy LZs. They came, they saw, and they invariably left, if not convinced, impressed.

General of the Army, Ohmar Bradley, takes time out to talk with Skytroopers during his 1967 visit to Vietnam.

General Dwight E. Beach, commander of U.S. Army Forces, Pacific, visited the division's area of operations in Binh Dinh Province in 1967.

Charley Black, war correspondent and columnist for the Columbus, Georgia, *Ledger-Enquirer*, who has covered the Cav from its early days at Fort Benning, definitely ranks in the "distinguished visitor" category.

Brigadier General (Retired) S. L. A. Marshall, the noted military historian and columnist, has made several visits to Cav Country since 1965, writing extensively on Skytroopers and the airmobile division in battle.

Secretary of the Army Stanley R. Resor visited Cav firebases for two days during August 1969. Mr. Resor talked with Skytroopers at LZs Grant, Kelly and Wescott.

General Creighton W. Abrams, COMUS-MACV and COMUSARV, visited Cav Country early in 1969 to attach the Presidential Unit Citation streamer to the guidon of Company A, 1st Battalion, 5th Cavalry. First Sergeant Salvatore Vizelli assists the general.

Terence Cardinal Cooke, Bishop of New York City and Military Ordinariate, visited the division's Camp Gorvad base December 24, 1969. As Military Ordinariate, Cardinal Cooke is the bishop for all Roman Catholics serving in the Armed Forces.

Colonel Alfred E. Stevens (Retired), registrar of the 1st Cavalry Division Association, inspects a LOH during his tour of "Cav Country."

General Ralph E. Haines, commander of U.S. Army, Pacific, talks with Specialist Four Samuel R. Faulk, a mortarman with Company E, 1st of the 12th, while the battalion was establishing LZ Cindy. Escorting General Haines are Major General George I. Forsythe (second from left), 1st Cav commanding general, and Colonel Karl Morton, 3rd Brigade commander.

Ron Ely, star of television's "Tarzan" series, made a USO tour of Cav firebases in December 1969. The former football star tried his hand at rappelling and found it "sort of like swinging from tree to tree."

U.S. House Representative George Cleveland receives a block of instruction in the use of the M-79 grenade launcher from a company commander of the 1st of the 8th Cav. Lieutenant Colonel James A. Graham, Jr., battalion commander, critiques.

Comedienne Martha Raye, starring in the USO production of "Hello Dolly," stops during her visit of Cav firebases to get acquainted with "Dum Dum," mascot of Battery B, 2nd Battalion, 19th Artillery, at LZ Geronimo.

General A. J. Goodpastor (above), deputy commander, MACV, attaches the Presidential Unit Citation streamer to the guidon of Company C, 1st Battalion, 5th Cavalry, in 1968.

Lieutenant General William B. Rosson, deputy commander of MACV, visited the Cav (below) for the assumption of command ceremony of Major General E. B. Roberts. On LTG Rosson's right is Brigadier General William E. Shedd, assistant division commander.

Congressional Representative Graham Purcell of Texas speaks with Cav personnel (above) during a visit in April 1969.

Republic of Vietnam President Nguyen Van Thieu (above) chats with Skytroopers during a tour of Cav firebases in 1969.

Lieutenant General Do Cao Tri, ARVN III Corps commanding general, and Major General E. B. Roberts, division commander, make an inspection (below) of a combined Cav-ARVN firebase north of Tay Ninh.

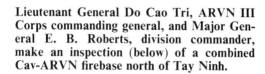

Bobbi, the AFVN weather girl, visits the 1st Cav weather detachment at the division's Camp Gorvad base.

Miss Marilyn Genz, "The Cav's Sweetheart," reads the latest issue of her favorite magazine, the FIRST TEAM, at the division's headquarters compound at Camp Gorvad.

Major General Harry W. O. Kinnard (second from left), division commanding general, discusses airmobility with Brigadier General Smith, USMC (second from right), Colonel William R. Lynch (center), 2nd Brigade commander, and with two Navy captains on a mountaintop near An Khe during Operation WHITE WING in February 1966.

Division History
(Continued From P. 42)

1969

The division continued Operation TOAN THANG II as 1969 began, interdicting enemy activity in the northern area of the III Corps Tactical Zone.

The new year opened with major military successes for the 1st Air Cavalry Division. From January 5 to January 12, 267 enemy were killed, and one of the largest munitions caches of the war, some 18 tons of arms and ammunition, was found near Tay Ninh on January 21.

Scout helicopters from C Troop, 1st Squadron, 9th Cavalry, initiated the weapons find when they spotted an ammo box on top of what looked like a bunker. They requested the 5th Battalion, 7th Cavalry, to move in and check the area. The enemy fought for three days to protect the bunker complex, but ARA, Air Force bomb strikes and artillery finally drove them to quieter parts of the jungle.

When the battalion landed, it found more than 100,000 AK-47 rounds, 35,000 heavy machinegun rounds, more than a ton of explosives and 643 mortar rounds.

The airmobile division went watermobile in January when the 1st Brigade carried out "NavCav" operations. Skytroopers rode the Vam Co Dong River and Bo Bo Canal network on Navy boats. Contact was light, but the effects of the boats and Cav observation helicopters resulted in the location of numerous munitions and weapons caches along the river bank.

In February the Cav's drive to deny the enemy his sanctuaries and supply caches continued in full swing. After the 2nd Battalion, 12th Cavalry, found 10,000 pounds of rice in a giant cache on January 31, an area roughly 25 kilometers northeast of Tay Ninh became the scene of repeated discoveries. During the action on the 31st, the division killed 47 enemy and captured 57,750 rounds of small arms ammunition.

The 2nd Bn, 12th Cav, found more than 37,000 pounds of rice on February 1 while the 1st Sqdn, 9th Cav, added another 20,000 pounds of grain. The next day 40,000 pounds were uncovered. The 2nd Battalion, 8th Cavalry, unearthed

157,400 pounds of rice February 9 and 11, some 23 kilometers north of Tay Ninh. Vietnamese Marines working with the Skytroopers found more than 100,000 rounds of ammo and a number of weapons on February 9 and 12. On February 12, 18 enemy soldiers were killed in a contact with the 1st Sqdn, 9th Cav, which also captured 1,000 pounds of rice that day. For some NVA units, it was going to be a lean year.

As the rice-denial and route interdiction operations continued in northern III Corps, some Cav units moved south to an area northeast of Bien Hoa. Their mission was to find and destroy enemy elements that had slipped past the division's cordon. The 2nd Battalion, 7th Cavalry, and the 1st Battalion, 12th Cavalry, with other 3rd Brigade elements, made the move on February 3.

Upon arrival in the new operations area, the two battalions straddled the major enemy infiltration routes. The 1st Bn, 12th Cav, assaulted into an area 13 miles northeast of Bien Hoa to establish LZ Cindy, while the 2nd Bn, 7th Cav, set up camp six miles further east at LZ

A machinegunner keeps his "gun" high, dry and ready as he fords a streams.

1st Brigade Skytroopers (below) keep watch for the enemy as they walk along the edge of heavy jungle during a mission in III Corps.

A hard day in the bush shows heavily on the face of this Cavalryman. A little Quan Loi red dirt is evident, too.

Liz. The Cavalrymen quickly spread out over the countryside in search of the enemy. They found the travelling easier than in the north, because of lighter vegetation. The new operation was dubbed CHEYENNE SABRE.

The first weeks of CHEYENNE SABRE were characterized by light contact, although numerous enemy bunker complexes and caches were located. The 2nd Bn, 7th Cav, fought a series of battles with enemy forces in fortified bunkers on February 27. The battalion killed 34 of the enemy. In a similar action on March 9 the battalion killed 15.

On March 12, the 2nd Bn, 7th Cav, joined the 3rd Brigade and began operations from LZ Lois. Two enemy platoons penetrated a battalion defensive position on March 17. The Skytroopers took 10 casualties, but killed 20 NVA as they pushed the enemy out of the perimeter. LZ Lois came under attack the same day by two reinforced companies who charged the base after a barrage of mortars and B-40s. The enemy lost 12 in the attack.

By April 19 the 3rd Brigade had returned to northern III Corps. More than 600 enemy had been killed in CHEYENNE SABRE.

While the 3rd Brigade operated near Bien Hoa, the rest of the division continued interdiction operations near Cambodia. Operation TOAN THANG II officially ended February 19 with more than 3,300 enemy killed and nearly a thousand individual and more than 300 crew-served weapons captured along with 900,000 rounds of ammo and 400 tons of rice. The spring and summer of 1969 were unique in the enemy's frequent attempts to overrun 1st Air Cav firebases. The scenario for these attacks seldom varied. Shortly after midnight the enemy would launch a barrage of rockets and

Air Cavalrymen of Company B, 2nd Battalion, 5th Cavalry, move out toward the treeline northeast of Tay Ninh City as their Huey lift birds nose forward to climb out of the assault area.

mortars at the base, then sappers and infantry would try to breach the perimeter. They might get no further than the wire; they might even succeed in occupying several bunkers, but inevitably they were thrown back, generally with heavy losses. No matter how many lives it took, the enemy evidently wanted to be able to claim a major victory over a 1st Air Cavalry unit. It was wishful thinking.

One of the hardest hit Cav bases was LZ Grant. Located northeast of Tay Ninh, the LZ was astride a major enemy infiltration route. The infantry companies of the 2nd Bn, 12th Cav, operating out of the landing zone were finding numerous enemy bunkers and caches, while C Battery, 1st Battalion, 77th Artillery, and A Battery, 1st Battalion, 30th Artillery, pounded his trails and sanctuaries with high explosives. The enemy decided to try to rid themselves of this obstacle.

The first attempt came on February 23 at 3:30 a.m. Sixteen of the enemy were killed. They tried again with 1,000 men on March 8. Despite a direct hit on the TOC that killed the battalion commander, Lieutenant Colonel Peter Gorvad, the battalion did not give way. The enemy had blasted through the outer wire with bangalore torpedoes, charging in after hitting the base with rockets, mortars, and nausea gas. A withering hail of small arms fire and point blank artillery stopped the enemy, and the appearance of aerial rocket artillery and Air Force gunships put him into retreat. At least 157 NVA died in the six hour battle.

An enemy battalion came back for more on March 11. Sixty-two of them

did not leave alive. Still the enemy did not give up. Perhaps they felt they had to make up for their earlier defeats. It was a vain quest. Two hundred NVA stormed Grant's berm May 12 and to be hurled back again with the loss of 45 men.

The division paused in its daily tasks on April 23 to say farewell to its fourth commanding general as MG Forsythe left to command the Infantry School at Fort Benning. On May 5th, the division, in a ceremony on the FIRST TEAM pad at Phuoc Vinh, welcomed back a former Skytrooper. MG E. B. Roberts, who had led the 1st Brigade in 1965 and early 1966, returned to command the division. MG Roberts, a 1943 graduate of West Point, served with the 101st Airborne Division in World War II. He had been the first chief of staff of the 11th Air Assault Division at Fort Benning. Most recently, the general had served as assistant division commander of the 9th Infantry Division in the Delta, and as deputy chief of staff (plans and operations), U.S. Army Vietnam. He had just returned from flight school where he earned his wings as a helicopter pilot.

MG Roberts scarcely had settled into his quarters when the division was embroiled in a major combat action. Early on the morning of May 6 the enemy hit LZ Carolyn and LZ Joe. The 2nd Bn, 8th Cav, fought the regimental-size enemy force at Carolyn for four hours, counterattacking to push them out of a portion of the perimeter they occupied. The enemy force was smashed, with 198 killed and 30 taken prisoner. They abandoned 81 AK-47s, 285 grenades and 325 satchel charges.

A 1st Brigade grenadier treds lightly as he eyes something suspicious on the trail ahead. A keen eye and quick reactions can save a man from an enemy ambush.

These are a few of the more familiar sights Cav soldiers see daily in Vietnam. Hardly any soldier who comes to Vietnam and gets beyond Saigon and Long Binh has been able to avoid filling and hefting the mainstay of defensive constructions, the sandbag (far left). It usually isn't hot water, but the field shower (left), just before turning in, can help take some of the grime off. In the war zone the workday starts as soon as there is light (below), and not infrequently it starts before dawn and runs well into the night. War knows no schedule, and "the enemy never sleeps," so the division runs 24-hours-a-day, seven days a week.

The weapons of war are numerous, and each passing defense budget sees newer and more advanced machinery and equipment trickle down the supply pipe. But for the infantryman in a firefight, his main weapons remain very much what they were for soldiers of the past; it isn't the same old "pineapple," but it is still a grenade (left), and there is still no greater immediate piece of comforting steel (bottom) than the machinegun.

In as great demand as the horse and mule of the old Cavalry ever were are the row upon row of the industructible jeeps.

At Joe, 5th Bn, 7th Cav, troopers killed eight of the NVA force that had made a ground probe.

On May 12, the same day as the attack on Grant, the enemy also assaulted LZ Jamie, LZ Phyllis and Quan Loi, the 3rd Brigade headquarters. Eighty-three enemy were killed in the unsuccessful attacks.

The 3rd Brigade was sent south again on May 19. Its mission was to interdict the movement of the 5th Viet Cong Division out of War Zone D toward the heavily populated and strategically crucial Long Binh-Bien Hoa area. Contact was light, but caches of supplies discovered were so large that intelligence indicated the enemy units were withdrawing to the north partially because of food shortages. Nearly 200 tons of rice were captured, 43 tons of salt, six tons of sugar, and 70 tons of other foodstuffs.

Specialist Four James Johnson keeps his M-79 grenade launcher at the ready during a recon mission by Company E, 5th Battalion, 7th Cav, near Song Be

The 3rd Brigade also killed 132 enemy and captured 77,070 rounds of ammo. The brigade returned to Quan Loi on June 1.

In the north, the 2nd Brigade discovered one of the largest single caches of the campaign on May 26. B Troop, 1st Sqdn, 9th Cav, first spotted parts of the cache in an area ripped open by a B-52 strike. LOH observers saw fresh trails and bunkers built less than 48 hours before. As 9th Cav "Blues" and elements of the 1st Battalion, 5th Cavalry, searched the area they found weapons and ammunition still in factory cases and bags of rice stacked neatly on logs and covered with green plastic. In all, the Skytroopers uncovered 45 tons of rice, 11 tons of salt, 23 cases of B-40 rockets, 10 cases of .50 caliber ammunition and numerous other supplies.

In southern War Zone C, the 1st Brigade dealt a crushing blow to the tenacious 95th VC Regiment in mid-June. With intelligence indicating an enemy build-up in the base area known as the Crescent, a company was inserted after a B-52 strike. It made contact and pulled back for two more strikes. Two companies were then reinserted and were heavily engaged by the enemy. Again pulling back, four more strikes were massed, edge to edge, one after another. Immediately after the last bombs, six airmobile infantry companies combat assaulted into the Crescent and sealed it off, Assisted by 11th Armored Cavalry Regiment tanks they swept the area and drove the enemy force across the Saigon River and deep into War Zone C, leaving more than 400 NVA dead.

The enemy launched several ground attacks on landing zones in June. LZ Joy was hit by a mortar and rocket attack of 300 rounds on June 11, followed by an infantry assault. The men of the 1st Battalion, 7th Cavalry, killed 35 NVA as they drove off the attack. Thirty-seven NVA died in an effort to overrun LZ Ike on June 18. The 2nd Battalion, 5th Cavalry, killed 90 NVA when the enemy attacked Ike again on June 20.

Despite the military challenge, the division still carried on a vigorous program of civic action. Tons of food were distributed to refugees. The division provided support in building schools, orphanages and dispensaries. Over a three month period division medics and doctors treated 4,566 patients in 48 Medcaps. A scholarship assistance program was instituted to help needy Vietnamese students. A community

relations council and friendship council were common features throughout the area of operations. The councils gave Vietnamese civilians and representatives of the division a chance to discuss mutual problems and their solutions. The division sponsored weekly trips to Saigon for children and teachers from the outlying rural areas, giving them their first view of the national capitol.

On the combat side, July was a relatively quiet period, Contact was sporadic and generally light as all three brigades carried on the interdiction campaign in northern III Corps. The calm was broken on August 12 when the enemy lashed out at towns throughout the division's AO.

LZ Becky, which had taken a smaller attack the night before, was blasted with 400 rounds of mortars and rockets, then attacked by two companies. Despite the heavy bombardment the infantrymen of the 2nd Battalion, 19th Artillery, rallied to defend the base, successfully keeping the enemy from penetrating the perimeter, and, with the help of ARA and Night Hawk birds, forced the NVA to retreat. Fifty-four NVA were killed.

The enemy also tried to take Quan Loi, LZ Jon, LZ Kelly and LZ Caldwell on the 12th. At each base they were repelled. As the enemy tried to melt into the jungle at daylight they were pursued by Cobra and Huey gunships. In a 24-hour period the enemy lost 452 soldiers. Another 242 would be added as the pursuit of the enemy continued over the next two days.

On August 26 elements of the 2nd Brigade began a series of engagements when Charlie Troop, 1st Sqdn, 9th Cav, spotted and fired on 50 enemy in the open. Air strikes, artillery and CS were employed in the area resulting in 12 NVA KIA. The next day 2nd Brigade scouts swooped down on enemy in the open, cutting down eight NVA. Delta Company, 5th Bn, 7th Cav, was fired upon on August 29. The enemy was answered with a devastating display of 1st Cav firepower. Organics, artillery, ARA and air strikes accounted for eight dead NVA. The following morning a sweep of the area revealed an additional 11 NVA KIA. The 5th Bn, 7th Cav, recon platoon atop Nui Ba Ra took small arms, mortar and B-40 fire on the night of August 30. The firefight flickered sporadically through the night and a first light sweep found 10 enemy bodies scattered on the mountain slopes.

LZ Ike came under enemy attack

again shortly before midnight September 3 when 100 mortar rounds slammed into the base. An estimated company-sized unit hit the wire. The defenders used point-blank artillery fire and Cobra gunships to crush the offensive, killing 33 NVA.

A significant action came September 15 when 2nd Brigade elements fought a fierce firefight with two NVA companies. Air strikes, the 1st of the 9th, ARA and tube artillery were employed during the skirmish with devastating results. When the defeated enemy withdrew they left behind 14 bodies and much ammunition and equipment. Numerous blood trails and discarded bandages indicated that many more wounded or killed enemy had been dragged away. The next day brigade units guarding a downed aircraft called in artillery and air strikes when they heard enemy voices. Ten dead NVA were found the next day, along with 126 mortar rounds.

The division's main task in the last three months of the year continued to be stopping enemy infiltration. The 3rd Brigade was extremely effective in this mission as its units blocked the Serges Jungle Highway, a network of trails hidden by triple canopy jungle. Sometimes the "trails" could more accurately be described as roads; at other times they were merely dirt tracks a few inches wide. They all were important as routes from Cambodia to complexes of supply and repair facilities in Vietnam.

The 3rd Brigade spread its battalions over the trail, placing them squarely in the path of enemy movement. Maneuver elements branched out through the jungle, finding numerous caches, bunkers, and often the enemy himself. By the end of 1969 the enemy had lost 800 men in the Serges area and 50 caches had been located and destroyed. Prisoners reported that the loss of the caches was forcing enemy units to concentrate their efforts on looking for food, thus drastically limiting their military potential.

In Phuoc Long Province, the 2nd Brigade was having a remarkable effect on the people. Phuoc Long had long been an enemy sanctuary, with the rural villagers forced at gunpoint to build bunkers and supply food to the NVA and VC units. The Skytroopers offered them a way out; freedom in secure areas. Twenty-seven individuals rallied at FSB Mary on September 29. More, many more, were to follow. The brigade's psyops units used the first ralliers to make heliborne broadcasts and write

Company B, 1st Battalion, 5th Cav, patrols the Saigon River. NavCav riverine operations proved successful during the first months of the division's operations in III Corps.

leaflets to appeal to those who had stayed behind. In the end, 546 Vietnamese deserted the enemy to come under Allied protection by the end of November. The enemy vented its anger at the 2nd Brigade with a sapper attack on the unit's FSB Buttons headquarters and other brigade firebases on November 4. Some 269 NVA died in the unsuccessful attempts.

The unique helicopter striking power of the 1st Sqdn, 9th Cav, ravaged the enemy ranks during the final months of the year. Week after week the squadron saw most of the action, its units sometimes accounting for more than half of the casualties inflicted on the enemy.

The division continued to carry out numerous civic action projects to increase the people's well being and ability to support themselves, showing them that the best hope for improving their lives was on the Allied side. The division put more medical teams into the villages than ever before, concentrating on "swing" districts, areas safe by day, but frequently visited by the enemy at night. The division band often accompanied the Medcap operations to entertain the villagers and help attract them to where they could be treated.

The division also supplied building materials and know how to help in construction and repair of schools. The 3rd Brigade civic action team distributed school supplies to the children at Quan Loi School. In Tay Ninh, donations from the 1st Brigade helped to build Tay Ninh Girls' High School, one

of Vietnam's most modern. Nearly 50 percent of the monetary contributions came from the brigade. The school enabled 1,100 students to leave the old, over crowded high school.

A demonstration farm was started, supported by funds from the division's voluntary civic action fund. The farm showed rural residents how to properly apply modern techniques of farming, concentrating on programs within the resources of the ordinary Vietnamese farmer. The 2nd Brigade imported rabbits and ducks to Phuoc Long Province to permit farmers there to experiment with them as possible new sources of income for the local economy.

In the spirit of Dong Tien, "forward together," the division was also working with the Vietnamese in the fighting itself. Rural Forces and Civilian Irregular Defense Group soldiers coordinated search and interdiction missions with division elements. Cav helicopters and artillery provided support for Vietnamese units when they made contact. ARVN Airborne brigades and artillery battalions moved into the AOs of the division's brigades, doubling the pressure on the enemy, who was then faced with the best of both the American and the ARVN forces.

The ARVN units made an important contribution to the division's ability to shut off enemy supply and infiltration routes. In the early months of 1969 the division had stopped the enemy threat from the 1st and 7th NVA divisions in the area near Tay Ninh. Further east the

2nd Brigade spoiled enemy plans to move down the Adams Road, while the 3rd Brigade blocked the Serges Jungle Highway in the Quan Loi area.

As the enemy continued moving east to escape the division's vise, Cav elements followed. The 2nd Brigade displaced to Song Be, astraddle Communist routes from Cambodia through Phuoc Long Province.

That, however, was about as far as the division could stretch its manpower. More spreading out would mean decreases in division effectiveness. Then the ARVN Airborne units came. With the 1st ARVN Airborne Brigade in the eastern region of the AO the combined allied forces could and did conduct operations all the way east to the boundary between III and II Corps. Along that boundary in November Bravo Troop, 1st Sqdn, 9th Cav, discovered the Jolley Trail, named after the troop's commander, Major Charles A. Jolley.

The enemy had spent nearly a year constructing the network of jungle trails comprising the highway, paving it with bamboo matting to keep it open during the rainy season, and building bunkers every few hundred meters as way stations and bomb shelters. The high speed trails were generally about four feet wide.

With the discovery of the trail enemy hopes of bypassing the 1st Cav were quickly dashed. Air strikes ripped off the concealing canopy, blasted the bunkers and blew away the trail's bamboo bridges. Cav helicopters constantly patrolled the route, looking for any signs of enemy movement.

The division had effectively sealed enemy routes through northern III Corps, and the combination of gunships, grunts and guns was making drastic cuts in enemy manpower. In November the division killed 1,808 enemy. That was the most casualties the FIRST TEAM had accounted for in a single month since the Tet offensive in February 1968, when 1,879 Communists were cut down. In December the enemy again paid a heavy price, with 1,555 killed. In two months the division had depleted enemy ranks by 3,434 men.

For the Communists in northern III Corps it had been an unfortunate year. Moving to bunker complexes to rest and replenish their supplies of food and ammo, they found the complexes destroyed and the caches gone. Walking down trails they had used for years, they met with ambushes on the ground while division helicopters harassed them from

A heavily-laden machinegunner leads the way as 1st Air Cavalrymen from 2nd Battalion, 5th Cavalry, cross a jungle clearing.

above. Entering villages whose residents had fed and sheltered them, they found that the villagers had fled to Allied areas where they could be protected from enemy exploitation. When the NVA hurled themselves against the division firebases that were the source of their troubles, they learned that the airmobile Skytrooper could be an immovable object if his mission was holding a position. What the enemy had taken for granted, domination of northern III Corps, had been taken over by the 1st Air Cavalry Division.

EPILOGUE

This, then, has been a brief review of

the accomplishments of the 1st Cavalry Division (Airmobile) from its activation on July 3, 1965, until December 31, 1969.

The division's history can be subdivided into five parts or phases, and, not surprisingly, these phases coincide pretty much with the tenure of each commanding general.

Each of these phases had flashy and spectacular moments, covered intensively by an omnipresent press corps; but much of the work in all the phases was done quickly, efficiently, and without fanfare. Heroism and dedication—to a cause, to a concept, to an organization—were the common threads throughout the tapestry that tells the Cav's story in Vietnam.

Any retrospective glance at the record

Skytroopers of the 2nd Battalion, 5th Cavalry, prepare to move out after taking a short respite from "humping the boonies." They were working in the bamboo-filled III Corps jungle.

of the FIRST TEAM in Vietnam should immediately reveal certain high points. Certainly the Pleiku Campaign, the relief of Khe Sanh, and the great move south to III Corps stand out as dramatic events. But who can say that the pacification of Binh Dinh Province, the second most populated province in Vietnam, was not equally or more significant in the final accounting. Nor can anyone deny that the complete mastery of the Cav over the North Vietnamese army units in northern III Corps ranks as a military achievement of remarkable proportions.

In the Pleiku Campaign MG Kinnard saw the triumph of the concept he pioneered, and then presided over the dramatics of MASHER/WHITE WING. But there were also for him the unspectacular but nevertheless productive operations called MATADOR, LINCOLN, MOSBY, and CLEARHOUSE.

MG Norton inherited a proven fighting team but soon had to face what every Cav commander since has had to weather—the rotational hump. His Operations CRAZY HORSE and PAUL REVERE were tough and violent and, alas, almost entirely ignored by the press. But THAYER and IRVING played to good audiences; and then there was the start of the long grind destined to end NVA/VC domination of Binh Dinh— Operation PERSHING.

It remained for MG Tolson to terminate that operation and begin others in the same vein. All were highly successful and few were noted by those outside the military family. A log, maintained by the division information office to record the names of news media representatives, reveals that the division appeared to have been forgotten by the press during some months of 1967. This was all changed during Operations PEGASUS and DELAWARE and it was for these that the unititiated best remember MG Tolson.

MG Forsythe, of course, engineered the move of the Air Cav south to III Corps. It had a flair and demonstrated the marvelous mobility of the airmobile division. But the defense of Saigon by the lightning ripostes of the Cav was equally impressive to those who observed and were aware of the implications of the tactics of those early days in III Corps.

Under MG Roberts the division settled down to a grinding, crunching and deadly efficient war of attrition in the three northern-most provinces of the III Corps Tactical Zone, punctuated during the summer and fall of 1969 by brief and violent episodes at the Cav's far-flung firebases.

Few in the division realized at the time that these fiery episodes were but the spasmodic twitchings of a strangling enemy war machine. The slamming of an iron door on three old and well-used infiltration trails has been well-told in this volume. It was done with the determined and tireless efforts of many small units, using arimobility as it never has been used before.

Perhaps this is the one message that comes across louder and clearer than all others. From the Ia Drang to the A Shau to War Zone C, the 1st Air Cav, successfully and repeatedly, changed its tactics and techniques to meet the challenges of terrain, weather and the enemy.

It is this very adaptability—this inherent propensity for doing precisely the right thing at the right time by a finely-tuned combination of men and machines—that has made the FIRST TEAM a consistent winner.

It has been said that the Pleiku Campaign was the triumph of the airmobile concept. In truth, every battle, every campaign, every year, has been the triumph of a concept.

253

2nd Brigade

(Continued From P. 51)

Vinh, the division basecamp in III Corps. Operating 11 miles north of Phouc Vinh, brigade elements found 10 well-fortified bunkers that contained 942 B-40 rockets, 300 57 mm recoilless rifle rounds, 60,000 small arms rounds, 150 RPG rockets, and several hundred pounds of medical supplies, rations and clothing. Ten enemy bodies were also found at the scene.

As 1969 began the 2nd Brigade was at Quan Loi, sharing with the 3rd Brigade the dusty camp in the midst of the Terres Rouge Rubber Plantation. On January 21 and 22 elements of the two brigades found one of the biggest caches of the campaign 23 kilometers southeast of An Loc. The NVA was deprived of the use of 112,000 rounds of AK-47 ammunition, 35,000 rounds of .50 caliber machinegun ammunition, 2,800 pounds of explosives, and thousands of other pieces of equipment. From Quan Loi the 2nd Brigade moved to Lai Khe, the basecamp of the 1st Infantry Division. The spring of 1969 was occupied with searches of the dense, B-52 strike-dotted foliage along the Saigon River as the brigade interdicted enemy infiltration routes.

In Lai Khe the brigade developed its "Rat Patrol." Whenever the base received incoming enemy rounds, members of the patrol would scramble to their jeeps, mounted with M-60 machineguns, and begin a search of the perimeter wire for possible breaks, entry of enemy personnel and booby traps or tunnels.

In August the 2nd Brigade moved its headquarters to LZ Buttons near Song Be City. The brigade's mission was to protect that province capital, to locate and neutralize the 5th VC Division, and to interdict enemy movement in Phouc Long Province. Throughout August brigade elements made frequent contact and significant finds of enemy material. In September units continued to effectively combine infantry, artillery, aerial rocket artillery, and air strikes to make life miserable for the enemy in Phouc Long Province.

Throughout this period the Blackhorse Brigade carried on a vigorous program of psychological operations and civic

action. In October it became evident that this program was highly effective. A record number of persons rallied to 2nd Brigade firebases and to units in the field.

On October 8, eight enemy soldiers rallied under the Chieu Hoi program and turned themselves over to B Company, 2nd Battalion, 12th Cavalry, while 11 more Vietnamese rallied to 2nd Bn, 12th Cav, at FSB Judy. Ninety-one individuals

came to the Blackhorse Brigade on October 11; that was only the beginning. By the end of November 546 Vietnamese had placed themselves under the protection of 2nd Brigade.

For five years the isolated, unmapped villages of the ralliers had served as vital supply points for the Viet Cong and NVA forces passing through. The villagers' reasons for leaving were many. They described life under the Com-

Skytroopers of Company C, 1st Battalion, 7th Cavalry, move down a hill in search of enemy base areas in northern III Corps.

munists as grim, with the VC closely controlling their economy, their religion and their actions. One third of the food they produced was "purchased" with bonds which, the VC said, would be redeemed after South Vietnam was "liberated". Another third of their produce had to be "donated" to the enemy. Brigade PSYOPs broadcasts from helicopters offered a way out.

The first refugees who came in the 2nd Brigade were used to make the PSYOPS broadcasts. Their words helped allay the fears that their fellow villagers had about rallying; fears the NVA and VC fanned with tales of beatings and bad treatment for Hoi Chanh. This was one factor in the growing stream of refugees. So were the civic action programs of the brigade, civic actions such as the airlift of rice to hungry villagers and the bringing of ducks and pigs to the people of the Song Be area to help them improve their agricultural economy. Word of these actions filtered back to the VC-held villages, and in some instances VC members themselves led the refugees to the firebases.

The success of the brigade's programs may have accounted for the desperate sapper attack the NVA launched against FSB Buttons on November 4. The Americans repulsed the attack, and 63 NVA died. Simultaneous attacks against other brigade firebases also failed. As 1969 ended the Blackhorse Brigade continued to block the enemy's plans for Phouc Long Province.

3rd Brigade
(Continued From P. 55)

away from the LZ. Firefights were frequent throughout November, as the brigade shifted to LZ Sue on the Song Be River. On December 3 the 2nd Bn, 7th Cav, air assaulted into a clearing not far from the Song Be River and was met by a battalion size enemy force equipped with heavy weapons. Outnumbered four to one, the Garry Owen troopers held against three enemy ground assaults and inflicted heavy casualties. Throughout December the

Members of the second platoon, Company D, 2nd Battalion of the 7th Cavalry, advance through a cloud of smoke during a search and destroy mission during Operation JEB STUART.

brigade interdicted the established jungle highways that honeycombed the area.

In January of 1969 the 3rd Brigade opened a VIP Center at Quan Loi, again the unit's basecamp. The VIP Center would serve as the home of Garry Owen troopers during two day standdowns, enabling them to enjoy steaks, beer and recreation.

On January 21 and 22 the 3rd Brigade combined with the 2nd to find one of the biggest caches of the campaign in a staunchly defended area 23 kilometers southeast of An Loc. Some 112,000 rounds of AK-47 ammo, 35,000 rounds of .50 caliber ammo, more than a ton of explosives, and hundreds of individual weapons were among the finds. A few weeks later Garry Owen companies found an NVA hospital that included classrooms, living quarters, mess and supply bunkers and medical supplies.

The enemy twice attacked the 3rd Brigade command post at Quan Loi in May, combining mortar and rocket attacks with probes by sappers. The enemy's efforts were futile and he sustained heavy casualties. Thirty-five NVA died on June 12 in an attack on LZ Joy.

On August 12, 1969, elements of the 1st and 7th NVA Divisions and the 5th and 9th VC Divisions struck 1st Cav Division bases throughout III Corps. In the heart of the fighting was the brigade headquarters at Quan Loi. At 1:20 a.m. NVA and VC troops from the 9th VC Division—spearheaded by a crack sapper platoon—threw themselves into the wire

and succeeded in penetrating it. A handful of sappers came within 175 meters of the brigade tactical operations center, but fell to the withering fire of eight medics who demonstrated that they knew how to use rifles as well as needles and bandages. By 4:30 a.m. the enemy withdrew, leaving 42 dead men inside the wire.

The 3rd Brigade's operations in the last four months of 1969 were concentrated on interdicting the Serges Jungle Highway, a vast network of trails spread over part of the southern and most northern halves of Binh Long and Phuoc Long Province. For years the trail had served as an NVA gateway from Cambodia to Vietnam. There were several different types of trails. Major trails were from eight to ten feet wide with hard packed surfaces often paved with bamboo matting. Numerous subsidiary trails branched off to provide easy access, exits and detours. These trails were sometimes only slightly smaller than the major trails, and sometimes merely dirt tracks a few inches wide. All of the trails were hidden from view by triple canopy jungle.

Hidden along the trail were the facilities of the enemy's 85th Rear Service Group, providing the supplies without which the NVA and VC forces to the south cannot effectively operate. The 85th RSG operated transportation, medical and repair facilities and maintained cache sites, bunker complexes and trail networks. The group serviced

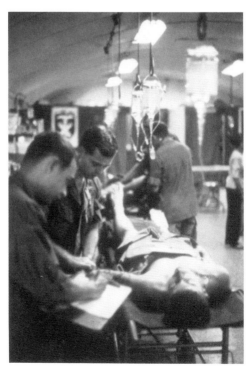

infiltrating troops and guided them to the south.

The brigade's intelligence section had used all the resources available to it to gather as accurate picture of the "highway" and its operation as possible. In September the division decided that interdiction of the highway was of prime importance if future enemy offensives were to be thwarted. The 3rd Brigade was given the task.

On the basis of its intelligence the brigade assigned each of its battalions a section of the trail to interdict. The first major finding came on September 24 when a brief contact by the 1st Battalion, 7th Cavalry, led to the discovery of six tons of rice that had been destined for enemy forces in the south.

That was only the beginning. As the operation progressed brigade units discovered numerous gardens that the enemy was cultivating. Destruction of crops was put off until just prior to harvest to keep the NVA planning on the yield.

Food was not the only thing the brigade was finding. On October 10 Delta Company, 1st Battalion, 8th Cavalry, found a cache that included 161 mortar rounds, 100 antitank mines, 300 Chicom grenades and other munitions. Later, in October a VC Hoi Chanh led the 1st Battalion, 5th Cavalry, to numerous caches and bunker complexes, including a VC district military headquarters. On its own, Bravo, 1st of the 5th found a complex of 100 bunkers.

As operations continued, the brigade became familiar with enemy transportation techniques. Bicycles were the primary movers, carrying 500 to 600 pounds of material. Porters were next in priority of use, followed by elephants. Cargo trucks were the least used and restricted to areas in close proximity to Cambodia. Brigade units would encounter and destroy elements of all these transportation modes as the operation progressed.

As 1969 ended the enemy had lost some 800 men in the Serges area, about 500 of whom were in rear service positions; 10 bunker complexes and nearly 50 caches had been located and destroyed; and 97 bicycles captured.

The 3rd Brigade had severely restricted enemy use of a vital lifeline. ✖️

Bruce, a black Labrador retriever, and his handler, lead Combat Tracker Team No. 1 and members of Charlie Company, 5th Battalion of the 7th Cavalry, back into the unit's firebase after a day's operation in III Corps' triple canopied jungle. And Bruce is still rarin' to go.

75th Rangers

(Continued From P. 197)

1969, North Vietnamese forces shattered a lull in battle activity with coordinated, widespread attacks throughout northern III Corps. Included in the enemy plans was an attack on FSB Buttons.

A Ranger team operating in the heavy jungle nearby tipped the base off to the attack when it spotted 45 NVA troops moving quickly toward the base, toting 107 mm rockets in addition to the ubiquitous AK-47s. It wasn't long before the enemy force was subjected to a shattering bombardment by both artillery and Cav gunships, called in by the Rangers. Forty-one of the enemy troops were killed. Other enemy units, reeling from their abortive assault on the firebase, were spotted after the attack. The Rangers brought artillery into play, further decimating the enemy ranks.

Late in 1969 the Rangers began running some of their patrols with members of the ARVN Airborne Rangers as part of the Dong Tien (Forward Together) program. After a brief period of mutual familiarization and missions, Captain Richard K. Griffith, the Ranger company commander, said, "The ARVNs are fully experienced and qualified. In my opinion, they're as qualified if not more so than our own teams."

Throughout the year the Ranger teams continuously reported enemy activity resulting in intelligence information that has been invaluable in spoiling enemy plans and keeping track of his movements.

Said one Ranger, "We don't just claim to be the best; we are." ✖️

Garry Owen troopers of the 5th Battalion, 7th Cavalry, keep watch for the enemy as lift ships arrive to extract them back to their basecamp.

1st Brigade

(Continued From P. 47)

Following Tet, the next distinct operation began April 5 when two battalions air assaulted into the PEGASUS AO as part of the relief of Khe Sanh, and the brigade command post went right along with them, setting up at LZ Snapper. Enemy resistance was only moderate and the brigade lifted the siege during the next 10 days. It then returned to the vicinity of Quang Tri to prepare for another move.

April 15, 1968 marked the beginning of Operation DELAWARE and the brigade displaced to LZ Stallion in the central A Shau Valley. Maneuver battalions conducted extensive reconnaissance-in-force missions throughout the valley, uncovering many enemy caches, and then redeployed back to the Quang Tri area in mid-May for Operation JEB STUART III.

November 1968 saw the division deploy from the I Corps Tactical Zone to III Corps. Establishing its command post at Tay Ninh, the 1st Brigade initiated offensive operations to interdict infiltration routes and to destroy enemy installations in Tay Ninh Province northwest of Saigon in anticipation of the 1969 Tet offensive. Deployed for the first time in a true cavalry role, screening across a broad front and conducting lightning raids deep into enemy areas,

the All the Way Brigade faced and met a new challenge.

Further redeployments were made in response to the enemy situation during this period as Task Force Duke, composed of elements of the 1st Bn, 8th Cav, moved to LZ Elrod in the Kien Tuong Province of IV Corps. This move made the 1st Cavalry Division, and its 1st Brigade, the only combat units in Vietnam to have operated in all four of the republic's corps tactical zones.

"Bushmaster" and "mini-cav" operations were stressed during this phase which emphasized the employment of numerous small unit ambushes designed to insure maximum interdiction and to deny the enemy his traditional sanctuary for movement, the night.

North Vietnamese elements immediately began taking immense losses in War Zone C. Besides personnel, they lost equipment of all descriptions, and—possibly more important—a vast amount of rice.

It should be pointed out that the only difference in the disposition of Allied troops in II Corps between the Tet periods of 1968 and 1969 was the presence of the FIRST TEAM. The failure of the enemy to launch an effective offensive in 1969 was in great part due to the pressure applied by 1st Brigade elements in what had previously been an NVA staging area and a major base area—War Zone C.

Indications are that the enemy's tactical back was broken by Cav interdiction and the loss of huge amounts of rice and other foodstuffs that had been uncovered by the 1st Brigade prior to Tet of 1969.

Operation TOAN THANG III commenced February 17, in AO Montana Scout in northeastern War Zone C, and the brigade continued to uncover the enemy's supplies. Some 190 tons of rice were captured in February as well as ammunition caches totalling some 20 tons, and another 77 tons of rice were uncovered in April.

Enemy activity during these months focused on LZ Grant which sat astride major NVA infiltration routes. The base was attacked once during February and twice again early in March. The latter two attacks on Grant alone cost the enemy 277 KIA and the total number of enemy killed by the brigade from February through April was 989, a severe and crippling blow in the enemy's strength.

Combat elements were moved as the enemy's posture and intentions shifted after April. When one spoke of the enemy in War Zone C at this time it was the 1st NVA Division that was mentioned with the 95C, 18B and 101D Regiments. These enemy units and the 1st Brigade came to know each other well.

Day to day operations were underlined by the tactical drama which pitted the brigade commander, Colonel Joseph P. Kingston, and his staff against the commander of the tough and tenacious 95C Regiment.

When the enemy tried to move, the brigade interdicted with a decentralized pattern of small unit operations along three critical avenues: the northwestern supply base system which was straddled by LZs Carolyn and Ike, the Mustang Trail in central War Zone C, and the Saigon River Corridor to the east.

When large enemy troop concentrations were spotted, however, the technique employed involved massed B-52 strikes followed by multi-unit exploitation.

Staggering and reduced to a flinching defensive posture, the enemy was damaged so severely that he was never able to muster a concentrated campaign.

Operations during this period included two in particular, one in the Crescent area and the other further north, which employed the "pile on" technique with great success against the 95C and 18B Regiments, inflicting such damage that these enemy units were ineffective for months afterwards. In the months of May and June an incredible number of 1,500 enemy soldiers were killed in combat with the 1st Brigade while another 39 enemy were taken prisoner

and six tons of rice were taken.

The opposition was the best that the North Vietnamese Army had to offer; they were not guerrillas or hastily mustered irregulars but experienced, battle-hardened and intelligently led troops. They were also particularly well-equipped, at least until the 1st Brigade brought the pinch to their supply lines.

The enemy licked his wounds during most of July, but apparently felt himself up to facing the brigade again in mid-August when FSB Becky, located close to the Cambodian border, was attacked on the nights of the 11th and 12th. North Vietnamese forces there suffered more than 70 killed.

During the autumn of 1969 increased emphasis was placed on Vietnamization of the war effort while the enemy reeled back from the grinding spring and summer campaigns. The 2nd Brigade of the ARVN Airborne Division joined the 1st Brigade in War Zone C and the two units coordinated operations in the area. New firebases were established, FSBs Vicky and Jackie, and FSB Carolyn was reopened under the flag of South Vietnam. The ARVN brigade's tactical operations center was colocated with the 1st Brigade's in Tay Ninh, and the ARVN maneuver units, mutually supporting with the three battalions of the All the Way Brigade, quickly adapted to the airmobile concept.

The two Allied brigades—the airmobile brigade that once was airborne and the airborne brigade that is now airmobile—were still conducting large scale operations and standing shoulder-to-shoulder in War Zone C through the end of 1969.

11th Air Assault
(Continued From P. 23)

tical integrity of infantry units. Thus a lift platoon would be able to move a rifle platoon, and a lift company a rifle company. This was, of course, before the UH-1D Hueys sprouted door guns and body armor for protection in an insurgency environment.

While waiting for the word from the top, the division kept busy with training in the Fort Benning area. In early 1965 some aviation and supporting elements of the division were deployed to the Dominican Republic. The task force, composed primarily of elements of the 229th Assault Helicopter Battalion, stayed in the republic during the summer and some did not return to Fort Benning until three weeks prior to the deployment of the Air Cav Division to Vietnam.

By early 1965 it was apparent that Army ground troops would be committed to Vietnam. It was also apparent, at least at Pentagon level, that either

the 11th Air Assault Division or the 2nd Infantry Division would be intimately involved in any major troop deployments to Southeast Asia. But because the divisions were so intermixed a decision would have to be made by Department of the Army . . . which one?

In February 1965 General Harold K. Johnson, then chief of staff of the Army, visited Fort Benning and conferred with commanders of both divisions. In the 11th Air Assault Division, GEN Johnson received a powerful and brilliant briefing from division staff officers.

During the summer months, the division, brigade and battalion staffs began war gaming situations pegged on a Vietnam mission. Because it was felt that the primary enemy threat at this

early stage was concentrated in the central highlands, the division staff placed most emphasis on this area, although the Delta, III Corps and I Corps areas also received attention in various studies.

On June 16, Secretary of Defense Robert S. McNamara announced in a nationally televised press conference that an airmobile division had been authorized for the U.S. Army force structure. This was not a surprise. Every Skysoldier in the division expected it. What did come as a surprise was Secretary McNamara's announcement that the famed 1st Cavalry Division had been chosen to carry the standards of airmobility beyond the test stage. He also gave the division a very short time to get organized and combat ready.

What was to happen was that the 11th Air Assault Division colors were to be retired. The 2nd Division colors were to be transferred to Korea and the colors of the FIRST TEAM brought back to United States soil for the first time in 22 years.

Appropriately, MG Kinnard was chosen to command the new division.

On July 3 the colors of the 11th Air Assault Division were cased and retired with a moving ceremony in Doughboy Stadium at Fort Benning. Then, to the rousing strains of Garry Owen, the colors of the 1st Cavalry Division were moved onto the stadium field.

Under the brilliant blue skies, MG Kinnard paid tribute to those who had served in the test division when he told them: "As a result of your efforts, the soldier is freed forever from the tyranny of terrain."

Skysoldiers suddenly had become

Skytroopers. A chapter in the history of airmobility had closed, but the book scarcely was begun and lingering but a page away was the beginning of a new and even more glorious chapter.

Troopers of the 1st Battalion, 8th Cavalry, proudly ride a Soviet truck which they captured in the A Shau Valley.

1st of the 12th

(Continued From P. 94)

On the 3rd of July, 1969, Delta Company found a 96-room North Vietnamese underground bunker complex in the jungle 13 miles northeast of Tay Ninh.

The Skytroopers also found the bodies of 32 enemy dead in the bunkers around the facility. They had been killed in artillery barrages and jet bomber raids which pounded the area the previous day and night after the infantrymen made contact with the enemy.

Inside, the Chargers discovered a mass of medical supplies. Also found were 25 gas masks, eight B-40 rockets, four claymore-type mines, and about 1,000 rounds of AK-47 ammunition. After searching the area, the men of Delta Company destroyed the bunkers.

On September 19, Delta Company had just finished setting up its night defensive position 20 miles northeast of Tay Ninh City when mortar rounds crashed into the third platoon's sector of the perimeter. Neither radio nor voice contact could be made with the observation post 50 meters in front of the platoon's position.

Sergeant Basil Clark called for his squad to cease fire. Then, under heavy NVA small arms fire, he carefully made his way out to the observation post and brought his men back to the safety of the perimeter.

As the mortar barrage continued, both the platoon leader and platoon sergeant were wounded, leaving the platoon in the hands of SGT Clark. He moved about checking wounded and restoring order during the battle.

"My platoon leader told me that if anything ever happened to the platoon sergeant and him, I'd be the one to take over," said the sergeant. "But I never expected it to happen."

The heavy mortar and rocket barrage was followed by a ground attack from all sides of the perimeter. The close-in fighting continued throughout the night, making it impossible to evacuate the 12 wounded until the next morning.

When morning came, the company was finally able to evacuate its wounded and search the area. Thirty-five NVA bodies were found. An estimated 50 more enemy were killed, judging from the numerous blood trails.

On September 28 the NVA made a small but fatal mistake when one enemy soldier tried to get a good look at a night defensive position manned by Charlie Company. He was spotted, along with his unit, and four days of hard fighting followed, resulting in 65 enemy deaths.

The first day's contact began soon after the company, operating in War Zone C about 18 miles northeast of Tay Ninh City, reached its night defensive position and began setting up perimeter defenses.

"Three of us went out to set up the claymore mines when I saw an NVA soldier pop his head out of some thick bamboo and take a good look around," said Private First Class Andy Giant. "I reported seeing him and the company reconned by fire. Then all hell broke loose!"

"They threw in Chicom grenades, B-40 rockets, and used both SKS and AK-47 rifles along with at least one machinegun," added Specialist Four Donavon Halderead. "The enemy covered the whole western side of our perimeter."

The firefight continued until well after dark. Flare ships guided bright red streams of lead from Cobra miniguns.

After an early-morning lull, the enemy again attacked the Skytroopers' position with hand grenades. While the company remained behind cover, artillery pounded the enemy positions and two light observation helicopters dove in with minigun fire.

The third day in the area Charlie Company moved 700 meters to the southeast and dug in again for the night.

On the morning of the fourth day, the company's resupply helicopter drew sniper fire. The renewed contact prevented the company from moving to another position for the night. Again, overhead cover was constructed and more air strikes were called in.

Two days later, a weary Charlie Company was happy to see the barbed wire and bunkers of LZ Grant. They had inflicted heavy casualties on the enemy and had captured a light machinegun, two AK-47 assault rifles, and two SKS rifles.

In an overnight position near Grant in the last week of October, Alpha Company troopers woke up to impacting mortar rounds and the pop of AK-47s. Air mattresses were the only casualties. The company immediately fanned out to search the area. By day's end 11 NVA were eliminated.

The battalion continued operations in the vicinity of Grant through early December, when they were released from the 1st Brigade. The battalion initially moved to the 3rd Brigade AO in western Phuoc Long Province, conducting operations from FSB Jerri near Bu Dop. In mid-December the Chargers began working for the 2nd Brigade when the battalion opened FSB Lee near the II Corps-III Corps boundary.

On December 31 Bravo Company discovered an enemy bunker complex near FSB Lee. The complex included 15 10 by 15 bunkers, two large bunkers used for classrooms, and a kitchen capable of feeding more than a hundred men. On the same day Echo Company killed four NVA in automatic ambushes near the fire support base.

As the new year began the battalion continued its mission of finding and destroying enemy shelters and caches, and of stopping enemy attempts to infiltrate through the division's AO.

5th of the 7th

(Continued From P. 79)

and chattered tracers toward the men. With one final grenade, Sprayberry crawled forward once more to the enemy machinegun bunker. He pulled the pin, let the lever fly and slammed the frag home. The explosion ripped through the bunker, killing all inside.

As dawn began to streak the sky, Sprayberry was moving the last wounded to friendly lines. Behind him in the barely visible outline of daybreak lay 12 enemy dead, two blasted machineguns and a string of quiet bunkers.

On October 9, 1969, James Sprayberry, by then a captain, stood before President Richard Nixon to receive the Medal of Honor for his actions on that dark night, for his relentless actions as a "lieutenant grenadier."

In the A Shau Valley the Skytroopers taught the enemy a hard lesson—that he had no area within the Republic of Vietnam that he could consider to be a secure base.

They also established LZ Jack. On May 6 the LZ endured an intense enemy mortar and rocket attack. Sergeant Michael A. Haviland of C Company managed to crawl out of his collapsed bunker and spied two injured Skytroopers trapped by debris in a nearby trench.

"I heard them calling for help; so I was determined to get them out," recalled SGT Haviland.

In spite of the enemy barrage the sergeant crawled to his comrades, dug them out and carried them to safety, an action for which he was later awarded the Silver Star.

The battalion moved with the rest of the division at the beginning of November to close out 1968 in northern III Corps. Shortly after New Year's, a helicopter pilot spotted what seemed to be an ammo box on top of a bunker, 23 kilometers southeast of An Loc. Charlie Company went to investigate.

"We tried to move in C Company but for the first three days we did not get in. Even though the enemy was well entrenched in his bunkers, with the help of aerial rocket artillery, Air Force strikes and artillery we were able to dislodge him and move in," the battalion

A 2nd Battalion, 12th Cavalry, machinegunner jumps to the ground from the skid of a Huey. Sometimes it was a long, long way down.

commander, Lieutenant Colonel John F. McGraw, recalled. It was 11 a.m. on January 21 when they penetrated what proved to be one of the most significant caches captured in the campaign—more than 18 tons of ammunition.

Combat activity up through April was scattered. Elements of the battalion pulled off a perfect night ambush April 14 about 20 kilometers southwest of An Loc. Four unsuspecting enemy soldiers wandered down a trail and paid heavily for their lack of security. Claymores and grenades halted their progress. All four enemy died without returning a single shot.

Later in the month on the 25th, a 5th Bn, 7th Cav, platoon was engaged by well entrenched enemy squad early in the evening. The platoon answered the heavy fire with its own automatic weapons, supported by tube artillery, ARA and tactical air strikes. Eight NVA were killed. Operating four kilometers away from the contact area the next morning, the same element spotted one enemy soldier moving down a trail and eliminated him. He was carrying two AK-47s.

Six men from Echo Company were

occupying a listening post the evening of May 5. Their vigil had just begun when they heard a sizable force moving in their direction. They called in a mortar barrage, blew their claymores and quickly returned to the landing zone.

The attack really began at 3:30 a.m. More than 200 mortar rounds fell on the base within 15 minutes. The barrage was followed by a ground attack but "only about 40 NVA hit the wire," said Captain Elvin Takata, commander of Alpha Company. The firebase was scheduled to be removed the next day. The enemy had lost at least eight of their number trying to dislodge the installation which was vacated by the following evening.

Searching in heavy jungle, Company A found six and a half tons of rice stored in a large bunker 34 miles north of Phuoc Vinh on August 2. The Garry Owen troopers also depleted Charlie's "motor pool" when they uncovered 12 bicycles in another bunker nearby. Many of the 112 bunkers in the complex were fortified with as much as four feet of overhead cover. Also captured that day by Alpha Company were 14 mines, 97 rifles, and a .51 caliber machinegun.

While on an operation in the dense undergrowth of Phuoc Binh District later in the month, Delta Company dug in when a large enemy force challenged with RPG rounds and small arms fire shortly after noon, just five miles southeast of Song Be.

Within minutes, the company's firepower turned from ground based tube artillery to airmobile as Cobras screamed down on the camouflaged positions.

After more than an hour of intense fighting, the enemy broke contact and scattered into the area to regroup for a second attack on Delta Company positions. Twenty-five minutes of quiet were broken when RPG rounds exploded near the Skytrooper position, signaling the second NVA attack in little more than an hour. It took only 20 minutes for the Garry Owen troopers to silence the enemy fire this time, with the aid of artillery support.

When the smoke had cleared, a company sweep of the battle site accounted for 19 NVA dead left behind by the fleeing, battered enemy forces. Also captured were 31 82 mm mortar rounds.

Cavalrymen surprised and killed seven NVA in a bunker complex on September 15, five miles southeast of Song Be. Bravo Company engaged the enemy and then called in helicopter gunships during the 45 minute battle ending shortly before noon.

The company continued to sweep the immediate area and two days later a recon patrol discovered a bunker cache.

One dead NVA was found along with 112 82 mm mortar rounds, 12 60 mm mortar rounds and one AK-47 rifle.

Alpha Company, working several miles away, killed six catching them in the open. It also discovered a bunker complex with a mortar pit and the ammunition cache.

Alpha Company was awakened on October 1 by incoming 60 mm mortar rounds pounding its night defensive position. The enemy broke off after they had pumped more than 30 rounds into the company's position. The Skytroopers fought back with artillery and used gunship support. When the smoke cleared

10 enemy bodies were found.

October 20 brought with it more mortars for Alpha Company. The Garry Owens were waiting for a lift on a pickup some 13 miles northeast of Song Be when the rounds started falling. The infantrymen returned fire and called artillery, gunships and tactical air support. The Skytroopers' response left 14 enemy dead.

No one in the battalion was left out of the action. When sappers breached the wire at FSB Buttons they were met at the berm by the battalion's clerks. It was the first firefight for the majority of the men but the enemy was quickly driven back, leaving 63 bodies behind.

At the end of the year the battalion was back at Phuoc Vinh patrolling the rocket and mortar belt around division headquarters. ✸

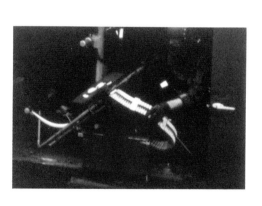

2nd of the 7th

(Continued From P. 75)

the Air Force were in constant action. Air strikes and 2.75 inch rockets filled the night with a "beautiful sound" in the words of one Skytrooper, and C-119 "Shadow" ships illuminated the contact area with their flares.

It was 6:15 a.m. before the enemy realized he had failed and broke contact. Fifty-three NVA were left behind inside the perimeter and as Delta Company swept around the landing zone that day, it found another 22 enemy bodies.

This was just one of several times that LZ Jamie was the target of NVA attempts to reopen their supply routes. Later that summer Delta Company was on base defense on LZ Jamie. It

had been a typical day on a landing zone, the usual patrols, searching out the enemy during the day, men checking the concertina wire on the perimeter, 105 mm howitzers occasionally booming support to nearby companies in the field.

While working around Jamie the battalion uncovered many North Vietnamese bunker complexes, food and weapons caches, and hospital complexes.

During a typical search operation in late July the battlion discovered one of these complexes. Searching a small cluster of fortifications 24 miles northeast of Tay Ninh, the Skytroopers of Bravo and Charlie Companies, 2nd Bn, 7th Cav, netted a lucrative assortment of enemy equipment, which included large quantities of drugs and first aid kits, rice, anti-tank mines, and a sewing machine.

The haul was the result of careful planning and experience gained during

FIRST TEAM operations in the same area in April and May.

"The last time we went in there," said the battalion commander, Lieutenant Colonel Godwin Ordway, "we were accompanied by elements of the 11th Armored Cavalry Regiment. Not only did we kill a large number of enemy, but we uncovered one bunker complex after another. The resistance we met there was quite stiff."

Tactics were changed significantly this time. Rather than pushing from north to south as they did in April, an "instant landing zone" was created by dropping a 10,000 pound bomb. Within hours of the "daisy cutter," elements of both companies air assaulted into the area.

The hospital complex was discovered soon after the assault. "We didn't see the bunkers until we were practically on top of them." said Specialist Four Ed Ranking, a rifleman with Company B.

And so went 1969. A year spent denying the North Vietnamese their critical infiltration routes. A year marked by hard fighting and quiet heroics by the men from the Garry Owen battalion.

1st of the 5th

(Continued From P. 60)

open; McWethy moved to help and was wounded a third time before he reached the injured man. As he began administering artificial respiration he was struck and killed by still another enemy round.

Meanwhile, SP4 Harvey was firing as fast as he could in an effort to subdue the heavy enemy fire. The enemy machinegun seemed to concentrate on him and bullets were bouncing all around his position. One round hit and armed a grenade attached to his belt. He tried to pull it loose but he couldn't get the grenade off. Realizing the danger to his comrades if he remained he jumped up and charged toward the enemy machinegun position. Before he reached the enemy, the grenade on his belt exploded, killing him and stunning the enemy machinegun crew. His two wounded comrades took advantage of the lull in firing to scramble to safety.

Harvey and McWethy were each awarded the Medal of Honor.

When Charlie Company troops jumped from their choppers March 18, 1968, they were right in the middle of Highway 1. They had flown from LZ Cindy to search the village of Thon La Vang just west of the highway.

Staff Sergeant Elray T. Ellender, the lead platoon's leader, recalled that his men started receiving fire from the village as the first men penetrated the outskirts. "The village was still, except for an occasional enemy round," Ellender said. "The NVA had chased the villagers out earlier."

Sergeant Ralph Wilson (above) of Company D, 1st of the 12th Cav, spreads his arms to guide a resupply helicopter to a landing zone near FSB Grant, and (below) two Skytroopers help a buddy climb a muddy embankment while on operations near FSB Grant.

After several fierce duels, the Cavalrymen pulled back to the railroad tracks which separate the village from the highway. They crouched behind the embankment as helicopters poured rockets into the Communist positions. The soldiers then went back into the village and encountered sporadic contact. Darkness forced them to withdraw to a safer position, but heavy artillery blasted the fortified emplacements during the night.

The next morning the company moved in and recovered 45 enemy bodies and 10 weapons.

The 1st Bn, 5th Cav, conducted Operation COMANCHE FALLS southwest of Base Area 101 from September 11 to October 2. It succeeded in denying the area to the enemy and disrupted his lines of supply. In addition to destroying several large basecamp installations (676 bunkers), the battalion killed 270 NVA soldiers and captured hundreds of weapons.

In what was the fastest and largest move ever in the Vietnam conflict, the battalion was ordered to move from northern I Corps to the III Corps Tactical Zone northwest of Saigon near the Cambodian border. As the end of 1968 approached the Black Knights were conducting operations southwest of Tay Ninh.

Members of the enemy's bicycle set literally lost their wheels after the new year when elements of the battalion came across their hideaway 12 miles southeast of Quan Loi. Companies B and E were searching through the area when they discovered the enemy complex, containing enough supplies and parts to construct some 40 bicycles—and a motor scooter.

"We were told there was probably a complex in the area, so we were just looking around," related Specialist Four Nathaniel Flowers, a fire team

leader with Company B. "Then there was this scooter leaning against a tree right out in the middle of nowhere."

"When we first saw it the reaction was 'Man, can you believe this?' One guy even tried to crank it up, but then we saw the claymores."

In anticipation of discovery, the enemy had placed claymore mines around the area. Everyone hit the ground, thinking it an ambush. But further investigation showed that they were not set to go off. Warm campfire ashes and dirty dishes indicated that the enemy had retreated in haste.

The complex, dubbed the "Motor Pool" by the Cavalrymen, contained 600 pounds of rice and 100 five-gallon cans of meat. In addition, numerous bicycle trails were found leading into and out of the complex.

Later in January the reconnaissance squad of Echo Company was sent to observe traffic along a highway 10 miles southeast of Quan Loi, following reports that the enemy had been waylaying Vietnamese travelers on the road. After not finding anything suspicious, the Cavalrymen moved further along the road to a new location to continue their mission.

"We had to set up and were just finishing the evening chow when we heard a noise like a chicken," reported Private First Class Gordon C. Swisher, a rifleman with the squad, "We flattened out on the ground, and then saw what was causing all the racket."

Up a nearby trail came a Viet Cong, kicking a chicken along ahead of him, evidently to spring any booby traps that might be there. Following the pointman

came several more enemy soldiers, each beating the bushes beside the trail for added security. The main element of the force then appeared, 140 in all, heavily armed with machineguns, B-40 rockets and small arms.

Waiting for a few minutes after the last enemy passed, the Cavalrymen called in artillery and air strikes on the unsuspecting enemy.

"That squawking chicken saved us," PFC Swisher said. "For a while I was wondering if we were going to make it, though, especially when they started beating the bushes. I was certain they would spot one of us."

February 2, saw one Skytrooper take on "Charlie" in a fast shooting contest. The rifleman, Private First Class Samuel Estep, was the pointman on a reconnaissance patrol which had been sent ahead to scout the trail prior to his platoon's departure from its ambush site near Chi Linh.

He had been told to be especially watchful since another friendly element had spotted enemy troops on the trail a few minutes earlier, and had radioed the information to Estep's platoon leader.

The patrol had not gone 20 meters when Estep rounded a corner of the trail and found himself face-to-face with the pointman of an enemy reconnaissance patrol.

It was then that the "quick kill" instruction—in which trainees learned to fire a rifle from the hip, without taking aim—came to PFC Estep's aid.

"It happened pretty fast," he recalled. "He ducked and I fired. The other two took off down the trail, but not before the platoon leader downed a second one. It was over almost as soon as it started."

Throughout the spring and into summer the battalion ecountered almost daily light contact and caches of enemy food and arms were found on a weekly basis. On June 14 Alpha Company uncovered 71 Soviet carbines, 10 mortar tubes, and six heavy machinegun barrels northwest of Lai Khe, while just down the road E Company troops were springing an ambush. They killed nine of the 15 enemy who crossed their path.

When Major General E. B. Roberts landed at LZ Lori on June 30 he reported that he and Command Sergeant Major Lawrence E. Kennedy had spotted some enemy during their flight. Observation helicopters killed one enemy and captured another when they went to check out the sighting. Charlie Company, 1st Bn, 5th Cav, diverted to make a sweep of the

A 2nd Battalion, 12th Cavalry, Skytrooper steadies himself by grabbing a stalk of bamboo while fighting his way (physically) through thick growth and "wait-a-minute" vines in the jungle north of Song Be.

area. They spotted six individuals who surrendered without a fight.

"Getting seven men to surrender without a firefight is very unusual," commented Lieutenant Colonel John Gibney, division G-3. "I can't recall the last time that such a thing happened in this division."

The battalion was patrolling the rocket and mortar belt around Camp Gorvad, doing its turn as "palace guard," when the big NVA offensive in Binh Long Province was unleashed on August 12.

The companies of the battalion were extracted from field locations around division headquarters, and air moved to Quan Loi. From there, the battalion was combat assaulted into blocking positions west of the An Loc-Quan Loi area to trap NVA elements fleeing back to their Cambodian sanctuary.

From August through September, the battalion combed the jungles of northwestern Binh Long Province, working its way northward toward the Bu Dop-Bo Duc area.

At FSB Vivian the battalion joined the 3rd Brigade's efforts at choking infiltration on the Serges Jungle Highway.

On October 5, Bravo Company and a recon element from Echo made a combat assault 40 kilometers north of Quan Loi. They were prepared to sweep the area of thick bamboo and double canopy jungle when the first platoon of Bravo aborted an enemy ambush.

"Our point element spotted the enemy ambush before anyone got into the killing zone," said Specialist Four Dean Sharp.

The contact then developed into a full scale firefight with the Skytroopers'

firepower forcing an enemy company to retreat into the thick jungle, dragging dead and wounded with them.

In mid-November the enemy again threatened Bu Duc and Bu Dop and Charlie Company combat assaulted into FSB Jerri to re-open the firebase and provide security for a corps artillery unit flown in to give needed fire support to the area.

Meanwhile, the mission of interdicting enemy infiltration continued unabated around FSB Vivian and when 1969 came to a close, companies of the Black Knight battalion were still giving the NVA fits on the Serges Highway.

Members of the 1st Squadron, 9th Cavalry's "quick reaction force," the Blues, blow 40 claymore mines and throw fragmentation grenades during an ambush training exercise near Phuoc Vinh in III Corps.

11th Aviation

(Continued From P. 154)

A 227th lift bird ferries a load of troops forward to yet another combat assault.

sible for assigned support aircraft to an operation, be it a combat assault mission, logistical resupply, or simply supplying a command and control helicopter.

Also under control of the 11th Aviation Group are the Path Finders—a unique combination of soldier and air traffic controller, a breed of men known as "Blackhats."

As their motto declares, the Blackhats are "first in and last out" on 1st Cav firebases. They must be on the first lift of a combat assault to open a new firebase in order to give radio flight instructions to the more than 200 aircraft that will flood the skies over a new firebase in its first 48 hours of life.

A Blackhat controller is easily identified. Besides the obvious black baseball cap that he wears in steel pot territory, the Blackhat has mannerisms that distinguish him from others in the field.

Most of the time he is standing, often on a water can, bunker or anything that will offer a better view. He will have a radio-telephone pressed to his ear and is constantly watching the sky for birds—big, noisy, metal birds.

On hot and cool LZs alike, their job is the same. They give navigational assistance to pilots approaching the LZ—wind direction, weather conditions, terrain features—and control the flight paths of aircraft in a crowded sky.

Admittedly, 200 aircraft in 48 hours does not equate the average LZ to O'Hare Field, but it is certainly enough traffic to be dangerous unless someone on the ground with an overall view knows what he's doing. And he must have absolute authority, despite the difference between his enlisted rank and the officer pilots he guides.

One afternoon over a Cav LZ a helicopter chose to ignore the Blackhat controller's approach directions. The Blackhat, watching the errant helicopter, got on the radio and chewed the pilot out, royally. The pilot recalled that when he landed the Blackhat was "embarrassed as hell when he found out I was a general, but I'll tell you one thing, he was right, and he stuck by his guns in the matter. Next time I did it his way."

228th AHB

(Continued From P. 149)

won another award. Brigadier General Frank Meszar, assistant division commander, presented LTC Bush with yet another safety award, honoring 22,500 accident-free flying hours totaled in a nine-month period. It was an all-time record of flying safety for the 1st Air Cavalry Division.

With 1969 coming to a close, the 228th Assault Support Helicopter Battalion was sending approximately 18 Chinooks in the air daily, flying from 110 to 120 sorties. Its mission in the division was air support—the backbone of airmobility.

Flight safety awards and records of hours flown and tonnage moved are all solid tributes to the men who fly, crew and maintain the Chinooks, but, sadly, these figures and testimonies do not measure sweat, fatigue and sheer bravery. The days for Chinook crews were long, long even by military flight standards and unbelievable by civilian aviation standards. Commercial airline pilots and crews are not permitted to average more than 85 hours per month. Pilots and crews of the 228th regularly flew up to 140 hours per month.

It had never been done before, in war or peace. Not even the pilots who "flew the hump" in China-Burma during World War II, or the veteran pilots of the Berlin airlift worked under such demands on a day-to-day basis, One of the 228th's pilots who could rightly make the comparison between the rigors of Chinook flying and combat flight in other years was Warrant Officer Ben R. Games of Union, Michigan, a veteran

from the flight decks of World War II B-25 and B-29 bombers who re-entered military service at a ripe age to volunteer for a year of flight duty in Vietnam. Games said of the Chinook missions he flew: "It's real flying, there's no question about it. It's constant flying, no auto pilot or anything, just plain honest stick time. I've never flown so much before in my life, even in World War II."

A flying day for Chinook pilots and crews began in the dark early hours when the crew arrived on the flight line to begin the pre-flight maintenance check. After an hour of crawling over the Chinook, the crew chief greets his pilots. "It'll fly okay," he reports.

At 7 a.m. they lift off, starting the actual flying day that will usually average out to about 10 in-flight hours, although some 12 hours will pass before they make their final landing that night. They will pick up troops and cargo at a score of different locations and deliver the cargo to another 20 locations.

Lunch is wherever the crew is at noon, and lunchtime is short. The bird is checked out and then takes off again.

The day ends between 7 and 8 p.m. Often the Chinook is landed after dark. When needed, the Chinooks make midnight runs to firebases under attack to deliver needed artillery and other ammunition.

It was by no means typical of the Hollywood glamor of combat flying. There was plenty of hard work and hour upon hour of flying, flying that keeps a division spread over 4,000 square miles supplied and functioning.

1st of the 21st

(Continued From P. 121)

sion was moving its AO to the III Corps Tactical Zone. By November the battalion and its units were in place in the Quan Loi area. Battalion headquarters was at LZ Andy at Quan Loi. The base received incoming enemy rounds frequently in November and December, and the battalion quickly responded with massive return fire. After the base received 36 hits from 107 mm rockets on December 9 the battalion fired 1,000 rounds against suspected enemy locations. Numerous secondary locations were observed.

The 1st Bn, 21st Arty, continued to center its operations in Quan Loi during the early months of 1969. As February began, the battalion's organic batteries were spread throughout the division AO. Alpha Battery was at LZ Jake, Bravo at LZ Elrod and Charlie at LZ Carol. Bravo Battery fired 300 rounds in one mission on February 3 to help a 9th Infantry Division unit break contact.

Bravo Battery helped drive back an enemy ground attack against LZ Joy on June 12. In two hours of heavy fighting the enemy lost 35 men. Alpha Battery was at LZ Joe when the base took 200 enemy rockets and mortars and a company sized ground attack, which was easily repulsed.

In late June the battalion headquarters returned to Quan Loi. It remained there for the rest of 1969, but the firing batteries of the battalion continued to make frequent moves.

227th AHB

(Continued From P. 145)

during resupply missions. Low-level flying proved to be the key to avoiding enemy gunners, and the pilots brought much-needed supplies in to ground troops usually without incident.

Occasionally, however, the helicopters met with stiff enemy resistance, and when this was the case it was not unusual to hear of outstanding deeds by the men of the battalion.

In fall of 1968 the battalion moved south to the division's new area of operations, the III Corps Tactical Zone. Here it supported the division as it interdicted the enemy infiltration routes from Cambodia. The terrain was thickly jungled, and the jungle frequently concealed enemy machinegun positions. The battalion supported the 3rd Brigade and the 2nd Brigade in Binh Long and Phuoc Long Provinces.

Extensive use was made of the battalion's Nighthawk helicopters in III Corps. With a infrared light coupled with a starlight scope, a powerful spotlight, three M-60 machineguns and a minigun mounted in the rear cabin, the Nighthawk seriously hampered the enemy's ability to take advantage of darkness. A typical demonstration of Nighthawk's effectiveness came in October 1969 when a Charlie Company bird used its equipment to spot enemy supplies and movement of the Song Be River. With the help of other choppers and an air strike, the Nighthawk silenced the enemy. Twenty-eight dead enemy were found at first light.

As with other aviation units in the Cav, the 227th found that III Corps flying was different than "aviating" in I Corps. Despite the flatness of the terrain, the heavy, tangled vegetation and the dearth of landing zones quickly reduced the size of the basic combat assault flight. Moreover, pilots soon found that the enemy used .51 caliber anti-aircraft weapons to deadly effect around jungle clearings where Cav ground elements were inserted. This in turn called for greater reliance on the escort Cobra gunbirds from the battalion's Delta Company.

These problems caused the development of the six plus two formation as the combat assault standard in III Corps. The six were Hueys packed with infantry,

the two were Delta Company gunships. The Cobras made gun runs on the LZ just before the troops were inserted, making it difficult for the enemy to take advantage of the hiatus between the ground assault prep fires and the actual landing. The Cobras also circled the LZ as the troops hit the ground, discouraging the enemy from firing on the Hueys at that most vulnerable moment.

The men of the battalion could meet the unique, once-in-a-tour challenge too. One downed Cobra, two trapped pilots and Sergeant Richard J. Korbel, a doorgunner with Company A, 227th Assault Helicopter Battalion, were the ingredients in a heroic history in August 1969.

A formation of 227th Hueys had just combat assaulted an infantry element near FSB Buttons when a "May Day" call flashed over the radio. A Cobra had just crashed nearby. The lead Huey, in which SGT Korbel was riding, flew to the scene.

"I had planned to rappel to the Cobra when we got close enough," said SGT Korbel, "but it turned out that we didn't have a rappelling rope. So the crew chief and I guided the pilots as close to the Cobra as we could and I hung from the skids and dropped about 15 feet to the ground."

The Cobra was lying on its left side. The two pilots, in a state of semi-consciousness, were still seated in the cockpit of their downed bird.

"The windows were jammed," said the doorgunner, "I looked around and spotted a part of the Cobra's radio lying on the ground. With it, I managed to break the glass and pull out the pilot." By this time a Medevac bird was hovering above and lowered its jungle penetrator. Korbel secured the pilot to it and returned for the co-pilot. "I was really exhausted," said Korbel, "The co-pilot's feet were caught on the control stick and I just couldn't pull him loose."

The sergeant signalled the Medevac to send down a man to help, and succeeded in extracting him. The Huey followed the Medevac bird to the aid station, where the sergeant told doctors what had happened. Then the sergeant and crew took off for Song Be. They were needed for a new mission.

Throughout 1969 the 227th Assault Helicopter Battalion continued to serve the division by providing rapid, flexible assault transportation to any terrain, the key to the division's airmobility.

requests for support did not have to go through infantry channels for clearance.

As 1969 ended, DIVARTY controlled three 105 mm battalions, one 155 mm battalion, 175 mm and eight-inch batteries, an aerial rocket artillery battalion and an observation battery. It was a combination of maximum flexibility and firepower, always ready for quick and massive support of division units in contacts anywhere in the area of operations.

1st of the 30th

(Continued From 125)

to incoming mortar and rocket rounds to shoot two sappers about to destroy a gun and its crew with satchel charges. That earned the sergeant a Silver Star, but it wasn't the first one. In the February attack on Grant the firing chief moved in the open from gun pit to gun pit to aid the wounded and keep the howitzers firing. That got him his first Silver Star. During the March 8 attack the "Chief of Smoke" won the Bronze Star for valor when he kept his battery blasting away at the enemy throughout the five and a half hour battle.

Charlie Battery was attacked at LZ Joy June 12. The battery's direct fire put nine of the attackers out of action. The NVA hit Alpha Battery at LZ Becky on August 11 and 12. In the latter attack the enemy concentrated their mortar and rocket fire on the 155s after the guns had started spewing out their deadly direct fire. The Redlegs continued to fire despite casualities, turning back a ground attack by two enemy companies. At first light 54 NVA bodies were found around the perimeter.

Ground attacks were not the everyday concern of the battalion, of course. Most days were devoted to providing support to infantry elements in contact, to preparations of landing zones, to protective fires for fire support bases and night positions and to fires on bunker complexes, enemy personnel and enemy infiltration routes. The battalion fired its 96 pound projectiles throughout III Corps, from Bien Hoa to the Cambodian border. The range and size of the 155 made it the most powerful gun organic to the 1st Cav Division, and it played an important role in the division's success in stopping the NVA.

DIVARTY

(Continued From P. 113)

to the citizens.

The Vietnamese government recognized DIVARTY's civic action program when the Vietnamese Cross of Gallantry was presented to S-5 Captain Fred R. Rowsee, Jr. The captain continued and expanded the medical and agricultural assistance program, and oversaw construction of a concrete schoolhouse to replace a wooden one being eaten away by termites. And he initiated the building of a bridge over the village creek to keep the village in communication with An Khe during the monsoon season.

For its activities from September 13, 1966, to July 31, 1967, DIVARTY Headquarters and Headquarters Battery received the Meritorious Unit Citation. The citation praised the unit for providing "superb artillery support" and for continually seeking improvements in artillery operations. The award specifically mentioned innovations by the intelligence section in determining targets and by the operations section in the training of new officers.

DIVARTY left II Corps in January 1968, as the division moved its headquarters to Camp Evans in I Corps. From here DIVARTY controlled the division's firing batteries as they helped

blast the NVA from the city of Quang Tri and also from the walls of Hue, which the enemy had controlled since their Tet Offensive.

The forward command post moved to LZ Stud on April 5 to coordinate artillery support for the division's relief of the Marines at Khe Sanh. The fire support coordination section shifted to the A Shau Valley on April 27 to support the division's assault on that NVA infiltration route and supply center.

The various moves failed to stop DIVARTY from continuing its civic action programs. Now it directed its attention to the hamlet of Tan Nguyen, located near Camp Evans. The unit's laundry was taken to the hamlet, giving the citizens a larger income to improve their living conditions.

In November DIVARTY found itself relocated at Phuoc Vinh after the division's move to a new headquarters in III Corps Tactical Zone.

They also found themselves in the unusual position of being responsible for base security at Camp Gorvad, the division's Phuoc Vinh basecamp. Because the base was outside the areas of operation of the division's three infantry brigades, DIVARTY had operational control of the infantry battalion assigned to protect the base. This unique arrangement enabled DIVARTY to provide artillery support to the infantry unit much faster than would normally be expected, because under this arrangement

Pacification

(Continued From P. 232)

arrival in Vietnam in 1965.

This rice and salt, as well as other foodstuffs found, is turned over to the civilian population in GVN controlled areas. This amount of rice is substantial, with an average of more than 10 tons per month being distributed.

The division's 1st Brigade has aided the people of Tay Ninh in many ways. Among its finer programs have been the construction of the Tay Ninh Girls' High School and the Tay Ninh Technical High School.

The girls' high school has been described as "Vietnam's most modern school." It was built with funds supplied by Free World Military Armed Forces. The division supplied 50 percent of the funds necessary for the completion of the school. It now boasts 20 classrooms and is attended by some 1,100 students daily.

The Tay Ninh Technical High School had thousands of dollars of equipment on hand, but no one to install the necessary power generators and electrical wiring. The 1st Brigade stepped in.

Volunteer workers from the 229th Assault Helicopter Battalion metal shop helped with the installation of the various technical tools. Generator mechanics from headquarters company helped by installing the generators and working with Pacific Architects and Engineers in installing electrical wiring. The school was soon operating, providing an education for many young men in Tay Ninh and the surrounding areas.

The 2nd Brigade also assisted in the building of schools. Through the donation of more than 100,000 piasters by the 1st Cav, Chon Thanh District's first high school was built.

In addition to these isolated incidents, the Cav has built hundreds of schools throughout Vietnam, the structures rising wherever it is that the Cav calls home.

The 1st Air Cav's pacification efforts have proven successful in every area in which the division has operated. The hard work of 1st Air Cavalrymen has brought a new life into reality for many people in the Republic of Vietnam.

This new life is evidenced in no better way than by an examination of the hamlet of Trung Loi in Binh Long Province. Through the efforts of the division, this hamlet, long under the terrorism of the Viet Cong, held its first free elections in its 172 year history in 1969.

A new hamlet chief and his assistant were chosen. All the people of the village voted, and were especially pleased to do so. Their former chief had been assassinated by the VC just a few months previously.

The selection of his successor marked a new freedom: Freedom to choose their own leader, and a freedom from the terrorism of the Viet Cong.

Late in 1969, with the increasing emphasis on "Vietnamization" in the war, the 1st Air Cavalry Division began a new phase in their civic action programs. Civic action work is now done exclusively by the Republic of Vietnam's Armed Forces, with the division civil affairs personnel acting in an advisory and support capacity.

With the Vietnamese forces taking charge of the nation's pacification programs, the people are easily able to identify with their government. It also serves to prevent the local nationals from developing a dependence on the American forces, a dependence that might prove disastrous when peace comes to the nation and the American forces are redeployed.

For example, rice now discovered in enemy caches by 1st Air Cavalrymen is turned over to elements of the ARVN forces which are working with the Cav in III Corps. They, in turn, distribute the rice throughout the villages and hamlets of the region.

Through this return to an advisory capacity, the FIRST TEAM is doing its part in establishing support for the Government of the Republic of Vietnam throughout Cav Country.

A 1st Cav doctor finds a placid means of getting to his patients during a MEDCAP mission near Song Be.

1st of the 9th

(Continued From P. 110)

22nd Regiment.

The enemy unit had built themselves camouflaged bunkers and slit trenches to serve as a base for attack against the 3rd Brigade. That attack would never take place. Less than 24 hours after the squadron's spotting, 1,000 allied troopers were in the area. When the battle ended the 22nd NVA regiment had lost 650 men and its effectiveness as a fighting force.

In late 1967 a squadron scout pilot described his job. The description could just as well have been any other year. Said Warrant Officer Dana A. Graham, "You learn something each day when you fly in this country. You have to keep your mind open and keep watching for new things that can help you."

Every day for several hours Mr. Graham was at the controls, flying first and last light reconnaissance missions for base defense, general reconnaissance missions, and screening missions for advancing infantrymen.

What was a general reconnaissance mission like? "They'll assign you an area, say 10 square kilometers, and tell you to check it out for bunkers, or fortified villages or, of course, troops. In a dangerous area like this, you fly at low altitudes in a special pattern. You don't like to go over the same area twice because it may give someone a second chance to shoot at you.

"If there are hills, you stay as close to them as you can, and if there are trees you try to stay close to them, so they give you cover from one side."

Mr. Graham always flew as close to the ground as the terrain permitted, often within 10 feet of the surface. "It permits better observation, for one thing. And we say there's a dead man's zone between 50 and 1,000 feet; that's where the other guy can take his best shot at you."

Operation PERSHING ended in January 1968. Over the length of the operation the 1st Sqdn, 9th Cav, was credited with killing 513 NVA and 1,214 Viet Cong, and capturing 602 enemy soldiers, 13 crew-served weapons, 190 individual weapons and 2,927 rounds of ammo. The small but elite unit had accounted for 38 percent of the division's kills during the operation.

Operation WALLOWA also ended in January, and again it was the 1st Sqdn, 9th Cav, that had scored the operation's greatest successes. Bravo Troop had dispatched 503 NVA and 412 Viet Cong for 915 kills, taken 305 prisoners and captured 37 weapons.

The 1st Cavalry Division moved to Vietnam's I Corps in January 1968, coincidentally arriving just in time for the enemy's Tet Offensive. The squadron immediately found itself carrying out missions as part of Operation JEB STUART, aimed at driving the Communists from the Hue-Quang Tri area.

Delta Troop had the top priority task of keeping Route 1 open to insure the uninterrupted flow of supplies into Camp Evans, the division's basecamp. The enemy had interdicted the road between Hue and Camp Evans and effectively shut off resupply by that route. The only seaport remaining open in the I Corps was Quang Tri-Dong Ha.

To keep critical supplies flowing from this source Delta Troop started minesweeping operations on the road before dawn each day, and provided convoy escort from LZ Evans to Dong Ha. Despite enemy contact and extensive NVA attempts to mine the road, two convoys daily made the trip between Dong Ha and Camp Evans.

In the battle for Hue, one squadron pilot and his doorgunner probably set a record for the briefest time in enemy captivity. First Lieutenant William Babcock flew over Hue just after much of the city had been taken by NVA troops. As he approached the area AK-47 and .30 caliber machinegun fire came at the ship from every bush and tree.

"Suddenly," said Babcock, "our ship started to shudder, to tremble, and I couldn't get enough power to stay in the air so I had to let her down and we spiraled to the ground . . . there were some farmers plowing and some cows, but the farmers left and the cows went away, and we started getting intense fire from behind a hedgerow.

"In a few minutes," he continued, "We were surrounded by a good-sized force and there was nothing we could do. They took us out of the chopper and set satchel charges to it."

Other squadron pilots had heard the lieutenant's radio calls for aid. Warrant Officer Thomas Maehrlein swooped out of the fog over Hue and saw the black smoke from the destroyed helicopter.

"There was no one near the ship," said Mr. Maehrlein, "but then as we jumped over a clump of trees bordering a flat, sandy field we dropped onto about

Bravo Troop Blues check out a bunker complex along the "Jolley Trail," a major infiltration route into the III Corps Tactical Zone discovered by B Troop, 1st Squadron, 9th Cavalry.

50 Viet Cong in black pajamas and carrying weapons.

"They were in two groups of 25 men and when they saw us they scattered. We went for the front group and flew by as my doorgunners cut loose with the M-60s. That's when we saw two Americans with the front group break in another direction, hold up their hands and drop to the ground. It's just lucky we didn't shoot them."

The chopper made a tight turn and landed about 150 meters from a place where the NVA had disappeared, and, while the VC began blasting away at the ship on the ground, Babcock and his doorgunner scrambled aboard and Maehrlein took off. The gunners on the ship killed 10 VC.

"I'd say there were about 30 or 40 VC in the group," Babcock said afterward. "They had full gear and plenty of weapons, but when that chopper came in on them it was so sudden they simply panicked and ran."

Then the pilot sat back in his chair and wiped his forehead. "It's just good to be back," he said.

The squadron's record for enemy killed for February was the highest yet for the unit, 536. In early March the squadron continued operations in the JEB STUART AO. The squadron conducted extensive reconnaissance for all three brigades into base areas 101, 114, the Ba Long Valley and the coastal plains area.

In the latter half of March the squadron was given six days to prepare the area around Khe Sanh for what was to be Operation PEGASUS, the division's drive to relieve the beleaguered Marine base. The squadron's mission was to detect and destroy anti-aircraft and automatic weapons positions and enemy troop concentrations, to select and prepare brigade landing zones, select the air corridors into the LZs and neutralize all enemy that could influence the corridors. Operating from LZ Stud on March 24, the squadron employed one air strike an hour and stepped that up to an air strike every half hour on March 29. On March 31, D-Day, the squadron was employing one air strike every 15 minutes.

The thoroughness of this preparation was demonstrated on D-Day when no assault aircraft were lost to enemy fire as they brought the infantry into the LZs. After the division's infantry battalions landed the squadron resumed its normal role of reconnaissance and support.

One of the biggest finds of the entire Khe Sanh operation was made by Alpha Troop on the morning of April 10. A scout team spotted a Chicom truck loaded with ammunition and supplies. An air strike blew up the truck and caused several secondary explosions. As the scout team went in to check the area they spotted the tracks of a vehicle. At the end of the trail the team found a PT-76 tank armed with a 76 mm gun and twin .30 caliber machineguns. The tank was destroyed by artillery and air strikes and 15 NVA soldiers were killed. Additional tank tracks were discovered leading to the Laotion border.

When Operation PEGASUS ended, the squadron had accounted for 142 enemy casualties and had been responsible for the major contacts of the battle.

No sooner had PEGASUS ended than the squadron was called upon to prepare the A Shau Valley for a division drive to clear it of the NVA, for whom it was a haven and a staging ground. The squadron conducted extensive reconnaissance missions and employed 308 air strikes to destroy enemy positions. The reconnaissance indicated that enemy had a well established road and supply system in the valley.

The enemy did not permit the squadron to operate unhindered. When the squadron began its A Shau reconnaissance, the ships were frequently the object of well-aimed or radar controlled anti-aircraft fire. Over the radio one day came the laughing call of a pilot,

"Help! They're shooting big beebees at me." When he returned to basecamp, it was discovered that the floor of his chopper had been ripped open by .50 caliber rounds.

A Charlie Troop scout team received heavy anti-aircraft fire from 37 mm cannons. Organic weapons and air strikes silenced the enemy guns. When the scout team checked the damage they found that the enemy position consisted of three cannons positioned in triangle composed of reinforced earthworks with numerous bunkers and fighting positions.

Heavy anti-aircraft guns were not all the squadron found in the A Shau Valley. Charlie Troop ships spotted five PT-76 tanks withdrawing from a truck stop. One of the tanks was destroyed before the rest escaped over the Laotion border. On the 25th of April squadron elements located 50 flatbed and five other trucks, all of which were destroyed or captured.

The squadron also made the sighting on April 26 that unearthed the first of A Shau's big caches. Among the items captured were 600 122 mm rockets, 315 Soviet AK-47 rifles, 225 pounds of medical supplies, 2,000 anti-aircraft rounds and 20,000 small arms rounds.

Delta Troop recoilless rifles provided anti-tank protection to the 3rd ARVN Regiment, working in the southern portion of the valley.

As the A Shau operation ended squadron elements returned to the Khe

Sanh and Hue areas.

Alpha Troop landed in the Da Nang area of operations on August 1 to help the Marines. On the first day of the joint action the troop initiated a contact that left 72 NVA dead. August 18, when the operation terminated, Alpha Troop had accounted for 159 enemy casualties.

In late August an Alpha Troop Pink Team was conducting Snatch operations with an infantry squad in a Huey. As the Huey landed so the infantry could pick up a suspect, they were attacked by an enemy battalion. An attempt to insert the rest of the platoon was aborted by heavy automatic weapons fire. Delta Troop, acting as a quick reaction force, was successfully inserted nearby, and in conjunction with other division elements inflicted 144 casualties on the enemy.

The squadron continued to provide general support for Operation JEB STUART III until it was completed in October. In the last week of October the squadron was given 24 hours notice to move its troops south to III Corps, the division's new area of operations. By November 1 Bravo Troop was operational at Quan Loi. The other troops quickly followed: Alpha Troop to Tay Ninh, Delta and Charlie Troops to Phuoc Vinh.

Squadron elements were on a general reconnaissance north of the Loc Ninh rubber plantation in late November when they spotted a small village containing approximately 40 military age males and 25 bicycles. An armored cavalry unit nearby was notified and began moving into the area, killing more than 60 NVA. The squadron placed air strikes and artillery on the enemy. The Communists responded with 12.75 armor piercing rounds. The Pink Teams remained on station until resistance broke and the battle ended. Results showed the enemy lost numerous soldiers and several crew served weapons.

The day after Christmas brought no cheer to one NVA unit near Loc Ninh. Charlie Troop pilot Warrant Officer John Jelich was flying his ship at treetop level when he spotted 45 to 50 individuals sitting below in what appeared to be a training class. Warrant Officer Michael Myhre, piloting the Cobra half of the Pink Team, lowered his bird's nose and rolled in, dumping three pairs of rockets on the location.

Despite enemy automatic weapons fire, Myhre struck again. "I rolled in and expended the rest of my rockets and sprayed the area with minigun and 40 mm

cannon fire."

By then a second Pink Team arrived from Phuoc Vinh. "I came into the area at what I thought to be a safe 2,000 feet when I started receiving a heavy volume of automatic weapons fire," said Chief Warrant Officer Thomas Harnisher of the second team's recon ship. "I could see the tracers whizzing all around my ship. I pulled out of the line of fire, dipped my nose toward the ground and sprayed the area with my minigun."

He was followed by his Cobra ship, which rolled in and expended its rockets on the fleeing enemy. The gunships accounted for 41 enemy dead.

The squadron was there for the first important action of 1969. East of Loc Ninh it combined with a long range reconnaissance patrol to kill 39 NVA attempting to infiltrate along the Serges Jungle Highway on January 5. Most of the squadron's activities were still centered around Operation TOAN THANG II, aimed at blocking enemy infiltration routes to Saigon and preventing any repetition of the Tet Offensive of 1968. By the time the operation was finished, the squadron's reconnaissance had resulted in numerous significant contacts, the uncovering of several large staging areas and bunker

complexes, and the destruction of rice and equipment caches. Squadron organic weapons were responsible for the deaths of 557 NVA and 101 VC.

Delta Troop smashed an enemy ambush on February 23 near Quan Loi. A Delta Troop platoon was making a recon-in-force through the wooded areas surrounding the 2nd Brigade basecamp when the enemy struck. The troop immediately returned fire from its jeep-mounted M-60 machineguns and 106 mm recoilless rifles. The mortar and infantry sections of the troop added firepower as the enemy began dropping RPGs into the midst of the American force.

Staff Sergeant John H. Hubbard learned that his platoon leader and medic were wounded. He hurried forward to help them and the other wounded, giving them first aid and making repeated trips under fire to return them to a safer area.

Another troop platoon moved in to provide relief. SSG Hubbard again exposed himself to direct the relief platoon into an effective firing position. Sergeant Richard A. Macleod wheeled his recoilless rifle jeep into place and got off five well-aimed rounds before his jeep was hit by an RPG. SGT Macleod repositioned his crew behind cover, then began carrying ammo to the forward

Every enemy mortar round captured means one less round to dodge later. This cache found by the 1st Squadron, 9th Cavalry, will result in a lot of peace of mind somewhere in Cav Country.

position.

As the jeep in which Specialist Five Charles J. Jackson was riding moved past the lead platoon, he saw a man trying to run to safety, Enemy machine-gun fire was closing in on him, raising splashes of dust. SP5 Jackson leaped from his jeep and knocked the man to the ground. When the fire let up he led the man to safety, returned and carried three more wounded men to safety, then returned and carried yet another three men to the rear.

The enemy withdrew and the division commander expressed the thanks of the 1st Cavalry Division a few days later when he pinned Army Commendation Medals for valor on SSG Hubbard and SP5 Jackson and a Bronze Star on SGT Macleod.

In March, the gunships of Charlie Troop teamed up with a company of Skytroopers to drive the enemy from bunkers spotted by troop scouts 11 kilometers northeast of Bien Hoa. Numerous secondary explosions were caused and the combined effort inflicted 46 enemy casualties.

Late in April, Alpha Troop Blues dented the enemy's transportation system when they discovered a fully-equipped bicycle factory, complete with 75 bicycles. They also found enough other bunkers to indicate that they had located an enemy regimental basecamp.

The Blues began to withdraw after blowing up the factory but were met by fire from an NVA platoon. A crossfire from the Blues' four machineguns scattered the enemy. Close to their extraction LZ the Blues met another enemy platoon. ARA and air strikes broke the enemy effort and the riflemen were extracted. That night B-52s made final work of the Communist position.

First Lieutenant David M. Stegall demonstrated the daring for which the squadron is so well known when, in May, his OH-6A LOH drew automatic weapons fire from a well-entrenched enemy force 10 miles north of Tay Ninh. Rounds or shrapnel not only hit each member of the crew, they severed the fore and aft push-pull lever, causing the chopper to lurch in and out of the tree line, narrowly avoiding a collision with the triple canopy jungle.

Despite injuries, the crew began to work to save the LOH. LT Stegall wrestled for control of the chopper, finally compensating for its shaking action by increasing lateral thrust, forcing the LOH to fly sideways. Meanwhile, crew chief Specialist Four Larry Kempers began throwing unnecessary gear and ordnance from the bird, anticipating a forced landing. The gunner, Sergeant John K. Binegar, sprayed machinegun fire at the enemy positions below.

After the helicopter staggered two and a half miles through the sky the crew saw a break in the treeline, a "clearing" covered with six-foot high elephant grass and 10-foot tall stumps. Stegall brought the chopper down, maintaining control and landing safely despite the sideways position. The bird and crew were soon evacuated to Tay Ninh.

The squadron deprived the enemy of important food and ammunition caches in May. Pink Teams spotted part of the large supply point in an area ripped open by a B-52 strike. Hovering at treetop level in their LOH birds the scouts followed trails as small as eight inches wide to find and judge the age of footprints, bicycle tracks, bunkers and the cache itself.

The tracks were only hours old. Some of the bunkers had been built less than 48 hours before. Rocket propelled grenades and AK-47 and mortar rounds were found in their factory cases. More than 10 tons of rice were spotted initially. Air Force bombers blasted the area again that night.

The next day the Troop B Blues were dropped in. Less than a kilometer south of the abandoned LZ they found 500 bags of rice totalling 50 tons, and more rockets, grenades and mortar rounds. Further down the trail they destroyed another 15 tons of rice. Similar finds by squadron elements were frequent during this period.

Throughout the summer of 1969 the squadron's reconnaissance served as the division's "eyes and ears" and frequently as one of its deadliest weapons, as when Charlie Troop discovered that you don't always meet the nicest people on a Honda.

A Charlie Troop Pink Team had been flying a bomb damage assessment run over a B-52 strike area. Suddenly LOH pilot Warrant Officer Clifford Lee spotted two enemy soldiers. As Captain Gayle Jennings' Cobra rolled in hot, killing both enemy, the LOH scooted away to avoid its companion ship's fire. From its new position the LOH crew spotted about 30 NVA, fully equipped with packs and riding bicycles and Hondas along a heavily traveled trail. Mr. Lee radioed for the Cobras to strike again. When the day was over 14 NVA were dead.

In the last four months of 1969 the units of the squadron saw much of the action as they made many important findings for other division units to follow up and carried on numerous small engagements on their own. In the last week of September the enemy kept making the mistake of firing on squadron helicopters. The squadron generally saw to it that they would never shoot

With the aid of an assistant gunner in a do-it-yourself boonie hat, a Cav machinegunner does his thing during Operation PERSHING.

Major General John Norton confers with Colonel Harold Moore, commanding officer of the 3rd Brigade, shortly after the Garry Owen forces moved to Dong Tre to begin Operation NATHAN HALE.

again. By the end of the week the squadron had accounted for 25 percent of the casualties inflicted on the enemy.

The next week the NVA lost 149 soldiers to the 1st Cav Division. One hundred of those casualties were caused by the squadron.

The last half of October was another outstanding period for the squadron. It again accounted for most of the action in the division AO. Alpha Troop, which made 74 of the division's 207 kills in the week ending October 24, discovered an elaborate NVA staging area 22 miles northwest of Tay Ninh. It included a barbed wire and trenchline perimeter encircling a 1,000 meter area in which were several sheet metal hootches and canvas tents.

In the last week of October the division saw more action than any other division in Vietnam, and the responsibility for most of the action was again the squadron's. One high point came when a Bravo Troop Pink Team spotted and killed three NVA near Song Be. An hour later the team killed four more enemy nearby.

Later that afternoon 15 NVA were spotted in the open and engaged. As artillery and air strikes were called in the scout helicopter remained on station, drawing the enemy fire to pinpoint their location. Before the day was over Bravo Troop had eliminated 41 NVA.

Three division fire support bases repulsed ground attacks on November 4, 1969. As the attackers retreated they were harrassed by squadron Pink Teams. Warrant Officer William McIntosh described the actions of three Alpha Troop Pink Teams as, "Just like a turkey shoot." Alpha Troop caught enemy forces withdrawing from FSB Ike.

Said Cobra pilot First Lieutenant Steve Justus, "We caught the first group in a trenchline about 300 miles north of Ike, then we just followed the trails to the north and kept picking them off."

"As they got farther away from the firebase, they started grouping together and heading for several small bunker complexes. Only one group fired at us; the rest appeared to be taken by surprise. One of them even looked up at me like he didn't believe we would shoot him," said Mr. McIntosh.

Later in November an Alpha Troop Pink Team was flying a routine reconnaissance mission over dense canopy jungle when the LOH received .30 caliber fire. Marking the suspected enemy position with smoke grenades, the LOH swung into a hard right turn as the Cobra rolled in, rockets and minigun blazing. The Cobra killed 15 of the NVA soldiers and destroyed their machinegun position.

A few days later another A Troop LOH spotted an enemy position. The Cobra made a pass but was about 100 meters off the mark. First Lieutenant Ronald Whitesides, the pilot, said it was easy to see just how far off he was when the entire woodline to his left opened up with AK-47 and automatic weapons fire.

"I thought they had me for sure," recalled the lieutenant. "It looked like bushel baskets of tracers coming up at me."

The tracers didn't keep the pilot from circling for another run. Before the action was over 21 NVA were killed, and Alpha Troop Blues found numerous blood trails and fresh bunkers. The Blues were extracted as the 4th Company, 11th ARVN Airborne, moved in.

Alpha Troop struck again in December, three of its Cobras blasting a group of 45 to 50 NVA soldiers seen setting up mortar positions northwest of FSB Jerri. Fifteen NVA were killed and the positions destroyed.

During the last weeks of 1969 Bravo Troop concentrated on interdicting the Jolley Trail, named after the troop's commander, Major Charles A. Jolley.

Elements of the troop discovered the enemy infiltration route in the Duc Phong area in November. The high-speed trail was generally about four feet wide, with bunker complexes every few hundred meters as way stations and bombshelters. Woven bamboo mats covered the trail, enabling wheeled traffic to pass over it in the rainy season.

Bravo Troop applied constant pressure to the trail, blasting away its overhead concealment, blowing up its bamboo bridges, and calling in air strikes and artillery on the bunker complexes. The Bravo Blues were frequently inserted to explore the network of trails and check the bunker complexes for supplies and signs of occupation.

The Jolley Trail had been the enemy's latest effort to find a safe way through "Cav Country." Bravo Troop was making sure the effort was no more successful than the others.

It was yet another instance of the outstanding performance—whether the assignment be reconnaissance, troop support, or lightning fast infantry operations—that typifies the 1st Sqdn, 9th Cav, an elite unit in an elite division.

Dong Tien

(Continued on P. 255)

the combined forces immediately made contact, killing five enemy as they jumped from the skids of the helicopters.

Throughout the mission, the CIDG troopers walked point for the Cavalrymen, their familiarity with the terrain a vital factor in the success of the operation. When the enemy opened up on the approaching Allied force the CIDG soldiers hit the ground, returned the fire and then assaulted the NVA positions.

At the end of the operation the force returned to their bases, a deep new respect for the CIDGs obviously in the minds of the Cavalrymen. "These guys really do a good job," said Private First Class William Duffey, the company RTO. "They move through thick bamboo like nothing I've ever seen; and they were great when we made contact. They didn't seem to be afraid of anything."

As 1970 begins the FIRST TEAM is heavily involved in working with Vietnamese forces. Adhering to the policy of letting the national forces assume more of the combat role, the Cav is constantly striving to provide all the assistance necessary to help the ARVN units fully establish themselves in III Corps.

Americans and Vietnamese are working side by side, looking forward to that day when peace will once again come to the war-torn Republic of Vietnam.

13th Signal

(Continued From P. 189)

A major project for the year was the physical improvement of the Hon Cong Mountain facility. The needs for a stable power system were met when two 100 kilowatt generators were installed with the aid of a CH-54 Flying Crane. During the year the residents of the hill remodeled and reconstituted the entire site. Conex containers, crude bunkers and makeshift shelters were removed and replaced with quonset buildings on concrete pads.

An airmobile command post for the division was maintained to enhance the overall tactical mobility. It took the form of two pods which were standard items designed to be carried beneath the CH-54 flying crane. When the pods were moved all signal equipment necessary to operate them was moved inside the pod, including FM radio remotes.

At the end of 1969 the nerve center of the division's signal operation was located at Phuoc Vinh.

The rear operations platoon had charge of all the signal facilities at rear locations. That included the communications center telephone switchboard and a radio network.

In the communications center tape punchers fed their hungry machines with perforated messages 24 hours a day, while at the same time, cryptographers coded and decoded top secret information.

The hub of the division's telephone system was set up in a small sandbagged bunker. Four telephone operators presided over the two switchboards of the "Skyking" and "Phuoc Vinh" systems. The "Skyking" telephone system is set aside as strictly a divisional level command and staff network, while the Phuoc Vinh system was integral with the Corps Area Communications System.

The realm of command and control was not the only activity of the battalion. They offered a personal service to every soldier in the division, known as MARS. MARS stands for Military Affiliated Radio Station, a name that still cannot describe the facility as well as to say that every soldier knew MARS was a place from which to make a phone call home. The signalmen dedicated to helping their fellow soldiers talk with their families and friends keep MARS operating 24 hours a day. The station at Phuoc Vinh was manned by a four man crew, and the station at Tay Ninh had two.

While the anxious soldier waited, the MARS station made contact with one of the thousands of private "ham" radio stations in the U.S. The radio hobbiest then hooked his equipment to his telephone and completed the connection with a telephone call to the soldier's home.

The station put a newer and larger transmitter into operation in April 1969 and nearly doubled the number of calls put through.

2nd the 12th

(Continued From P. 99)

of the map board. Our intelligence sergeant was lying wounded under a table. A radio operator was wounded and flat on his back but still talking on the radio."

Brown quickly took command. Nearly 1,000 NVA were assaulting the base behind the mortar and rocket barrage. They had also hit the base's defenders with nausea gas. Brown called in air strikes, artillery and an Air Force ship armed with miniguns.

The Communists blasted through the outer perimeter wire with bangalore torpedoes. Saving their claymores in case of a second assault, the men of Delta Company held the enemy off with small arms, M-60 fire, and their own artillery, cranked down to fire point blank into massed enemy troops charging the perimeter berm.

Sergeant Major Leland Robinson was in the command bunker when the rocket exploded. He was literally blown outside. "It just turned dark in there all of a sudden and I wound up outside in a pile of sandbags," Robinson said. He ignored two shrapnel wounds in his foot and ran back into the bunker, helping the wounded and joining MAJ Brown in organizing the base defense.

The enemy had failed to take Grant and had lost 157 men in the unsuccessful attempt. They tried again three nights later, and once more failed, losing 62 men.

The enemy was tenacious. On May 12 Alpha and Echo Companies at Grant were bombarded by rockets and mortars, then 200 NVA troops stormed toward the berm, breached the western perimeter and succeeded in occupying two bunkers before being pushed back. In the morning 45 NVA lay dead around Grant. Once more the 2nd Bn, 12th Cav, had stymied a desperate attempt by the Communists to capture Grant.

Bloody battles did not prevent the battalion from paying attention to the other side of the war. The battalion's civil affairs section, operating from Tay Ninh, paid weekly visits to the companies, rounding up unused sundries, and distributing the articles to eager children at Co Nhi Vien Orphanage. Candy and personal hygiene items usually comprised the bulk of the gifts. Among other things, 350 toothbrushes and 485 bars of soap were distributed.

If there is anyone home, he's probably not friendly, so Staff Sergeant Robert Teague, a platoon leader with Delta Company, 2nd Battalion, 12th Cavalry, has a "no knock" policy. This bunker was found north of FSB Buttons.

According to Sergeant Jesse D. Raley, of the battalion civil affairs office, "We try to give them items having a lasting impact on them. A toothbrush will have far more beneficial effect on the kids in the long run than will a candy bar."

In June it was business as usual for Companies A and B. Combining airmobility with the firepower of tanks they surrounded and crushed an NVA force entrenched in a large bunker complex east of Tay Ninh.

Hours after an early morning B-52 strike, 11th Armored Cavalry Regiment tanks and three companies of the 2nd Bn, 12th Cav, swept toward the northeast into the woodline surrounding the bunker complex.

As the operation drew to a close, more than 100 NVA had been killed and the bunker complex was destroyed.

On July 6 the battalion moved to LZ Dolly. The move was soon followed by shifts to LZ O'Keefe and LZ Caldwell, as the battalion continued its efforts to find the enemy and interdict his supply routes.

Numerous small contacts were made, as on August 12 when a Delta Company platoon successfully ambushed and engaged an enemy force moving toward Duc Phong. Another platoon reinforced the American element and contact continued through the night. A search of

the area showed 15 NVA killed with blood trails indicating more enemy losses.

On August 17 the battalion airlifted to LZ Alvarado, near Song Be, capital of Phuoc Long Province. For the rest of 1969 2nd Bn, 12th Cav, operations would center around Song Be, protecting the city and its airstrip, and blocking enemy movement with the command post alternating between FSB Don, FSB Judie and FSB Buttons.

On October 19 Company B made contact with an unknown size enemy force north of FSB Judie. Despite enemy mortar fire, the Skytroopers inflicted 20 NVA casualties.

At the end of October Bravo Company found 13 tons of rice 12 miles northeast of Song Be. The rice was lifted out and distributed to Vietnamese citizens in the Song Be area.

Action through the last months of 1969 was intermittent. Perhaps no more successful sign of success in the war could be found than the steady flow of Viet Cong and former VC sympathizers who, sometimes in handfuls and sometimes in scores, rallied to the battalion and other elements of the 2nd Brigade to escape the enemy.

1st of the 7th

(Continued From P. 71)

troopers grip on the land by attacking their command posts. One such attack was launched against LZ Eagle.

At a "temporary" firebase several miles to the west of Quan Loi, the battalion held fast against a vicious enemy mortar bombardment and ground attacks.

The 200 defenders at LZ Eagle from Companies C and D, aided by helicopter gunships, fired point blank artillery and 81 mm mortars to smash the attack by a reinforced company-sized NVA force.

Thirty-one NVA bodies were found outside the single strand of barbed wire after the two hour battle. Ten Skytroopers were wounded.

"If it wasn't for our mortars, we'd be fighting them now," said Sergeant John May after the determined enemy had been turned back. "The mortar tubes pounded the woodline so hard that the NVA never had a chance to get close."

The attack was not a total surprise since the firebase, opened only two days earlier, was designed to blunt an expected assault on Quan Loi. "I can not understand why they waited until 5 a.m.," said Specialist Four Russell Maxwell, "but they sure came prepared."

Bangalore torpedoes, 60 and 82 mm mortars, 75 mm recoilless rifles, small arms and various kinds of explosives were found in the woodline after the battle.

In the early morning on the 12th of June, LZ Joy, in the heart of War Zone D, came under heavy rocket and mortar attack. Companies D and E were defending the LZ while it received more than 300 incoming rounds of indirect fire.

A battalion-size enemy force then launched a ground assault on the landing zone. The battle raged hard and long with the Skytroopers utilizing artillery, ARA, and a C-119 "Shadow" gunship to repulse the attack. A few NVA managed to make it through the barbed wire fencing but were killed by the Garry Owen Skytroopers before they could make it to the bunkerline.

After three hours of heavy fighting, the NVA forces broke contact. It was

The affinity between an infantryman's stomach and the ground when the crackle of small arms fire breaks the silence is demonstrated here as Skytroopers get acquainted with the monsoon mud during the battle of Hue.

4:45 a.m. and the end of a long night for the men of Delta and Echo Companies.

The next morning 35 enemy dead were found in the barbed wire along with 22 AK-47 rifles and assorted rockets and explosives.

Often in the rush of movements, operations and battles, the day to day life of the Skytrooper is overlooked. The individual infantryman depends heavily on his squad leader for guidance, tips to help make life in the bush a little more bearable, and alertness in case of attack. When a new Garry Owen trooper arrived in his company it was his squad leader who taught him the ropes. His squad leader showed him how to set a good perimeter with claymore mines, trip flares, and, of course, how to dig the all-important foxhole.

The squad leader was one of the most dependable veterans in the company. He was picked because he knew what he was doing, like this Garry Owen squad leader.

James W. Krudop, sergeant, squad leader, veteran of 16 months in the field, was a cool hand in the wilderness.

Like a gangling pied piper, he walked point for his squad, his platoon or his company on a regular basis. Moving cautiously, confidently, M-16 gripped loosely in his right hand, the six-footer

appeared keyed at every step.

He was good and he knew it. He didn't ask for point. He took it and no one questioned him.

"Well, let's get this thing over with," he said as his platoon from Company E, 1st Bn, 7th Cav, dismounted their armored personnel carriers and moved out of the rubber plantation in two columns, Krudop at the front.

"Damn it, not like that!" he barked at those behind him who had bunched up. "Stagger, man, stagger. Let's get it right."

"I would rather be here than pulling guard and KP in the rear," he said later. "Here you are on your own, man. These are my people," he said referring to his squad—the Mod Squad as he calls it. "They are all crazy, but they get the job done."

Krudop, 23, extended six months to serve with the 1st Air Cav, "because they are airmobile, man."

The company moved through a small valley, climbed and descended the next hill, maneuvered through a rice paddy, searched an abandoned village, then came full circle back to the track vehicles. They had traveled two kilometers that afternoon.

About one kilometer out, the platoon leader offered to change points. "I'm all right," Krudop replied, as if offended.

"No, I mean change point squads,"

the lieutenant added.

"Naw, we can handle it."

"OK."

When Krudop climbed the last hill and re-entered the rubber plantation, the tracks were directly in front of them, 50 meters away.

"Well I guess we get an 'A' for land navigation," Krudop said, brushing back his dust-red colored hair. He grabbed a soda from the track, popped it open and downed it.

When a company made contact with the enemy, it was the platoon leader who kept the platoon working together. A good platoon leader was exposed to more contact than just about anyone else in the company. It's not difficult to see why platoon leaders often found themselves in some tight situations, and, if they were courageous and had the respect of their men, why they often won honors for themselves and the Garry Owen battalion.

On March 17, 1969, a Garry Owen platoon leader found himself in one of those tight situations. It was just getting light enough to see. Suddenly there were several loud explosions as enemy rocket-propelled grenades (RPG) pounded into the company's night position. Following the rockets, a heavy volume of small arms fire and the company was assaulted by the enemy.

One of the first things that First Lieutenant Thomas A. Ciccolini, a platoon leader, noticed was that one of the defensive positions had taken several casualties. Exposing himself to enemy rockets, mortars and small arms fire, LT Ciccolini gathered a couple of men from other positions to fill the gap in the perimeter.

Realizing that the wounded men needed immediate medical attention, the platoon leader quickly set up a position where they could receive first aid and later be evacuated.

After taking care of the wounded, LT Ciccolini returned to the battle to redistribute available ammunition.

After the enemy had withdrawn, the company swept the battle area around its position and found 123 enemy bodies, 20 AK-47 rifles, three radios, and 17 crew-served weapons.

Later, Brigadier General Richard L. Irby, the deputy commander of the 1st Air Cavalry Division, awarded LT Ciccolini the Silver Star for his valorous actions.

Bravo Company elements were at Quan Loi August 12 when the 3rd Brigade headquarters was attacked. Sergeant Douglas Chappell saw the enemy occupy two bunkers and then move toward his. "The NVA were standing on top of them, firing at our bunker," said the sergeant. "About 25 of them started coming at us. "For two hours SGT Chapell and a medic shared the bunker and held off the attackers.

"I started throwing frags as fast as I could and laying down a base of fire with my M-16. I guess I threw about 60 frags," said the NCO, who at one point dodged enemy fire to run to a nearby bunker for more ammunition. At first light a dozen dead NVA were found at the side of his bunker.

The battalion command post moved in August to the Bu Dop CIDG Camp. The Garry Owen troopers concentrated on stopping the infiltration and activities of the 141st and 165th NVA regiments. The enemy hit Bu Dop with several mortar and rocket atacts in August and September. To increase effective artillery support for the battalion, Alpha Company opened FSB Jerri south of Bu Dop on September 7.

September 15 the battalion moved to FSB Westcott. With Westcott as a base the Skytroopers moved into the jungles, finding numerous enemy weapon and food caches. In November Echo Company located a cache that included 30-caliber machineguns and B-40 and B-41 rockets. On November 16 Alpha Company came under fire from small arms, automatic weapons and B-40s in the jungle southwest of Bu Dop. With the help of artillery and ARA the unit killed 16 of the attackers before they fled. On a patrol three miles northeast of FSB Fort Compton, the unit's new command post, Charlie Company discovered a huge arms cache on December 14 in an NVA bunker complex. The cache consisted of 50 Chicom submachineguns, more than 300 rocket propelled grenades, 86,000 small arms rounds, nearly 500 60 mm mortar rounds, a Soviet flame-thrower and numerous assorted individual weapons.

The arms find was fitting conclusion to a year in which the battalion played a major role in interdicting the enemy infiltration and supply system near the Cambodian border.

2nd of the 20th

(Continued From P. 138)

artillery batteries. The Cobra can pack 76 rockets and has a mini-gun capable of firing 4,000 rounds per minute. Added to the mini-gun in later models was the 40 mm grenade launcher, which can chuck out 400 rounds per minute.

The battalion fired its 750,000th rocket in Vietnam in July 1968; however, the unit had not forgotten the other side of the war. That summer it also adopted an orphanage in Quang Tri, helping expand the orphanage's space, building beds and providing medical care.

In addition to their regular fire missions, the ships of the battalion carried out regular mortar patrols at the division basecamp and brigade headquarters. Within seconds of mortar attacks ARA would pound the area where the flash of the tubes had been spotted. The mortar patrols added considerably to base security. The enemy continued to develop a well-founded fear of ARA. Documents found on dead NVA soldiers told them not to fire at helicopters with the "things on their sides," the "things" obviously being rocket pods.

In November 1968 the battalion, with the rest of the division, moved to a new area of operations, the III Corps Tactical Zone near the Cambodian border north of Saigon. The unit was soon in action. That same month the NVA assaulted LZ Dot, located 43 kilometers northwest of the new division basecamp

at Phuoc Vinh. Some 2,000 enemy hit the tiny LZ at midnight with a human wave assault after a mortar and rocket attack. ARA was called in, decimating the enemy just as they penetrated the outer wire. At 6:30 a.m. the enemy broke contact, leaving 287 dead.

Charlie Battery performed a rescue mission on a smaller scale on a December night when two of the unit's Cobras were in the air minutes after being scrambled. Their mission on the dark and rainy night was to rescue a long range patrol team of six men who were evading an NVA company. The red glimmer of a flashlight pointed through an M-79 grenade launcher pinpointed the patrol's position. The patrol radioed

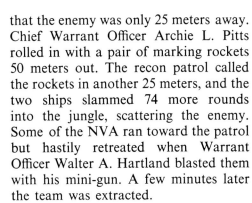

that the enemy was only 25 meters away. Chief Warrant Officer Archie L. Pitts rolled in with a pair of marking rockets 50 meters out. The recon patrol called the rockets in another 25 meters, and the two ships slammed 74 more rounds into the jungle, scattering the enemy. Some of the NVA ran toward the patrol but hastily retreated when Warrant Officer Walter A. Hartland blasted them with his mini-gun. A few minutes later the team was extracted.

By the end of 1968 the 2nd Bn, 20th Arty, helicopters were known throughout the 1st Cav as "Blue Max," a fitting tribute to pilots and crewmen whose skill and daring at least matched that of the World War I flying aces with whom the award originated. The blue Maltese Cross on the original medal was adopted by the battalion as a symbol.

In 1969 the Cobra completely replaced the Huey as the main force of the battalion. Each battery consisted of 12 Cobras. There were three platoons of four aircraft each in a battery. A service platoon maintained the Cobras. An ARA section consisted of two Cobras, and usually nothing less than a section would carry out a strike. Among the many other firsts to its credit, the battalion added that of becoming the first all-Cobra unit in Vietnam in January.

In March the Cobras came to the aid of the 1st Battalion, 7th Cavalry, when one of its units was attacked on Hill 54, a small forward operations base northeast of Bien Hoa. The ARA was restricted in its fires, however, because two listening posts were outside the perimeter.

The battalion again came to the defense of a base under attack in May. Alpha Battery Cobras were in constant flight

around the perimeter of LZ Carolyn, spraying the attacking 900 NVA with rocket and mini-gun fire. "All of our sections went out at least two or three times," said Warrant Officer Richard A. Chapman. "There were .51 caliber positions all over the place with a lot of people down there shooting at us. One slug almost put my ship out of action."

The enemy also tried to attack the division basecamp at Phuoc Vinh in May. Enemy forces were spotted approaching the camp just after midnight. ARA ships worked out, driving back the Viet Cong and following them step for step. The next morning nine enemy bodies were found around the base.

In August two Alpha Battery Cobras were escorting a formation of troop-carrying Hueys when four anti-aircraft positions opened up. Warrant Officer Thomas G. Porter rolled in hot on one emplacement. On his second pass the aircraft took a hit. As .51 caliber tracers filled the air the other pilot, Warrant Officer David R. Watson, looked straight down and saw two guns firing at the formation. Said Mr. Watson, "Tracers were coming from my rear. I rolled in under the formation and knocked out one position." Although Watson was wounded he also got the other position. The section made eight more passes on enemy .30 caliber positions, expending all of their ammunition. Mr. Porter received the Silver Star for the action.

The NVA launched a major effort against division firebases in early November. ARA responded to help keep the efforts from succeeding and inflict 269 casualties on the enemy.

It was a new instance of the battalion's performance of its old mission, quickly bringing devastating firepower on the enemy with maximum accuracy.

A pair of Cav history makers, Major Generals John Norton (left) and John Tolson pose in front of the commanding general's quarters at Camp Radcliff in July 1966. MG Tolson was on a liaison visit to Vietnam. Less than a year later, he returned to command the FIRST TEAM.

1st of the 77th
(Continued From 129)

In early March a blast from one of Alpha Battery's guns marked the battalion's 150,000th round since the move south. The battalion shifted its headquarters from Quan Loi to Lai Khe, following the 2nd Brigade as it moved further south to interdict enemy routes to Saigon.

During the summer the Blackhorse Brigade and the 77th Artillery turned their attention northward again, moving to FSB Buttons near Song Be, Phuoc Long Province capital.

Phuoc Long had been a prime enemy infiltration route for some time. So effective was the combination of the 77th Artillery and the 2nd Brigade in interdicting those routes that on November 4, 1969, the enemy attacked the brigade headquarters at FSB Buttons in an attempt to rid themselves of this obstacle.

The early morning attack put the clerks, cooks, mechanics and commo men of the On Guard battalion's Headquarters Battery into the midst of a firefight. From 1:30 a.m. until first light the battery's men stayed on the berm, refusing to yield to enemy grenades, B-40s, satchel charges and small arms fire. With M-16s and grenades the battery kept the enemy from broaching its sector of the perimeter. Several NVA actually reached the berm, and the "redlegs turned rifemen" stopped them

with point blank fire from the top of the berm. Specialist Five Graciano Hernandez, a cook, preferred a bow and arrow to an M-16. When dawn broke, only four of the eight shafts he shot could be found.

When the enemy retreated, Headquarters Battery, other men on the berm and artillery and gunship fire had accounted for 63 enemy dead.

As 1969 ended, the battalion headquarters was still at Song Be. Both Alpha and Bravo Batteries had joined Charlie as opcon to the battalion's headquarters. All of the On Guard batteries were now supporting the 2nd Brigade in blocking enemy movement in Phuoc Long Province. ✠

545th MPs
(Continued From P. 193)

bined operations with the Vietnamese National Police in traffic control and "populace and resources control."

The MPs performed many liaison functions with local Vietnamese military and civilian police forces. The MPs patroled the highways and villages near basecamps. A typical patrol consisted of one MP, his interpreter, a member of the regional forces and a civilian official. Thus composed, a team could arrest or apprehend any suspect—American, ARVN or civilian.

The MPs were, after all, the keepers of the peace within the Cav community.

This was an awesome responsibility in view of the high level of anxieties and frustration inherent in the combat environment. The 1st Cav is a community of 21,000 individuals each of whom is armed to the teeth with the best weapons available.

The peaceful, even sleepy, atmosphere of the division's headquarters and three brigade basecamps belies the potential for trouble. This is so because the MPs, by their very presence, are fulfilling their primary duty of preserving law and order.

Whenever elements of the Cavalry needed to move large amounts of supplies and vehicles along roads the MPs would be called. The MPs helped to arrange the vehicles into a convoy.

The progress of the war meant an increase, rather than a decrease, in the duties of the MPs. There were fewer prisoners to care for and fewer hostile hamlets to search but the relative peace of 1969 increased many fold the need to control traffic on the roads and maintain tranquility in the civil and military rear areas.

The 545th MP Company shares with the rest of the division the Presidential Unit Citation for the Pleiku Campaign and has a Meritorious Unit Commendation for the period February 12, 1967, to January 1, 1968. ✠

Artillery pumps out counter battery fires during a brief mortar attack on a temporary Cav firebase.

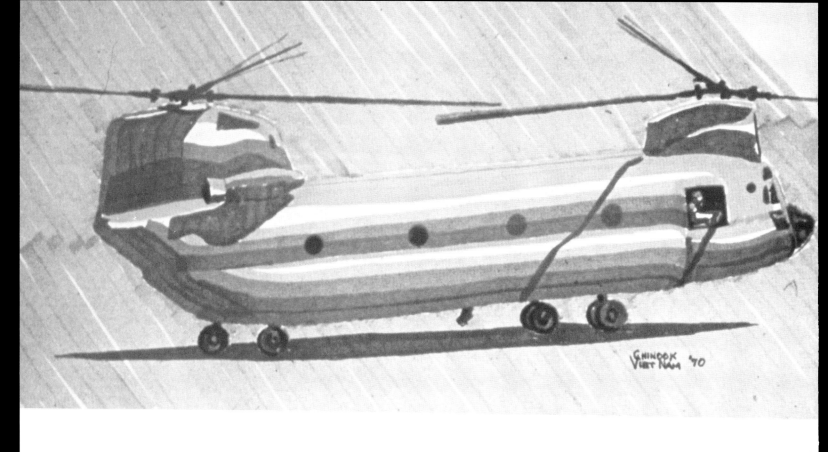

Chinook
Viet Nam '70

2nd of the 5th

(Continued From P. 65)

the Demilitarized Zone. Despite defeats suffered during the first two weeks of Tet, the enemy soldiers appeared to be high in morale and they were well-equipped and supplied.

The first blow struck in the battalion's effort to choke off the enemy's supply traffic and freedom of movement was made by Company B, conducting a cordon and search operation around and in the village of Pho Trach in Phong Dien District.

The village itself was less than a mile from Camp Evans. The enemy had placed command-detonated mines along the trail leading to the village, and when Company B's point element was into the kill zone, the enemy kicked off an ambush by detonating the mines and engaging the infantrymen with small arms and machinegun fire. Company B reacted immediately, returning fire with its own small arms, machineguns and 90 mm recoilless rifles, while the commander, Captain Robert Carroll, called for gunship support. Having suffered only one casualty, Company B moved on line against the ambushers, but the enemy broke contact, taking their dead and wounded with them.

The end of February found Alpha and Bravo Companies closing in on Churchville, a river bank hamlet seven miles northeast of Camp Evans. The village was dominated by a towering cathedral, its militant congregation consisting of an enemy regimental commander, his staff and a large security force. There was an ammo dump in the basement, machinegunners in the vestibule and forward observers in the belfry.

On the morning of March 4, both companies combat assaulted into the vicinity of the church with the plan of establishing a cordon around the remaining enemy force. The previous night some 1,000 rounds had been fired into the area, but nonetheless the Cavalrymen began to receive fire almost as soon as they touched down. Snipers were everywhere and it took almost two hours to maneuver the various infantry units into place.

Additionally, the Cavalrymen were subjected to a nightmare of crossfire. Two enemy soldiers were in the trees to their left, placing effective AK-47 fire on them. One alert Skytrooper spotted them, killing both instantly with his M-79 grenade launcher. With the crossfire eliminated the situation improved, but the tide really turned shortly after, announced by the unmistakable drone of a Cobra, accompanied by a Huey gunship, both loaded with rockets.

The gunships expended their rockets directly into the church and surrounding

bunkers, setting off several secondary explosions. After the first run, enemy fire subsided sufficiently for the Huey gunships to land and take out most of the wounded men. After three more passes by the Cobra, the church was a lifeless gutted shell and more than 20 enemy were dead.

On April 3, the 2nd Bn, 5th Cav, left LZ Jane and moved further north to join other elements of the division in relieving the Marines at Khe Sanh (Operation PEGASUS).

In November the battalion moved to its new III Corps home at Phuoc Vinh, 52 miles north of Saigon. The remainder of the year was spent helping to clear and secure the new division headquarters basecamp.

The battalion was committed to Operation NAVAJO WARHORSE in February 1969. Company B was on a night ambush patrol on March 9 when an enemy battalion paraded into its kill zone. Bravo took them on, killing 36.

On June 22 a routine patrol of Echo Company's recon platoon was pinned down 18 miles northwest of Tay Ninh. As the intensity of the contact increased the platoon began to head toward an old bomb crater, Sergeant Jesus S. "Poncho" Duran providing cover all the way with his machinegun.

Tactical air strikes were called in, forcing the enemy to flee, leaving an estimated squad-size element to cover their retreat.

"We were pinned down pretty tight and we needed a Medevac bird pretty badly," said Lieutenant Danny G. McGrew, the platoon leader. "On top of that we were getting ready to be extracted."

As the Skytroopers prepared for extraction an enemy machinegunner

While a buddy lays down covering fire, the Skytrooper (picture top right) unlimbers a strong right arm and a frag during a firefight near LZ Baldy in Quang Tin Province. During the same firefight, in which more than 100 NVA died, a radio operator trades communications for instant firepower from an M-16.

attempted to sneak up on their position. His efforts were frustrated when Poncho jumped from the bunker and, firing his M-60 machinegun from the hip, cut the enemy gunner down.

"I knew he was up there so I let him have it," Poncho said later. "That's when I saw the muzzle flashes from the squad that had us pinned down." Running toward the enemy positions, a virtual one-man assault, he fired his remaining ammunition while other members of the unit supported him. The onslaught was too much for the enemy, as they broke contact and sought asylum in the thick jungle surrounding the bunker complex.

The recon platoon was inserted into the same area a week later to check some cooking pots that a pilot said he thought he had seen. As they approached the area where the pots and pans had been discovered, Cavalrymen found a large bunker complex, complete with mess halls, classrooms and drinking wells.

"I've never seen anything like it," said Staff Sergeant Michael DeHart, the platoon sergeant. "The mess hall was big, and it had about three feet of overhead cover. There were benches in there, a large cooking area with a hearth in the middle of it, and rice was still cooking on the stove when we busted in on them." They also discovered many bunkers equipped with hammocks, slits for their weapons and ammunition and shelves for their personal possessions.

"And everywhere we went," said DeHart, "we found NVA rucksacks. Some were filled with AK-47 ammo, others with extra fatigues and even spare Ho Chi Minh sandals."

Suddenly, while pushing through the enemy complex, they encountered intense small arms and rocket propelled grenade (RPG) fire.

"We opened up on them," said LT McGrew, "but they were hitting us from three sides. I immediately called for air strikes, and attack helicopters were on station all the time. If it hadn't been for their rocket fire holding the enemy back, our luck might have run out."

Soon after the contact began, the force began seeking cover in preparation for the air strikes.

"When the Air Force got there, they provided close air support which sent the enemy running," said SSG DeHart.

A sweep through the area revealed six dead NVA. Bunkers and fighting positions were destroyed.

An NVA battalion assaulted LZ Ike on June 18, defended by A and E Companies. When they had cut the wire and at least 10 of the enemy were inside the first barrier, the Cavalrymen began receiving small arms fire and hand grenades from the determined enemy. By detonating their claymores and returning a heavy volume of fire toward the enemy, the Skytroopers drove the enemy back from the wire. One NVA soldier was detained and 13 bodies were found in the wires.

During October and beyond, the Black Knights sponsored the 11th Battalion of the ARVN Airborne Division, conducting a series of missions designed to acquaint the Vietnamese unit with airmobile concepts. The continued success of these combined activities prompted the battalion to take greater part in the program to increase the Vietnamese ability to take over the war.

15th Admin

(Continued From P. 179)

base, naturally enough, moved too. And with it came the ever increasing slice of the 15th Administration Company.

Then the division moved south to III Corps, and again, the forward elements of the 15th Admin moved, except by this time, few could tell what was forward and what was rear.

During late 1968 and early 1969, the permanent rear of the division remained at Camp Radcliff. But in April 1969, as the 101st Airborne began to vacate Bien Hoa Army Base, the division ripped out the records kind of roots and brought its administrative tail back into the general neighborhood of the fighting body.

Despite all the organization, reorganizations, moves and shifts, the individuals within the company continued to provide the division with the administrative support required to accomplish the mission. Skytroopers were processed in and out; were promoted, sent on leave and R & R; paid; entertained by Special Services; had legal services rendered; had their image polished; and, perhaps, even had a chance to voice a complaint or two.

During FIRST TEAM operations in III Corps, weapons and rice caches were being turned up daily. The best kind for the soldiers, were the semi-automatic and bolt action rifles which made great war trophies.

Medevac

(Continued From P. 175)

As the chopper passed over the crash site for the fourth time, a thick cloud of white smoke erupted from the bamboo below, and there was a bright red flash from to ground.

"Hey, man, our ship just blew up!" the wounded doorgunner shouted. He turned to the medic with his eyes wide and fearful. The medic talked into his radio mouthpiece, listened, and then looked up at his patient.

"He's all right. The Blues got him out. He's okay."

The helicopter circled down to land in a yellow meadow close to the crashed and burning chopper. The rescued doorgunner looked past the medic. A big smile shot across his face as he flashed the "V" sign at the freed pilot, now sprinting toward the ship.

"You're the greatest. You're the greatest," the rescued pilot cried to the Medevac crew as he climbed aboard. Then he turned and lunged at his own two crew members who caught him in a wild embrace.

1st of the 8th

(Continued From P. 85)

stration of the unit's tremendous fighting ability, the 1st Bn, 8th Cav, was later awarded the Presidential Unit Citation.

In October, the battalion accounted for 31 Viet Cong killed during Operation IRVING along the sea coast. THAYER II in the Soui Ca Valley commenced December 16. Two days after Christmas, Companies B and C established contact with an NVA battalion and Delta Company fought another, inflicting heavy casualties.

THAYER II continued into 1967, terminating on February 11. The next day the battalion began Operation PERSHING along with other division maneuver battalions—an operation that lasted through one year.

On February 16 the first platoon of Company C was deployed in a night ambush near Bong Son when it was suddenly hit with an intense and accurate grenade barrage. A number of men were injured. To aid those wounded, Private First Class James H. Monroe, medical aidman, moved from position to position, oblivious to the hail of grenades and shrapnel about him. While treating the wounds of the platoon sergeant and his RTO, Monroe saw a live grenade land directly to his front and behind the two men he was treating. He gave off a shout, pushed the two men aside and dove on the fragmentation grenade just as it detonated, absorbing the blast and shrapnel with his body. He became the battalion's second recipient of the Medal of Honor—awarded posthumously.

The 1st Bn, 8th Cav, operated in the Bong Son Plain until May when it provided security for LZ Geronimo. The battalion assumed the entire Bong Son Plain AO on June 23 and remained there until August 2 when the command post moved to LZ Sandra to initiate operations in the An Lao Valley. The Jumping Mustangs returned to Bong Son and LZ Santana 17 days later.

The battalion operated in the Cay Diep Mountains through mid-September while headquartered at LZ English. Operations were resumed in the Bong Son area on September 17. A fight was quick in the coming and Bravo Company that day made contact with local VC guerrillas in an all day engagement. The VC lost 31 dead.

Contact was sporadic throughout the month. In October the battalion killed 16 NVA and 20 Viet Cong while detaining two NVA and 14 VC.

The last heavy contact of the year was concentrated in the villages of Tam Quan and Dai Dong December 6-8.

After assaulting into the area, Company B was engaged by enemy fire from camouflaged spider holes, trenches and bunkers. By morning Alpha Company had joined the fight, and a mechanized platoon was brought up as well. Even after artillery and air strike poundings, repeated attempts to take the well-prepared positions met with heavy resistance.

On the morning of December 8 Company C began the final assault through Dai Dong and remained to police the battlefield. The two-day and night fight had pitted fierce fighters from both sides. It was close and quick fighting. When the men of C Company walked through the finally quiet village they counted 204 NVA dead as evidence of the heated fighting.

April 5, 1968, marked the beginning of Operation PEGASUS—the relief of the beleaguered Khe Sanh—as the Jumping Mustangs air assaulted west of the camp at LZ Snapper. The 1st Bn, 8th Cav, compiled a remarkable record in the nine days it remained near Khe Sanh. The Cavalrymen were engaged in seve-

ral sharp fights as they pushed north and then west toward the Laotian border and the CIDG Camp at Lang Vei. Every day in their sweep was marked with a find of large enemy supply caches including equipment and ammunition.

The A Shau Valley is a slit in the mountains 45 kilometers west of Hue, close to the Laotian border, remote and usually hidden from air view by the thick canopy of jungle. It was a major NVA base area and a primary way station on the Ho Chi Minh trail.

Operation DELAWARE changed all this. The Jumping Mustangs, fresh from their relief of Khe Sanh earlier in the month, converged on the valley with two other airmobile battalions and set up LZ Stallion to secure the A Luoi airstrip in central A Shau.

Toward dusk on the 25th the hills around Stallion echoed with excited shouts and the rumble of a truck engine. From the north bounced a green vehicle covered with waving Skytroopers. Men of Delta Company had found five Russian made trucks one kilometer north of the landing zone and were driving one back.

"We had a little trouble getting supplies," said Specialist Four Joe McClure. "When we first got into the valley we had to get water out of a bomb crater. But later we used those Russian trucks to haul supplies for us."

Tipped off by helicopter sightings, Delta Company unearthed the first of the A Shau's big caches on the 26th. Captured were 315 Soviet K-44 rifles, a 60 mm mortar tube, 36 Soviet mine detectors, 30 flamethrowers, 202 Chicom protective masks, 225 pounds of medical supplies, 600 122 mm rockets, 2,000 23 mm anti-aircraft rounds, 100 pounds of dynamite, six tons of rice, 60 cases of canned meat, 70 37 mm anti-aircraft rounds and three B-40 rockets.

The last big battle in I Corps prior to the move south was near Quang Tri over August 20-22. Alpha Company, on a standard "Swooper" assault mission, had landed on two sides of a village and right into an NVA battalion.

Two platoons on the northern side were forced to seek refuge in an abandoned building. "We were drawing fire from every direction," said Specialist Four Donald Ferguson. "The only thing we could do was head for this building about 100 meters away."

On the opposite side of the village, the company commander, Captain Thomas McAndrews, and the two platoons with him also made heavy contact. "I wanted to sweep toward my other people," he said, "but we drew a heavy wall of fire every time we tried to move out."

During the night—while the two isolated platoons sweated it out—Companies Alpha, Charlie and Delta were brought up. At dawn they struck, sweep-ing across the area at a run, firing as they rushed in, and relieved the 39 surrounded men. In their charge the massed companies had killed 85 enemy and captured four others.

In late October the battalion moved, with the entire division over land, sea and air to III Corps.

It was in III Corps in December that the battalion became the first Cavalry-men to become "watermobile." On December 21 they began conducting NavCav operations with the Navy, a combination of techniques utilizing both sea and air power and a minimum number of troops to cover a maximum number of locations.

The Navy provided as assortment of river craft including assault patrol boats, armored troop carriers and "Monitor" gunboats. Some of the ships sported helicopter pads on their foredecks and all were heavily armed.

As the mini-armada motored up river, the patrol boats would turn into the shoreline at irregular intervals to land troops. NavCav operations were a daily occurrence on the Vam Co Dong and Vam Co Tay Rivers, and their success was weighed in the high tonnage of enemy caches found in these areas.

For the men in the battalion NavCav work was a welcome change of pace—although just as dangerous as their prior experience of walking and cutting through the jungle on foot. "It's really something," said Specialist Four Charles Baggett, machinegunner with Company B, "and it sure beats walking."

On January 20 the 1st Cavalry Division was given the mission of cutting enemy routes in the Kien Tuong Province of IV Corps. Charlie and Echo Companies from the 1st Bn, 8th Cav, were formed into Task Force Duke and swept into the province, marking the first entry of a 1st Cav unit into IV Corps. With that move the Cav had left its mark in all four corps areas in the Republic of Vietnam.

In May and June the battalion was targeted against a specific enemy, the 5th VC Division. In the COMANCHE WARRIOR AO, the Jumping Mustangs cut into the enemy's southerly movement through Long Khanh Province—from War Zone D to heavily populated areas in the Long Binh-Bien Hoa region and along known crossing points on the Dong Nai River.

A few sharp contacts were initiated but the period was characterized by large cache discoveries, forcing enemy units to withdraw to the north due to food shortages. The first big find was on May 28 when Company B air assaulted into a rear service element in a bunker complex, routed them and uncovered the enemy's food and ammunition stores. The next day Charlie Company found a huge supply of sugar, salt, rice and peanuts totaling over 60,000 pounds. Nearby, Company B unearthed and destroyed a large ammunition dump. And on May 31 Bravo Company turned up still more salt and rice. The enemy's supply system was hurting.

The most significant contact of the period came on June 2 when Company A was engaged and pinned down just north of the Dong Nai as it moved into a bunker complex. For reinforcements, Company B was airlifted over the river by platoons. After ARA and air strikes softened the complex, the two companies moved out again to approach the complex under heavy sniper fire. They engaged the enemy at the bunkerline and fought through the night. At dawn they swept the enemy position to find 54 NVA dead and their comrades gone. As a matter of interest, Company A was commanded in that action by Captain Walt-

A patrol makes contact and for the first few vital seconds, its fire first and seek cover later.

er J. Marm, winner of the Medal of Honor for his heroism in the Ia Drang Valley one day in 1965.

While working in the COMANCHE WARRIOR AO, the battalion command post was located at LZ Rock, possibly the only LZ that was named for an individual soldier while he was still a member of the unit, and certainly the only LZ that really did not take the name of the man it honored.

Sergeant First Class Joseph Musial was the reconnaissance platoon leader of Echo Company, a second-tour veteran and highly decorated. His second Silver Star was earned on LZ White where he personally assaulted three enemy sappers attacking the firebase after dodging grenades and incoming mortars to care for wounded comrades. He had been known as "Sergeant Rock"

to the men of the 1st Bn, 8th Cav, for so long most of them didn't even know his real name. When the firebase was opened the battalion commander needed to come up with a name and he opted for LZ Rock. "I guess I called this place Rock because that sergeant is the hardest charging soldier I have ever seen," he said.

On September 6, as Company C searched an area of numerous ground-to-air firings southeast of LZ Wescott, the men spotted and pursued about 30 NVA regulars and engaged them with small arms and machineguns as artillery and ARA gunships provided blocking fire. The enemy was armed with two .50 caliber and one .30 caliber machineguns and an 82 mm mortar. They retreated at nightfall, but the Cavalrymen caught up with them at dawn and re-

sumed fighting for almost two hours. When the shooting stopped the enemy had left 12 of their dead and both .50 caliber weapons behind on the battlefield.

In mid-September the battalion operated around the Bu Dop CIDG Camp and the Bo Duc district headquarters—a change of location that also marked by one of the largest reciprocal repositioning of troops ever attempted in III Corps. The move was completed in less than 48 hours and involved more than 1,200 men and their equipment.

Directing a major effort to interdict the Serges Jungle Highway, a reconnaissance mission headed by Delta Company some eight miles from the Cambodian border and northeast of LZ Deb uncovered three quarters of a ton of salt and eight and a half tons of rice. The find was turned over to GVN authorities for redistribution to needy civilians in Bu Dop and Loc Ninh.

FSB Ellen, located six miles west of Song Be, was reopened on October 9 by the battalion, which departed its former location at FSB Jerri. One month later Ellen was attacked.

The sapper attack at FSB Ellen was stopped just short of the third strand of wire as helicopter gunships, direct fire artillery and Air Force jets straffed the perimeter. The date was November 4, and the attack was opened at 1:30 a.m. "We were watching the light show at FSB Buttons (under attack) and wondering when we were going to get hit," said Captain Rocco Allessandro, Echo Company commander. "Two minutes later we got our answer."

"The fire was so heavy," said Staff Sergeant Casey Connelly, "that we had to fire our mortars while lying on the ground." The Cavalrymen killed 35 enemy in the battle, beating back the ground attack in the first hour. No Americans were killed.

Two weeks later enemy sappers attempted a light ground probe on the firebase at 10:15 p.m., preceded by RPG and mortar fire. Three NVA were killed and no friendly casualties were sustained. When dawn broke, a fully

Master of all he surveys, Private First Class Tom Decelles can cover one side of LZ Laramie with his M-60 machinegun.

assembled and armed flamethrower was found just outside the last strand of concertina wire. Apparently things had gotten too hot for the NVA sapper squad member who had humped the weapon through two strands of wire.

In the last month of 1969, elements of the battalion were involved in four significant actions. The first, on December 2, involved Company B in ground reconnaissance six miles east of FSB Jerri. In that fight the company killed 12 enemy soldiers.

On December 9 a two-pronged battle left 11 enemy dead at the hands of Delta Company men who had infiltrated into an NVA basecamp shortly after 9 a.m. One platoon lay in ambush on a trail to the rear of the camp while the forward ambush sprung its trap on a small group of the enemy and the rest of the company opened fire in the bunker complex. Five enemy were killed in the double ambush and six others died in the bunker fighting. The camp was located 12 miles south of Bu Dop.

As the year 1969 drew to a close, it found the 1st Bn, 8th Cav, in sporadic contact with the enemy. On December 14 Alpha Company clashed with 16 NVA soldiers near FSB Ellen, killing five in the mid-day battle. Seven days later the same company killed five additional enemy soldiers in an ambush waiting for the enemy battalions to move—and awaited the new year.

2nd of the 8th

(Continued From P. 89)

recover their wounded. Following intense artillery and close air support fires, Delta Company swept the village with the tanks. More than 90 of the enemy were dead.

On September 17, in Phu Yen Province, the 2nd Bn, 8th Cav, task force went under the operational control of the 173rd Airborne Brigade for Operation BOLLING, conducting search and clear missions in the western portion of the Tuy Hoa-Phu Hiep coastal plain, which terminated on October 14. The battalion had sustained no casualties and killed 21 of the enemy. Twelve had been detained and 3,000 pounds of rice and 208 fortifications had been destroyed. The battalion closed on LZ Uplift the 25th day of the month.

The battalion initially released two companies to the 1st Brigade, 4th Infan-try Division, for the defense of Dak To (Operation MACARTHUR) on November 15. Company C made contact with an NVA battalion in well-fortified positions on a ridgeline nine kilometers east of the Dak To basecamp the next day.

After three days of fighting, the company occupied the first of a series of jungle-covered hills that commanded a sweeping view of the installation, directly above Highway 14, the land supply route to the camp.

At the beginning of 1968, the battalion was still engaged in Operation PERSHING with the 1st Brigade. Line companies were securing LZ Laramie, as well as pulling base defense at LZ English and LZ Geronimo. All companies were engaged in search and clear or cordon and search missions in the Bong Son Plain area.

At the beginning of March the battalion command post moved from LZ English to Quang Tri, joining Operation

JEB STUART. For one day, the 27th, Bravo Company was under the operational control of the 3rd Marine Regiment, air assaulting into LZ Stud.

On the 15th of March the battalion trains area received 15 incoming mortar rounds, killing two. Lieutenant Colonel Howard Petty, the commanding officer, was one of the men killed.

The battalion began Operation DELAWARE throughout the southern A Shau Valley on April 24, airlifting into LZ Cecille. The operation terminated May 16, and the battalion moved back to LZ Sharon, beginning Operation JEB STUART III. A new company, Echo, was formed the next day, having the mission of providing a mortar section for fire support and a reconnaissance element.

In a 10-day period, in late September and early October, the battalion uncovered, bagged and transported more than 57 tons of enemy rice to Trieu Phong District headquarters, where it was distributed to needy civilians. Charlie Company found more than 43 tons. For about a week the unit had been turning up caches on a daily basis, accumulating 30,200 pounds of the grain.

During the next two days, the company found 55,040 more pounds of rice. In one instance Private First Class Frank E. Sinkovich, an RTO, began digging a position for the night after the company had made a long, tiring march across the sandy coastal plains six kilometers northeast of Quang Tri.

"I dug down about a foot and a half and I saw some plastic," he explained. "It was a rice cache." The unit remained in the area to check for other hidden stores.

"When we left our night location we were supposed to go two kilometers to the northwest and then work back toward the CP," said Second Lieutenant Fred Shaffert, "but before we got 20 meters away we found five separate caches. It was like that all day, we just kept finding rice everywhere."

While visiting the rice hunters, Major General Truong, the 1st ARVN Division commander, remarked that Company C had found enough rice that day to feed an NVA division for an entire month.

The battalion began packing on October 27, strapping conex containers tightly to wooden pallets, forklifting them onto trucks and driving them to Hue for transport on Navy LSTs. On the 28th, the Skytroopers were camped on the Quang Tri airstrip, waiting for the C-130 flights south, to begin Operation LIBERTY CANYON. The Cav was moving to III Corps.

They reached Quan Loi on the 29th, sorted out their combat gear and inspected their weapons. On the 31st, they air assaulted into LZ Joe with artillery preparation, air cover and waves of supply choppers bringing up the rear.

It was Halloween, but for the enemy there were to be no treats. Aerial rocket artillery (ARA) ships blasted the woods and the battalion rapidly began turning a former NVA base area into Cav Country. The occupation of Joe was the first combat assault for the Skytroopers in III Corps. Many more were to follow.

On New Year's Day, 1969, the battalion was still on LZ Rita near the Cambodian border in the vicinity of the "Fishhook" in War Zone C. Since November 7, 1968, the battalion had conducted offensive operations as a part of TOAN THANG II, which was to continue until February.

The first significant engagement of the year involved Alpha Company, 10 kilometers from the landing zone on January 24. The unit clashed with a reinforced NVA company. The enemy left 27 bodies behind. All elements of the battalion were making frequent contacts and turning up lucrative caches.

The battalion command post and all maneuver elements moved to LZ St. Barbara on February 1. Significant contacts were made immediately and huge rice caches were discovered during the month. On the 10th Company D uncovered 61,400 pounds of rice and 4,100 pounds of salt. Bravo Company, six kilometers from St. Barbara on February 12, discovered 165 bags of rice—some 33,000 pounds. Two days later Delta Company uncovered 22 100-pound bags of rice in a bunker.

The battalion was also finding enemy hiding places and equipment. One 350-bunker complex, 20 miles northwest of Tay Ninh, revealed some prize trophies, including a pair of 12.7 mm anti-aircraft guns. The weapons were so new that the enemy hadn't had time to remove the cosmoline protective coating from them. Included in the complex was a hospital still under construction. The medical center boasted five operating rooms and six wards capable of accommodating 15

An Alpha, 229th Assault Helicopter Battalion, slick is guided in by a Skytrooper in central War Zone C.

to 18 persons each.

The trend continued through March and April. An indication of the battalion's success were the parting words of outgoing commander Lieutenant Colonel Frank L. Henry. "While I have been commander," he said, "you have killed more than a battalion of North Vietnamese Army soldiers and captured enough rice to feed two divisions for 40 days."

On April 9 another huge rice cache was discovered, this time by Company C. Fifty-two 200-pound bags of rice were found on a wooden pallet.

In mid-April LZ Carolyn was established northwest of Barbara, deep in the jungles of War Zone C at Prek Klok, a former CIDG camp. High on the priority list for repairs was the 2,500 foot runway. Soon the 5,500-pound capacity C-7A Caribous made their first nine sorties to the landing zone, marking the first time in more than a year that fixed wing aircraft had landed there.

Maneuver elements of the battalion began making contacts daily after Carolyn was established and patrols were initiated.

At LZ Carolyn the perimeter guards peered silently into the darkness, expecting something to happen. Shortly after midnight May 6, a trip flare went off outside the wire and a B-40 rocket slammed inside the perimeter. The LZ was under attack.

The explosion was followed by many more B-40 and 107 mm rockets and heavy automatic weapons fire. A regimental-size ground attack from the southwest and north followed.

"At first there was nothing within my sights," said Specialist Four Gordon R. Loder, a rifleman with Charlie Company, "but the next thing I knew, there were large groups of them coming directly toward us. I put my M-16 on rake and just started firing into the masses."

Although the enemy eventually succeeded in penetrating the perimeter and occupying six bunkers, the fierce counterattack launched by the Skytroopers

convinced the NVA that their attempt at seizing LZ Carolyn was lost.

The decimated enemy force began to withdraw at 4 a.m. and contact was broken by 6 o'clock. At first light, three companies were air assaulted to block and interdict avenues of escape to the north and west. Delta Company saw 30 individuals carrying their wounded away and killed 18. Alpha got five and Company D killed six more later that day.

What was once an NVA regiment was out of business. The enemy left 198 of their soldiers dead on the battlefield and 30 were detained.

The unit deployed north, close to the Cambodian border, to interdict the "Mustang Trail" on July 9. The battalion began the construction and security of LZ Becky.

Sporadic action was seen throughout the month. On August 7, Charlie Company uncovered a rice cache totaling 5,800 pounds.

August 11 marked the beginning of a demanding 48 hours for the battalion. At 3 a.m., LZ Becky received incoming 60 mm and 82 mm mortars, rocket propelled grenades (RPGs) and then a ground attack launched by a company-

size NVA sapper unit. The battle was short. Fifty-five minutes later 17 sappers were dead outside the wire. Later that day, Bravo Company discovered two NVA artillerymen setting up 107 mm rockets near Becky, killed them, and captured a 60 mm mortar tube. It was an indication of what was to happen the next morning.

An eight week "lull" was shattered throughout the FIRST TEAM's AO on August 12. LZ Becky was the scene of what was perhaps the fiercest fighting.

Enemy activity was observed on radar at 1:45 a.m.—what appeared to be a truck discharging personnel near the LZ. It was engaged by tube artillery and a secondary explosion resulted.

The enemy attacked at 4:10 a.m., following a mixed mortar and rocket barrage that destroyed an artillery ammunition storage area, causing the only friendly casualties of the battle.

The attack was termed by a gunship pilot as "the most intense stand-off attack on a firebase I've seen since the Cav moved to War Zone C."

Some 400 enemy mortar and rocket rounds repeatedly riveted holes in the surface of the LZ, as the enemy battalion launched a ground attack from the

A typical NVA fighting bunker is examined by a Cav grenadier. The bunker, with up to three feet of overhead cover, is well camouflaged and, when filled with a determined enemy, is a tough nut to crack.

north.

In the next 40 minutes the landing zone was silhouetted with the flashing glow of a massed firefight. The enemy reached the wire, but never breached the perimeter. When they withdrew, 101 of their number had died in the attempt and one other was captured.

The battalion left Becky later that day. The 1st Brigade commander, Colonel Joseph P. Kingston, decided that major enemy forces had withdrawn to regroup and prepare for future attempts to the southeast. To preclude this, and to maintain close observation of the enemy and find prepositioned fortifications and stores, the battalion was shifted to LZ Ike.

The enemy was, indeed, moving into that area. The battalion was in for more heavy fighting in the month to follow.

On August 25 Delta Company, near Ike, engaged an NVA element in bunkers and received heavy automatic weapons and B-40 fire in return. Searching the contact area the next day, Cavalrymen found the bodies of 33 NVA soldiers. Five days later Company B, which had ambushed two NVA on the 30th, engaged several in two separate contacts, killing 28.

On September 1 Company C, discovering a strand of enemy communications wire, followed it and ambushed two NVA signalmen setting up a field phone. Tapping the wire, it hooked into an enemy battalion net and directed artillery on an unsuspecting NVA command post.

Bravo Company continued to make contact. On September 2 it took one individual prisoner, pulling him out of a spider hole. Later it was again engaged by the enemy. Air and artillery support killed nine, Company B accounted for three.

LZ Ike was hit September 5, with A and E Companies securing the berm. More than 160 shells pounded the LZ, followed by a reinforced NVA company. Fifty-one caliber machineguns filled the air with enemy lead, making air support a hazardous proposition at best. The attack was repulsed by 3 a.m., but incoming rounds continued to hit the LZ until 10 o'clock. A search of the area revealed 46 dead enemy soldiers and one wounded man who was detained.

LZ Ike was again the target of the enemy in mid-September. Stoney Mountain Skytroopers from Charlie and Echo Companies beat back a determined as-

Heavily laden Skytroopers from the 1st Brigade leap from slicks to climax a Cav Charlie Alpha. The action occurred during Operation JEB STUART.

sault on the LZ in the early morning hours September 14, killing 34 and detaining another.

The battle erupted shortly before midnight when 100 mortar rounds hit the firebase. An estimated company-size unit then hit the wire while the defenders used point blank artillery fire and Cobra gunships to crush the offensive.

Ike was probed again two days later, but an alert trooper picked up movement through a starlight scope just after midnight. Seven NVA were found lying outside the wire the next morning.

The 2nd Bn, 8th Cav, left War Zone C September 23, moving to Camp Gorvad to secure the division basecamp at Phuoc Vinh. On the 25th the battalion became operationally controlled by Division Artillery and conducted operations in AO Chief, patrolling and mortar belt surrounding Camp Gorvad and securing Song Be Bridge. In mid-December it moved to FSB Mary in the 2nd Brigade's AO.

2nd of the 19th

(Continued From P. 117)

millionth round in Vietnam.

In the few months since arrival in III Corps the battalion had already established 16 firebases, the battalion FDC had moved five times and the battalion headquarters three times.

The battalion's Charlie Battery was on LZ White March 21 when NVA sappers hit the base. The battery fought off the attack with direct fire. On May 6 the NVA hit LZ Carolyn. Alpha Battery mowed down the enemy with 800 rounds of direct fire, 198 NVA dying in the attack.

It was Bravo Battery's turn on May 12 when the enemy attacked LZ Jamie. The attackers used bangalore torpedoes to penetrate the perimeter wire and occupied a bunker, with at least 12 NVA inside. Seventy NVA were killed in the battle.

The battalion's batteries proved invaluable in other ground attacks in 1969, too, helping stop enemy attempts to overrun LZs Becky and Ike. Throughout the year the batteries performed their basic mission of supporting the infantry as it searched the jungle for the enemy, his bunkers and his supplies.

Editor's Note: History of the History

Phuoc Vinh, Vietnam
February 12, 1970

This volume is the result of a happy juxtaposition of circumstances, decisions and events. The publication of any unit history depends on financing, and in early 1969 the financing picture was pretty bleak. Non-appropriated funds were being curtailed sharply, and club funds, which had been used in the past by other units for yearbooks, no longer were available in this division. The only means of financing available was through the division association, and its funds were meager.

Concurrent with wrestling over decisions on the scope of a history, MG Roberts decided to boost the financing of the division association's education foundation through a powerful drive within the active division. The key decision in this case was to raise money through a business organization, called "FIRST TEAM Scholarships," rather than through solicitations in the paylines.

This business organization, dedicated to raising money for scholarships through sound business and promotion practices, was in an ideal position to act as publisher of this volume.

But a business organization needs capital to operate, and it was not until November 1, 1969, that we were sure that a history of the 1st Air Cav was going to move from the dream to the reality category.

Some advance work had, of course, been done, but it was a mere scratch on the surface. First Lieutenant Donald B. Ashton was given the mission of researching and writing the unit histories. We found that while the division's story was well and fairly told in records available, there were gaping holes in the subordinate unit histories.

Moreover, unit histories, while factual and detailed, also were dry and dull. To personalize these histories, we turned to stories published in the *CAVALAIR*, the division's weekly newspaper; the quarterly magazine of the division; news clippings accumulated in our files; and personal interviews with second-tour FIRST TEAMers.

By late November, sufficient material was available to begin writing in earnest, and three writers were assigned to begin weaving the threads of the division's story into a cohesive fabric. Eventually, nearly every writer in the information office got into the act. Specialist Five Joe Kamalick, a wordsmith on TDY with *Pacific Stars & Stripes*, was plucked back to the fold to shape and polish the written drafts. And then, completing that, he stayed on to play a major role in the picture selections and final layout.

Captain James Ryan, an artist in his own right, supervised the art staff and also played a key role in picture selection and layout.

All photographs appearing in this book are Department of the Army photos, taken either by Department of the Army Special Photographic Teams or by the photographers organic to the FIRST TEAM. We have listed what we recognize as only a partial list of photographic credits. It simply was impossible, from the resources available to us, to determine the name of every individual whose pictorial contributions appear in this volume, and for this we apologize.

Acknowledgment is given to the dozens of talented writers who labored in the FIRST TEAM vineyards during the past five years. Their imaginative offerings, preserved in division publications, enabled us to breathe some life into the dusty after-action reports. Special thanks are rendered to two artists, Specialists Five Larry Collins and Ron Doss, whose art work appeared in past division magazines and is reproduced here.

And, finally, my personal thanks to the book staff that worked so hard. Long work hours are expected in a combat zone and, in the Cav, the 16-hour work day is an article of faith. But even so, in the 90 days that went into the research, writing, editing and makeup of this book, there were still a lot of letters home that didn't get written, movies that didn't get watched and clubs that didn't get patronized.

J. D. Coleman

J. D. Coleman
Major, Infantry
Information Officer

Book Staff

EDITOR-IN-CHIEF

MAJ J. D. Coleman

ASSOCIATE EDITORS

CPT James W. Ryan
1LT Donald B. Ashton
SP5 Joseph A. Kamalick

RESEARCHERS AND WRITERS

SP4 Jerry W. Norton
SP4 James D. Egan
SP4 Jay W. Saul
SP4 Barry H. Bjornson
PFC Charles W. Petit

GRAPHIC DESIGN

SGT Douglas L. Crow

COMBAT ARTISTS

SGT Douglas L. Grow
SGT Stephen E. Wilson
SGT Richard R. Cooper
SP5 Lee Napoleon
SP4 Ted Fairbanks
SP4 Glenn Thompson
SP4 Don E. Chapman
SP4 William E. Stransky

STAFF PHOTOGRAPHY

SP4 R. Dean Sharp
SP4 Leonard W. Fallscheer
SP4 Robert J. Conway

LAYOUT ASSISTANT

SP4 Glenn Thompson

PRODUCTION EDITORS

SP5 David A. Wolfe
SP4 Dennis Keenon

PHOTOGRAPHY:
COMBAT PHOTOGRAPHERS
1965–1969

MAJ J. D. Coleman
1LT Marvin Wolf
1LT William D. San Hamel
SFC Jack H. Yamaguchi
SSG Lyle V. Boggess
SSG Lewis Dacurro
SSG Howard C. Breedlove
SSG Hector Robertin
SSG Gilbert L. Meyers
SSG Barney Wilson
SP6 Samuel L. Swain
SP5 Ross P. Jones
SP5 Steve Robinson
SP5 Bill Larson
SP5 Paul J. Romine
SP5 Ed Koehnlein
SP5 Herb Denton
SP5 H. A. Klein
SP5 David Frank
SP5 Terry Moon
SP5 A. J. MacLean
SP5 D. J. Meyers
SP5 Paul Sgroi
SP5 Carl C. Hansen

SP5 Dave Wolfe
SP5 Steve Caldwell
SP5 Phillip Blackmarr
SP5 Luther Wolfe
SP5 Travis Holden
SP5 Joe Kamalick
SP5 Thomas Benic
SP4 Stanton R. Pratt
SP4 Pat Christian
SP4 Charles Hoover
SP4 Robert Borchester
SP4 James McCabe
SP4 William Ahrbeck
SP4 Cornell Coe
SP4 Chuck Harris
SP4 Michael Miller
SP4 Don Graham
SP4 Archie Bonyam
SP4 Richard S. Durrance
SP4 Douglas Fuller
SP4 Andy Rust
SP4 Eric White
SP4 R. Dean Sharp
SP4 Len Fallscheer
SP4 Robert Conway
SP4 Ron Merrill
SP4 Tom Scott
SP4 Bruce Montoya
SP4 Gregory Cormany
SP4 James Caldwell
SP4 Richard Hawkins
SP4 Steve Matalon
PFC Robert F. Fromm
PFC Jeffery Cohen
PFC Thomas Baroody

This publication, entitled THE FIRST AIR CAVALRY DIVISION, VIETNAM, Volume 1, 1965-1969, is an authorized publication of the 1st Cavalry Division (Airmobile), APO San Francisco 96490. Views and opinions expressed are not necessarily those of the Department of Defense or Department of the Army. Unless otherwise indicated, material and photographs may be reprinted provided credit is given to the 1st Air Cavalry Division. Individuals desiring a copy of this publication should send check or money order in the amount of $7.00 to: FIRST TEAM SCHOLARSHIPS, in care of the Information Office, 1st Air Cavalry Division, APO San Francisco 96490. All proceeds from the sale of this book accrue to the scholarship fund of the Education Foundation of the 1st Cavalry Division Association.

PRINTED BY DIA NIPPON PRINTING COMPANY, LTD., TOKYO, JAPAN.